55 *years of* MERCURY

The Complete History of the Big "M"

by John A. Gunnell

Published by

krause
publications

700 E. State Street • Iola, WI 54990-0001

Please call or write for our free catalog of automotive publications.
Our Toll-free number to place an order or obtain a free catalog is 800-258-0929.
Please use our regular business telephone 715-445-2214
for editorial comment and further information.

Library of Congress Catalog Number: 94-77500
ISBN: 0-87341-311-3
Printed in the United States of America

Contents

Introduction

The inspiration for *55 Years of Mercury* came to me from book seller Ken Ohman, by way of writer "Doc" Howell, thanks to auctioneer Mitch Silver. It was at Mitch Silver's "Hot August Nights '93" auction that I met "Doc" for the first time. He, in turn, introduced me to Ken Ohman, who operates Automobilia Books in Ocean Shores, Washington. I was looking for projects to put on the books schedule for 1994, and Ohman suggested a Mercury history. He said that he had been receiving a inordinate number of requests, from Mercury enthusiasts, for a book about their favorite marque.

"They don't want a Lincoln-Mercury book," Ken Ohman advised. "And they don't want a book about only one Mercury model. They want a book that's pure Mercury, and tells the history of the company from the beginning, to the current time."

That is the purpose of *55 Years of Mercury*. The idea of a Mercury book seemed interesting to me, since I have driven several Mercurys over the years. None of these cars was particularly "collectible," but I loved them all, and recall little stories about each one.

The first Mercury I drove was a dark Blue, 1966 Comet 202 four-door Sedan. This was a salesman's car leased by a company I worked for in New York City. I recall bringing my oldest son home from the hospital in it. I also vividly recall the night before I turned it in to the company. Its odometer didn't quite match the mileage on my records, so I had to jack the car up and run it in reverse, all night, to make the numbers match! The company had given me a similar White car to use. It had bad tires, and the Blue car had brand new tires. I was told to switch them. To save a few bucks, I decided to switch only the wheels. Both cars were in the air, the dark Blue one with the White wheels mounted, and the White one with dark Blue wheels on it, when a police squad car pulled up. I had a job convincing "New York's Finest" what they were seeing, especially since one car had New York tags, and the other had New Jersey tags. On top of that, they were both registered to a Maryland leasing company!

My next Mercury was also a company car. It was a 1969 Montego four-door Sedan with a six-cylinder engine. As a business car, it was one of the cheapest available, but it sure looked nice with dark Olive-Green paint, and a black vinyl interior. I picked it up at a Mercury dealership in Brooklyn, New York, and drove it home to Staten Island, a distance of 11 miles. When I turned it off, it would not start again. The starter had gone bad. To make matters worse, the Ford service people were on strike and the car couldn't be fixed under warranty. My boss was not very happy. Over the next three years, I put more than 100,000 miles on that Montego. It was a pretty good car, except that it "ate" a new starter about every six months.

One time, while the Montego was laid up, I borrowed a 1964 Comet that my boss had as a spare. I remember that he had a big sales meeting, and asked me to show up at his house, in Northern New Jersey, early in the morning. When I got there, he tossed me the keys, and said, "I have to rush." I told him, "You'd better not leave that fast ... I can't drive this car ... it's a stick." Instead of attending his meeting, Joe spent the next three hours teaching me how to use a clutch, and a manual gear shift!

The last Mercury that I drove was a 1973 Monterey Custom four-door Sedan. This is the only car that ever belonged to *four* members of the *Old Cars* staff. I purchased it from an area collector who had bought it from research editor Ken Buttolph. Ken bought from then-*Old Cars* editor Mary Sieber. It had belonged to Mary's father for many years. Eventually, I sold the car to *Old Cars* advertising representative Paul Katzke. He made a $22 repair, and sold the car for a 100 percent profit a few weeks later. As far as we know, it's still running. Maybe it will return to Iola some day, so the newer *Old Cars* staffers can have a crack at it!

As I said, I loved driving all of these Mercurys, and I now enjoy remembering the experiences, both good and bad, that I had while I owned them. Hopefully, you will enjoy reading about the Mercurys that you used to own as you leaf through the pages of *55 Years of Mercury*. It covers the company's complete history, and the great products that it has built for more than half a century.

John A. Gunnell
July 1994

4

The Mercury was one of the first products styled in Ford's new in-house Design Department and this is a front view of the final prototype. (Dick Dance)

A Ford Design Department photo showing a 1939 Mercury prototype in close-to-production format. (Dick Dance)

Styling the first Mercury 1935-1938

The 1939 Mercury was the first car to be created by Ford's styling studio. E.T. "Bob" Gregorie established that department in 1935. Between 1932 and 1943, Gregorie designed cars for Edsel Ford. Edsel had been given responsibility for styling, by his father, Henry Ford. He hired Gregorie and gave him sweeping authority over the appearance of a various products, from tractors, to cars to buses.

Gregorie was trained as a naval architect. He had worked for Cox and Stevens, and the Submarine Boat Company (now General Dynamics), before getting into automotive design. Gregorie put in brief stints with the Rolls-Royce Brewster Body Company and the General Motors (GM) Art and Colour Section. Then he joined Ford Motor Company.

Gregorie enjoyed a direct pipeline to Edsel Ford. He had a great appreciation of Edsel's artistic sensitivity. Edsel Ford respected Gregorie's artistic ability, his communications skills, and his understanding of engineering principals. Gregorie knew what Edsel liked. His design work did not have to please many other people, although it often did. Gregorie was given authority comparable to that of a corporate vice president.

Since he was "in the loop," Gregorie did not need advisors and management committees to approve his concepts. He had, more or less, the final say on styling. This allowed him to maintain a staff of no more than 50 people at a time. When the Mercury was being designed, the staff was composed of only 19 men.

This pilot model for the 1939 Mercury four-door Sedan is close to the final production version, although it lacks chrome body side moldings and a hood nameplate. (Dick Dance)

Front end lacks hood side nameplates, moldings and red-painted highlights. (Dick Dance)

Bob Gregorie was called chief designer. Edward A. Martin was in charge of drafting and planning. Martin Regitko handled body surface development. Instrument panels were the responsibility of John H. Walter. The task of designing interior trim fell on Walter Kruke.

Ford Design Department hadn't worked out rear details at this point. (Dick Dance)

Willys P. Wagner took care of bumpers, lights and exterior hardware. Grilles and sheet metal were designed by Bruno Kolt. James Lynch was shop foreman. Richard Beneicke was head of clay modeling. Bud Adams, Ben Barbera, Frank Beyer, Frank Francis, John Najjar, Emmet O'Rear, and Robert Thomas were apprentices. Rounding out the staff were Ross Cousins, Tucker Madawick and Duncan McRae.

In addition to the new Mercury, this group had several other vehicles in the studio at the same time. They ranged from 1940 Ford cars to a cab-over-engine Ford truck. The Lincoln Zephyr and 1940 Lincoln-Continental can also be seen in photos of the styling department taken by Willys Wagner. The Zephyr was being restyled and the Continental was in its initial development under Edsel Ford's personal direction. Gregorie was also working on a school bus design for Henry Ford.

Apparently, Henry Ford left the styling department alone most of the time. The work that came out of it was primarily a reflection of the thinking of Edsel Ford and Bob Gregorie. In 1974, illustra-

There's no "Mercury" nameplate on the hood of this 1939 pilot model Convertible and the hubcaps vary from production style hubcaps.

This Convertible is nearly finalized. (Dick Dance)

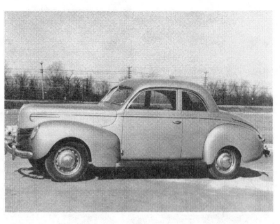

This pilot version of the Sedan-Coupe also lacks the "Mercury" name on its hood. (Dick Dance)

These women seem to like the Ford Design Department's work. (Dick Dance)

This pilot model has hood nameplate and "Ford-Mercury" stamped on hubcaps. (Dick Dance)

This pilot version of the 1939 Sedan-Coupe has "Ford-Mercury" hubcaps. (Dick Dance)

A bird's-eye view of the 1939 Mercury pilot model. (Dick Dance)

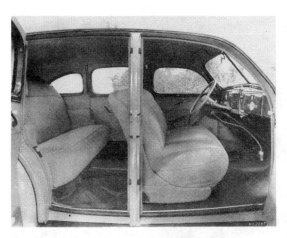

Ford Design Department worked on the 1939 Mercury interior, too. (Dick Dance)

tor Ross Cousins told *Special-Interest Autos* magazine, "Henry didn't like us too well, but Edsel was our godfather and patron saint."

The 1939 Mercury was the first Ford production car that was developed from a full-size clay mock-up to a real car. It became one of the most aerodynamic automobiles of its era. Talk of a "big Ford," to fill the gap between Fords and Lincolns, began in July 1937. Engineering work, carried out under the direction of Larry Sheldrick, got underway immediately. By late in the year, the Mercury's V-8 engine was ready to make its first appearance in Ford trucks.

Two hand-built Mercury prototypes took only a year to complete. They were finished and running by July 1938. One was a two-door Sedan and one was a four-door Sedan. They got a thorough workout on Ford's new Dearborn test track and later were taken on trial runs all over the country.

Pilot production of Mercurys began on September 21, 1938, with dealer introductions on October 17. One week later, there was a press introduction. The public introduction was held on November 4. These cars, as well as later pilot production cars, had obvious differences from showroom Mercurys. These ranged from Ford-Mercury nameplates to a variety of hubcap and taillamp designs.

Bob Gregorie spent almost 15 years in charge of the Ford styling department. He was already working on postwar Ford models when Edsel Ford died, suddenly, in 1943. That same year, Grego-

The back of this photo was stamped "Ford Design Department." The Sedan looks close to the one that appeared on the cover of the first sales catalog, with "Ford-Mercury" hubcaps. (Dick Dance)

Prototype 1940 Mercury four-door Sedan has painted hubcaps. A "Mercury" nameplate is under the trunk handle, instead of above it. The bumper has 1939 guards and "Mercury" stamped on it. (Dick Dance)

rie left Ford Motor Company for six months. He was rehired, but things were never the same again. Henry Ford II took over the company. He hired Ernest Breech, a former GM executive, who worked at Bendix Corporation. Breech started to reorganize Ford in the GM mold. This entailed a complete revamping of the styling department's structure. Bob Gregorie had no desire to work within a system where committees and corporate politics governed the work of designers.

As Gregorie states in *The Art of American Car Design*, "All design activity was placed under chassis engineering — a 10-year step backward. Due to these conditions, I decided to inform Mr. Ford that I was leaving the company. This was understandable, and my departure was mutually agreeable." Gregorie retired to Florida, where he did some boat designs. He maintained a cordial relationship with Ford Motor Company and was later, officially honored for establishing the company's original styling department.

The Mercury photographs illustrating this chapter originally came from the Ford styling department. They show pre-production versions of 1939 and 1940 Mercurys, plus some other projects carried out in the years Bob Gregorie ran the department. The photographs are now part of a collection assembled by Dick Dance.

This 1940 Sedan has different hubcaps on front and rear. (Dick Dance)

Close-to-production 1940 dash has starter button on panel, instead of below it. (Dick Dance)

A postwar Mercury dashboard design proposal. (Dick Dance)

The "X" on the license plate may stand for "experimental," but this four-door Sedan is very close to 1939 production form. (Dick Dance)

This looks like an early clay model of a 1941 Mercury design proposal. (Dick Dance)

Another view of a late prototype 1939 Mercury. (Dick Dance)

Styling of the exterior and interior was locked-in by the time Ford Design Department snapped this picture. (Dick Dance)

11

Mercury before the war 1939-1942

Edsel Ford created the Mercury expressly to fill the market gap between the Ford Deluxe and the Lincoln-Zephyr. There was a "black hole" in the Ford pricing ladder. In 1938, for example, the most expensive Ford Deluxe, the Station Wagon, was $825. The lowest-priced Lincoln-Zephyr, which was a three-passenger Coupe, sold for $1,295. General Motors could plug this gap with any Buick Special (other than the Phaeton); any closed Buick Century (except the four-door Touring Sedan); any Oldsmobile (both sixes and eights) and any Pontiac six or eight (except the Convertible Sedans). The LaSalle Opera Coupe was right at the $1,295 mark. Even this "baby Cadillac" could slip into the "gap-without-a-Ford," if a Cadillac dealer was inclined to a $1 discount.

Car buyers who could afford something better than a Ford Deluxe, but who did not have the extra money needed for a Zephyr, were buying medium- or upper-medium-priced automobiles. Most of the cars in these brackets came from General Motors. GM was taking thousands of sales away from Ford by offering so many models (37 in all) in the middle price ranges. Dodges and DeSotos, as well as some Studebaker models, were other worthy competitors. All this added up to millions of dollars in lost business for Ford.

Ford dealers must have been very happy to hear the September 29, 1938, announcement that a "new-from-the-ground-up" car was coming. Within a week of that date, Ford gave the car a name and revealed that it would be V-8-powered. Certainly, no one was surprised by this choice; Ford was the biggest builder of V-8s anywhere.

Edsel Ford picked the Mercury designation. Over 104 names had been suggested for the new car, from Cyclops to Pharaoh. Even Ford Falcon was a consideration. Mercury was the name of the winged messenger of the gods in Roman mythology. He was also the god of commerce who symbolized dependability, eloquence, skill and speed. The Mercury 8's official press introduction was held on October 24, 1938, at Ford headquarters in Dearborn, Michigan. "There's something as new as the Spring in the clean, sweeping lines of the Mercury 8," said the advertising copywriters. "It is a wide, remarkably roomy car, but skillful design has made its bulk beautiful."

The Mercury was the first car to come from Ford's in-house styling department, which opened in 1935. It was also the first vehicle adopted from a clay model done expressly by Ford designers. Those designers reported directly to Edsel Ford. Henry Ford was there, too, looking over Edsel's shoulder, of course.

"New 95 hp Ford line is called Mercury," said the headline of an article about the all-new car. It appeared in America's *Motor* magazine for November 1938. Two pictures showed how the Mercury looked in four-door Sedan and two-door Sedan formats. Two additional detail photos showed the radiator grille and the instrument panel. The early models shown even had "Ford-Mercury" hub-

Model number 70 was generally referred to as "the Sedan." It had two-doors and a streamlined roof. (Mercury)

caps. Later in the year, the hubcaps were stamped "Mercury 8" instead.

Mercury production had begun at an assembly plant in Richmond, California on September 21, 1938. Initial sales were strong. On October 8, regular production started at factories in Chicago, Illinois; Louisville, Kentucky; Kansas City, Missouri; and Edgewater, New Jersey. Showroom introductions took place on November 4.

"The Ford Motor Company has brought out a new model called the Mercury 8, priced between the Deluxe Ford and the Lincoln-Zephyr," explained the article. "It has a wheelbase of 116 inches, roomier bodies and more luxurious appointments than the Fords. Its V-8 engine develops 95 hp at 3600 rpm, an increase of 10 hp. This increase was secured by enlarging the bore 1/8 inch. Bore and stroke are 3.185 by 3.75 inches and the piston displacement is 239 cubic inches. With the

Adventurer Lowell Thomas with his 1939 Mercury Convertible Coupe. (Mercury)

addition of the new model, the company now offers three lines of cars, the other two being the Ford V-8 and the Deluxe Ford V-8."

An advertisement of 1939 boasted, "The history of the Ford Motor Company is written in ever-increasing motoring values. The Mercury 8, an entirely new car, is another chapter in that history. Priced between the Ford V-8 and the Lincoln-Zephyr V-12, the Mercury brings to the price field many advantages of both these Ford-built cars ... advantages that are best expressed in the phrase 'top value.'"

Four Mercurys, each suitable for five passengers, were offered. Model 70 was the two-door Sedan; Model 72 was the Coupe-Sedan; Model 73 was the four-door Town Sedan; and Model 76 was the Convertible Coupe. Their prices were $916, $957, $957, and $1,018, respectively. They all weighed in the neighborhood of 3,000 pounds. The Coupe-Sedan looked quite sporty, with a slim

A 1939 Mercury AACA Senior four-door Sedan restored by R. Dale Miller of Hickory, North Carolina. This car was originally purchased, by his father Cloyd L. Miller, in Lander, Wyoming in July 1939 for $600. (R. Dale Miller)

This is how R. Dale Miller's car looked when his uncle Larry Miller and spouse Connie presented him with it in 1984. (R. Dale Miller)

The 1939 Coupe-Sedan looked sporty, with a slim window pillar and stainless steel window trim that suggested the evolution of hardtop styling. (Mercury)

window pillar and stainless steel window trim that suggested the coming evolution of postwar hardtop styling.

The Mercury 8 resembled the Ford in general design. Its body was approximately six inches wider, though. This reduced the size of the running boards. Mercurys had flatter fenders than Fords and semi-skirted wheel openings. The body was mounted on a new type of frame. The flanges of the X-member pointed outward, with the legs of the X running the full length of the frame side rails to form stiff, box-section girders. "The size of the Mercury is not an illusion," Ford advertised. "This is a big, wide car, exceptionally roomy, with large luggage compartment. Note these generous dimensions: wheelbase 116 inches; over-all length 16 feet 2 inches. The front compartment in sedan body types is 54 inches wide, and the rear compartment measures 56 inches from side to side."

Styling highlights included a modern, streamlined look with headlamps that were flush with the fenders. "It's long and low ... as streamlined as a ribbon in the wind," said one poetic sales pitch. "And it's luxuriously large inside ... completely cushioned for lounging ... remarkably silenced for rest."

The increased slant of a non-opening windshield added to its sleek appearance. Since the windshield did not swing open, the windshield wipers could be mounted in a modern new location, at the bottom. The nose had a solidly enclosed radiator covering with a chrome ornamental center rail. It also had a low, Ford-shaped grille opening. However, the Mercury used a horizontal-bar grille, rather than the Ford Deluxe's vertical-bar grille. The top and side panels of the hood were made of one unit. Its rear was hinged to the cowl. It lifted, from the front, in "alligator" style.

Exterior paint colors for early Mercurys were Black; Jefferson Blue; Gull Gray; Dartmouth Green; Tropical Green; Mercury Blue Metallic; Folkestone Gray; and Bright Coach Maroon. Spring colors, added later, were Cloud Mist Gray and Claret Maroon.

Inside, the Mercury featured comfortable, triple-cushion upholstery with flexible, rolled-edge seat cushions. There was an up-to-date, two-spoke steering wheel ... the first ever seen in the industry. "All its appointments are as modern as the new steering wheel and instrument panel," said one promotion. The upholstery was done in taupe Bedford cloth or striped broadcloth, except in Convertible Coupes. The "ragtop" featured hand-buffed, antique-finished leather. Initially it came in Mahogany Red only, but it was later offered in Light Russet, as well. Convertible tops came in Black with Vermilion beading or Tan or Gray with Tan beading.

"The Mercury 8 offers you remarkable freedom from noise and vibration ... thanks to thorough soundproofing," said a color advertisement showing a two-door Sedan. "All the resources of modern technology have been used by Ford research engineers to track down and eliminate engine, body and chassis noises. New materials and many rubber mountings also contribute to making the Mercury 'as silent as the night,' restful and relaxing."

The Mercury engine had a larger bore. Therefore, it had a heavier, cast alloy steel crankshaft than the Ford V-8 employed. It came with 2.14-inch (instead of two-inch) diameter crank pins. Due to the use of steel expander rings in the second and third grooves of the pistons, the Mercury V-8 promised improved oil economy. Valve seat inserts were installed on both intake and exhaust valves. A six-blade fan was attached to the front of the crankshaft. The engine had cast iron heads and required 14-millimeter spark plugs.

"Driving this Mercury is sheer delight!" a California buyer stated in one letter to Ford. "My wife is particularly pleased with the steering, (it) makes the car so easy to park. On our first trip, we did better than 20 miles to the gallon of gasoline. In traffic (we) have not fallen below 17 miles to the gallon."

A blocker-type synchronizer, similar to the one in the Lincoln-Zephyr, was featured in the Mercury's transmission. It was a three-speed manual gear box with a floor-mounted gearshifter. A nine-inch, single-plate, semi-centrifugal clutch carried the power rearward. Overdrive was an available option. The torque tube drive components and 3.54:1 rear axle were also of the same design as those employed in the Lincoln-Zephyr. The use of a numerically lower rear axle ratio, than that of the Ford, added to the Mercury's "zippy" performance.

Several changes, introduced on the 1939 Ford Deluxe, were also standard on the Mercury 8. Hydraulic brakes, of a simple two-shoe design, were one such improvement. They produced a 55/45 front-to-rear distribution of braking effort, with all four front brake pistons larger than those at the rear. Twelve-inch drums with 162 square-inches of braking area were riveted to all four steel hubs with cast iron rivets. The hydraulic brake tubing was routed above the rear radius arms, to shield it from damage caused by stones tossed up by the front wheels. At the front of the torque tube, short rubber tubing connected the rear hydraulic system with the master cylinder. The cylinder was rigidly mounted, with the pedal bracket bolted to it.

Like the 1939 Ford Deluxe, the Mercury 8 used a battery condition indicator in place of a conventional ammeter. This was a special voltmeter, with a scale marked H (high), N (normal) and L (low). It told a motorist the condition of the battery at a glance. Both cars had a voltage-controlled generator with a maximum charging rate of 30 amperes.

A two-spoke steering wheel was the first ever seen in the industry. (Mercury)

Fred Jones, Oklahoma's largest Ford dealer, was an early Mercury dealer, and is still in business. (Fred Jones)

In 1939, the 115,514 residents of Spokane, Washington could visit the Day-Majer Company's showroom to see the new 1939 Mercurys. (W. McKiernan)

15

Additional standard equipment in the Mercury included a trip mileage indicator; front and rear ashtrays; and twin air-electric horns. Extra-cost options ranged from a heater and defroster to a new type of Ford radio. This radio had a single push-button, which was pressed from one to six times to tune in any of five radio stations or to bring the manual dial into use. Deluxe wheelcovers, fog lights and spot lamps, and even a set of matched luggage, were also available.

The MoToR, an English magazine, did extensive road tests of American vehicles at this time. It analyzed the new Mercury 8 in its March 21, 1939, issue, praising its performance, roadability and rugged construction. It was credited with being one of the best buys on the British market, due to its "lightning acceleration." In actual road tests, it went from 0-to-60 mph in 13.3 seconds and showed a top speed of 90 mph. Handling was also rated highly. The Mercury 8 compared favorably to contemporary British sports cars.

In the United States, Mercurys were spotlighted at the 1939-1940 New York World's Fair and the Golden Gate Exposition in San Francisco Bay. At the New York event, the entrance to the Ford pavilion had a 25-foot-high, stainless steel statue of the Roman guard Mercury. Fair-goers could also ride over Ford's "Highway of Tomorrow" in new Ford Motor Company cars of various brands.

While introduced as a "new 95 hp Ford," the first Mercury 8 was clearly superior to the

The "ragtop" featured hand-buffed, antique leather seats. It first came in Mahogany Red only, but was later offered in Light Russet. (Bernard Pranica)

The top and sides of the 1939 hood were one unit. It was hinged at the cowl, and lifted from the front. Photographer Leroy Byers snapped this photo of a car he owned at a 1966 car show in Denver. (Leroy Byers)

Leroy Byer's and Rick Comin's cars (left) show Mercury's horizontal-bars grille. The 1939 Ford (right) had vertical-bars grille. (Leroy Byers)

Leroy Byer's former convertible shows how 1939 Mercurys had flatter fenders than Fords, and semi-skirted wheel openings. (Leroy Byers)

1939 Fords in size, power and roadability. The articles in trade magazines seemed to pitch it, to car dealers, as the "big Ford." However, just about any single-line or multi-line dealer could sell the Mercury, whether they handled just Fords, just Lincolns, just Mercurys or any combination of the three car-lines. "The New Mercury 8," read a headline appearing in many advertisements. "A Product of the Ford Motor Company."

The dealers must have lined up to handle the new Mercury, too. According to *Ward's Automotive Yearbook* 1942, there were 3,500 Ford Motor Company dealerships selling Mercurys, in the United States, by as early as 1941. These figures compared to a total of 7,200 dealers selling Fords and 2,300 selling Lincoln-Zephyrs. Duplications were approximately 33-1/3 percent for the dealer body as a whole, with Chrysler Corporation "duals" and Ford/Mercury/Lincoln-Zephyr combinations accounting for the greatest share of the duplications. Mercury's main competitors were De-Soto, handled by 2,500 Chrysler Corporation dealers and Pontiac, a brand which 3,500 General Motors dealers carried, many as an exclusive line.

Actually, it made most sense for FoMoCo dealers to sell the Mercury as an up-scale Ford. Pushing it as a cheaper Lincoln went against the grain. Was the Lincoln salesman supposed to tell his customers, "Why don't you move down the ladder and spend a little less with us this year?" Hardly! There was more to be gained by telling Ford shoppers, "I can give you fine-car features for a few dollars more than the lowest-priced models, just like GM does." Ford salesmen now had a weapon to use in fighting for a larger share of the market.

Some folks still did not understand where the emphasis was supposed to go, though. *The New York Times* wrote, "Modernly streamlined, the car has a family resemblance to the Lincoln-Zephyr." Maybe the *Times* saw a similarity, but the resemblance was a loose one. In all honesty, the Mercury 8 was a unique product. None of its body panels interchanged with those of either the Ford or the Lincoln-Zephyrs. The Mercury really was all-new.

Although Ford did not represent the Mercury as a Lincoln, it did sometimes blend it smoothly into the corporate family. "Thirty-five years ago, the Ford Motor Company manufactured its first automobile," read a color advertisement for the Convertible Coupe. "The accumulated experiences of all those thirty-five years now finds new expression in an entirely new car, the Mercury 8 ... designed to extend Ford-Lincoln standards of mechanical excellence, progressive design and outstanding value to a new price field."

In the end, Ford probably did not care if buyers moving up the ladder saw the 1939 Mercury as a "big Ford" or as a "baby Lincoln. What counted most was that they bought it. The new marque had a successful first year, with 69,135 assemblies for the model run. That included 13,216 two-door sedans; 8,254 Coupe-Sedans, 39,847 Town Sedans and 7,818 Convertible Coupes. Out of the total, 10,621 cars were built overseas.

While the later Mercurys of 1949 to 1951 are well-known popularity leaders in the custom car industry, the 1939 model was also very attractive to automotive enthusiasts who modified vehicles for increased performance or improved eye appeal. The Mercury's larger flathead V-8 accepted much of the same speed equipment readily available for Ford flatheads, but produced more horsepower after being "hopped-up." In a similar fashion, customizers found Fords readily available and affordable and came to appreciate their styling lines. The "Mercs" had a family resemblance, but still provided some distinction for the modifier seeking something that stood out from the crowd. In the very first edition of *Motor Trend* (September 1949), a 1939 Mercury Convertible that had been customized by Jack's Trim Shop, of Detroit, was featured. Updates to this car included a smoothened hood and turtle deck, leaded-in fenders, concealed controls and Oldsmobile bumpers with parking lights and taillights in the bumper guards. The same magazine was filled with ads for customizing parts, most of which were designed for Fords and Mercurys.

"Ford and Mercury More Attractive and More Comfortable," *Motor* announced in October 1939. The trade magazine noted that some new features of the 1940 Mercury trickled down to the Ford Deluxe, while a redesigned and restyled Lincoln-Zephyr shared some of its new features with the Mercury. However, one thing that Mercury shared with no one was a new Convertible Sedan. This Mercury body style was an exclusive offering from the Ford "family" that year.

All three car-lines had new sealed beam headlamps; a steering column-mounted gear-shift; a controlled All-Weather ventilation system with window ventilators; and rear compartments with four inches of additional leg room, thanks to thinner seat backs. There was also more elbow room, thanks to a change in the trim on the side panels. The Mercury sported a revised front bumper, with a lower center section; new rectangular taillamps (replacing 1939's barrel-shaped units); and an instrument panel with blue and silver finish.

Rick Comin's 1939 Mercury Convertible took first place in Lincoln-Mercury class at Ford Nationals, in Detroit, circa 1975. (Leroy Byers)

Exterior colors for the second year were Black; Cloudmist Gray; Folkstone Gray; Lyon Blue; Sahara Sand; Yosemite Green; Mandarin Maroon; Cotswold Gray Metallic; and Garnet. The colors Como Blue Metallic and Acadia Green were added at midyear. Interiors were upholstered in Blue-Gray body cloth accented by Silver garnish moldings. They had blue door handles, knobs and escutcheons.

A slightly revised grille featured horizontal chrome bars, on either side of center, on the lower half of the front end. They met at the center rail. Stylist Willys Wagner designed the new headlamp rims, which were wider at the top. In addition to looking just great, they accommodated the new sealed beam headlights without changing the 1939 front fenders.

Other changes included a hood with new trim and a revised latching system; a deck lid with "clock-spring" style supports; redesigned rear armrests; better insulation; an improved lock on the lighted trunk compartment; and the relocation of the headlamp high beam button to the left of the clutch pedal, instead of between two pedals.

Mercury retained its flathead V-8, which was rated for 95 hp at 3600 rpm. Its top speed was again somewhere around 90 mph. The X-braced chassis continued to ride a 116-inch wheelbase and the car's overall length was 195.9 inches.

Technical changes were of mostly a minor nature. Mercury switched to wheels with a smaller 5-1/2-inch bolt circle (with no change in tire size) and curved disc "spiders." A stabilizer bar was added up front and coupled directly to the axle ends, without the use of a linkage. This provided lateral stabilization, to keep the frame in proper relationship to the axle, and reduced body roll on turns. Metal spring covers were standard and shock absorbers now had self-sealing glands, eliminating the necessity of filling them.

Here's a good rear view of Rick Comin's 1939 Mercury Convertible. (Leroy Byers)

Other mechanical improvements included a voltage- and current-regulated generator, which was of larger capacity, plus a new 120-ampere-hour battery with a 20 percent increase in cranking capacity. The clutch pedal linkage was also redesigned so that accurate control of the clutch was unaffected by any movement of the engine on its rubber mountings.

The Convertible Sedan was added to the model lineup with a $1,212 price tag. Mercury historian Tom LaMarre once wrote about this model as Mercury's "better late than never" car. "Photos exist showing a 1939 Mercury Convertible Sedan prototype," LaMarre noted in *Old Cars*. "But the body style did not go into regular production until the 1940 model-year. In addition to being the most expensive Mercury, it was the heaviest at 3,138 pounds."

Other prices for 1940 Mercurys climbed $61 for the Convertible (now called a Convertible Club Coupe) and $30 for each of the other body styles. The Mercury Deluxe 8 Convertible Club Coupe was equipped with a vacuum-operated top at no extra cost. The automatic top system operated from vacuum developed in the engine's intake manifold. The top was much like the manual type, with a linkage designed to receive the piston rod from the operating cylinder. The power unit consisted of two vacuum cylinders at each end of the rear seat. There were three latches, at the windshield, to hold the top down, on metal pegs, at its center. Pulling out as dashboard-mounted control knob lowered the top. Holding the control valve in raised it.

Convertible tops came in Black with Vermilion beading or Tan/Gray with Tan beading. Richard Defendorf owns this restored ragtop. (Milton Gene Kieft)

In its second year, the Mercury caught the eye of at least one hearse and ambulance builder. The Shop of Siebert, located in Toledo, Ohio, introduced a Mercury-based "Aristocrat" funeral coach and several other models. Siebert had previously utilized the Ford chassis, so the switch to Mercury was logical, the "Merc" having more power to move heavy caskets and finer appointments to fit the occasion.

In 1940, the worldwide production of Mercurys climbed to 86,685 cars. This total included at least 1,083 Convertible Sedans, of which 979 were sold in the United States. They were the last regular production open phaetons made by any of the Ford marques until the Lincoln-Continental four-door convertible of 1961. There were 9,741 Convertible Club Coupes built; 42,806 four-door Town Sedans; 16,189 Sedan-Coupes; and 16,243 two-door Tudor Sedans.

The 1941 Mercury lost some of the marque's original exclusiveness. Mercury now shared, with Ford, an all-new family of body shells. This gave the two brands even more commonality than in 1939 and 1940. They were larger, higher, wider and, generally, roomier than the previous models. They also had deeper windshields. In overall appearance, they looked like a "squatting down" 1940 model with squared-off fenders. Thinner roof pillars, increased glass area and a one-piece backlight enhanced visibility for drivers.

Identical widths revealed the commonality of the Ford and Mercury bodies, although the Merc's 118-inch wheelbase and 129.38-inch spring base were each four inches longer than those of the Ford. The overall length of 200.61 inches was 6.2 inches more than the Ford stretched from bumper-to-bumper. The Mercury's longer measurements were due to a longer front end. The steering worm shaft had to be made longer than the Ford type. Special brackets set the

The 1940 Mercurys sported a revised instrument panel with blue and silver finish. (Tim Howley)

Some 1940 Mercury features were shared with a redesigned Lincoln-Zephyr, but one thing Mercury shared with no one was a 1940 Convertible Sedan. (*Old Cars*)

The Mercury Deluxe 8 Convertible Club Coupe was equipped with a vacuum-operated top at no extra cost. The automatic top system operated from vacuum developed in the engine's intake manifold. (Mercury)

engine back four inches. The front suspension was moved four inches forward through use of a special plate. From the cowl area backwards, the bodies were virtually identical.

Size, of course, qualified as a selling feature in 1941. Ford did not overlook this fact. "The big car that stands alone in economy," said one advertisement of the year. Mercury pushed economy, too, claiming that some owners got 20 mpg. Another advertisement hit the same themes, boasting, "A driver's dream come true is the superb new Mercury 8. A car as big and commanding as you'd wish ... yet lively and full of the high spirit of travel. A car of deep, satisfying comfort and apparently unlimited power. And above all, a big car that is really economical to drive."

Round headlamps and fender top-mounted parking lamps were among front styling changes. In this year only, Mercurys had parking lamps on top of the front fenders. The hood was lower, broader and more plain-sided than in 1940. Lower, broader fenders carried a horizontal bead all around and had a vertical bead delineating hefty front "catwalks." Low grilles, with fine, horizontal blades, were seen on both sides of a vertical center piece, which tapered slightly towards the bottom. The hood was trimmed with a horizontal nose band up its center and a vertical center molding. The front bumper was more bowed than the 1940 bumper. It had twin guards directly in front of the grille, instead of flanking the sides of the grille.

Body improvements included wider doors; concealed running boards; a gas filler cap hidden below a flip-up door; an inside-the-car hood release; the addition of new rear fender gravel deflectors; and redesigned wraparound taillamps. Adding a neat touch was the manner in which the outside door handles blended in with the design of the belt moldings. The body and fender moldings used on Mercurys built early in the year were of a different design than those used on late-production cars. There were a number of running changes, because the 1941 models sold better than expected and inventories of certain parts were depleted. Ford then used different parts to assemble additional cars. Since 1941 Ford sales were not exceeding projections, some Ford parts were used to complete Mercurys.

Mercury collector Bernie Roehrig did an extensive study of variations between early- and late-production 1941 Mercurys. It was published in the March/April 1991 issue of *V8 Times*, the Early V8 Ford Club of America's wonderful magazine. In brief, some of the variations between the two types of cars are as follows:

Early Cars	Late Cars
Double U-joint front spring plate	1941 Ford style spring plate
1940 Ford style drag link	1941 Ford style drag link
Smaller radiator surround	Larger radiator surround
19A Special front park light	11A-1941 Ford front park light
Oval inside rearview mirror	Rectangular inside rearview mirror
Radio speaker grille with red "M"	Radio speaker grille without "M"
Starter button left of steering wheel	Starter switch on dash
Horn ring with protruding spokes	Smooth horn ring
Door panels with one strip and medallion	1946-1948 Mercury style door panel
Bullet-tipped fender and body moldings	Pointed-tip fender and body moldings
Three-piece front fender	Two-piece front fender
Single-piece hubcap	Two-piece hubcap w/ attaching insert
Hood hinges bolted to "flat" on firewall	Hood hinges bolted to side of firewall

Inside all 1941 Mercurys was a new instrument panel and larger seats with foam rubber padding. The interior color was changed to brown, for most models. There was a restyled "Easy Vision" two-spoke steering wheel with a half-moon horn ring. The radio grille was built into the instrument panel. The windshield wipers were revised, with a new motor and linkage being used. The wiper control switch moved from the base of the windshield, at the center, to the instrument panel.

The Mercury V-8 was basically unchanged, although a high-compression head was made available. There were new hardened valve stems, tungsten steel valve seats and improvements to the manifold and the fuel pump. New, three-ring steel pistons were employed. The fan blade shaft was four inches longer to make up for the "set-ahead" front axle. A larger, 10-inch diameter "Velvet-Action" clutch was adopted, along with clutch linkage revisions. Other refinements were a newly designed "Perfected" stabilizer bar and a "Center-Poise" balanced chassis with a box-sectional frame and longer, softer-acting springs. The body mounts and front shock absorbers were improved, too, and larger 6.50 x 16 tires were mounted.

Seven body styles were now offered in the Mercury line-up, the new ones being a Station Wagon and a "Coupe A/S," which designated the Coupe with Auxiliary Seats. The Convertible Sedan was gone, but a five-window, two-to-three-passenger Coupe was new. While not actually listed as a "Business Coupe," it had a behind-the-seat luggage space and parcel shelf, which were well suited for commercial users. Its roof was more streamlined than that of the Sedan-Coupe (sometimes called the "Club Coupe") and it had a one-piece backlight.

As in the past, each body style had a numerical model designation, which was often written following the 99A Mercury motor number. Thus, Model 99A-77 was the $910 five-window Coupe; Model 99A-67 was the $936 A/S Coupe; and Model 99A-72 was the $977 Sedan-Coupe. Other models and prices were: Convertible Club Coupe 99A-76, for $1,100; Tudor Sedan 99A-70, for $946; Town Sedan 99A-73, for $987; and Station Wagon 99A-79 for $1,141. The 99A-74 model designation for the Convertible Sedan was no longer used.

Paint color charts reveal that there were eight colors offered for 1941 Mercurys at the beginning of the model-year: Black; Cotswold Gray Metallic; Capri Blue Metallic; Cayuga Blue; Mayfair Maroon; Lochaven Green; Harbor Gray; and Palisade Gray. By spring, Mercury added Conestoga Tan Metallic; Sheffield Gray Metallic; Florentine Blue; and Seminole Brown. Two-tone paint combinations were introduced late in the model year, along with a projectile hood ornament.

In 1940, Mercury built 16,189 Sedan-Coupes. They again featured stainless steel window frames, and had a "hard-top" look. (*Old Cars*)

A revised 1940 grille had horizontal chrome bars. New headlamps held sealed beams without changing the 1939 fenders. (Mercury)

The 1940 Mercury had a 95 hp flathead V-8. Its top speed was again somewhere around 90 mph on dry pavement, but it was not quite that fast in the snow. The X-braced chassis had a 116-inch wheelbase. (Mercury).

The most popular 1941 Mercury, as might be expected, was the perfect-for-the-family four-door Town Sedan, of which 42,984 were assembled. The rear doors on this model were still of front-opening, "suicide" design. (Mercury)

Closed cars had tan interior trimmings and brown hardware. Convertibles offered tan, red, or blue leather seats and a choice of a black top with vermilion beading or an olive top with olive beading. Wagon seats came with tan, blue or red leather trim. They were "interchangeable," which meant they could be set up four different ways. Essentially, this meant that the rear two seats could be removed or either one could be installed, alone, in either position.

The Station Wagon featured maple body framing with birch panels. It had a truck-style taillamp that swiveled, so it could be seen, at night, with the liftgate and tailgate open. The spare tire mounted on the tailgate. To allow clearance for the tire, when the gate was down, the rear bumper was identical to that used on Ford Deluxe models. While all other 1941 Mercurys weighed-in at 3,000 to 3,225 pounds, the Station Wagon was a hefty 3,468-pounder.

Other Mercury body styles also had distinctions. The Model 99A-67 A/S Coupe included fold-down rear seats and lowerable rear quarter windows. The Tudor Sedan had rear vent windows. Unlike its thin-pillared, hardtop-like predecessor, the new Sedan-Coupe had standard type roof supports. Its rear quarter windows pivoted outwards in "wind-wing" style. The Convertible Club Coupe now had a hydro-electric mechanism to supply power for rising and lowering the automatic convertible top. In the two/three-passenger Coupe, the quarter windows were fixed and the one-piece seat back lifted for access to the storage area behind it.

Siebert again offered hearse and ambulance conversions for the Ford or Mercury chassis, with 18 separate models available. The same firm also constructed an eight-door, 11-passenger tourist bus from a Mercury Town Sedan. It had a 190-inch wheelbase and weighed 5,100 pounds. Overall length was 22-1/2 feet. Naturally, a vacuum-assisted brake system was needed to stop this monster. It had a roof rack, large 7.00 x 15 truck tires and a $2,280 price tag.

The new-for-1941 Station Wagon came with tan, blue or red leather seats that were "interchangeable." (*Old Cars*)

There was a pair of coupes in the 1941 Mercury line. The (Business) Coupe was $885, and the Sedan-Coupe was $950. (Lowell E. Eisenhour)

Several other contemporary customs were made from 1941 Mercurys. One was a six-door, 11-passenger woodie, also constructed by Siebert. Another was a Sedanca deVille built by Paul Stengel of Coachcraft LTD., a Hollywood, California coach building shop that did a lot of conversion work for motion picture stars.

Common folks liked Mercurys as well as Hollywood hot shots and Ford had a winner again in 1941. In only its third year on the market, Mercury ranked 11th in industry sales. That put it ahead of Nash; Hudson; Packard; Cadillac; Lincoln-Zephyr; and Willys. The year 1941 was the second best production year in automotive history, after 1929. Model-year production of Mercurys rose for the third straight time, peaking at 98,412 cars worldwide.

Early in the calendar-year, on February 13, Mercury produced its 200,000th car. "So right is the Mercury's combination of motoring's good things, that it has won more than 155,000 owner-friends in just 25 months," the advertising copywriters gushed. The most popular Mercury, as might be expected, was the perfect-for-the-family four-door Town Sedan, of which 42,984 were assembled. It was followed by the Tudor Sedan with 20,932 made and the Sedan-Coupe, with an 18,263-unit production total. The Convertible Club Coupe, with 8,556 made, was also fairly popular. Bringing up the rear were the all three of the new models, the five-window Coupe with 3,313 orders, the Station Wagon with 2,291 and the A/S Coupe with 1,954.

"Liquamatic Drive," increased horsepower, better riding comfort and improved braking highlighted the 1942 Mercury story. The new Mercurys, along with their Ford "cousins," started production on September 10, 1941. They were "announced" on October 4, the same day as Lincolns and one day after the introduction of the 1942 Fords. For the first time, *Motor* (October 1941) featured Mercury's press announcement separate from that of Ford. The magazine depicted two- and four-door Town Sedans, the attractive new instrument panel design and the broad, new grille with the parking lamps moved to the catwalks, alongside the front of the hood.

Prices increased $115 for the Convertible Club Coupe. The open cars offered leather seats. (Mercury)

The 1942 fenders were lower, with narrower catwalks, but wider tops. There was a bead line, below each headlamp, curving around to the wheel openings. The upper and lower grille sections had wide horizontal bars. (Mercury)

Prices increased $115 for the Convertible Club Coupe. (*Old Cars*)

For an enhanced "Sky Ride" 1942 Mercurys had wider 58 inches front, and 60 inches rear treads. Only 857 wagons were built. (*Old Cars*)

The 1942 wagon came with a choice of red, tan or blue leather upholstery. (*Old Cars*)

The Mercury's fenders, grille and bumpers were restyled for 1942. The fenders were lower. They had narrower catwalks, but wider top surfaces. There was a horizontal bead line, below each head-lamp, at the level where the grille's bottom section started. They curved around the body corners, to the front wheel openings. The grille consisted of upper and lower sections with wide, horizontal bars. Eight bars crossed the upper grille sections, from just inside the headlamps. They were bisected by a vertical center molding. Five longer bars, running below the center of each headlamp (and also bisected by a vertical center member) filled the lower grille section.

On top of the grille was a chrome header bar, with a decorative center ornament. Above this was a molding with the Mercury name stamped into it. The rectangular parking lamps flanked each side of the nose. Directional signals were optional. There was a double bead molding along the hood's sides and nose, plus a hood ornament. The front fender tops had chrome moldings on them. There was a more massive bumper, with a license plate holder in its center, and bumper guards on either side. Splash shields were added between the bumper and the body.

While the Mercury's wheelbase stayed at 118 inches, its overall bumper-to-bumper length jumped four inches. Most, if not all, of this was due to the larger bumpers. The spring base remained unchanged, too, as did body width. All models, except the A/S Coupe, returned to the Mercury lineup. Prices increased from $78 to $94 for coupes and sedans, $115 for the Convertible Club Coupe and $119 for the Station Wagon. Sedan-Coupes had a revised turret top, which was now interchangeable with that of the 1942 Ford Sedan-Coupe. Both the two- and four-door "slant back" Sedans were now called Town Sedans.

Interiors in Coupes and Sedans were cloth with tan imitation leather trim. The Convertible Club Coupes offered leather seats, while the Station Wagon came with a choice of red, tan or blue leather upholstery. Mercury was big on designing steering wheels. There was another new one, with a full-circle horn ring. It had a large center insert with the Mercury head on it, and plastic spoke inserts with "Mercury Eight" lettering. The redesigned instrument panel sported what Mercury called the "balanced look." It had a central radio speaker grille flanked by a large, circular clock and speedometer. Other gauges were set in a panel on the left, which was balanced by the glove box on the far right. There were twin ashtrays, near the top of the panel, on either side of the speaker.

Many 1942 Mercury publicity photos showed cars with women drivers. This may have been part of an effort to promote the Liquamatic Drive option. This system consisted of a liquid coupling, in place of the conventional flywheel, and an "automatic" transmission. The gear-shift lever con-trolled the conventional, manually-operated low and reverse gears. The second speed position could be used to lock-out the automatic shifting feature of the transmission. It kept it from shifting into high gear and permitted using the engine as a brake, through second gear. The former high gear position put the transmission in "driving" range, where the start was in second gear and the shift to high was achieved automatically. An accelerator kick-down switch was provided to permit temporarily down-shifting to second gear, at 11 to 38 mph, for more passing power.

With the gear-shift lever in high, the car would start from rest, in second gear, whenever the accelerator was depressed. It then shifted into high, when the foot was lifted off the accelerator

For just $1,126, the 1942 Mercury Town Sedan was a lot of car. Mercury was America's 14th largest automaker in its fourth season. (Bob Thatcher)

above a speed of 12 mph. A shift back down to second occurred when the speed dropped below 10 mph. The second gear ratio in Liquamatic Drive was 1.83:1, instead of 1.74:1. The clutch had to be disengaged, when the gear-shift was moved, but almost all driving could be done with the shifter in high. With Liquamatic Drive, the transmission was actually in two gears at once, when the lever was in high, but second gear would freewheel, unless the driver down-shifted into second gear for engine braking.

Mercury advertisements called the 1942 model "The Aviation Idea in Automobiles, More Power Per Pound." Dimensions of the flathead V-8 remained unchanged, but horsepower increased to 100 at 3800 rpm. There were several contributing factors, but an improved flow of gases in both the intake and exhaust systems was credited for most of the year's increase in power. A new Chandler-Groves carburetor replaced the original Ford carburetor. The compression ratio was also boosted to 6.4:1. Mercury relocated the coil from the distributor, to the engine block. More uniform cooling was achieved by revising the size of the fluid passages. Both intake and exhaust valve seats were now made of 15 percent chrome-molybdenum alloy, instead of chrome-tungsten steel. The old chrome-nickel valves were replaced with high chrome alloy types.

For an enhanced "Sky Ride" and more comfort, the 1942 Mercury had an increase in tread width to 58 inches up front and 60 inches at the rear. In addition, new five-inch-wide (instead of four-inch-wide) wheel rims were used. The front stabilizer bar, added in 1941, was joined by a transverse radius rod running from one end of the axle to the opposite side stabilizer bracket. Also new was an anti-sway bar to improve the car's equilibrium. The front of the Mercury was lowered a total of 1-1/2 inches, one inch by a new axle with less spring camber and an additional 1/2 inch through a switch to 6.50 x 15 size tires.

Better body insulation and rubber-bushed spring eyes increased the Mercury's quietness. Each spring leaf had one large oil groove (instead of two smaller ones) for more effective lubrication. There were two new rear engine mounts to provide better front-to-back stability and to eliminate the use of vibration-prone brace rods between the engine, frame and body.

Braking effectiveness was upped via a 15 percent decrease in the minimum brake pedal operating pressure required to halt a Mercury. This was achieved because the larger diameter front brake pistons divided the braking effort 60/40, front-to-rear, instead of 55/45.

Cars with conventional, manual transmissions had easier gear-shifting, because longer levers were used on the side of the transmission case. Also, a heavier steering column tube, with a ball bearing at its upper end, improved steering action. The standard rear axle ratio was lowered (made numerically higher) for even better road economy.

Due to the outbreak of World War II, the manufacture of Ford Motor Company models ground to a halt on February 10, 1942. By March 2, passenger car rationing began throughout the nation. Naturally, the shortening of the model-year caused Mercury production to drop for the first time ever. Only 24,704 units were assembled. They included 11,784 four-door Town Sedans; 5,345 Sedan-Coupes; 4,941 two-door Town Sedans; approximately 969 Convertible Club Coupes; 857 Station Wagons; and 800 three-passenger Coupes. Only 774 cars had Liquamatic Drive, which did not return after the war.

Mercury during the war 1943-1945

The outbreak of war in Europe and Asia brought drastic changes to the American way of life. Millions of men willingly took up arms to join in the battle for world freedom. On the "homefront," everyday life was affected. The conflict brought the rationing of gasoline, tires, food, and many other items normally taken for granted.

New-car production in the United States was halted in early February of 1942. Thereafter, no brand new cars or trucks were constructed for civilian buyers until approximately July 2, 1945. A number of unsold 1941 and 1942 vehicles were "mothballed" for people who were considered "essential users." This classification included doctors, munitions plant workers, government oficials and Civil Defense officials, etc.

Ford Motor Company, like other auto manufacturers, converted its assembly lines to the production of war goods. During World War II, Ford was probably best known for making B-24 Liberator bomber engines, the GPW Jeep (based on Willys-Overland specifications) and amphibious Jeeps. It also made military Command Cars, Pratt & Whitney aircraft engines and dozens of other military vehicles and parts.

Monart Motors Company hired designer Brooks Stevens to create its conversions. He is on the right, in the center. (Brooks Stevens)

Lincoln built tank engines, amphibious Jeep bodies and B-24 bomber parts. Since Mercury was not yet a distinct division of the company, it played no specific role in war goods manufacturing. However, one Mercury-related program that was conducted on the homefront, did contribute, indirectly, to the nation's ability to struggle for freedom.

With car assembly lines halted, there developed a severe shortage of automobiles, even for essential users. This prompted one Mercury dealer, Monart Motors Company of Milwaukee, Wisconsin, to create a special vehicle conversion program. It was designed to provide multi-passenger, Carry-All Station Wagons to school bus operators, ambulance services and other groups that critically needed a reliable means of mass or special transportation.

Monart's "Conservation in the War Effort" program converted stock Mercury automobiles into large, wood-bodied Station Wagons. The

Original design rendering for Monart Station Wagon indicates "styled by Brooks Stevens 8-42." (Brooks Stevens)

Monart-Mercury Carry-All Station Wagons started out as Coupes, two-door Town Sedans or four-door Town Sedans that had been built to standard factory specifications. They were originally designed to carry from three to six passengers. After the Monart Station Wagon conversions, they were capable of carrying nine to 12 passengers each.

Monart Motors' sales brochure discussed the need for Station Wagons, administrative "Carry-Alls" (Suburbans) and ambulances during World War II. It noted that all of the new 1941 and 1942 Station Wagons had been sold. Throughout the United States, car dealers' stocks of such vehicles were completely exhausted. Even the highest-priced Station Wagons, such as those made by Packard, could no longer be obtained.

"The fact that most of these were purchased by governmental agencies is proof of the preference for and the utility of Station Wagons over all other body types," noted Monart. "Sedans were bought (by the agencies) only after exhaustion of the supply of available Station Wagon models."

The Mercury dealer further pointed out that ordnance plants, the Red Cross and other businesses engaged in the war effort, throughout the nation, had bought Station Wagons whenever they could get their hands on one. "It was quickly recognized that not only could more persons per unit be transported, but also that the Station Wagon provided a vehicle that served as an all-pur-

The Mercury Sedan on the left is what Monart began with. When converted, the car would look like the Station Wagon on the right. (Brooks Stevens)

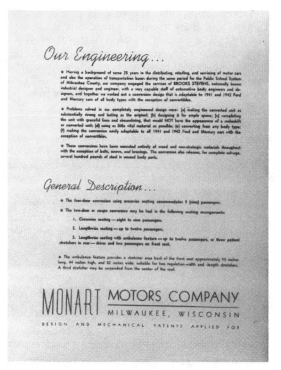

The "Conservation in the War Effort" brochure for Monart Mercury had a patriotic look. (Brooks Stevens)

A full-page announcement in the Monart Motor's brochure outlined the company's background and reliability. (Brooks Stevens)

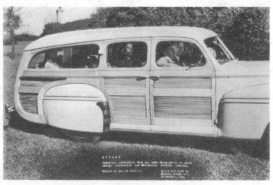

Comparative costs of conversions on a cost-per-seat basis were outlined in the brochure. (Brooks Stevens)

This is Monart's nine-passenger with skirted rear fenders. (Brooks Stevens)

In civilian trim, the Monart Motors Station Wagon had the appearance of a rich estate wagon. Nine- and 12-passenger versions were offered. (Brooks Stevens)

pose utility car," explained the sales booklet. "This (is) because all or a part of the seats are easily removable and the unit can serve the multiple purpose of a light-truck, ambulance or passenger car."

Although these Monart Carry-All Station Wagons were no longer vehicles completely engineered by the original manufacturer, neither were they shoddy conversion units. Monart Motors Company had a 25-year-long history in distributing, retailing and servicing motor cars in Milwaukee. It also operated transportation buses for the Public School System of Milwaukee County during the same period. It was, in short, a well-established firm with a solid reputation to back its newest product.

To protect its reputation, Monart Motors Company hired Brooks Stevens, the internationally-known industrial designer and engineer, to help create the conversions. Working with a capable staff of automotive body engineers and designers, Monart and Brooks Stevens came up with a conversion design specifically adaptable to all types of 1941 and 1942 Fords and Mercurys, except Convertibles.

During the creative process, a number of important challenges were closely considered. First, the design engineers tried hard to make the converted units as substantially strong and long-lasting as the original cars. They carefully planned the vehicles to provide ample space, while trying to maintain the graceful appearance and stream-lining of the "factory" design. They did not want the Carry-All Station Wagons to look makeshift, as was too often the case with converted vehicles. Brooks Stevens also tackled the task of making the conversion easily adaptable to all 1941 to 1942 Mercury closed-model cars. This meant that there would be a larger pool of "donor" vehicles to use as platforms for the Carry-All Station Wagon conversions.

In one part of the brochure, the sales pitch claimed that a conversion suitable for two-door cars actually freed up four-door cars for sale to essential users. This was seen as an advantage, because four-door Sedans generally held more passengers. The thinking was a four-door Sedan held six passengers, while a typical Coupe held three. Thus, it would take just one

An ambulance with siren, roof rack, and "black-out" trim. (Brooks Stevens)

This Monart Carry-All Station Wagon conversion was used as an ambulance by the medical staff at a United States Army Air Base Headquarters. (Brooks Stevens)

Sedan to transport as many people as two Coupes. That suggested that every Sedan Monart Motors saved, by converting two-door cars instead, cut the number of vehicles needed for essential users in half.

It was also important for the conversion work to consume as little vital material as possible. The supply of raw goods was still under strict rationing and patriotism was a big factor. Earnest attempts by industry to conserve commodities for the war effort were viewed as good for business, while wasting materials could drive many customers away.

The conversion unit was said to be "executed entirely of wood and non-strategic materials throughout, with the exception of bolts, screws and bracings." Monart Motors added, "The conversion also releases, for complete salvage, several hundred pounds of steel in unused body parts."

When four-door model cars were converted, the accommodations included crosswise seats holding nine passengers. The Mercury two-door Sedans or Coupes came in a choice of conversions with several different seating arrangements possible. The first featured crosswise seating for eight to nine passengers. The second featured lengthwise seating for up to 12 passengers. The third featured lengthwise seating with ambulance equipment to accommodate up to 12 passengers, or a driver and two passengers on the crosswise front seat and stretchers in the rear.

The ambulance model provided a stretcher area, in back of the front seat, that was approximately 95 inches long, 44 inches high and 52 inches wide. It was suitable for a pair of regulation-width and regulation-length patient stretchers, while a third stretcher could be suspended from the center of the roof.

Monart Motors' sales brochure did not specifically state how much a conversion cost. Instead, it said, "The comparative expense of conversion on a cost-per-seat basis reveals some interesting figures. Lumping all body types in the lower price car field would bring the average cost of a 'basic car' to around $1,150 which, allowing six passengers per unit on a cost-per-seat basis, would be approximately $190 per seat. However, many of the basic, cars will not accommodate six passengers. Adding the above cost of approximately $1,150 to the cost of the Monart conversion, the resulting cost on a per-seat basis would then be approximately $217 for the nine-passenger Carry-All Station Wagon or approximately $163 for the 12-passenger Carry-All Station Wagon."

Simple algebra tells us that these figures suggest the basic price of a Monart Station Wagon was $1,953. Using the $1,150 basic car price, the conversion cost can be calculated at just over $800. These, of course, are probably rounded-off figures, since we're assuming that the nine-passenger model cost less than the 12-passenger and that the latter cost less than the ambulance.

The Monart Carry-All Station Wagon conversions may not have sold very well, as little is known of them and there is no hint that any of the vehicles survive today. They do not seem to have played a very crucial role in Mercury history.

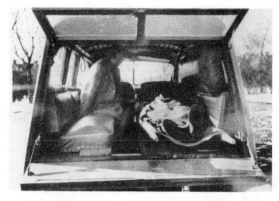 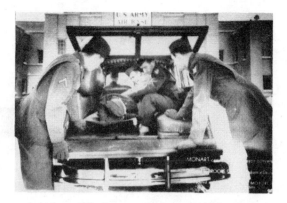

A nurse uses a lengthwise seat to watch over a patient cot. (Brooks Stevens) **GIs demonstrate how two medics could attend to a patient. (Brooks Stevens)**

Three crucial things *did* happen, during the war years, at Ford Motor Company. All three had a significant impact on the postwar history of Mercury. The first occurred when Edsel Ford died at the age of 49. Edsel had been only 25-years-old when he became president of Ford, but Henry Ford, Sr. gave him little real power and lots of pressure. Early in 1942, he had undergone abdominal surgery. Ten months later, he was hospitalized with undulant fever. His ulcers became cancerous and inoperable. He was sent home to die, which he did on May 26, 1943.

The Lincoln-Zephyr and the Mercury were Edsel's most important contributions to Ford Motor Company. His untimely death meant that others would have to guide Mercury's future when the war was over.

Also paving the way for an era of revolutionary corporate and product changes in the postwar era was the retirement of Henry Ford, Sr. on September 21, 1945. Burdened by Edsel's death and old age, Ford had allowed his company to fall into disarray. Edsel's widow, Eleanor, threatened to sell her Ford Motor Company stock, unless Henry Ford, Sr. would step aside and permit his grandson to replace him. Twenty-eight-year-old Henry Ford II was released from the U.S. Navy to return home and salvage the firm. Under his guidance, Ford Motor Company would be reorganized and expanded, with many of the revisions having a direct impact on the future of the Mercury.

Monart wagons seemed at home on the estate...

... or on a military base.

Mercury after the war 1946-1948

In its October 1945 issue, *Motor* magazine announced that a Mercury line of five models would be produced for 1946. A sixth model, the wood-bodied Sportsman Convertible, was added later in the model-year. Production of 1946 models began on November 1, 1945. Some sources indicate the number of available models was limited at first, but the announcement in *Motor* does not support this. Most likely, any inability to get a certain model from a local dealer was due to the fact that full national distribution had not been re-established. It took until February 8, 1946, for things to get back into full swing. Production of 1946 models then continued until approximately February 1947.

Even before the postwar assembly lines started rolling, a significant event took place. The Lincoln-Mercury Division of Ford Motor Company was established on October 22, 1945. It was to be

National distribution of 1946 cars was not re-established when model-year 1946 began. It was February 8, 1946, when Mercury was back in full swing. (Mercury)

responsible for all Mercury planning, parts, service and manufacture. Construction commenced on two new Mercury production plants. As a marketing move, work on starting an independent dealer network began. This was a serious effort, on the part of Henry Ford II, to divorce Mercury from Ford, as much as was possible under a shared corporate umbrella. The goal was to complete the separation by the start of model-year 1947.

Like other automakers, Mercury did a quick warm-over of its 1942 model to speed its return to production of a 1946 model. It was publicized as the "Mercury," not as the "Mercury 8," although the front of the car was stamped with both terms. The brand name appeared, on a chrome-plated ornament at the upper center of the grille frame, against a red-painted background. The letters E-I-G-H-T were stacked on the center piece of the lower grille, on a black-painted vertical "stripe." The upper hood ornament had red-painted grooves. The front bumper guards were the same ones used in 1942. They had short, horizontal grooves near the top, which were striped with red paint.

The 1946 Town Sedan was advertised as "More of everything you want with Mercury!" (Mercury)

Although, there were no changes to body dimensions or general appearance, the company's sales slogan promised "More of everything you want with Mercury!" Under the hood was a flat-head V-8, which seemed very similar to the prewar motor. However, the power plant had unseen changes, brought about by technological advances that the war speeded up.

Advertising copywriters boasted that the postwar Mercury "is styled to perfection, with distinguished smartness (and) flowing low-slung lines." In reality, other then some very minor details, the 1946 to 1948 Mercurys were essentially the same as the last prewar cars. The starting motor number for 1946s was 99A-650280. The 1947s began with number 799A-1412708. Early 1947s looked like 1946 models. A chrome upper grille frame which had the Mercury name against a black-painted background, can be helpful in spotting late 1947 and 1948 models. These also lost the red

This 1946 Sedan-Coupe shows the painted upper grille frame. A center piece with four vertical elements said "Eight" on it. Above the center piece was a chrome-and-red Mercury nameplate. (Robert Twohey)

Only 6,044 of the 1946 Mercury Club Convertibles were made. (*Old Cars*)

stripes on their upper hood ornament and had different front bumper guards. The motor numbers for 1948 began with 899A-1990957.

The 1946 upper grille consisted of a body-color rectangular frame filled, on each side of center, with four distinct clusters of very thin, diecast vertical louvers. Dividing the upper grilles was a center piece with four thicker vertical elements and "eight" lettered down the middle. On the grille frame, directly above the center piece, was the chrome-and-red Mercury nameplate. The lower grilles, were also of "split" design, with two horizontal bars running across each opening. Feature lines were restyled and the moldings on the side of the hood no longer ran around the car's nose. The front bumper was the same used in 1942 and was also continued through 1948. Bumper end guards, which were optional, were also the same from 1942 to 1948.

A distinction of 1946 Mercurys and early 1947 Mercurys was a bright metal rub molding running along the belt line, from the front of the hood to the rear of the body. Wide, lower moldings were seen on the front and rear fenders, while new "Mercury Eight" nameplates were added to the rear deck lid. The head of the Roman god Mercury appeared on the new hubcaps, inside three rings, with the head and the rings highlighted with red paint.

Probably the biggest model design change of the year was the introduction of a wood-bodied convertible called the Sportsman. This car was based on the renamed Club Convertible, but it had mahogany wood panels attached to the doors and trunk lid steel panels and the quarter-frame and wheelhouse extensions. Power windows, a first for Mercury, were standard equipment on the $2,263 Sportsman. The hydraulic operation of the windows was accomplished by an internal-rotor pump driven by a unit adapted from a standard passenger car starting motor. It was mounted on the dashboard and controlled by a three-position electrical switch on the doors and the quarter trim panels. A block of switches on the left door trim panel allowed the driver to control all of the windows. The convertible top was operated by the same pump and motor as the windows.

Eight colors were initially available in 1946: Black; Light Moonstone Gray; Navy Blue; Dynamic Maroon; Botsford Blue-Green; Dark Slate Gray Metallic; Greenfield Green; and Silver Sand Metallic. In April, the Navy Blue choice was replaced by a color called Modern Blue. There were midyear decorative changes, too, such as the addition of stainless steel taillight housing trim. In addition,

Mercury's wood-bodied 1946 Mercury Sportsman was a new model. (*Old Cars*)

dual windshield wiper equipment was reinstated on later cars, as a running change.

As in the past, the Mercury continued to feature a color-coordinated interior with revised design details. "New two-tone interiors and a colorful new modern look," were promised in 1946 advertisements. "Makes you want to be inside behind the wheel ... lounge back in those restful seats ... stretch out your legs ... plenty of leg room, plenty of elbow room and head room for six people." A plastic steering wheel with a full horn ring of improved design was seen. Smartly styled hardware and beautifully appointed plastic fittings were used. Handsome new, metallic maroon lacquer, highlighted the interior. The starter button, now located on the instrument panel was, Mercury said, "Fully appreciated when starting on a hill."

In 1946, Mercury built 13,108 Sedans, which was the official name for the two-door version. (Mercury)

Closed cars were upholstered in a choice of cord or broadcloth fabrics with genuine leather accents. Two color schemes, rust or gray-green, were offered. Club Convertibles and Sportsman convertibles featured tan, red or gray-green leather seats and matching door panels. Station Wagon leather interiors were described as gold-tan, red or gray. Five colors were available for the instrument board and interior moldings, to harmonize with the upholstery color schemes. There was a new "Mercury" glove compartment nameplate.

Again, dozens of technical improvements were "hyped" by Mercury ad copywriters. Cylinder heads were now interchangeable. The engine had improved, cam-ground aluminum pistons with four piston rings. There was a bigger oil pump; tri-alloy connecting rod bearings; chrome-nickel valves; an oil bath air cleaner; and other revisions. Many of the changes evolved from technology developed for the war effort. There was a new Holley dual-barrel carburetor, but Stromberg carburetors were also used on some cars. The horsepower rating did not change in either case.

As usual, the 49-1/2-inch long "Slow-Motion" springs; the Wagner Lockheed "Self-Centering" hydraulic brakes; and the front suspension were all slightly upgraded, to further enhance Mercury's

A handful of Mercury Station Wagons even got Marmon-Herrington all-wheel-drive conversions. Naturalist Don Bleitz purchased one such car. (Courtesy *Collectible Automobile*)

An obvious change to the front of this "true" 1947 Town Sedan is the chrome upper grille frame. The nose ornament, with the Mercury name, had a new black background. The upper hood ornament now had red stripes. (Mercury)

Ron Handy, of Tuxedo, New York, spent three years restoring his 1947 Mercury Convertible from a basket case to a trophy-winner. (Ron Handy)

"Full-Cushioned Ride." Mercury used a hypoid rear axle with a 4.22:1 gear ratio as standard equipment on cars with the standard three-speed manual, helical gear transmission. The clutch was a 10-inch outside diameter type sourced from Borg-Warner's Long Manufacturing Division. A fluid coupling was optional.

Major selling features of the 1946s included "Mid-Section" seating, extra luggage compartment roominess and big, adjustable, double-acting hydraulic shock absorbers. Other Mercury attributes ranged from "balanced" weight distribution and torque tube drive, to "Two-Way" chassis stabilization. Metal spring covers and a dynamically-balanced, rugged special alloy crankshaft were also promoted as things buyers should look for in their next car.

Postwar prices rose significantly. The October 1945 issue of *Motor* carried a number of industry news items. Several addressed the fact that automakers had delayed the release of their 1946 prices beyond the United States Government's Office of Price Administration deadline. The magazine included charts indicating prices of $951 for the Mercury (two-door) Sedan, $982 for the Sedan-Coupe, $992 for the Town Sedan, $1,105 for the Club Convertible, and $1,146 for the Station Wagon.

Of course, most new cars were already selling at above their list price. This was due to a continued shortage of both used and new vehicles. The problem of a new-car shortage was compounded by material shortages and labor strife. This situation kept car inventories low for nearly two years, and the law of supply and demand soon sent even the factory-list prices skyrocketing. By the time sales really got rolling, the two-door Town Sedan was up to $1,448. The new Sportsman (not listed in October) was the most expensive model. Other post-introductory factory list prices were $1,495 for the Sedan-Coupe; $1,509 for the four-door Town Sedan; and $1,711 for the Club Convertible. No longer tops in price, after the Sportsman came out, was the Station Wagon. It then listed for $1,729. Production totals were 13,108 Sedans; 195 to 205 Sportsman Convertibles; 24,163 Sedan-Coupes; 40,280 Town Sedans; 6,044 Club Convertibles; and 2,797 Station Wagons.

Total model-year production came to 80,858 units, including some rare ambulances and hearse conversions, most of them done by Siebert. A handful of Mercury Station Wagons even got Marmon-Herrington all-wheel-drive conversions. Naturalist Don Bleitz purchased one such car, which appeared in *Motor Trend* in October 1952. Coachcraft LTD., of Hollywood, California, patterned the wagon after a 1942 Ford designed by Walter Dupee, of Bel Air, that it also built. The top was customized by the addition of a luggage rack. Metal storage compartments were installed beneath the floor. Bleitz used the Mercury for wilderness trips to the Sierra Mountains. Also a little different were Ford-based Canadian Mercurys, both cars and trucks, that became available following the war. (A history of Canadian Mercurys is featured elsewhere in this book.)

The 1947 "model-year" actually began on February 19, 1947, but there were no changes in

Convertibles came in regular colors, plus the exclusive hues Pheasant Red and Maize Yellow. (Bud Josey)

The 1947 Station Wagons had tan or red leather interiors, the same offered in convertibles. (Dennis Adler for *Car Exchange*)

This snapshot of a 1947 Mercury Sedan-Coupe was taken in San Diego, California in 1947. (John Nevestich)

39

On late-1947 to 1948 Mercurys, like this 1947 Sedan-Coupe, the hood side molding was shortened. It extended only about one foot onto the hood. In front of it was a "Mercury" nameplate. (Mercury)

This Town-Sedan ad ran after April 1947, when the "chrome grille" Mercs arrived. (Mercury)

The 1948 ads showed whitewalls. A Town Sedan ad in the January 24, 1948 *Saturday Evening Post* also showed a chauffeur. (Mercury)

Only 24,283 Town Sedans were made in the short 1948 model-year. This one carries an accessory sun visor. (*Old Cars*)

Car Collector Ron Donatt restored his 1948 Mercury convertible with Pheasant Red paint.

The 1948 Mercury Club Convertible sold for $2,002. Despite the shortness of the 1948 model run, 7,586 ragtops were made. (Robert R. Ziemer)

The interior of the 1948 Mercury Convertible had a rich, natural look. (Robert R. Ziemer)

Although the 1948 Mercury (left) and Ford (right) shared a family resemblance, the Merc looked richer and bigger. (Ray Donatt)

The 1948 Mercury Sedan-Coupe had a $1,645 price and weighed 3,218 pounds. (*Old Cars*)

Mercury built a total of 16,475 Sedan-Coupes in 1948. (*Old Cars*)

This 1948 Mercury Town Sedan is parked outside the Lincoln-Mercury Administration Building. (Mercury)

The interior of Ron Donatt's 1948 Mercury convertible shows trim details.

Mercurys at this time. "So-called face-lifting, resulting in small appearance changes, is not necessary to designate a yearly model," explained Ford Motor Company vice president J.R. Davis. "It is up to the manufacturer to designate changes for the purposes of registering a car as a yearly model. We have done this so current buyers of Fords, Mercurys and Lincolns will get the benefit of 1947 titles."

The main difference between the 1946 and early 1947 Mercurys was pricing. Model-for-model, the cars went up $150 to $300. Also, the slow-selling Mercury Sportsman was dropped from the lineup. Ford advised buyers to refer to serial numbers to tell a 1946 Mercury from an early 1947 model. It wasn't until early April 1947, that the "true" 1947 cars appeared.

"Graceful as a yacht!" is how one advertisement described them. "Always so smooth — so easy to handle — such satisfaction to be seen in — Mercury now gives you even more of everything you want," the copy continued. "Famous among young moderns as *the* smart car." The ad mentioned a newly designed two-tone interior, a smarter outside, and lively, all-around performance. "Beginning with the front grille," the advertising copywriters boasted, "The 1947 Mercury look is more massive, lower, sleeker than ever."

The most obvious change to the front of the car was a chrome-plated upper grille frame. The center hood ornament, with the Mercury name, now had a black background, instead of red. Parts manuals tell us that the 1947 upper hood ornament had a different part number than the 1947 part. Both looked the same, but the red striping in the grooves was gone. The hood top panel was a new part. The 1946 and early 1947 cars had a hood top panel that interchanged with the Ford's. The late-1947 to 1948 part was exclusive to Mercury. The main revision was to the side of the hood, where the belt molding no longer ran full length. Instead, it extended only about 12 inches onto the hood. In front of the shorter molding was a "Mercury" nameplate. The headlamp doors were also smooth, instead of "rippled." The optional front and rear bumper guards were of a new design. They looked straighter and narrower. The front guards had three short horizontal grooves, but they were no longer red-striped.

Ford Motor Company's Lincoln-Mercury Division medical personnel used this 1948 Station Wagon, equipped with Red Cross decals, emergency flashers and Venetian blinds, for ambulance duty. (Mercury)

Standard equipment on all 1947 Mercurys included an electric clock; a cigarette lighter; a locking glove compartment; twin electric horns; two sun visors; armrests on each front door; dual windshield wipers; twin stop/taillamps; and a power-operated top on the Club Convertible.

Only a few parts applications were revised for 1947. The oil pressure gauge, the battery charge indicator and the fuel gauge were among them. There was also a new generator regulator and battery cable going to the starter switch. The light switch, the headlamp foot switch, the horn and some transmission parts (including the gear shift lever) were new, as were a few steering gear components. Late 1947 models had new ignition switches, as Briggs & Stratton's number 600180 was substituted for its number 80935, a change carried over to 1948 models. New windshield wiper equipment was also installed on late-in-the-year Mercurys.

Colors that 1947 closed cars came in included Black; Taffy Tan; Tucson Tan; Parrot Green Metallic; Feather Gray; Glade Green; Monsoon Maroon; Barcelona Blue; and Rotunda Gray. Convertibles were also available in the exclusive shades Pheasant Red and Maize Yellow.

Station wagons had tan or red leather interiors, the same offered in Club Convertibles. Cloth trim was standard in closed cars. The instrument panel was finished in an attractive new Gunmetal Gray color.

The early postwar years continued to bring shocking developments that affected the history of Ford Motor Company. On April 7, 1947, Henry Ford, Sr. died in his sleep at the Fairlane Estate in Dearborn, Michigan. How strange that this automotive pioneer would meet his maker in the year that the industry was officially celebrating its "Golden Jubilee." Henry was 83-years-old.

Model-year production of Mercurys moved upwards again.

A total of 86,383 vehicles were turned out. This included just 34 two-door Town Sedans; 29,284 Sedan-Coupes; 42,281 four-door Town Sedans; 10,221 Club Convertibles; and 3,558 Station Wagons. About 1,000 additional cars were built for special purposes, such as hearse and ambulance conversions.

"Whether it's a picnic, taking the children to school, shopping, or driving home from the office — the hours spent in your Mercury are hours of solid motoring enjoyment," said a September 6, 1947 advertisement. The Mercury is *thrilling* to drive and ride in. It's so easy to handle, hugs the road so

Since the early postwar era the 1942-1948 Mercurys have been popular with customizers. (*Old Cars*)

Grant Motor Car, of St. Petersburg, Florida, sold Fords and Mercurys in late 1947 or 1948. Of 7,000 Ford dealers then, one-third sold Mercurys. (Mercury)

safely, levels out the bumps so *gently*, slows down so *surely*. The Mercury is *thrifty, too* — giving you more mileage, more dependability, month after month, year after year. You owe it to yourself to see and compare this new Mercury. It gives you everything you want — *and more!*"

The car depicted in the ad looked much like the late-1947 model. However, the front bumper guards were changed again. They no longer had three grooves near the tip. Instead, they were completely smooth. Also, the hubcaps clearly showed the Mercury name in the center, with the letters finished in black. And, for the first time since before World War II, the advertisement pictured a car ... the four-door Town Sedan ... with white sidewall tires.

The radiator's grille frame was again chrome-plated, like the late-1947 type. By the way, the chrome frame carried an over 50 percent higher price than the 1946 and early-1947 style painted frame. The side radiator grille and the lower grille frame remained identical to the ones in use since 1946. The hood side moldings were the shorter ones, with Mercury nameplates in front of them.

Very few mechanical changes were made for 1948. However, there was a new speedometer head and a different directional signal flasher. Most other parts were the same as used on 1947 Mercurys. Overall, there was very little changed from 1942 specifications.

The model lineup was down to four choices for 1948, which made sense, as an all-new Mercury was due in 1949. The company had no desire to wind up with an inventory of slow-moving cars, so phasing out the least popular body styles was a way to "clear the decks." For $1,645 you could have a Sedan-Coupe. A Town Sedan was $15 more. Considerable costlier was the $2,002 Convertible and the $2,207 Station Wagon.

One 1948 Mercury Sedan-Coupe earned a little fame as a racing car. In the early 1950s, American hot rodders Troy Ruttman and Clay Smith purchased the car, for $1,000, from a used car lot. Smith, a mechanic who had prepped "bathtub" Mercurys for the Mobilgas Economy Run, bored the car's engine block and added things like Edlebrock heads and an Edmund's two-carb manifold. After running up a total tab of $2,500, the two men entered the car in the 1952 Panamerican Road Race. They finished fourth behind Bill Sterling's big-bucks-backed, hemi-powered Chrysler New Yorker and a pair of $11,000 Ferraris driven by the winner, Taruffi, and second-place finisher Ascari.

The 1948 grille frame was chrome-plated as in late-1947. The side radiator grille and the lower grille frame remained identical to 1946. (Dale Peltier)

The old Merc could do 115 mph. By the end of the grueling Mexican contest, it trailed Sterling's third-place Chrysler by one minute and 57 seconds. Ruttman and Smith won 50,000 pesos ($5,795 at the time) from the race backers for their performance. In addition, they picked up 40,000 pesos from Lincoln-Mercury and $500 from Mobiloil. They netted a total of $11,600. "Everyone seems to be interested in the fact that the car that Clay Smith and I ran to fourth place in the race was probably the cheapest car entered," wrote Ruttman in the March 1952 edition of *Motor Trend*.

For model-year 1948, Mercury slipped to 10th rank in industry sales, from ninth rank in 1947. Output totaled 50,268 units. This included 16,475 Sedan-Coupes; 24,283 Town Sedans; 7,586 Convertibles; and 1,899 Station Wagons. On April 29, 1948, an all-new Mercury was introduced. Best-known as the "bathtub" or "James Dean" Mercury, the totally revised models was a sensation then, and still is today.

One 1948 Mercury Coupe earned fame as a 1952 Mexican Road Race car. Troy Ruttman and Clay Smith paid $1,000 for it and came in fourth. (Courtesy Petersen Publishing Company).

"James Dean" Mercs 1949-1951

The "James Dean" Mercurys of 1949-1951 were far from "rebels without a cause." Although they became a symbol of rebellious, car-crazy teenagers, they were actually aimed at more conservative buyers than earlier Mercurys. Their "cause" was to turn around a downward-pointing trend on Mercury's sales charts. They handily accomplished this goal.

Prototypes for the original, 1939 Mercury, had worn "Ford-Mercury" nameplates. Through 1948, the identities of the two marques were intertwined. Mercurys seemed like Fords with larger wheelbases, peppier power plants and richer appointments. The similarities increased after 1941, when Fords and Mercurys began sharing the same body shell. The role of the "James Dean" Mercury was to change the marque's image and to make it more Lincoln-like.

Despite a rebel image attached to customs like a 1949 Coupe with a "shaved" hood, stock "James Dean" Mercs were conservative cars. (BHMA)

Ford styling chief E.T. "Bob" Gregorie had designed the original Mercury for Edsel Ford. During the early days of World War II, Gregorie's studio was already at work on designing Ford's postwar cars. Six car-lines were envisioned at first: Small Ford; big Ford; small Mercury; big Mercury; standard Lincoln (or Zephyr); and Continental. In 1943, artist Ross Cousins did a sketch of a "big" Ford with fade-away fenders. He didn't know it then, but the car he sketched would eventually evolve into the 1949 Mercury.

After Henry Ford II took over at Ford, he brought Ernest R. Breech in from Bendix Corporation. Breech helped him revamp Ford Motor Company. Breech, to his credit, saw no need for six postwar car-lines. The small (100-inch wheelbase) Ford went to Europe, where it became the Vedette model, sold by Ford of France. Cousin's big Ford, now with a 118-inch wheelbase, seemed like a viable product. However, it was too large to compete, price-wise, with a Chevrolet.

Breech decided to rush through a new 114-inch-wheelbase Ford. (It became the 1949-1951 "shoe box" model.) He then earmarked Cousin's design to be the one and only new Mercury. The proposed "Zephyr" was turned into a standard Lincoln. It had the new Mercury's body, but a longer front end and wheelbase. A larger Lincoln Cosmopolitan finished Breech's four-car lineup.

Harold Youngren, a newly-promoted Ford vice president and director of engineering, was given the job of bringing the Mercury from Cousin's drawing board to the showroom in less than a year. This was about half the time it normally took to develop such a product. An article in the May 1948 issue of *Science Illustrated* magazine discussed the two major considerations that governed the project. The first was to create a new car aimed specifically at the postwar buyer's market. The second was to produce a product that would combat Mercury's image as a bigger and fancier Ford.

The work began with countless pencil sketches to nail down details. Stylists like Joe Unsicker, of the Mercury studio, made numerous drawings. Final approval of the early design work came from

Mercury's 1949 two-door six-passenger Coupe is often referred to as the "Club Coupe" or the "Sport Coupe." Sport Coupe was the "factory" designation, but is not used in this book to avoid confusion with Hardtop Sport Coupes. (Mercury)

Ford design chief Bob Gregorie. Then, a full-scale drawing that looked very close to the final car, was completed in full color. At that point, Fred Hadley, Mercury's 26-year-old head modeler, designed a 1/4-scale clay model. In the spring of 1947, after the "clay" was approved, plaster models were cast.

By this time, Bob Gregorie had resigned from Ford. Tom Hibbard, the well-known custom coach builder of Hibbard & Darrin fame, took over management of the corporate styling studio. He guided the Mercury from the clay and plaster model stage to the full-size mock-up stage. Meanwhile, engineers and draftsmen were working out power train details. Some of the new drive line parts were fitted to 1947 and 1948 Mercurys. These cars were driven around the country, for test purposes. The testing went well.

The first all-new Mercury body, made by hand, was mounted on the new chassis in July

The 1949 Mercury Sport Sedan had "suicide" doors and vent windows front and rear. (Mercury)

1947, only nine months after the project began. According to *Science Illustrated*, "That car and 14 other handmade cars cost more than $50,000 each, for a total engineering cost of three-quarters of a million dollars." Photos accompanying the magazine's story showed one of the early prototypes, complete with black-out trim, during a road test in the snow.

Once development of the new Mercury was completed, selling the car became the responsibility of the Lincoln-Mercury sales force. This branch was, then, under the direction of 28-year-old Benson Ford. On April 22, the standard Lincoln hit the showrooms. It was the first all-new postwar car to come from a major "Big 3" automaker. The 1949 Mercury bowed one week later. It shared the body shell of the standard Lincoln. This made it five inches longer, 3-1/2 inches wider and 4-1/2 inches lower in overall height, than the 1948 Mercury. It also weighed an average 132 pounds more than the previous season's model. As an observer noted, "This car is no longer a 'glorified Ford,' it's an 'Everyman's Lincoln.'"

The smooth, round, streamlined looks of this design would eventually achieve "cult" status, based on the customized car that actor James Dean drove in the motion picture "Rebel Without a Cause." Playing the role of Jim Stark, a swaggering young "hunk" with a chip on his shoulder and a penchant for speed, Dean cruised the streets in a jet-black, 1949 Merc that was "nosed," "decked" and lowered. That car soon became the symbol for a "lost generation" of young Americans caught up in the nation's changing, postwar culture.

"Rebel Without A Cause" was released in 1955, but customized "bathtub" Mercurys were commonly seen by late 1949. That was when a Los Angeles company named Trend, Incorporated began publishing a magazine named *Motor Trend*. By 1950, several other car enthusiast magazines were on the newsstands. They carried numerous ads for aftermarket auto accessories specifically designed for Fords and Mercurys. By 1950, Southern California Muffler Service, of Culver City, was using a sketch of a rebellious-looking, "hot rod" Mercury convertible in its advertising.

Naturally, the rebel image was not among Mercury's official promotions. The company simply advertised its 1949 car as "Not a 'new model' ... the All-New Mercury" and said it was "designed for down-front visibility." The rigid, heavily reinforced, all-steel body was directly related to that of small Lincoln. However, the Mercury was on a three-inch shorter wheelbase. Its shorter front end sheet metal made it easier to see the road ahead. It also made it possible to have a Mercury two-door Station Wagon, a model that shared its "woodie" body with the 1949 Ford Station Wagon.

The Mercury model lineup included a Convertible Coupe, a six-passenger Coupe, and a Sport Sedan. Each 1949 model was interesting in its own way. The Convertible Coupe had a power top, power windows and a power seat as standard equipment. The six-passenger Coupe had "butterfly" style quarter windows. Featuring new notch back styling, the Sport Sedan included "suicide" doors and ventipanes in all doors, front and rear. Each model had different door panels. The six-passenger Coupe and the Convertible Coupe shared the same rear fenders and moldings, but the Sport Sedan had different versions of these parts. The front fenders were the same on all models.

"The '49 Mercury ... longer, lower, wider," boasted sales literature. "Its broad-beamed sturdiness is artfully combined with fleetness of line." The six-passenger Coupe and the Town Sedan had different upper body sections, but similar-sized backlight (back window) openings. Both models started the long model-year with a three-piece backlight. It consisted of small pieces of side glass that cost $4.75 each and a large center section that retailed for $16.75. On late-1949 models, a one-piece back window, costing $30.50, was substituted.

There were other running production changes, too. Early lever-type door handles, which pulled out from the door, were found to develop linkage problems. Push-button door handles replaced them about the same time the backlight design was changed. Also at that time, a stronger chassis was incorporated. It was designed to overcome some undesirable flexing experienced with the early 1949 models. All models had a new fresh air ventilation system dubbed "Fingertip Weather Control." A counter-balanced trunk lid was used on all 1949s.

"It's got plenty of get-up-and-go!"

—THAT'S WHAT OWNERS SAY ABOUT THE EXCLUSIVE NEW MERCURY ENGINE!

New owners say it's a whirlwind on wheels! They just can't get over its terrific power on hills...its split-second response on the highway... its watchtick smoothness. They claim it's the "sweetest" power plant ever engineered for any car in its class. And it is!

White side-wall tires and rear wheel shields are optional

Make your next car MERCURY

LINCOLN-MERCURY DIVISION OF FORD MOTOR COMPANY

MERCURY'S NEW 8-CYLINDER, V-type engine is really something to talk about. And so is the surprising *economy* it gives you. But there's more —much more than that to Mercury!

The 1949 Mercury is all-new *all over!* You get all-new *springing*, an all-new "comfort-zone" *ride*, all-new easier *steering*, all-new "super-safety" *brakes*, all-new broader, softer *seating*, all-new increased *visibility!*

Yes, and you'll get all-new *styling* that will steal your heart! See it—and you too will say: *It's Mercury for me!*

"It's got plenty of get-up-and-go!" boasted ads for the Mercury Convertible. White sidewall tires and rear wheel shields (fender skirts) were optional. The convertible had vacuum-operated power seat and windows. (Mercury)

Clean, rounded lines and a touch of panel sculpturing characterized the all-new body with its fade-away fenders. The "electric razor" grille had four distinct vertical segments, on either side of a vertical center piece bearing an "E-I-G-H-T" designation. The parking lights were set into the sheet metal, just outside the grille ends, and directly below the single, round headlamps. They looked round at a glance, but were actually "squarish," with very rounded corners. A winged ornament sat on the nose, above a Mercury hood emblem. There was Mercury lettering along the hood lip. A wraparound bumper was seen.

A shorter wheelbase made possible a Mercury two-door Station Wagon that shared its wood body with 1949 Fords. (*Old Cars*)

Only one car-line was offered, the 9CM Mercury series. It came in just one trim level. All cars had body side moldings, with the Mercury name near the front. Skirted rear fenders were common. Hubcaps had the word "Mercury" stamped around the circumference, on one end, and the word "Eight" stamped around the circumference on the other end. Most, if not all of the 1949 models, came with accessory wheel trim rings.

Body colors for 1949 were Royal Bronze; Maroon Metallic; Black; Berwick Green Metallic; Dakota Gray; and Lima Tan Metallic for all models. Alberta Blue and Biscay Blue Metallic were available on all models, except the Convertible. Bermuda Cream was offered for the Convertible and the Station Wagon only. Tampico Red came only on the ragtop. Two-tone paint combinations were Banft Green Metallic over Berwick Green Metallic and Lima Tan Metallic over Haiti Beige. All wheels were painted black.

Inside, the cars featured chair-high seats. They were positioned well forward, to give "Picture-Window" visibility through the deep, wide windshield. There was a two-spoke "Clear View" steering wheel. The driving instruments were conveniently grouped in plain sight, in front of the driver. Foam rubber-cushioned seats were a new option.

Plain-looking woven broadcloth or cord fabric upholstery choices were offered for six-passenger Coupes and Sedans. Colors included pale green checked, gray striped, and beige. Convertible

A total of 8,044 Station Wagons were assembled in 1949. The Station Wagon used a different rear bumper than other Mercurys. It was actually a Ford part. Its design allowed the tailgate, with the spare tire mounted on its outside, to be lowered without bumping the bumper. (Mercury)

Coupes and Station Wagons had tan, green or red genuine leather seat surfaces (with whipcord trim in the ragtops). Power windows and a power seat adjuster were optional for Coupes or Sport Sedans.

While some automakers were switching to overhead valve V-8s in 1949, Ford stayed with the flathead type. The Mercury did get a larger and more powerful version of this tried-and-true engine design, with its stroke increased to four inches. However, its bore remained at the Ford's 3.1875 inches. This came out to 255.4 cubic inches, which helped the Merc's motor generate 110 hp at 3600 rpm. It had three main bearings and a 6.8:1 compression ratio. There

Berl Berry, on Wilshire Boulevard, in Los Angeles, California, was the world's largest Lincoln-Mercury dealer in 1950. (Jay Katelle)

Coupes and sedans had one-piece rear window. All '50 Mercs had a "cockle-shell" trunk ornament and "Mercury" on bumper guard cross-bar. (James L. Gwaltney)

were other engine improvements, including a new carburetor; auto-thermic pistons; an automatic choke; locked-in connecting rod bearings; a conventional type distributor with full vacuum control and single breaker points; redesigned intake and exhaust manifolds; new cylinder heads (no longer interchangeable); and cooling system advances.

"It's got plenty of get-up-and-go!" Mercury quoted its customers saying, in an advertisement illustrating a yellow Convertible with a red

Mercury ads compared the features of the 1950 Sports Sedan to golfing. "Rides and handles like every road's a fairway," they said. Production for this model was 132,082 units. This one has an accessory spotlight. (Jerry Eica)

The Coupe came in two models for 1950. This is the fancier 72B. The 72A model had black rubber window gaskets, fixed rear side windows, no clock (standard on other models) and no wheel trim rings. (John Gunnell)

"Mercury's smoother, livelier 8-cylinder, V-type engine is precision-built to go farther with less maintenance," said a 1950 ad.

For those attracted to General Motors' sporty hardtops, Mercury created the Model 72C Monterey. (Mercury)

This 1950 Monterey has Cortaro Red Metallic paint and a black vinyl roof. (Harrison Snell)

The 1950 Mercury Monterey also came in Turquoise Blue with a dark blue vinyl roof. (Old Cars)

interior, white sidewall tires and fender skirts. "New owners say it's a whirlwind on wheels! They just can't get over its terrific power on hills ... its split-second response on the highway ... its watchtick smoothness. They claim it's the 'sweetest' power plant ever engineered for any car in its class. And it is!"

A three-speed manual transmission with column-mounted gear-shift was standard. It came with a 3.9 1:1 rear axle ratio. "Touch-O-Matic" overdrive, made by Bendix, and a 4.27:1 ratio rear axle were optional. A Hotchkiss open drive shaft replaced the previous torque tube drive system. The permanently-lubricated rear springs were of a new semi-elliptic design. Mercurys did retain an X-type chassis, which contributed to their sturdy construction, but it also added weight.

The hood ornaments were the same in 1949 and 1950. Instead of Mercury lettering, the 1950 hood molding had "Mercury" stamped in it. (Mercury)

The independent front suspension featured "Soft-Acting" coil springs. "Sea-Leg" telescopic shock absorbers were mounted in the center of the springs. Another selling point was the use of 7.10 x 15 "Super-Balloon" low-pressure tires. Mercury advertised that its revised parallelogram-type steering linkage "virtually eliminates road shock vibration." The front tread, at 58-1/2 inches, was a half-inch larger than in 1948. The rear tread was unchanged and still at 60 inches.

The 1949 Mercury was tested by *Mechanix Illustrated* magazine in a story that lead off, "It's turtle-nosed, squat and fast and McCahill says it holds the road like no other Mercury has before." Test driver "Uncle Tom" McCahill found it capable of speeds approaching 95 mph. He gave it his seal of approval.

Popular Mechanics put Floyd Clymer behind the wheel of a 1949 Mercury six-passenger Coupe for a high-speed test run from Omaha, Nebraska to Cheyenne, Wyoming. He was able to cover the 484 miles, with traffic lights and all, at an average speed of 66.6 miles per hour. At times, he reported that he did 95 miles per hour! Clymer found the front springs a bit soft, but liked the handling of the car at high speed. "It has all that anyone could ask for," said Floyd. He made reference

"Rain or shine, this sleek, new Mercury Convertible laughs at the weather," said promotional verse. "The snug-fitting automatic top, safety glass windows, and wide front seat are all push-button operated." (H. Shea)

New, smart fashion Convertible interiors were available with all-leather or leather-and-nylon upholsteries. There was a wide choice of beautiful colors for the exterior of all Mercurys. (Mercury)

to a survey of 3,000 Mercury in which 83.6 percent rated the 1949 model good to excellent. Only 0.8 percent described it as poor.

Not every 1949 Mercury owner was totally satisfied. George A. Remington, of Long Island, New York, wrote to *Motor Trend*'s "Sound Off!" column about his Merc's poor fuel economy. National advertising, showing a picture of a bearded Scot in kilts, had boasted, "Imagine getting 18...18...19 miles per gallon and up! Owners say this long, low, road-proven Mercury does it every day! They claim it's the thriftiest, most-practical-to-own-car they've ever driven.!" The ad even had a footnote,

"and even more with Overdrive." Mr. Remington felt otherwise. "I own a 1949 Mercury ... and so far as gasoline consumption is concerned, I get 10 mpg in city traffic and 17 mpg with overdrive in the country. We have tampered with this one (engine) until we're exhausted, but that is the maximum mileage to date."

A big fan of the 1949 Mercurys is Mike Rollins, of Canadian, Texas, who wrote a letter to *Old Cars* about running production changes made in the cars. "How excited we were, at Rollins Motor Company, in El Paso, Texas, in April 1948, when we introduced the first Ford-built postwar designs ... 1949 Lincoln and Mercury cars," he recalled. "Announcement date ushered in what was to become one of the longest production runs in history for a single model-year." Rollins remembered that late 1949 Mercurys were much like the 1950s that followed, except for their peculiar instrument panel and exterior ornamentation. "The late '49s and the '50 model Mercurys were the most trouble-free cars that we ever had the privilege to represent," he said.

If the 1949 Mercury was bigger and better, it was also more expensive. Closed car prices were up about $335 to $370. Convertibles jumped by over $400; wagons by over $500. Nevertheless, buyers saw the "baby Lincoln" as a good value. Sales took off like a rocket. Model-

Harold T. Youngren (standing) explains the detailed operation of forthcoming Merc-O-Matic transmission to FoMoCo engineers. (Ford Motor Company)

year production, at 301,319 units was over three times higher than the company had ever achieved before.

Naturally, part of the increase was due to a long model-year that stretched 20 months. Still, Mercury became America's sixth largest automaker, up from 12th or 13th. Ford assembly plants in St. Louis, Missouri and Metuchen, New Jersey had to be converted exclusively to building Mercurys. Production included 120,616 six-passenger Coupes; 155,882 Sport Sedans; 16,765 Convertibles and 8,044 Station Wagons.

This ad announced automatic transmission for 1951, but showed 1950 cars. (Lower left) Benson Ford and Harold T. Youngren in 1950 Merc-O-Matic Convertible. Other photos show controls and 1950 Merc-O-Matic Sedan. (Ford)

In Toledo, Ohio, professional car builder Siebert came up with a new "Sky Coach" line. These early airport limousines were based on the Sport Sedan, but were stretched to fit either a 154-inch or 190-inch wheelbase. The smaller version had three doors on the passenger side. The front two were forward-hinged and the third was hinged at the rear. The larger car had twin sets of "suicide" doors on its right-hand side. Ambulances and funeral vehicles were also constructed on the new Mercury platform.

Another special 1949 Mercury was built for United States President Harry S. Truman. It seems the head of state wanted an inconspicuous Sedan to use on local trips, in place of his Lincoln Cosmopolitan. Ford Motor Company put together a specially-stretched Mercury Sedan. It was made on the small Lincoln's 121-inch wheelbase chassis. The Mercury was black and had no official markings.

The Truman Mercury had a standard cloth rear seat. The front seat, designed for a chauffeur, was covered with leather. A partition was bolted to the floor, behind the front seat, for privacy or protection. Truman discovered he couldn't stretch his legs out to a comfortable position, due to the partition. He used the car just once, then returned it to Lincoln-Mercury.

Ford offered incentives to any dealer able to sell the car. One knew of a wealthy woman, with a prewar Cadillac, who wanted a new limousine. A deal was made. The next day, the woman's chauffeur returned. She wanted her roomy 1940 Cadillac back. Even she complained that the partitioned Mercury was short on leg room.

Mercury won trophies for its performance in the Mobilgas Grand Canyon Economy Run. (General Petroleum Company)

The dealer got the car back. In fact, he was stuck with it. Lincoln-Mercury wasn't as understanding as he had been. The company would not take it back. The dealer removed the partition from the interior, put in a new floor mat, and shoved it back in the showroom. It sat there for several months, attracting no buyers. Then one day, an Arab came in to the dealership. He bought the car, for cash, and drove it off. Neither the buyer or his car were ever seen again.

The 1950 Mercury entered production in November 1949. Factories in Dearborn, Michigan; Los Angeles, California; St. Louis, Missouri; and Metuchen, New Jersey built 294,658 cars to model-year specifications. On a calendar-year basis, an all-time record of 334,081 units was built. June 1950 was Mercury's all-time peak month. It made 33,664 cars then. There were 2,750 autoworkers in New Jersey and 2,300 in Missouri building *only* Mercurys. Another 1,050 in Los Angeles and 5,050 in Detroit made both Lincolns and Mercurys. Con-

Benson Ford drives the 1950 Mercury pace car for the Indy 500. Beside him is Wilbur Shaw, general manager of the Indianapolis Motor Speedway in 1950. (Indianapolis Motor Speedway Corporation photo)

struction of a new assembly plant, in Wayne, Michigan, also began during 1950.

The 1950 Mercury models were introduced in dealer showrooms on November 29, 1949. In May, a yellow Mercury convertible paced the Indianapolis 500-Mile Race. On June 23, the Monterey "hardtop" was added to the 1950 line, along with the Lincoln Lido and the Lincoln Cosmopolitan Capri. (The Ford Crestliner didn't arrive until July 29). In August, the one-millionth Mercury was made.

Ad copywriters boasted of "new flowing lines" and said "the beautiful new front end treatment is most attractive." Promotional copy unabashedly claimed many improvements. "There's no mystery about Mercury's ever-increasing popularity today. For Mercury — a great car last year — is now *better than ever in everything*!," said one announcement. "Better in *styling* — with new advanced design! Better in *comfort* — with 'Lounge-Rest' foam-rubber cushioned seats. Better in *performance* — with 'Hi-Power Compression!' Better in *safety* — with 'Super-Safety' brakes. Better to *drive* and *park*!"

Actually, there were very few significant changes in the cars for 1950. Even the obviously face-lifted Mercury frontal treatment cleverly utilized many of the same components as 1949 models.

Many sheet metal panels, for cars of the same body style, had the same part numbers in 1949 and 1950. This included bolt-on items like

Actor Clark Gable, an Indy 500 fan, stands by a 1950 Mercury "Official Car" assigned to S.A. Silberman, director of Magnafluxing. (IMSC photo)

doors and trunk lids, as well as entire rear quarter panel assemblies and turret top panels. Front fenders, and the "Mercury" moldings on them, were new for 1950. So was the front bumper face bar. However, the front bumper guards were the same as in 1949. A horizontal bar between the bumper guard was optional both years. All 1950 Mercury six-passenger Coupes and Sport Sedans had the one-piece backlight and push-button door handles used on late-1949 models. The six-passenger Coupe was promoted as a "Sport Coupe." However, it was not a pillarless hardtop, like a General Motors Sport Coupe.

The Mercury hood top ornament and hood front ornament were the same both years. Instead of Mercury lettering, the hood lip had a molding with the Mercury name stamped into it. Apparently, this molding attached to some of the same holes as the letters did in 1949, since the part number for the hood was the same both years. The new lip molding rose up and "surrounded" the bottom of the hood front ornament, making it look different, although it really wasn't changed. Other revised front end parts included the headlamp doors and the center grille upright. The latter no longer said "E-I-G-H-T." The same radiator grille used in 1949 was back for 1950. However, new grille extensions were added on either side. They stretched to below the headlamps and held slightly smaller, circular parking lamps at their centers.

Six-passenger Coupes and Convertibles, of both 1949 and 1950, had the same rear fenders and moldings. The Sport Sedans shared different versions of these parts in the same two years. There was a new trunk handle/ornament that resembled a sea shell. The rear taillamp assembly, lens, and door were the same in 1949 and 1950.

Mercury Station Wagons shared many of the same parts from 1949 to 1951. Some front end parts from the wagons interchanged with those of other Mercurys. However, from the cowl back, most of the "Station Wagon" parts interchanged with those of Ford Station Wagons. Only a few small rear end trim parts were exclusive to Mercury wagons. Aftermarket parts books do not always list Mercury Station Wagon parts applications, since they were sourced from Ford. Therefore, all of the parts applications discussed in this chapter may not apply to Station Wagons.

For instance, Station Wagons had their own rear bumper. It allowed space for the spare tire, when the tailgate was lowered. It was used from 1949 right through 1951. Rear bumpers and guards used on other Mercury models were the same in 1949 and 1950, but changed in 1951. A horizontal bar between the bumper guards, with the Mercury name stamped into it, was new in 1950. The 1949 and 1951 versions were plain. Also identical for 1949 and 1950, on all non-Station Wagon models, were the dash panels, front body assemblies, windshield glass and radiators.

Another thing that was revised was the "Safe-T-Vue" instrument panel. The fuel gauge; ammeter; ignition switch; light switch; oil pressure gauge dash unit; water temperature gauge; and speedometer were all new parts. The instrument panel no longer resembled a box with the instruments tunneled into it. It was flatter. The gauges were arranged horizontally, except for the hooded speedometer directly in front of the driver. The bottom section of the instrument panel was curved. There was a bright metal trim panel on the left two-thirds of the dashboard.

In addition to this Lincoln Presidential Limousine, Harry S. Truman had a special Mercury limo that he used for a short time. (Truman Library)

This long wheelbase Siebert Ambulance, constructed on a 1950 Mercury chassis, has double "suicide" doors on its right-hand side. (Phil Skinner)

Starting with the engine, mechanical changes were either very minor or non-existent. The three-main-bearing V-8 again had a 3-3/16 x 4 inch bore and stroke and 255 cubic inches. The compression ratio stayed at 6.8:1 and solid valve lifters were used again. The horsepower was again 110 at 3600 rpm and torque remained 200 pounds-feet at 2000 rpm. Some people say that a new camshaft was used in 1950, but early production cars, at least, had the same camshaft (part number 8CM-6250B) that was used in all 1949 Mercurys. There was a different oil filter; upper radiator hose; fan and pulley assembly; water pump; radiator core; fuel and vacuum pump; fuel tank; electrical starter; and carburetor assembly. New rubber drive belts were required for the new fan and generator. Otherwise, just about everything else below the hood was unchanged.

The 1951 "Econ-O-Mizer" carburetor was a model number 885FFC Holley two-barrel. It got a big promotional push. "Owners reported 17, 18, 19 and more miles per gallon last year and this year, better than ever economy is obtained with the 'Econ-O-Mizer' carburetor," said Mercury's ad men. "Its design prevents vapor lock and stalling and assures greater economy." In actuality, the biggest change in the carburetor was a new main body. The float, the needle valve and seat, the air horn and the throttle body and shaft were all exactly the same as in 1949.

Transmissions offered *in production models* were the same both years. However, a two-page advertisement, previewing the introduction of automatic transmission for 1951 Mercurys, appeared in a national magazine. It showed photos of a 1950 Mercury Sport Sedan with captions indicating that the car had automatic transmission. There was also a photo of Benson Ford sitting in a Convertible with Harold Youngren. In Benson's hand was an automatic transmission gear shift lever!

Getting back to the production Mercury with manual transmission, the clutch was slightly changed. However, other clutch parts, like the disc and the throw-out bearing, were the same as in 1949. Also unchanged were all of the manual gear-shift mechanism components. The optional Touch-O-Matic overdrive, made by Bendix, was the same, except for its control cable. The propeller shaft assembly was also carried over from 1949. As in 1949, three rear axles were available. The standard ratio was 3.9:1. Cars with overdrive featured a standard 4.27:1 axle ratio. A 4.58:1 axle was listed, too. Wheels and brakes matched in both years, except for the parking brake, which was redesigned for 1950.

Steering and suspension part numbers had no changes, even though Mercury promoted a supposedly-new "Stedi-Line" steering system with a new steering wheel, "high-ratio" steering, and narrow-tread tires that, ads said, "all contribute to easier steering." Front and rear tread widths were identical from 1949 through 1951 and 7.10 x 15 tires were used all three years. All 1949 to 1951 models listed the same turning radius. (The outer wheels turned to 17-1/2-degrees when the inner wheel was turned to 20-degrees.) However, front caster settings were revised for 1950, which may have helped inspire some of the (apparently) way-out advertising claims. As for the "new" steering wheel, it was, again, of two-spoke design. It had a restyled hub and center piece. The color was changed from black to white.

Two coupes were added to the 1950 lineup, one on the low end and one on the high end. The 72A model was a "loss leader" with a $1,875 price tag. It had black rubber window gaskets, fixed rear side windows, no clock (standard on other models) and no wheel trim rings. For people attracted to General Motors' sporty new hardtops, Mercury created the Model 72C Monterey. It sported canvas or vinyl roof coverings at $2,146 or $2,157, respectively. It was not a pillarless coupe, but it looked nice enough to compete with the hot-in-the-marketplace GM "hardtop convertibles" and the word "hardtop" was used to describe the Monterey in several instances. *Ward's Automotive Yearbook* called it the "Monterey hard-top." Unfortunately, it proved a poor competitor and few were sold.

A well-known, current "James Dean" modified is "T-Ski's Merc." This radical custom was created by John Tomaszewski, the operator of T-ski's Kustom Touch, a customizing and restoration shop in Stevens Point, Wisconsin. (John Gunnell)

Standard with the Monterey, besides the vinyl roof coverings, were leather facings for the seats; a simulated leather headliner; wool carpets; a gold-winged hood ornament; chrome-plated inside garnish moldings; fender skirts; a black custom steering wheel; a two-toned dashboard; dual outside rearview mirrors; and full wheelcovers. An all-leather interior was optional for $10 extra. The Monterey came in Black with a yellow Landau-grain vinyl roof; in Cortaro Red Metallic with a black vinyl top; or in Turquoise Blue with a dark blue vinyl roof.

Offered again was a single open car. "Rain or shine, this sleek, new Mercury convertible laughs at the weather," said a snippet of promotional verse. "The snug-fitting automatic top, safety glass windows, and wide front seat are all push-button operated. New, smart fashion interiors are available with all-leather or leather and nylon upholsteries. And there's a wide choice of beautiful colors." The Station Wagon carried Mercury's highest price of $2,560.50. In midyear, the wagon was changed from a "true" woodie and got a new interior with fold-away, instead of removable, center and rear seats.

Colors for the 1950 Mercs were Black; Royal Bronze Maroon Metallic; Trojan Gray; Roanoke Green Metallic; Everglade Green; Maywood Green Metallic; Dune Beige; Laguna Blue; and Banning Blue Metallic. Four two-tone color combinations were offered: Penrod Tan over Dune Beige; or Banning Blue Metallic, Roanoke Green Metallic and Laguna Blue under (or over) Trojan Gray.

"Mid-section Seating" was promoted again. "Look at the room in this broad, foam rubber-cushioned front seat!" said another advertisement. "Almost a full five feet of 'better than ever' comfort!" The bench seats were said to have "Cushion Coil" front springing. There were new interior trim moldings and ornaments. Standard furnishings included armrests, courtesy lights and a map light. The interior ventilation system was improved. "Handsome trim has been used to create 'customized' interiors," said the 1950 Mercury salesman's guide book. A variety of nylon-and-broadcloth fabrics combinations was used to cover the seats in the closed cars. The Station Wagon continued with leather seats. New fiberglass insulation was used, in the headliner and under the dash, for improved sound-proofing. Safety door handles on the inside doors and an inside hood release were other selling points.

In the late summer of 1950, Mercury's sales department said that the six-passenger Coupe was "Popular as a series ticket" in a World Series/baseball-themed ad that also stressed the car's thriftiness. It pointed out that the "Sweepstakes Winner of the Mobilgas Grand Canyon Run was 'America's No. 1 Economy Car!'" This event was featured in the April 1950 edition of *Motor Trend*, which stated, "best mpg economy was by Studebaker (26.6), Mercury (26.6), Nash Ambassador (26.4),

Willys Jeepster (26.1), and Nash Statesman (25.5)."

The Mercury, with the second-best mpg figure, won by averaging the highest ton-mpg. It was named "Sweepstakes Winner" and Mercury picked this up in its later advertising. This was very interesting, in that official support of this effort was granted rather reluctantly, and only after the fact. According to an article in the June 1993 issue of *Special Interest Autos*, it was a Long Beach, California dealer, named Art Hall, who pushed Mercury into this revival of the old, prewar Gilmore Oil Company Economy Runs, in February 1950.

Apparently, Hall was able to get the nod from Benson Ford to enter the trial, but received no promise of financial support from Lincoln-Mercury. Undaunted, he then hired race car builder Bill Stroppe and camshaft designer Clay Smith to build him a winner. The two mechanical geniuses pulled out every trick in the book and took advantage of all loopholes in the contest's

Another "chopped-top" Mercury radical-custom, named "Knight Rider," is active in the nostalgia kustom-kar scene today. (*Old Cars*)

rules. They went through an elaborate procedure to plot and test the course, ahead of time, to avoid as much stopping and starting as possible. A weatherman was hired, to ride ahead of the car and monitor wind conditions. These were relayed back to the driver, Stroppe, by flag signals. Of course, the Mercury won. After Hall phoned Benson Ford to tell him of the win, the general manager volunteered to reimburse all his expenses.

On March 27, 1949, entertainer Ed Sullivan made an exciting announcement on his "Talk of the Town" television show. His sponsor, Lincoln-Mercury, would be supply a specially-trimmed convertible to Indianapolis Motor Speedway, to pace the race there on Memorial Day. Naturally, Benson Ford was seen driving the pace car around the "Brickyard." Benson also posed, at the speedway, with race driver Joe James, who piloted the "Bob Estes Special" in the 1950 race. This car, sponsored by a Lincoln-Mercury dealer, had a modified V-8 engine.

Providing Official Pace Cars for the annual 500-Mile Race at Indianapolis carried a total cost of approximately $50,000 in the early 1950s, which was quite expensive for a fleeting (less-than-three-minutes) exposure to 150,000 speedway spectators at a speed of 90 mph. There was no live television coverage in those days, as the race broadcast was delayed 48 hours. So the pace car got less media exposure.

Speedway manager Wilbur Shaw personally selected an Official Pace Car each January. The "lucky" automaker was expected to pick up the tab for a pace car party and press parties in New York and Chicago. In addition, the company was required to supply the speedway with 25 official courtesy cars; two Station Wagons; (for ambulance and utility use); three pickup trucks (for fire protection); and two pace cars. The lettered-up courtesy cars were used, by the officials, for one year. They then had to be offered to each official, for purchase at cost. The wagons and trucks were returned to the manufacturer, to be refurbished and sold as used vehicles. The actual pace car was presented to the winner of the Indy 500.

The 1951 grille had "scoops" behind the bumper guards. Wraparound end pieces held new parking lamps. The molding had a slashed tip and larger lettering.

New for 1951 were longer rear fenders, vertical taillamps, "rippled" bumper extensions, a cross-bar without Mercury name and wraparound backlight.

The 1951 Mercurys did look more glittery, especially with bright metal accessories like the combination front mud guard/rocker panel molding. The six-passenger Coupe weighed 3,485 pounds in base trim. (*Old Cars*)

The sponsor was required to put up 10 lap prizes, of $200 per lap, in exchange for publicity announcements on race day. The automaker also had to take out a $250 two-color advertisement in the Indy 500 program. The speedway reserved two blocks of seats, costing $1,392, for 116 guests of the sponsor and gave the automaker garage space at the track. (This was for storing the cars, as well as for partying.) In addition, the sponsor had to buy about 200 lunches for media reps. They cost about $2 each. Also available to the pace car suppliers (for varying fees) was billboard space near the speedway and radio and televising advertising opportunities.

Despite all the costs involved, Ford was always anxious to supply the Indy 500 Official Pace Car. In the postwar years, the company did so in 1946 (Lincoln-Continental); 1950 (Mercury); 1953 (50th anniversary Ford Convertible); 1957 (Mercury Convertible); 1961 (Thunderbird); 1965 (Mustang); 1966 (Mercury Comet); 1968 (Ford Torino); 1979 (Mustang); and 1994 (Mustang Cobra).

In addition to pacing racing events, 1950 Mercurys competed in some of them. Eleven Mercurys ran in the original Carrera PanAmericana, or Mexican Road Race, in 1950. One of them, car number 11, was a 1949 model and the rest were 1950 models. They had the numbers 15; 32; 39; 57; 60; 64; 82; 84; 93; and 104. The number 64 car, driven by Marcelo Quintanilla S. of Mexico, was wrecked. The number 32 car, piloted by Mexico's Olegario Perez P., took third place in the eighth leg of the event and won $500. The 1949 Mercury, driven by B.A. Hemesby, and the number 60 car, driven by S.S. Barragan, were from the United States. Cars number 95 and 104 were sponsored by the Republic of Colombia. Judging by the drivers' names, the rest of the Mercurys all seem to have been Mexican entries. Only five of the 11 cars completed the race.

Mercurys also won two NASCAR stock car racing events in 1950. One of them was among the West Coast's biggest events of the year ... the 250-lap Stock Car Race at the 5/8-mile Oakland Speedway. It drew big name competitors, including eight Indianapolis drivers. Marvin Burke piloted his 1950 Mercury to victory at an average speed of 77 mph, winning on the basis of skill and pit stops. However, the Mercurys were not standouts as racing cars. The "baby Lincoln" body was too big and the flathead did not have the power to match a Cadillac or Oldsmobile with an overhead valve V-8. Even Plymouth, with an inline, L-head six, took twice as many races as the Mercurys did. Plymouths, however, won because they could run a lot further, than any other competitor, on a set of tires. Plymouth pilot Lee Petty (father of Richard) was another contributing factor.

Walt Woron, a prolific automotive writer who test-drove many now-collectible postwar cars, wrung out the 1950 Mercury, for *Motor Trend*, in May 1950. His Royal Bronze Maroon four-door Sport Sedan had the 4.27:1 axle and overdrive. Woron described the appearance of the Merc as "streamlined, yet functional." He appreciated the restrained use of chrome, its headroom and the interior design, but suggested that a larger backlight would enhance rear vision. He also noted that the key had to be left in place, when the trunk was unlocked.

Woron found the soft suspension contributed to a comfortable ride, but said it detracted from cornering ability in sharp turns. He suggested that a faster steering ratio would be an improvement. Initially, the brake pedal had a soft feel, but the binders worked excellent. They stopped the car,

The six-passenger Coupe (a.k.a. Sport Coupe) was the most economical Mercury, with its $1,947 price tag. (*Old Cars*)

from 60 mph, in 173 feet, without "burning rubber."

Performance-wise, the Mercury took 15.98 seconds to get from 0 to 60 miles per hour. The quarter-mile required 20.88 seconds and got the Merc moving at 69 mph. According to the magazine, the car had a top speed of 83.75 mph, but Woron thought that seemed conservative. "With better tuning and a longer approach distance, it is certain that the Mercury could turn a higher top speed," he wrote.

Woron tried some hill climbing on his return trip to Los Angeles. "Returning the 1950 Mercury to the factory after eight hours on the road, having traveled 120 miles on open highway, over mountainous terrain, and through city streets, we felt that Mercury had lived up to its advance billing," he said. "It is a car that any owner could well be proud of."

Mercury built its one millionth car — a four-door Sedan — during 1950. By the end of the year, Mercury had clinched ninth rank in overall industry sales. Model-year production included 1,746 Station Wagons, 8,341 Convertible Coupes, 132,082 Sport Sedans and 151,489 coupes of all types, combined. It has been estimated, but not confirmed, that the Monterey Coupe sold somewhere from just under 1,000 copies to as many as 5,000.

The four factories began cranking out 1951 Mercurys in October 1950. Showroom introductions were done on October 24. In May 1950, Lincoln-Mercury Division was awarded a multi-million dollar contract to build J-40 jet aircraft engines for the United States Navy. These were to be produced in the new, $50-million-dollar factory near Wayne, Michigan. It was scheduled to open in mid-1952 and be completed by the spring of 1953. In December 1950, Mercury assemblies at the Rouge, Michigan factory were terminated. Mercury production was then transferred to the "Detroit Lincoln" factory. In mid-1952, the assembly lines were scheduled to start moving to the Wayne plant. However, this move was ultimately delayed until the fall of 1952.

There were no changes in models at the start of the 1951 model-year, but the 72A Coupe (the one with the black rubber windshield gasket) didn't last long. Most reference sources don't show it at all. Others list it with a $130 lower price. All other Mercury prices dropped a bit. The six-passenger Coupe, Convertible Coupe, Sport Sedan, Monterey Coupe and Station Wagon were all down about $30. Mercury advertised the lower retails as part of a "Down to Earth" pricing promotion.

Rear fenders on the 1951 cars had a higher, longer shape. They protruded out, past the trunk. "Notice how the fenders sweep gracefully out, almost to the bumper line, and give the 1951 Mercury a completely new look," said one ad. The fenders had fluted ornaments, on the bottom, that looked like extensions of the bumper. The taillamps were now made of plastic. They were vertically-mounted, instead of horizontal.

A new, full-width grille assembly appeared. It had an "electric shaver" look, somewhat like the 1950 design, but without a vertical center piece. (Some accessory houses sold an aftermarket center section that could be used, in place of the 1949-1950 vertical center piece, to update the look of the older Mercury models.) All louvers in the 1951 grille were of approximately equal width, but the louvers did not go fully across. Instead, there were new "air scoop" grille pieces directly behind the bumper guards. The large, chrome air scoop sections had a "hooded" design that integrated with the shape of the bumper guards. A "bowling pin" look characterized the new front bumper guards. Extensions on each end of the grille were narrower, but wider, and wrapped fully around the corners of the body. They incorporated parking lamp doors and new parking lamp lenses made of plastic. The front bumper face bar was new, with a crease at its center, instead of along the bottom.

There was a new hood lip ornament and a medallion that resembled the 1950 trunk handle. The medallion had a sort of "notched sea shell" shape with the Mercury name, in black, stamped around a red plastic insert bearing a gold Mercury-head logo in its center. "The new front end appearance will delight you," boasted Mercury. "So simple, so balanced, so graceful."

The front fender moldings had a blunt look at the front, like the 1949 moldings. However, the Mercury lettering on them was much larger than in 1949, running completely over the wheel opening and further. Mercury door moldings were the same, from 1949 to 1951. Rear fender moldings varied according to body style. The 1950 and 1951 Monterey Coupes had a distinctive rear fender molding. All other Coupes and Convertibles used the same rear fender moldings all three years. The 1949 to 1951 Sedan rear fender moldings also had the same part number. New headlamp doors were used in 1951. The front fenders also had new part numbers and probably had small changes to accommodate the redesigned grille. They were the same for Coupes, Sport Sedans and Convertibles. The hood was unchanged. Full wheelcovers were fitted to all models, not just Montereys.

The 1949 to 1951 Station Wagon windshields were the same, and were not shared with Ford wagons. All other Mercurys of the three years shared their windshields with small Lincolns. The 1951 closed cars used a new semi-wraparound rear window with more than 1,000 square inches of safe viewing area. Mercury said it had "See-ability." This change did not affect the rear door glass or rear door window glass. These parts were the same all three years and interchanged with Lincoln models.

There were nine two-tone color choices for 1951. A Coventry Green-Gray/Everglade Green combination was depicted in this ad. These colors could be had with either on top and bottom. (Mercury)

This 1951 Mercury Sport Sedan has 18,000 original miles. The Fulton sun shield is an aftermarket accessory. (Paul Ferguson)

Original photo from mid-1950s shows Michael Pateuk's grandfather's 1951 Mercury Sports Sedan in Wildwood, New Jersey (M. Pateuk)

The colors available for 1951 models were the carryover hues of Black; Banning Blue Metallic; and Everglade Green; as well as the all-new colors Luxor Maroon Metallic; Coventry Green-Gray; Kerry Blue Metallic; Tomah Ivory; Mission Gray Metallic; Sheffield Green; Academy Blue; Monterey Red; Turquoise Blue; Brewster Green Metallic; Yosemite Green Metallic; and Vassar Yellow (Convertible Coupes only).

There were nine two-tone color combinations. Black over Tomah Ivory was offered. The other combinations could be had with either color on top and the other on the bottom. The colors were Sheffield Green/Coventry Green-Gray; Sheffield Green/Tomah Ivory; Mission Gray Metallic/Banning Blue Metallic and Coventry Green-Gray/Everglade Green.

The interior again featured the "Safe-T-Vue" instrument panel and fiberglass insulation. Foam rubber seat cushions were used on the so-called "Cushion-Coil" seats, which offered "broader, softer seating and extra roominess." There was a new "Medallion" steering wheel and a cable-operated parking brake. "From stitches in its seats to head bolts in its power plant, Mercury is precision-built for the years ahead of it," said one ad. "New colors and fabrics let Mercury set the pace for style and beauty." Cloth interiors came in tan; tan-and-gray; gray; gray-and-rust; blue; tan-and-rust; green; brown; brown-and-turquoise; and white-and-green. Nine leather trims were offered: red-and-black; tan-and-brown; blue-and-ivory; blue; red; green; black-and-red; brown-and-turquoise; and white-and-green.

The Mercury "Hi-Power Compression" V-8 had the same basic specifications, but two additional horsepower. Surprisingly, no big thing was made of this in advertising. A new automatic transmis-

Vassar Yellow was a color reserved for Convertible Coupes only. This model had a $2,380 list price and weighed 3,760 pounds without options. Only 6,759 of the 1951 ragtops were built. (Old Cars)

sion generated most of the hyperbole this season. The engine did have a better-balanced crankshaft, new roto-type valve retainers, exhaust valve inserts, and a vacuum-booster fuel pump. To quench the flathead's tendency to run hot, a higher pressure radiator cap was used. The throttle linkage was improved as well. Shorter engine valves were used and higher-pressure valve springs. Naturally, the flathead had different valve clearance settings and timing revisions. It used the same two-barrel carburetor as in 1950, and again had 6.8:1 pistons. It was rated for 112 hp at 3600 rpm and 206 pounds-feet of torque at 2000 rpm. "Test the whisper-hustle of its great 8-cylinder, V-type engine," was about the only promotional reference to the power plant.

The 1951 Mercury Station Wagon was the year's rarest body style with a 3,812-unit production run. (Jon DeMars)

There were a number of 1951 chassis refinements, such as a new rear engine mount and transmission cross member; a revised front suspension idling arm, and a ball-bearing type clutch pilot bearing. A new 3.31:1 rear axle was used on cars with the optional Merc-O-Matic transmission. This included approximately 33 percent of all Mercurys built in 1951. In fact, demand for the automatic transmission was even stronger, but Korean War materials shortages prevented Mercury from producing more Merc-O-Matic gear boxes.

Other new-for-1951 options included a lighted ashtray; a visor-vanity mirror with a built-in reading lamp; and a three-legged jack. The long list of extras also included a "Merco-Therm" heater, an AM radio, and white sidewall tires. Of course, dealers were always anxious to add spotlights, No-Mar fuel door guards, exterior sun shades, fender shields (skirts), wheel trim rings, fog lights and many other extras.

The Monterey was back for 1951, but with less extras than it had in 1950. It still came in cloth-top and vinyl-top models. It sold for $2,314 and tipped the scales at 3,485 pounds. A second version, with genuine leather upholstery, was $2,325. The 1951 Monterey had many of the same extras featured in the model in 1950, but a Custom steering wheel and chrome window garnish moldings were deleted from the standard equipment list. However, many Montereys did get the optional Merc-O-Matic transmission.

Although 1949 and 1950 Station Wagons shared the same back lower panel, the 1951 panel had a new part number. The back window glass (clear only) was also changed. The spare was carried on the tailgate for the last time. (Jon DeMars)

"It's here now! New 1951 Mercury with Merc-O-Matic Drive — the Drive of Your Life!" was the bold way Mercury announced its new transmission. And why not ... Mercury was the first brand to get the new Ford automatic (called Ford-O-Matic when installed in Fords). As already mentioned, several 1950 Mercury test cars had this feature, which Ford had been working on during the previous decade. The company said that its engineers had experimented with "every known principle of automatic transmissions" and that they had built "dozens of them." All were found to have one of the following drawbacks: slipping; jerkiness; excessive heat build-up; too much power loss; or poor fuel economy characteristics. Working with Borg-Warner, a unique combination of various proven principles resulted in Merc-O-Matic Drive.

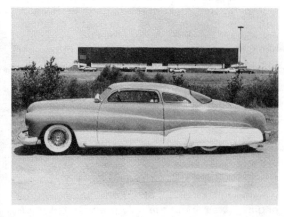

With their extended rear fenders 1951 Mercury "lead sleds" have been popular with customizers since they were new. (*Old Cars*)

"We have spent 4-1/2 years achieving this drive," said Ford engineering vice president Harold Youngren. "We could have had one (automatic) at any time, but we refused to compromise until we had a drive that would do all the things we believe an ideal automatic drive should do. Now we have it, and I sincerely believe it is as fine a drive as engineers know how to build today."

Merc-O-Matic had a P-R-N-Dr-Lo shifting pattern, like the one that's standardized today. For normal driving, the lever was slipped into "Dr." The driver could go straight from neutral to reverse, without going through forward speeds. This was handy for rocking a car out of mud or snow. This was unique to Ford at the time. Also uncommon, on automatics of the era, was a Park gear. It locked the wheels, when the car was parked, even on a steep hill. Cars with Merc-O-Matic had a small script on the rear fenders. It was under the gas filler door on the left side and in the same position on the smooth, right rear fender.

The automatic transmission featured a climbing gear, for use going up hills, and provided engine-braking action when the car was descending a hill. This transmission was fairly smooth, though not quite a match for GM's four-speed Hydra-Matic. Cars with the option were slow, too. In *Mechanix Illustrated*, Tom McCahill said, "I'll bet you a 100-year subscription that no Merc-O-Matic Drive Merc will ever win a stock car race or an economy run."

Unlike Floyd Clymer and Walt Woron, McCahill seemed far from a die-hard Mercury fan. However, he liked his 1949 stick-shift car. If he had purchased a 1951 model, he surely would have ordered it with the "Silent Ease" standard transmission and, probably, with the optional Touch-O-Matic Overdrive. Even so-equipped, a 1951 Sport Sedan that McCahill drove, took 16 seconds to go 0-to-60 and 20.8 seconds to cover the quarter-mile, with a terminal speed of 69 mph.

Walt Woron, and his technical editor Don Francisco, did better with their overdrive-equipped Mercury Sport Sedan in an April 1951 *Motor Trend* "Motor Trial." This car went from 0-to-60 mph in 19.21 seconds and did the standing start quarter-mile in 21.74. Naturally, Woron liked the larger rear window, a change that he had actually suggested in his 1950 Mercury "Motor Trial." This time, the automaker made sure that the car was tuned-up, too. As a result, it turned in a higher average top speed of 91.18 mph. It's fastest one-way run was 92.49 mph.

Woron's article addressed the fuel economy questions that many Mercury owners raised, after they heard of the phenomenal figure of 26.52 mpg that Mercury registered in the Mobilgas Economy Run. He explained how cars competing in the run were "set up perfectly" for the contest. "We did approach it, however, with 25.80 mpg at a steady 30 mph," he noted. "While the poorest mileage was through heavy traffic (without overdrive) — 8.38 mpg." In light traffic, Woron achieved 18.75 mpg with overdrive, but this dropped to 15.50 mpg in medium traffic and 13.38 mpg in heavy traffic."

Motor Trend did approve of the 1951 Merc's high-speed stability, visibility and comfort. Brake stopping distances were slightly better than with the 1950 model. Criticisms included an instrument layout that was hard to read at a glance, a lack of foot room (for rear compartment passengers) below the front seat, tire rumble, and "spongy" steering. Overall, the car was considered improved from 1950.

Most automotive evaluators gave the Mercury high marks. In addition, it took first place in Class C in the Mobilgas Economy Run. The 1951 trial ran from Los Angeles to the Grand Canyon, via Death Valley and Las Vegas. *Motor Trend* published a detailed article, by Walt Woron, about the run. It appeared in the magazine's June 1951 issue. Woron did a taped interview with 1950 overall winner Bill Stroppe (Mercury) and 1951 overall winner Les Viland (Lincoln). For 1951, the Class E Lincoln Sweepstakes winner hit 66.484 ton-mpg, while the Mercury was third with 59.868 ton-mpg. (Between them was, believe or not, a Chrysler Crown Imperial with 63.289 ton-mpg!)

Henry Ford II was the proud owner of this "Mercury" Coupe that was specially-built to his order in 1951. It was exhibited at a show in Turin, Italy, before being shipped to the United States. (Dick Dance)

The basically positive magazine reviews and the very heavily promoted economy run results made Mercury feel confident enough in the car's ability to invite people to "Road Test it! Make the Mercury 2-Way test for the buy of Your life. Coming or going, it's a smooth and balanced ride in a Mercury — as you'll discover once you sit behind the wheel. Easy handling? You'll wonder if Mercury's reading your mind, so quickly does it respond to your every wish. Riding Comfort? Special bump-smothering springs turn the roughest road into 'easy street.' And performance? Great performance! You've simply got to drive it to believe it."

The 1951 ads put a lot more emphasis on economy; value; low prices; good gas mileage; low upkeep; long life (92 percent of all Mercurys ever built were still on the road); high trade-ins; and solid values. Nearly all of the cars shown in ads had black sidewall tires. "For long-run investment, you're smart to put your money in this penny-pincher," one slogan suggested.

Model-year production of 1951 Mercurys hit a new record for the young company. Despite controls on output due to the Korean conflict, it was the second best year in Mercury history. The company said that it had built 1,390,000 cars in its first 12 years and that 81 percent of them were built since 1946. This strength also came despite several major work stoppages at different factories. The Los Angeles plant shut down for two days, in July, due to a railroad strike. In St. Louis, Missouri and Metuchen, New Jersey, the National Price Administration prompted a four-day shutdown, in mid-August, to maintain production within Korean War quotas. Plant adjustments shut the Rouge plant, in Dearborn, for one day in October and one in November. In December, between the 10th and the 17th, all Mercury plants shut down (for eight to 11 days) to make the 1952 model changeover. Model-year production figures for 1951 revealed that 310,387 cars were built. Of these, 157,648 were Sport Sedans; 142,168 were Coupes (of all models); 6,579 were Convertible Coupes; and a mere 3,812 were Station Wagons.

"For long-run investment, you're smart to put your money in this penny-pincher!" a 1951 Mercury ad claimed. (Mercury)

Mid-century Mercurys 1952-1956

With Benson Ford at the helm of Lincoln-Mercury Division, the 1952 Mercury entered production later than usual, in January 1952. This was probably necessitated by several factors. The first had to do with production facilities. When the changeover to the all-new 1952 models was done in December 1951, Mercury's assembly line at Ford's Rouge factory was temporarily moved to the Detroit Lincoln factory. The reason for this was that the modern, $50 million assembly plant being erected in Wayne Township, Michigan, was still not completed. In addition, raw materials restrictions, related to the Korean War, may have caused some problems.

Mercury's general sales manager, J.E. Bayne, was finally able to schedule dealer introductions for January 30. That put A.H. Crowley and R.R. Nadal to work. Crowley was the manager of product promotions and distribution, while Nadal was product sales and service manager.

An all-new body shell was shared with Ford, although Mercury's chassis had three additional inches of wheelbase. Mercury advertisements described the new look as "Forerunner Styling." Indeed, there was a crisp smartness to the "Guideline" fenders" and "Air Foil" feature lines of the new FoMoCo body. It obviously drew much of its design inspiration from jet aircraft of the early 1950s. In fact, copywriters working for R.F.G. Copeland, Mercury's advertising and sales promotion

For 1952. Mercury finally had a two-door Hardtop or Sport Coupe and it was a dandy. The Custom version even came at a modest $2,100 list price. (Mercury)

manager, boasted of "sweeping, jet-lined grace." Other modern-looking design elements included a "Jet-Scoop" hood, a "Monopane" windshield (with 17 percent greater visibility), a centralized "Hide-Away" gas cap, and an "Interceptor" instrument panel.

The new body was definitely Ford-like in its appearance and general proportions. Although the 1952 Mercury had a 118-inch wheelbase (same as 1951), versus the 1952 Ford's 115 inches, it was still some five inches shorter, three inches narrower and 100 pounds lighter than a 1951 Mercury. The new Mercury's overall length was 202.2 inches. That made it 4.6 inches shorter than the 1951 Mercury, but 4.4 inches longer than a 1952 Ford. The only measurement unchanged from 1951 was the Mercury's height. Despite being generally down-sized, the Mercury was up-graded when it came to trim and appointments. It had a Lincoln-rich feeling about it. "Eye America's No. 1 Styling Car," advertisements boasted.

A second car-line was introduced this year. The base Mercury series included two- and four-door Sedans, an all new two-door Hardtop Sport Coupe and six- and eight-passenger Station Wagons. Prices started at $2,004 and went to $2,591. Higher up the scale was the new, three-car Monterey series. These fancier cars had the word Monterey (in place of Mercury) on the rear fenders and added a "curb-buffer" strip (rocker panel molding) along the bottom of the body sides. Offered with Monterey trim were the Hardtop Sport Coupe, the four-door Sedan and a Convertible. They were priced between $2,133 and $2,390. The Hardtop had a wide chrome trim plate with horizontal scores on the roof rear quarters, and bright vent window frames. Monterey Sedans also had rear roof pillar trim plates, but they had more vertical, slanting score lines. There were chrome-framed vent windows front and rear. The Convertible no longer came standard with power windows, as it had since 1949. It was available with all-vinyl or vinyl-and-nylon upholstery. A fabric top boot was included.

All Mercurys featured "Frenched" headlamps and a unique, massive, integrated bumper grille characterized by an upper "air foil" and a horizontal center bar that wrapped around the body corners. The lower bumper pan was bright metal with a second air foil opening and circular parking lamps located just outside the lower opening. Near the center were tall uprights with circular "lights" at the bottom and a strange, 1950 Buick-like "buck tooth" center piece.

Road tester Ted Koopman, of *Speed Age* magazine, made reference to this in his 1952 Mercury review, saying, "If credit lines were customary in the automobile industry, the Mercury's would include: Air scoops by Cadillac; taillights courtesy of Oldsmobile; windshield by Studebaker; and grille dentures by Buick."

If the large, simulated air scoop on the hood made the Mercury look racy, there was a reason for it. Originally, a functional scoop had been

Mercury's Custom four-door Sedan cost $1,987. A total of 83,475 Sedans were made, including Montereys. (Mercury)

Mercury's 1952 Monterey Sport Coupe had bright rocker panel moldings, and a "Monterey" chrome script. (Bill Nappi)

The 1952 Sport Coupes, like Bill Nappi's Monterey, had three-piece rear windows. (Bill Nappi)

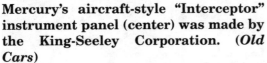

Mercury's aircraft-style "Interceptor" instrument panel (center) was made by the King-Seeley Corporation. (*Old Cars*)

The 1952 taillamps incorporated stop lamps, turn signals, a reflector, and a white back-up lens. (Bill Nappi)

scheduled to "co-star" with a planned overhead valve V-8. The new engine wasn't ready in time and the flathead V-8's air cleaner didn't fit under the lower hood. So, engineers closed the scoop's air intake, made the "bump" bigger, and decorated the front edge with a large chrome wind-split molding. The word "Mercury" was also spaced across the hood lip, under a crest emblem on the upper front of the hood.

The simulated hood scoop wasn't the only concession that Mercury made to changes in plan. In addition to the original plan for an overhead valve V-8, the new model had carefully been designed to accept several significant revisions over its three-year styling cycle. They included a ball joint front suspension, power steering, power brakes, and a glass-top Sun Valley hardtop. Harold Youngren engineered the 1952 Fords and Mercurys to survive three annual changeovers. In contrast, General Motors got only two years out of its major 1953 restyling. Ultimately, this meant more profits for Ford Motor Company.

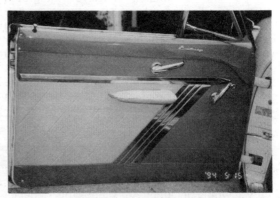

Wheelcovers had winged Mercury head symbol in center. These Firestone tires look very correct on restored car. (Bill Nappi)

The 1952 Monterey Hardtop had neat door panels. Note nomenclature tag on jamb, between door hinges. (Bill Nappi)

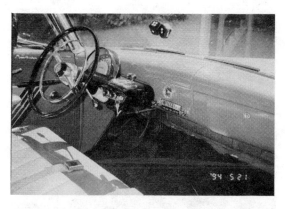

Glove box was plain. Clock and radio mounted in center of dash. Hanging dice were not standard equipment. (Bill Nappi)

Simplicity was part of the 1952 to 1954 design's staying power. Sweeping around the body corners, the 1952 to 1953 Mercury bumper ends had horizontal indentations to keep them from looking too bland. The plain front fenders had "squarish" wheel openings. The front doors were plain, too. The rear quarters of two-door models and the rear doors of four-door models had "Air-Scoop" trim. This consisted of a wide, forward-slanting, simulated chrome air intake (with ribbed indentations). It met a horizontal spear that ran to the taillamps. In the corner, where the "slash" intersected the horizontal molding, was a chrome "Mercury" or "Monterey" script. Montereys also came standard with full wheelcovers; bright rocker panel accents; chrome rain gutters; fender skirts; two-tone finish; and leather-and-vinyl interior trim.

Cars in both series featured a new wraparound rear window, which accentuated and complemented the simplicity of the overall styling. The vertical taillamps were encased in massive chrome housings that capped the backs of the rear fenders. In the rear, the gas cap was hidden in the center, under a hinged license plate holder. At the time, this was a very popular feature of FoMoCo models. A large, circular ornament decorated the center of the rear deck lid. It had concentric ring embossments and a red center with the god Mercury's head. Station Wagons had a liftgate/tailgate arrangement and an inside spare tire. The Mercury name was stamped into the rear bumper, between the bumper guards. Wagons did not have bumper guards to permit lowering the tailgate.

L. David Ash, who became a well-known Ford designer, gets credit for the 1952 Mercury's Interceptor instrument panel. It brought all of its "pilot-like" controls within easy reach of the driver. The temperature, oil pressure, fuel and battery gauges were housed inside a hooded, half-moon shaped console which rested on a horizontal "shelf" directly in front of the driver. All dials and gauges could be read at a glance, while driving the car. Below the console were four levers that moved horizontally, to the front or rear, as integral controls for the "Dual-Duct" heating and ventilation system. Two "Joy-Stick" controls marked "air/vent" and "inverse" jutted from slots on the left-hand side of the shelf. On the right-hand side were two additional Joy-Sticks to control the blower speed and heater/vent. The optional radio speaker, clock, and radio were stacked, top-to-bottom, in the center of the dashboard. A lockable glove box took up the right-hand side. Unfortunately, it

If you wanted a 1952 Mercury Convertible, you had to move up to the fancy Monterey series. That gave you rocker panel moldings and full wheel discs. The ragtop listed for $2,370 and just 5,261 examples were built. (Mercury)

didn't have much storage space. The steering wheel was a two-spoke type with full horn ring. It had the Mercury head in its horn button.

Colors offered for the new Mercury body were Newport Gray; Admiral Blue; Coventry Gray-Green; Academy Blue; Lakewood Green; Lucerne Blue; Vassar Yellow; Pebble Tan; Fanfare Maroon; and Hillcrest Green. The all-steel Station Wagon came with simulated DI-NOC wood-grain trim.

Mercury upholstery selections decreased from 21 to 19. Cloth trims included brown-and-white, gray, green, brown, blue and black-and-gray. All-vinyl interiors were black-and-red, green-and-ivory (two options), blue-and-ivory, bittersweet-and-ivory, red-and-ivory, and tan-and-brown. Cloth-and-vinyl options were ivory-and-green, and red. Leather trims came in black-and-red, green-and-ivory, blue-and-ivory or bittersweet-and-ivory.

Fall 1952 photo shows Mercury Monterey Hardtop on the street. Note the blackwall tires. (Bernie Roehrig)

No changes in bore, stroke or displacement were made in 1952. This was probably because Mercury expected to have the overhead valve V-8 ready and didn't quite make it. The flathead did go up to 125 horsepower at 3700 rpm and 211 pounds-feet of torque at 2100 rpm. A 7.2:1 compression ration helped in this regard. "There's something our engineers knew you never wanted changed," said one advertisement that attempted to turn the missed deadline into a sales benefit. "And they were able to keep it and increase horsepower (12%) and compression at the same time."

The 1952 Mercury engine also had revised piston clearances, a one-quart smaller crankcase capacity, a 1/2-gallon smaller, center-fill fuel tank, and a 3/4-quart smaller cooling system. There was a new "Centri-flo" carburetor, too. It was a Holley 1901FF dual downdraft model with an automatic choke. A dashpot was provided for cars with Merc-O-Matic drive. This type of carburetor had no air horn. The air cleaner fit over the main body and mounted on the throttle body, serving as both an air cleaner and air horn. The engine also had rotating valves, weatherproof ignition, vacuum spark control and a floating oil filter.

Speed Age found the 1952 Mercury four-door Sedan, with overdrive, capable of going from 0-to-60 mph in 13.57 seconds with a top speed of 97 mph. The magazine calculated 21 mpg fuel economy at a steady 60 mph. *Motor Trend* also tried the same model. It recorded an 18.6-second 0-to-60 time, a 93.75 mph top speed and only 17.4 mpg at a steady 60 mph speed. Another sedan with the Touch-O-Matic overdrive took class honors at the 1952 Mobilgas Economy Run. The car -- specially prepped by Bill Stroppe and Clay Smith -- registered 25.4093 mpg. In stock car racing, the Mercurys made no headlines this year. None finished in the top five at any big NASCAR, AAA or USAC events.

Other technical changes for 1952 included a suspended clutch pedal. A new chassis, with a stabilizer bar, was engineered for extra strength and smoother roadability. Mercury called it their "new Supersafe double-braced frame." It featured a box-type design with five supporting cross members, and cradled the riders between the axles. Mercury described this as, "the Comfort-Zone of the car." Live-rubber body mounts, "Cushion-Coil" front springs and 53-inch rear springs minimized jolting and jarring. The front tread of 58 inches was within a half-inch of the 1951 specification, but the 56-inch rear tread was a full four inches narrower.

Mercury's "Auto Action" brakes had smaller primary linings, front and rear, than the 1950-1951 models. The same size secondary linings were used all around. On the smaller, lighter cars, this added up to improved overall braking performance. A "Soft-Touch," floor-free brake pedal was suspension-mounted. Mercury also promoted a "Tip-Toe" braking system with one square inch of brake lining surface for every 23.06-pounds of car, an improvement over 1951.

Motor Trend tested the 1952 Mercury four-door Sedan in its October 1952 issue, reporting a good initial impression that survived through 1,000 miles of driving. The magazine noted the car's smaller size, due to changing from the Lincoln body to the Ford body. It summed up the results as "generally improved." The car moved from 0-to-60 in 18.6 seconds and did the quarter-mile in 20.1 seconds. Its fastest top speed run was 93.75 mph, while its four-run average was 91.71 mpg. Both performances were up from 1951. The Mercury, with overdrive, averaged 16.7 mpg in normal driving. The engine was quiet. Stopping, from 60 mph, required 194 feet, plus an inch. The pendulum type pedals were reported to be an improvement.

Writer Fred Bradley found the Merc comfortable, with a soft ride, firm steering and better ride control than earlier models. However, objectionable road shock was noted, too. The front seat did not have enough rearward adjustment to keep Bradley happy and his rear seat passengers complained of side sway. Steering and braking were good. The car was well-constructed, in general, but the large 1950s-style license plates did not fit well in the holder and covered the "Buick" teeth up front. *Motor Trend* liked the fact that the rear door glass went all the way down, flush with the window sills. Overall, the review of the Mercury was positive.

Overall the public liked the Mercury, too. However, the company endured a steel strike, government-mandated work stoppages (due to Korea), supplier strikes, and parts shortages in 1952.

Model year production, although still above prewar levels, dropped 18 percent. The annual figures would probably have been even much worse, except for the opening of the Wayne factory. It began operations in October. All Detroit Lincoln and Mercury assembly was transferred there, with no loss in production. In total, the division's fourth-quarter ran 35 percent higher than the same period a year earlier.

With this end-of-the-year push, Mercury increased its share of the domestic auto market to 4.5 percent, up from 4.47 percent in 1951. Half of all 1952 models had Merc-O-Matic transmission and 32.5 percent were hardtops. Total model-year output, according to body style, was: Mercury two-door Sedan, 25,812; Mercury and Monterey Custom four-door Sedans, 83,475 combined; Mercury two-door Hardtop Sport Coupe, 30,599; Monterey Hardtop Sport Coupe, 24,453; Mercury Station Wagon, 2,487; and Mercury Monterey Custom Convertible, 5,261.

Ford Motor Company celebrated its 50th anniversary in 1953. Every car it built had a special steering wheel horn button commemorating this milestone. FoMoCo vice president Benson Ford continued as the general manager of Lincoln-Mercury Division. R.E. Krafve was his new assistant general manager. R.P. Powers replaced N.S. Brown as general manufacturing manager, and Brown took the title of production manager. (Both men moved on by 1954, by which time D.J. Bracken became manufacturing chief). J.E. Bayne continued as general sales manager. Bayne's department selected December 9, 1952 for new-model introductions. Annual price increases averaged $17.

Mercury's advertising emphasis was on "Unified" styling and "Forward-Looking" design. "Get the facts -- and you'll go for the new 1953 Mercury," the copywriters promised. Most ads had the various features and options "windowed" in small photos. Value was stressed with slogans such as "Move ahead with Mercury -- get more for your money," and "Save with Mercury now -- get back more later, too!" Positive reviews from the automotive media and continued success in the Mobilgas Economy Run seemed to back up all of the promotional claims. This also made it easier to get

Ford's Advance Styling Studio looked like this in 1953. Both Lincolns and Mercurys were designed in this facility. (Ford Motor Company)

The 255.4-cubic-inch flathead V-8 was used again in 1953 and had the same 125-hp rating introduced the previous year. (John Gunnell)

buyers into the showroom for a test ride. "Just look -- we won't say a word," was the theme in an ad for a bright red Monterey Convertible. "Next -- let Mercury do the talking on the road!"

Three models were offered in the Mercury Custom series. The two-door Sedan was $2,193.50; the four-door Sedan was $2,250.50; and the Hardtop Coupe was $2,315. The four-door Sedan and Hardtop Coupe also came as Montereys, for $2,332.50 and $2,451.50, respectively. Other Montereys included the Convertible, with a $2,609.50 list price, and the Station Wagon for $2,825.50. All models introduced what Mercury called "Two-Stop Doors." They stayed in position either halfway open or fully open and were a great convenience in narrow places like garages and driveways.

Advertisements for 1953 Mercurys highlighted stunning new interiors; the widest choice of colors in the field; metallic paints; two-tone finish; 30 cubic feet of trunk room; "Pilot" controls; a V-8 engine; exhaust system improvements; ride and handling; and economy. Motor Trend's Jack Campbell said, "It has comfort and looks, economy and liveliness. It comes closer to being the compromise car than any of the new cars we've tested." His "MT Research" road test report went on to praise the Mobilgas Economy Run-winning Mercury for its combination of design, roominess, top speed, and fuel efficiency.

Specifications sheets showed an unchanged 118-inch wheelbase. Overall length was listed at a shorter 202.2 inches, probably due to not counting the length of bumper guards or to changes in grille design (the bumper-grille no longer had the Buick-like "buck teeth"). Also slightly smaller was a width measurement of 74 inches. Perhaps some chrome trim was not as wide as 1952, but the body shells were virtually identical. The height was 62.2 inches. Standard tires were again size

Benson Ford poses with a 1953 Mercury Monterey Convertible and Lincoln Capri Sedan in the styling showroom at Ford's engineering laboratory. Benson was vice president and general manager of Lincoln-Mercury Division. (Mercury)

7.10 x 15, with 7.60 x 15s specified for Monterey Convertibles and Station Wagons. The six-passenger Station Wagon was dropped, but the eight-passenger model was still offered.

Styling changes from 1952 were seen in the chrome trim parts and interior trim details. The grille was revised. According to *Motor's Flat Rate & Parts Manual*, only two grille components (the "Dagmar" style bumper guards) had the same part numbers as in 1952. However, the thin upper molding, the full-width horizontal center-bar, and the lower bar (which housed the circular parking

The 1953 Mercury Custom two-door Sedan had a 50,183-unit production run. This one is owned by J. Stanley Stratten. (*Old Cars*)

The 1953 Monterey Sport Coupe looked good from all angles, as well as from the driver's seat. Trim distinctions included "Mercury" on rear fender and behind top wind split molding, plus front fender badge and "Monterey" script. (Mercury)

The 1953 Monterey Sport Coupe had ribbed trim plate on roof pillar. Tail-lamps and bumper were same as 1952, but trunk ornament was new. (Mercury)

The 40,000,000th Ford vehicle produced in the company's 50th year was a Mercury. (Imperial Palace)

Advertised as a product costing "just a few dollars more than low-priced cars," the Monterey four-door Sedan listed for $2,133. Model-year production of this car was 64,038, making it the most popular 1953 Mercury. (Mercury)

The 40 millionth vehicle built by FoMoCo was a bright red 1953 Mercury Monterey Convertible with appropriate gold lettering on its side. It is now part of the Imperial Palace Auto Collection in Las Vegas, Nevada. (IPAC)

lamps) all looked very close to the previous parts. They had similar part numbers with different prefixes, perhaps indicating that only minor changes were made to their designs. For instance, the 1953 deflector had four buffer bars attached to it, while the 1952 deflector featured seven "bumps" that were integral with it. Also, the 1953 lower bar had horizontal ribs in the center, where the 1952 grille had "buck teeth."

All Mercury models used the same hood in 1952 and 1953. The hood air scoop was still non-functional. The front hood ornament (Mercury emblem) was also identical to 1952. In addition, the "hood wing assembly" (what most people would call the "hood ornament") was the same both years. However, the hood molding had a different part number and very slight changes. The 1952 Mercury dashboard panel and cowl side panel were identical to Ford parts. In 1953, these parts

The inexpensive Custom Station Wagons vanished in 1953. This model was offered only as a Monterey with six-passenger seating. (John Gunnell)

Jay Findley got a $750 1953 Mercury ragtop with 49,000 miles as a graduation present in 1959. He still owns it. The car now has 193,000 miles. (Jay Findley)

Production of Monterey Convertibles saw a healthy increase in 1953, with 8,463 made during the model-year. The "ragtop" had a base price of $2,390 and tipped the scales at 3,585 pounds. (Mercury)

were modified and no longer the same used on Fords. All models also used different rear quarter panels and trunk lids in 1953 and neither interchanged with similar Ford components. In addition, 1953 four-door Sedans had different rear doors. As the glass was unchanged, the door skins must have been modified to go with new mud guard trim.

The rear mud guard trim had a small "fluted" chrome gravel guard on the bottom and two more flutes (short, tapered chrome moldings) above. A full-length chrome mid-body side molding ran from just ahead of the front wheel opening to near the taillamps. The 1953 Mercury bodies came in a choice of 15 colors: India Black; Superior Blue Metallic; Mohawk Maroon Metallic; Glenwood Gray; Beechwood Brown Metallic; Brentwood Brown Metallic; Banff Blue; Tahiti Tan; Sherwood Green Metallic; Pinehurst Green; Asheville Green; Village Green Metallic; Bittersweet; Yosemite Yellow; and Siren Red.

Cars in the base series had chrome "Mercury" scripts on the rear mud guards, just behind the top flute molding. Two- and four-door Sedans had a narrow, chrome trim plate at the rear roof quarters. These trim plates had three diagonal scores. Neither model had rocker panel moldings or chrome frames on the side window, and the two-door Sedan also lacked what Mercury called "rear wheel pants" (fender skirts). The Sport Coupe had a horizontally scored rear roof quarter trim plate, but no side window frames. Hardtop Coupes represented 39 percent of production.

In 1953, most Mercs delivered to East Coast buyers were made at this Metuchen, New Jersey plant built in 1948. The Mercury factories in Los Angeles, California and St. Louis, Missouri date from about the same time. (Mercury)

Ernest R. Breech, Ford Motor Company executive vice-president, was one of the company's postwar "Whiz Kids." (Ford)

Top-of-the-line Mercurys had the same "Mercury" name on the rear mud guards, and the "Monterey" name on the front fenders. Standard features included bright accents on the rocker panels, skirted rear fenders; full wheel discs; and chrome-framed side windows. The four-door Sedan had wide, multi-scored chrome rear roof quarter trim plates, while the Special Custom Coupe had horizontally-scored chrome rear roof quarter trim plates, and heavier chrome side window moldings.

Windshields and door glass specifications varied by body style. In most cases, glass for Coupes and Convertibles had the same part numbers. Back window glass part numbers were the same for Sedans, Station Wagons and Convertibles, but the three-piece backlight used on 1952 Coupes was replaced with a one-piece style. Convertible folding top parts saw no changes. However, some cars of both years had two-terminal top lift control switches, while others of both years had three-terminal switches.

The gas gauge (except Station Wagons) was different, but the speedometer, battery indicator, oil pressure, and temperature gauges were the same. The 1952 and 1953 ignition switches matched, but the headlight switches were not identical. The 30 interior trims included seven (two solid-color) all-cloth options; eight (one solid-color) all-vinyl selections; 10 vinyl-and-cloth two-tone combinations; and five extra-cost two-tone leather options for Sport Coupes and Convertibles.

Mercury's 1953 engine was again a 255.4-cubic-inch flathead V-8, which produced 125 hp at 3800 rpm. It had a 7.2:1 compression ratio and a power-to-weight ratio of 27.2 pounds per horsepower. Most engine parts were the same both years, including the carburetor. Exhaust pipes and mufflers were different. A straight-

Henry Ford II (right) leans on Mercury XM-800 "dream car." Benson Ford strikes a similar pose with the Lincoln XL-500, which William Clay Ford is "driving."

through muffler replaced the three-pass design used in 1952 and the tailpipe had a larger two-inch diameter. These improvements were said to reduce back pressure as much as 50 percent. There was also a new, low-restriction air filter silencer.

According to *Motor Trend* (August 1953) the Mercury power team delivered 57.6 percent of its gross horsepower to the rear wheels. This was enough to push a Merc-O-Matic-equipped four-door Sedan through the quarter-mile in 20.8 seconds, with a terminal speed of 65.5 mph. The car moved from 0-to-60 mph in 19 seconds and had an average top speed of 88.52 mph. The Merc consumed an average of one gallon of gas for every 12.5 miles it traveled in traffic, but got 22.5 mpg at a steady 30 mph.

Transmission options included three-speed manual, Touch-O-Matic overdrive or Merc-O-

Northeast Lincoln-Mercury dealer-ship, in Philadelphia circa 1953. There were 1,824 Lincoln-Mercury dealers in operation then. (Jay Katelle)

Matic. The three-speed was a synchromesh unit using helical gears and had ratios of 2.77 in first, 1.61 in second, 1.00 in third, and 3.63 in reverse. Touch-O-Matic featured a planetary type unit with manual lock-out and accelerator-activated downshift. It had a 0.70:1 ratio and a 2.87:1 overall ratio. The automatic was a torque convertor type with planetary gears for low and reverse ranges and intermediate gear drive. Standard rear axle ratios were 3.90:1 with the conventional three-speed; 4.10:1 with overdrive; and 3.31:1 with automatic. Both manual transmissions and the Merc-O-Matic drive assemblies were slightly revised for 1953.

In *Motor Trend*, the Mercury was found to be one of the easiest cars to drive without power steering. It held the road well and drifted, in the rear, only under extreme conditions. While not overly plush or spongy, the Merc gave a firm, pleasing, comfortable ride. The powerful engine gave good performance and braking was better than cars in the same weight class, as well as many lighter cars. The magazine's interior appointments expert, Dale Runyan, rated the Merc "good" to "excellent" on most points inside the car. The wool-and-nylon upholstery was good-looking and had a high-quality feel. The seat adjusted easily.

Motor Trend liked the aircraft-style instrument panel. "The only major improvement necessary to make this one of the safest dash panels in the industry would be to relocate the radio control panel and the clock (mounted in the center of the panel), and to pad the surface facing the passengers," it said. However, the glove box was criticized for being too small. The Merc's driver had an excellent view and the heating and ventilation system worked well. The car was determined to be well-built, durable and easy to service. "We've often said that no car can strike a perfect balance of performance, economy, comfort, durability and appearance," said the tester. "The statement still stands; but, after driving, comparing, and evaluating the Mercury, we feel this car comes closer to being the 'compromise' car than any of the new cars we've tested."

On April 10, 1953, power braking became a new Mercury option with a $43 price tag. Exactly one month later, optional power steering was offered for $150.50. Although the two options were available for only five or six months, 15 percent of the 1953 cars had power steering and eight percent had power brakes. Other extras included white sidewall tires ($32.35 additional); heater ($72.26); full disc hubcaps; a bumper grill guard; windshield washers ($10.55); tinted glass ($23.13); Merc-O-Matic Drive ($189.81); Touch-O-Matic overdrive ($109.70); radio ($105.95); and a "4-Way" power seat adjuster and power windows (combined only) for $136.93.

Eleven Mercurys competed in stock car racing events in 1953, but none of them were top five finishers. Mercurys did not place high in the 1953 Mobilgas Economy Run, although *Motor Trend* writer Walt Woron used a 1953 Merc press car to cover the test. For the second year in a row, Lincoln-Mercury scored big at the Mexican Road Race, but it was Lincolns that placed one, two, three in the big/stock class. In an interesting test, Goodyear Tire & Rubber Company drove a 1953 Mercury almost one million miles (just over 950,000 miles to be more exact) on railroad ties. "This test gives dramatic proof of the miracle strength and safety of All-Nylon Cord Tires," said an advertisement, picturing the two-tone blue car speeding down railroad tracks.

Model-year assemblies began in November 1952 and totaled 305,863 cars by year's end. Although buyers started slowly, Mercury smashed production and sales records by the fall of 1953, as it posted the second-best performance in its 16-year history. The 1,500,000th Mercury was built on August 17, 1953. An all-time-high weekly production total of 9,193 units was achieved on August 22. For the calendar-year, the division built 320,369 cars (5.22 percent of total industry), which was almost 64 percent more than in 1952. Amazingly, this occurred despite a five-week strike at the Wayne, Michigan plant and a 10-week work stoppage at the Borg-Warner transmission factory in Muncie, Indiana.

In September, Mercury hit a new one-day production record, building 1,855 cars on the 10th of the month. It was also one of just a handful of automakers to pick up market share in 1953. Production was less than five percent behind 1950's all-time record. The company moved from eighth rank to sixth rank in the industry. A $13,000,000 expansion of the Lincoln-Mercury plant in Metuchen,

New Jersey got underway, while the Los Angeles, California, St. Louis, Missouri and Wayne, Michigan factories were all altered to increase their production capacity.

An all-new overhead valve V-8, a ball-joint suspension and a hardtop with a tinted, plexiglass roof panel made news at Mercury in 1954. The "V-161" engine had "Twin Tornado" combustion chambers, aluminum alloy pistons and a four-barrel carburetor. It generated 161 hp. Although Mercury was rarely shy about coining a trade-name, the new front suspension did not have any special label. "Presenting the Sun Valley, America's first transparent-top car," said an ad for the new, see-through Monterey.

Mercury's redesigned front was dominated by a restyled bumper-grille with no carryover parts. The upper molding widened in the center and had "Mercury" block-lettered on it. Attached to the molding was a new hood front ornament that was also used in 1955. (The 1956 ornament was changed to show the Mercury head emblem in its center.) The grille bars had a full-width horizontal center bar. Its center section had 14 indented "stripes" with black-painted finish in them. The lower bumper face bar had a simple, curved design, with the edges wrapping around the body corners. Large bumper guards had a "stove pipe" look. Tucked between the two bars, at the outer edges, were the parking lamps, which curved slightly around the front body corners. Extending from them, just above the bumper ends, were filler plates with horizontal scoring.

The hood and front fenders of all models were the same parts as used in 1952 and 1953. A new hood top ornament was seen, as well as a new hood ornament wing. The two pieces were now made of pot metal, instead of the stainless steel used in 1952 and 1953. The hood lock assembly was also revised. Front door shells were again different for four-door Sedans, Station Wagons and Coupes/Convertibles, though unchanged from the 1952 and 1953 parts for the same body styles. Sun Valley models had their own front door window glass, which interchanged with glass on Ford Skyliner Hardtops. The body side moldings were straight and almost full-length again. A new circular medallion appeared near the front tip of the Monterey front fender moldings only. It was finished in black with a gold emblem.

Rear doors on four-door Sedans were changed again. Those on wagons were the same. The rear quarter panels of all models were slightly different than 1953 panels. The most noticeable change was to the upper rear fenders. They had curved-over upper sections, just above the taillamps. The vertical taillamp assemblies, which matched for 1952 and 1953 models, also changed in 1954. They were shorter and set into the notch in the restyled rear fenders. The rear compartment lid was the same as 1953, as was the rear lid handle and handle medallion. The rear quarter panel ornaments and moldings were changed, too. The basic design followed the same theme, with chrome mud guard shields and three tapered moldings. These items were larger in size, however, and there was no "Mercury" signature behind the top molding. Instead, the series names, "Mercury" or "Monterey," appeared on the sides of the rear fenders, above the body side molding.

The 1954 Mercury models included a two-door Sedan ($2,194), a four-door Sedan ($2,251), and a Sport Coupe ($2,315). The Monterey series offered a Special Custom four-door Sedan ($2,333), a Special Custom Sport Coupe ($2,452), a Special Custom Convertible ($2,610), an eight-passenger Station Wagon ($2,776), and the Sun Valley Hardtop ($2,582). "Anyone who has seen travel posters of Vista-Dome trains winding their way through the Royal Gorge must have envied the passengers; they can look up, as well as out, in any kind of weather," said Walt Woron in *Motor Trend* (January 1954). "So can you, if you're riding in the new Mercury Sun Valley."

The Sun Valley Hardtop was added to the Mercury line on December 10, 1953. The front portion of this car's hardtop roof was made of Plexiglas, trimmed with a stainless steel trim molding. It was tinted the shade of sunglass lenses. Sun Valleys came in just two color combinations at first: Dark Green over Light Green or Dark Green over Cream. Later in the year, additional color schemes were added. A limited number of color-coordinated vinyl-and-cloth or all-vinyl upholstery trims were offered. Despite the fact that testing in the Arizona desert showed that the "glass dome" raised interior temperatures only five degrees, Mercury offered a snap-on, interior sun shade as an option for Sun Valleys. Offered as a dealer sales aid, a see-through Plexiglas panel for the hood was available for the similar Ford Skyliner model, but not for the Mercury Sun Valley.

Mercury Custom base models had body side moldings without front medallions, no trim on the roof rear quarters, no rocker panel moldings, and chrome windshield frames only. Rear fender skirts were extra. The fancier Mercs said "Monterey" in script on their front fenders, which had front fender spears with round medallions. Smaller round medallions with red and silver finish dressed-up the roof quarter panels. All body types in this series, except Station Wagons, were referred to as Monterey Customs, a somewhat confusing designation.

The 1954 instrument panel had a more rectangular shape, but retained the "joy-stick" type heater controls. Most trims were two-tone. (Norman F. Abston)

80

For a little as $2,333 (plus the cost of whitewall tires and two-tone finish) these lovely ladies could purchase this 1954 Monterey four-door Sedan. It was the second most popular model of the year and 65,995 were built. (Mercury)

The taillamps were "notched" into the rear fenders and served as side marker lamps. The Monterey two-door Hardtop Sport Coupe listed for $2,452 and weighed 3,520 pounds. With 79,533 assemblies, it was the most popular 1954 Merc. (OCW)

The 1954 Monterey featured its name, written in chrome, above the side spear on the rear fender. (*Old Cars*)

Simulated wood-grain exterior trim was included in the $2,776 price of the 1954 Mercury Monterey Station Wagon. (Ron Kowalke)

Special wide chrome trim was used on the windshield and side windows of all Montereys. Rocker panel accents and fender skirts were standard on all, except the non-Custom Station Wagon. New wheel discs, with larger red centers, were also seen.

Exterior colors for 1954 dropped to 14 solid colors: India Black; Atlantic Blue Metallic; Lakeland Blue; Mohawk Maroon Metallic; Granby Gray; Country Club Tan; Bloomfield Brown Metallic; Brentwood Brown Metallic; Glenoaks Green Metallic; Parklane Green; Bittersweet; Yosemite Yellow; Siren Red; and Artic White. However, there were 21 two-tone combinations of these colors. This gave a grand total of 35 paint choices.

Inside, Mercurys had a dashboard that, despite a new look, retained the "Interceptor" airplane-type instrument panel with "joy-stick" controls. The instruments were grouped nicely, with the speedometer in a long line above the oil pressure, water temperature, battery indicator and gas gauges. Two types of speedometers were used in 1954. One had numbers in a fan shape. On the other style, the numbers were straight up and down. There were three solid and one two-tone all-cloth-trim interiors; seven two-tone vinyl-and-cloth options; eight all-vinyl selections (one solid-colored); and seven genuine leather, two-tone trim combinations.

Mercury's new over-square, overhead valve V-8 was the big news. The company revealed that 640 hand-built, experimental engines had proceeded the production versions. These were subjected to over a quarter-million hours of dynamometer testing and four million miles of road use. The prototype engines were rebuilt an average of eight times each. The V-161 had a 3-5/8 x 3-3/32 inch bore and stroke for 256 cubic inches. Advertised horsepower was 161 at 4400 rpm. Torque was 238 pounds-feet at 2200 to 2800 rpm. It had a 7.5:1 compression ratio and a Holley model 2140 four-barrel carburetor.

The January 1954 issue of *Motor Trend* had a picture of the new engine and the Sun Valley Hardtop on the cover. Inside, Walt Woron gave his early driving impressions. Some of the nice things he said were: ... "You'll like the 1954 Mercury, particularly if you like power that'll make you sit back in your seat when you stomp the throttle" ... "I checked the ability of the car to take off from scratch, in drive range, on a 17 percent grade, which it was able to do" ... "The car wouldn't start forward on the 30 percent grade from a standstill in drive, but it burned rubber taking off in low." Woron also praised the Mercury for lack of wind-wander, a firm-and-comfortable ride, and rapid suspension system recovery over sharp dips.

For the magazine's May 1954 issue, Woron gave the Monterey four-door Sedan with Merc-O-Matic a complete "MT Research" road report. The car went from 0-to-60 mph in 14.9 seconds and covered the quarter-mile in 19.4 seconds, with a 69 mph terminal speed The average top speed, over four runs, was 97.7 mph. One run hit 99.7 mph. Over a 1,359-mile test, the car averaged 16.3 mpg. At a steady 30 mph, it hit 22.4 mpg. Gone was the "Ford sound" of the flathead V-8 era. The new engine was rated "exceptionally quiet" and easy-to-service.

Vital statistics for 1954 were: Wheelbase, 118 inches; front tread, 58 inches; rear tread, 56 inches; overall width, 74-13/32 inches; overall length, 206 inches; overall height, 62-13/64 inches and curb weight (Sedan) 3,850 pounds. The car had a 41-foot turning circle and 5-1/4 turns lock-to-lock. Weight was distributed 57 percent to the front and 43 percent to the rear. Tires were again 7.10 x 15 or 7.60 x 15, depending on model.

As in the past, manual, overdrive and Merc-O-Matic transmissions were offered. Rear axle ratios were 3.91:1 with standard shift (4.09:1 optional); 4.09:1 with overdrive (3.91:1 optional); and 3.54:1 with Merc-O-Matic (3.31:1 optional). *Motor Trend* found that the automatic transmission in its test car functioned better and had "more oomph."

The new ball-stud front suspension was basically the same as that introduced on 1953 Lincolns. There were two simple ball-and-socket joints attaching the front wheels to the frame. Compared to the old king pins, with 16 grease fittings, the ball-joint suspension had four. Mercury's brakes were

HOW MERCURY'S SALES RECORDS CAN PUT MONEY IN YOUR POCKET

MERCURY'S GROWTH means you save when you buy. With a 480% increase in Mercurys on the road since 1946, Mercury dealers sell more cars per dealer than their competition. This higher volume means they have lower overhead expense per car sold, can give you a better deal—even on the Sun Valley shown above.

YOU SAVE WHEN YOU SELL—The same features that make Mercury so popular now help *keep* it in big demand. You can command a better price when you eventually trade. Proof? Mercury consistently leads its class for trade-in value according to independent national market reports of used-car prices.

IT PAYS TO OWN A MERCURY. Its all-new 161-hp V-8 engine is one of the most efficient in our economy-famous history. You save as you drive. And you get new ball-joint front suspension for even easier handling. Better see your Mercury dealer for a trial drive. MERCURY DIVISION • FORD MOTOR COMPANY

A two-tone green 1954 Sun Valley Hardtop was one of three Montereys depicted in this advertising art (the others were a yellow Convertible and a white-over-red Sport Coupe). It promised a "good deal" on the "glass-top." (Mercury)

Only 7,293 of Mercury's 1954 Monterey Convertible were produced. This one was photographed at the company's Dearborn, Michigan Proving Grounds. Without optional equipment, the ragtop had a suggested price of $2,610. (Mercury)

also upgraded to go with the more powerful overhead valve engine. They stopped the car, from 60 mph, in 167 feet. The stopping distance was 21 feet shorter than that of the 1953 model.

Test driver Woron had some difficulty getting used to his Monterey's Bendix power steering. Actually, he didn't trust what turned out to be a good system. Power steering was only three years old at this time, and manufacturers were still refining the option. He described Mercury's as a cross between Chrysler's finger-tip control type and GM's "when you need it type." In the end, Woron admitted, "It's the best power setup we've yet driven." Bendix also supplied the Mercury's power brakes.

The power brakes cost $40. Power steering added $140. Other option prices were $190 for Merc-O-Matic; $110 for overdrive; $106 for a radio; $72 for a heater; $167 for the "4-Way" power seat and power windows; $129 for a "2-Way" power seat and power windows; $78 for optional Sedan trim; and $32 (additional) for white sidewall tires. According to *Ward's Automotive Yearbook*, new options for the year included factory dual exhausts and air conditioning.

With the new motor, Mercury's had a bigger impact in 1954 stock car races. The nameplate was ranked fifth in the competition. Although no checkered flags were captured, Mercs took two second-place awards; two fourth-place berths; and captured fifth-place honors three times. In 20 different races, the Mercurys were in the top 10 finishers. Mercury also did better in the 1954 Mobilgas Economy Run, taking second among low-medium price V-8s with standard transmission and overdrive. The Monterey went 21.48 mpg overall and registered 49.98 ton miles per gallon.

A fiberglass-bodied factory dream car called the Mercury XM-800 made the rounds of automobile shows in 1954. It was a four-passenger Hardtop Coupe. Its low overall height of 55.6 inches was predictive of the "Low-Silhouette" Mercury models that would be arriving in 1955. Its long, 207.4-inch overall length accentuated its forward-canting hooded headlights and straight-line styling. Unlike the production model, the show car had a *functional* hood air scoop to provide additional air flow to the high-compression, overhead valve V-8 engine. This car reflected the basic styling motifs used on 1955 and 1956 Lincolns. It still exists in a private collection of dream cars.

Model-year production of 1954 Mercurys, which began in November 1953, slipped to 259,306 cars. Of these, 85,067 were Mercury Customs and 174,238 were Monterey/Monterey Custom models. Calendar-year production stood at 256,729 cars or 4.66 percent of industry. In the low-medium price class, Mercury had 19.3 percent of sales. That put Mercury seventh on the sales charts.

The year's highest weekly output was the 8,220 cars made between January 4 and 9. January was also the year's best month, as 30,772 cars were built. In all, there were 1,824 Lincoln-Mercury dealers operating in 1954. The largest number in a single state were the 142 dealers in Texas. On St.

Patrick's Day, Mercury hosted 102 Lincoln-Mercury salesmen, who together sold a total of $40 million worth of cars in 1953. Each received an all-expense paid vacation. In March, a 120,000 square-foot addition to the Metuchen factory was announced. Sales were strong at the start of the year, setting a record for any first quarter. They tapered off in August and September. A strike at St. Louis hurt production. The company said the labor dispute cost workers $1,200,000 in wages and cost Mercury 14,000 assemblies.

The year 1955 marked an important milestone in Mercury's corporate history. On April 15, Ford Motor Company established separate Lincoln and Mercury divisions, along with a new Special Products Division. A public announcement of the change was made three days later. F.C. Reith remained vice president and general manager of Mercury Division (Benson Ford had been appointed a FoMoCo vice president in late 1954.) J.E. Bayne was again general sales manager and D.J. Bracken kept his role as chief of manufacturing. The advertising and marketing departments saw some title shifting and several personnel changes. Kenyon & Eckhardt Company remained Mercury's advertising agency.

The 1955 Mercury model run began the week of October 25 to October 30, 1954. There were two series at first, but a third was quickly added. When Mercury Customs and Montereys bowed on December 2, prices were also reduced on several options, including a radio, which cost $97, and power steering, which sold for $108. Other options included Merc-O-Matic Drive ($189); Touch-O-Matic overdrive ($110); power package ($43); power brakes ($41); power seat ($70); electric window lifts ($103); heater ($73); and air conditioning ($594).

The new Mercury look was squarer, with higher fender feature lines. A sleeker roof line with a lower arch was seen on several models. New Montclair two-door Hardtops, Sun Valley Hardtops, Sport Sedans and Convertibles had lower roof lines and shorter windshields than other Mercurys. A "Full-Scope" wraparound windshield and forward-canted, hooded headlamps were other new styling characteristics that were obviously inspired by the XM-800 show car. Massive "pontoon" style rear fenders bulged out further in the middle than on the bottom. Separate trim plates were used at the forward edge of each bulge. The new styling was designed to unshackle the Merc from its "big-Ford/baby-Lincoln" personality conflict of earlier years. "Exclusive styling," bragged advertisements. "You don't have to look twice to tell it's a Mercury."

The Custom series offered two- and four-door Sedans, a Hardtop Coupe and a new eight-passenger Station Wagon. They were priced from $2,218 to $2,686. Three Montereys came in four-door Sedan, Hardtop Coupe and eight-passenger Station Wagon body styles. Mercury introduced the

The 1955 Mercury Montclair Sport Coupe was 58-1/2 inches high. Drop-moldings, under the window sill, lowered the belt line to door handle level. The area framed by these models had a contrasting "panel-of-color." (Jim Carlson)

The 1955 Mercury dashboard had a new fan-shaped instrument panel. Shape of steering wheel horn ring was unique. (Jim Carlson)

Mercury's "Far-Advanced Full-Scope" wraparound windshield had 17 percent more glass area for better appearance and greater safety. (Jim Carlson)

new Montclair series at the Chicago Automobile Show, which opened on January 8, 1955. At first, this line included a Hardtop Coupe, a Sun Valley Hardtop and Convertible with prices between $2,631 and $2,712. The latter was the cost of both the "ragtop" and "glasstop" models in the Montclair line.

It didn't take long for Mercury to add a Montclair Sedan. "We'll stake our April paycheck on the appearance of a low-slung, hardtop-like four-door in time for the spring selling season," said Don MacDonald in *Motor Trend's* "Spotlight on Detroit" column in January 1955. The new spring model was a four-door sedan (later called a Sport Sedan). It was a full-pillared model, but wide, chrome frames surrounded all of the side windows. "Billed as a Hardtop, though pillared, these (Montclairs) are chromed to resemble collapsible pillars of classic Convertible Sedans," said MacDonald. "The 'Convertible' effect is further enhanced by wide chrome frames on the edge of front and rear windows nearest the center pillar."

The Montclairs introduced "Low-Silhouette" styling. This term was coined to describe the lower-than-standard height of the Montclair. They also sported what Mercury called its, "striking panel of color under the windows." Drop-belt moldings started at each windshield pillar. They slashed down and back several inches, before running horizontally to the rear roof pillars. From there, they slanted back up to the window sills. The body between the window sills and the drop-belt moldings was painted a contrasting color.

This treatment had the effect of visually emphasizing the cars' low height and "dropping" the belt line to door handle height. Montclairs were also decorated with round medallions and "Montclair" scripts over the body side moldings, above the front wheel openings. The circular chrome medallions were black-finished inside a chrome outer ring, with a shield emblem in their center. The body side moldings ran around the front body corners, where they mated with the full-width moldings above the grille. The hood lip had "Mercury" spelled-out in block letters, with a shield-shaped emblem (the same used in 1954) above the letter "C."

Like all Mercs, the Montclairs had a large, winged, chrome hood ornament and new chrome wheel discs. These had a smooth, conical shape with chrome and red circular bands around a red center circle. In the middle of the red center was a chrome Mercury head emblem. Montclairs also came with bright rocker panel moldings, and dual exhausts with "flattened-oval" chrome extensions. The Montclair Hardtop was available with the Sun Valley roof treatment, too. This model did not get much exposure in advertising or the media. Only 1,787 Montclair Sun Valley Hardtops were made in the model-year.

Mercury Montereys lacked the "panel of color" window sill treatment and bright rocker panel accents of Montclairs. The side windows of Monterey Sedans did not have the Montclair-like chrome window frames. Otherwise, the two series shared the same exterior trim, but the front fender scripts said "Monterey." The Monterey Station Wagon featured simulated wood-grain side trim, which was applied in an unusual fashion. A small wood-grained panel decorated the larger, mid-section of the pontoon rear fenders. A separate, larger wood-grained panel decorated the doors and the front fender behind the wheel opening. On the rear door section of the wood-grained pontoon was a Monterey script and a large chrome trim plate with a circular medallion. The Station Wagon front fenders had no namescript.

Mercury's base series was the Custom. "Mercury" scripts decorated the front fenders of Custom models, but there were no round medallions on these cars. The rear fender sweep spear moldings were higher than those of the other series and the fan-shaped trim plates, on the front tips of the fender pontoons, were smaller. Customs had no rocker panel moldings and skirted rear fenders were optional.

All models had a new "Dual-Beam" bumper-grille and redesigned vertical taillamps. Overall size was about the same as 1954 models. Station Wagons even retained the 118-inch wheelbase, while passenger cars had a one-inch longer stance. Overall lengths were 201.78 inches for Station Wag-

The only Mercury Convertible offered in 1955 was in the top-of-the-line Montclair series. It had a $2,712 price tag and 10,668 examples were assembled during the model-year. (Mercury)

ons and 206.3 inches for cars. The overall width was 76.4 inches. Heights for different models varied from the Montclair's ground-hugging (for the time) 58.6 inches to as high as 62.5 inches. Standard tires, now of tubeless design, were size 7.10 x 15, while Convertibles and Station Wagons used 7.60 x 15 rubber.

Mercury offered buyers a choice of 18 colors: Tuxedo Black; Biltmore Blue; Gulfstream Blue Metallic; Kingstone Gray; Rockdale Gray Metallic; Forester Green Metallic; Springdale Green; Canyon Cordovan Metallic; Lime; Tropic Blue; Yukon Blue; Arbor Green; Alaska White; Glen Lake Blue Metallic; Sea Isle Green Metallic; Carmen Red; Persimmon; and Sun Glaze. An amazing 34 two-tone color selections were available.

The Mercury interior was highlighted by a novel and beautiful instrument panel. The gauges were arranged, in tiers, in front of the driver, with the heater controls, clock and radio grouped asymmetrically on either side. There were three solid-color all-cloth trims; 23 cloth-and-vinyl selections (one solid-colored); and five all-vinyl options, with three in single colors. Fabrics available included tapestry-weave nylon; Chromatex woven plastic; plain nylon; and vinyls. Leather was no longer offered. Montclairs had an adjustable center armrest in the rear.

Mercury engine wizard Vic Raviolo was credited with improvements to the overhead valve V-8 introduced in 1954. Actually, there was a pair of new "Super-Torque" V-8s. Both motors featured porting, a higher lift camshaft, and a new "open-wedge" cylinder head design. Camshaft, valve tappet and push rod materials were changed for better metallurgical compatibility and quieter operation. Aluminum alloy pistons were fitted. Engine noise was further reduced by redesigning the air cleaner, valve covers, and timing chain and by the provision of a pressure relief pocket in the oil pump. Both had five main bearings. The valve train featured adjustable solid lifters with adjusting screws found on the rocker arms.

Both motors had the same 3-3/4 x 3-19/64-inch bore and stroke and 292-cubic-inch displacement. Holley supplied the model 4000 four-barrel carburetor, which featured an automatic choke. This carburetor had improvements from 1954, including larger venturis and the relocation of the choke plates over the throttle body. The first engine was standard in all Customs and Montereys and Montclairs with stick-shift. It had a 7.6:1 compression ratio and 188 hp at 4400 rpm (193 hp in late 1955). The torque rating was 274 pounds-feet of torque at 2500 rpm. Engine number two, standard in Montclairs with Merc-O-Matic, used an 8.5:1 compression ratio. It produced 192 hp at 4400 rpm (198 hp in late 1955) and 286 pounds-feet of torque at 2500 rpm. The lower horsepower V-8s were used with standard transmission and the higher horsepower engines were used with automatic transmission attachments.

Cars with three-speed manual transmission came with a standard 3.73:1 ratio rear axle (a 4.09:1 axle was optional). Adding Touch-O-Matic overdrive changed the 4.09:1 to the standard axle and a 3.73:1 rear was optional. Merc-O-Matic cars came with a standard 3.15:1 axle and 3.54:1 was optional. The 1955 Merc-O-Matic transmission was completely revamped to give smoother up and down shifting and to provide automatic low gear start with the gear-shift selector in drive. When used in Mercurys, this was called the MX transmission. Ford called theirs the FX. (Most transmission rebuilders thought of these as "small" and "medium" case transmissions). The 1955 Thunderbirds, as well as 1956 Thunderbirds with "312" V-8s, used the Mercury transmission. The new "Low End Torque" feature gave improved performance under traffic and cruising conditions, where most normal driving was done. The automatic also had a new casing and hydraulic controls.

An improved ball-joint front suspension was another 1955 innovation. It eliminated the binding common in old-fashioned king pin suspensions and permitted easier, steadier steering, plus better control and freer action in cornering. The Mercury Montclair had a 42.37-foot turning circle. Hotchkiss drive was retained to make the "Low-Silhouette" styling feasible.

Other technical revisions included the mounting of electrical fuses and the turn signal flasher in a fuse block under the dashboard, near the steering column. The Mercurys still used six-volt, posi-

Mercury offered 11 beautiful, "super-powered" models for 1955. These drawings show 6 of them. (Mercury)

Early Medalist two-door Sedans were part of Custom series and had this "abbreviated" trim. Both series and trim design changed later. (Mercury)

tive-ground electrical systems. They had 2HN/2N batteries. There was a new weather-proof ignition system; new over-size hydraulic brakes; and 18 mm. spark plugs. The latter were new, conical-seat, "Turbo-Charge" spark plugs supplied by Champion Spark Plug Company. A wider space between the insulator and outside shell minimized fouling. They were also easier to install, because the conical seat was not as torque-critical as old-style gaskets.

Motor Life road tested the 1955 Montclair in its May 1955 issue, achieving a 0-to-60 mph time of 11.7 seconds and a 19.5-second quarter-mile run. The big Hardtop Coupe turned in a fast run of 107.9 mph and averaged 103.1 mph for four runs. Fuel consumption was 21 mpg at a steady 30 mph and 15 mpg at a steady 60 mph. The car took 149 feet to stop, on dry pavement, from 60 mph. The magazine noted performance improvements over past years and much better steering. "The Montclair went through winding roads, cornered and parked with a degree of control that may cause it to be classed as tops for the year in this department said the article. "Factors which contribute to this apparently are the lower center of gravity, wider (by three inches in the rear) tread and mounting of the shocks at a horizontal angle, to reduce body sway."

Motor Trend did a "Driving Around" report on the Merc, by Walt Woron, in January. "Looks and feels entirely different from '55 Fords," he concluded of the 198-hp car he tried at Ford's Dearborn Proving Grounds. "The ride is definitely softer, while handling has not been noticeably affected; body lean is apparent only on the sharpest of curves." Woron praised the car's better visibility over a sloping hood and said it was "a cinch to park." He speeded up from 0-to-64 mph in 13.5 to 14 seconds, a second less than the 1954 Merc took to achieve the same speed. The car shifted into second at 35 mph and into third at 65 mph. Upshifts and downshifts were both smoother and the '55 had better hill-climbing abilities than the '54, said Woron. He also noted that the larger brake linings, "Seem to have some effect on fast brake stops; the Merc seems to squat down to a stop considerably quicker."

In April, Fred Bodley did a full-range test for *Motor Trend*. This time a Custom four-door Sedan equipped with the 188-hp V-8, Merc-O-Matic, manual steering and manual brakes was reviewed. This car did 0-to-60 quicker than the Montclair (11.4 seconds) and covered the quarter-mile in 18 seconds, going 78 mph at the finish. That was also faster than the Montclair. This car had an average top speed of 105.3 mph over four runs and a fastest one-way run of 107.9 mph. It got 20.6 mpg at a steady 30 mph and 16.2 mpg at a steady 60 mph. The manual brakes required 153 feet to stop the Merc from 60 mph. Like other automotive journalists, Bodley praised the car's power, ride, roadability and improved (over 1954) fuel economy.

Carl Kiekhaefer, of Fond du Lac, Wisconsin, who was well-known for racing Chrysler 300s, also had Mercurys in his stock car racing fleet in 1955. One famous photo shows a fleet of Kiekhaefer's delivery vans with a 1955 Chevrolet, 1955 Chrysler 300 and 1955 Mercury sticking out of them. The industrialist liked to win the races that he entered and the best way to do so was to use all of the fastest cars of the year. Since Kiekhaefer owned Mercury Marine Corporation, a manufacturer of outboard boat motors, the "Big M" race cars were a natural for him. They were tops in their particular racing class and Kiekhaefer loved taking the checkered flag.

Car-buyers liked the 1955 Mercury, too. In April, the same month Mercury "divorced" Lincoln, a record of 43,354 cars were built. Model-year output was also an all-time record, at 329,808 units. For the calendar-year, the production total was 434,911 cars, which was 30 percent higher than the previous record set in 1950. Sales were counted as 394,948 units, 50 percent higher than in 1954 and 25 percent over the record set in 1950! Mercury's share of total industry production was 5.48 percent and 5.2 percent of all cars registered in the United States, during 1955, were Mercurys.

The company noted that nine out of every 10 Mercurys built since 1939 were still "going strong" in 1955 and said that total production, since the start of the brand, had hit 1,250,000 units of which, 800,000 came at the expense of other makes in the same price field. In November, Mercury announced plans to boost plant capacity, in St. Louis, Missouri, by 25 percent. In addition, construction of a separate Station Wagon body plant, at Wayne, Michigan, was put on the schedule to start in February 1956 and the ground-breaking for a huge new plant, in Rosemead, California, was set for March.

On September 29, 1955, Mercury dealers nationwide took the wraps off their new 1956 models. The introductory cars were updated versions of the 1955 products, except that the Sun Valley Hardtop was discontinued. A number of ongoing additions and changes took place during the model-year. An interesting option was automatic chassis lubrication, which classic cars of the 1930s had once featured. The Mercury system, called "Multi-Luber," was manufactured by Lincoln Equipment of St. Louis, Missouri. It was operated by merely pressing a button on the instrument panel.

All 1956 Mercury Hardtops and Sport Sedans were considered "Low-Silhouette" cars, but only Montclairs had drop-belt moldings and

The 1956 Custom four-door Sedan listed for $2,410. Mercury built 15,860 of these in the model-year. (Mercury)

Mercury built 20,857 of these 1956 Custom two-door Hardtops in 1956. This model sold for $2,485 and weighed 3,560 pounds. (Old Cars)

color panels under their window sills. Hardtop Coupes stood 58.6 inches high. Phaetons and Sport Sedans were 58.8 inches high. In contrast, conventional Sedans and Station Wagons had a height of 60.6 inches.

The initial Mercury line up included several new models. A plain-trimmed, low-end Medalist model was introduced as part of the Custom line. A six-passenger Custom Station Wagon was new, too. In addition, a Monterey version of the Sport Sedan (first introduced as a Montclair in mid-1955) was released. All other models seen in the fall were carried over from 1955. However, more changes were coming.

Once the calendar flipped over, several other model additions were made. These new body styles were released in an attempt to increase an industry-wide sales slump in the medium-priced market. They actually did a fairly good job of keeping the Merc's popularity near record levels. In fact, Mercury's share of the medium low-price field actually increased from 14.5 percent in 1955 to 17.2 percent in 1956. Total model-year output for the 10 marques in that group went down from 2,274,000 units in 1955 to 1,914,500 in 1956. Mercury, however, lost only 2,000 units, while its rivals Pontiac and Buick (Special and Century models) lost both 154,000 and 104,000, respectively. It definitely paid for Mercury to expand into the lower price brackets with the new Medalist.

A pillarless four-door Hardtop, with the misleading name Phaeton, was the first midyear addition. It was released on January 2, 1956. "Announcing a big advance in 4-door hardtops -- The Big M Phaeton," said a two-page color advertisement in national magazines. It pictured this latest body style with the Montclair-style drop-belt molding and "below-the-window-sill" color panel in two-tone Carousel Red-and-Classic White paint. The four-door Hardtop (which was offered in all four levels of trim by year's end) replaced the four-door Sport Sedan. Discontinuing the Sport Sedan made the new Monterey version, which was marketed only in 1956 model, into a half-year-only model. However, nearly 10,000 were made in that short time.

On February 1, 1956, Mercury added a Medalist four-door Sedan and two-door Hardtop to the line. The company then created a separate Medalist series. At this time, the "abbreviated" body side trim used on early Medalist two-door Sedans was changed and upgraded. Like the two new Medalist models, it was given the same "lightning bolt" body side moldings that other Mercurys had. The new Medalist four-door Sedan also had some distinctions in hubcap design and in roof and window frame finish.

The rarest car of 1956 was the Custom Convertible. It listed for $2,712 and weighed 3,665 pounds. Only 2,311 examples were manufactured. Full-wheel discs were an extra-cost item on this model. (Mercury)

There were two four-door Sedans in the 1956 Mercury Monterey series. This is the model 57 type, with a conventional height. The Sport Sedan, model 58, had the "Low-Silhouette" styling and was offered only in the fall. (Mercury)

On March 9, 1956, a Medalist four-door Phaeton-Hardtop was added to the Mercury line up. At $2,458 this was one of the lowest-priced V-8-powered four-door hardtops offered in the industry. Externally, it had just a bit plainer trim than the Custom and Monterey Phaetons. The front fenders had "Medalist" scripts and it came with small "bottle cap" hubcaps. These were the same as the 1952 style hubcaps, with the centers painted white, instead of red.

Also on March 9, a Convertible was made available in the mid-range Custom series. Its $2,712 price tag was also attractive. It came with the same side trim as other Mercury Customs. The interior was trimmed with all vinyl, the same as a Monterey two-door Hardtop. It had rubber floor mats, instead of carpets. Only 2,311 of these ragtops were made, making them the rarest cars of the year.

The 1955 Custom four-door Sedan listed for $2,410. Mercury built 15,860 of these in the model-year. (Mercury)

With these additions, the total number of distinct 1956 Mercurys a collector could find came to 20. However, not all 1956 models were available concurrently.

All of the new cars had a new grille with "Mercury" spelled out in block letters attached to the horizontal upper grille bar. The deflector behind the upper bar had smaller, louver-like slots, and three larger chrome "bumps." The bumps lined up directly with the three large grille uprights, when viewed from the front. The bumper guards (optional on Medalists) were redesigned. From the front, the vertical sections of the guards looked like grille uprights and the upper sections looked like "horseshoes" with horizontally-ribbed plates in the center. Three vertical bars, spaced widely apart, attached the upper grille bar to the bumper face bar. These had the same part number as the three 1955

"Gel Cap" taillamps and "handle-bars" trunk ornament were new for 1956. (Jim Carlson)

grille uprights. On many models, the thin moldings above the grille were the same for both years, too. The shorter outer moldings, which attached to the fenders of 1956 Custom and Medalist models, had the same part numbers as the moldings used in 1955. The longer center molding, which attached to the hood lip, was the same on all 1955 and 1956 Mercurys.

Most parts numbers for body panels used on 1955 and 1956 Mercurys of a single body style had similar or same parts numbers. For instance, the part numbers used on four-door sedan "cowl top panels" were number B6A-7002010A for all 1955 models; number BU-7302010A for 1956 Montereys; and number B6A-7002010A for 1956 Customs, while the deck lids for the four-door sedans had part number BV-7040110A in 1955 and BU-7040110B in 1956. Identical numbers meant the same parts were used both years, but the similar numbers (which were more common) indicated that the panels were modestly changed for 1956. In some cases, the "changes" were no more than holes punched in different locations for trim attachment, as several decorative bright metal items were redesigned.

The hood had a new "Big M" crest in its center. This emphasized the marque's first year as a separate division of Ford Motor Company. However, the airplane-shaped hood top ornament was the same part used in 1955. The rear bumpers were the same as in 1955, but there were three different types. One was the standard bumper, one was the dual exhaust outlet bumper and the last was for Station Wagons. The only difference between the standard bumper and the dual exhaust bumper was the bolt-on exhaust extensions on the dual exhaust bumper. The bumpers had the "Mercury" name on an indented center section and short "guard rails" inside the bumper guards (except on Medalists). The taillamp clusters were restyled, rising vertically up the fender. They were

Selling for $2,630, the 1956 Mercury Monterey two-door Hardtop had the lower vehicle height, but not the color panel on its window sills. This was the year's second most popular model, with a production run of 42,863. (Mercury)

A standard 1956 Mercury Montclair two-door Hardtop was $2,765. Two-tone paint was a little bit extra. This car illustrates the "Flo-Tone" paint treatment with the same color on lower body, window sill and roof. (Jim Carlson)

wider than the 1955 style, with an oval outer housing and vertical, "gel-cap" shaped lenses. A ribbed back-up lamp lens was seen at the bottom.

Size-wise, the Mercs were about the same as the previous year. However, the new "lightning bolt" side trim used on all models (except early Medalists) gave the 1956 Mercurys a longer, more modern look. It emphasized the forward haunch of the rear fender bulges, giving the cars a "fast-standing-still" appearance. The upward slash of the body side molding, as it traveled from the rear fender "vent" ornament to the front fenders, perfectly complemented the arch of the Hardtop roof lines. This really enhanced the look of the cars, especially when they were two-tone finished. Near the front of Monterey, Montclair, and Custom Station Wagon models, the body side molding had a large, round medallion.

After the Medalist series was established, there were four separate car lines. Each had its own exterior decorations. In addition, certain models had trim distinctions, too. The new Medalists were Mercury's lowest-priced cars. Early Medalist two-door Sedans exhibited a more frugal use of side chrome. This "abbreviated" trim consisted of a straight molding running from the chrome, simulated air vent on the rear quarters to the taillamp area. The Medalist standard equipment list also lacked the front bumper guards found on more expensive models, although they could be added as a low-cost option. These low-end Mercs did have the "Big M" hood crest, a front fender "Medalist" script, a chrome windshield molding and chrome mud guards. Plain, gray-textured vinyl material was used to upholster the Medalist's seats. When the two new models were introduced in February, the Medalist series was established and all three models got the same body side moldings used on other Mercs, but without medallions near the tips of the front fender moldings. In March, came the Medalist Phaeton, which has already been described above. Prices for the full range of

The 1956 Montclair two-door Phaeton's rear seat included a fold-down center armrest. (Jim Carlson)

The "Safety-Surge" V-8s of 1956 had a new combustion chamber design, full-vacuum spark control, and larger four-barrel carburetors. (Jim Carlson)

Medalist models ran from $2,313 for the four-door Sedan to $2,458 for the four-door Phaeton Hardtop. A total of 45,812 Medalists were produced during the model-year.

Customs (except early Medalists) had "lightning bolt" side trim right from the start of the year. There was a "Custom" script on the front fender of all models, except the Medalist two-door Sedan. The new six-passenger Station Wagon even carried the large, Monterey/Montclair-style round medallions on its front fender moldings. This is said to be related to the fact that Mercury wagons had Ford bodies (on a Mercury frame with a Mercury front end) and had to have trim that fit into the same holes as Ford trim. According to Gary Richards, of the International Mercury Owner's Association, the Mercury wagons also had a Mercury dashboard, taillamps and side trim. "All the body components were interchangeable with Fords, except the front fenders and hood," Richards explains. "The Mercury had a longer wheelbase than the Ford and the difference was due to the Mercury front fenders. If you were to measure from the front edge of the front door to the center line of the front wheel, you will find the difference in wheelbase between a Ford and a Mercury." The Custom Station Wagons also lacked chrome mud guards and the "vent" decorations on the rear fenders were flatter.

This 1956 ad showed how Ford improved upon the traditional Roadster, Ragtop, and Convertible Sedan. The "Roadster" (T-bird) became a sporty Convertible in a size reminiscent of classic roadsters. The convertible (Ford Sunliner) became a six-passenger open car. The "Convertible Sedan" (Mercury Montclair Phaeton) became a four-door closed car with Convertible-like looks. (Mercury)

80 MERCURY PHAETONS FREE

...10 EVERY WEEK IN

ED SULLIVAN'S $425,000 MERCURY CONTEST

SPECIAL BONUS AWARDS

$10,000 CASH to new Mercury buyers
Awarded *instead* of new Phaeton if you buy a new Mercury during contest and *before* being advised of winning one of the top 10 weekly prizes.

$2,000 CASH to used car buyers
Awarded in *addition* to new Phaeton if you buy a used car during contest and *before* being advised of winning one of the top 10 weekly prizes.

(See Official Entry Blank for details)

2,680 PRIZES IN ALL—EASY TO ENTER—YOU CAN ENTER EVERY WEEK—HURRY! LAST CONTEST ENDS AUG. 4

EACH WEEK THESE PRIZES WILL BE AWARDED

1ST PRIZE—Mercury Montclair Phaeton plus an all-expense paid weekend trip to New York for two via American Airlines DC-7 Flagship with suite at famous Waldorf-Astoria Hotel, special guests of Ed Sullivan at his television show.

2ND-10TH PRIZES—9 Mercury Monterey Phaetons—Like all Phaetons, the Monterey features distinctive low silhouette styling and 4-door hardtop beauty.

11TH-35TH PRIZES—25 General Electric portable TV sets—Compact, smart, latest model, light and easy to carry. Colorfully two-toned.

NEXT 300 PRIZES—Beautiful Elgin American Signet automatic cigarette lighters with winners' initials . . . autographed by Ed Sullivan.

HERE'S ALL YOU DO TO ENTER!

1 Go to your Mercury dealer today
2 Pick up Official Rules and Entry Blank
3 Complete last line of Mercury Phaeton rhyme
4 Mail Official Entry Blank to "Mercury Contest".

GO TO YOUR

MERCURY DEALER

92

Television host Ed Sullivan helped Mercury give away 80 Mercury Phaetons in a 10-week contest in the summer of 1956. (Mercury)

With a $2,900 list price, the Montclair Convertible was the next-to-highest-priced 1956 Mercury (the Monterey Station Wagon was $2,977). It was also the next-to-rarest model, with 7,762 assemblies in the model-year. (Mercury)

The Custom four-door Sedan had a thin strip of the roof color extending down the rear window pillar to the body belt line and a section of the front door, between the windshield pillar and the vent window, was painted, rather than chrome-trimmed. In Custom trim, the Phaeton looked very much like the Medalist Phaeton with front bumper guards, "Custom" front fender scripts, and full-wheel discs. It did not have a full wrapover rear roof band or below-the-window-sill color panel of Montclair Phaetons.

The added Custom body styles brought the series' model count up to seven, making it the largest Mercury car-line. Prices started at $2,351 for the two-door Sedan and ran to $2,722 for the fancy new Station Wagon. The Custom series had a production run of 85,328 units.

The second-largest number of 1956 Mercury models was offered in the Monterey series. It offered five body styles during the year, but only four at one time. Front fender scripts on these cars said "Monterey." All had round medallions on the body side moldings, at the forward ends of the front fenders. The four-door Sport Sedan had the same shape rear vent window as the similar Montclair model, but sections of the window and upper door trim had a painted finish. The Monterey Sport Sedan and Monterey Phaeton both lacked below-the-window-sill color panels and the Phaeton did not use the Montclair-style full wrapover rear roof band. Monterey Station Wagons were distinguished by their simulated wood-grain trim, which also seemed to coordinate better with the shape of the new body side moldings. Monterey prices started at $2,555 for the four-door Sedan. The highest-priced car in the line was the four-door "woodie" wagon. This was a three-seat Station Wagon. Early in the year, Mercury listed such models as "eight-passenger" jobs, but they were later reclassified as "nine-passenger" wagons. This was done to make the Mercurys more competitive with Chevrolet's nine-passenger Beauville Station Wagon. Montereys were Mercury's most popular offering, with model-year production counted at 105,369 cars.

A "Montclair" front fender script identified the top-of-the-line cars. They also had the full front-to-rear "lightning bolt" molding treatment. Full wheel discs and fancy interiors were standard equipment, too, along with such items as a clock and more interior brightwork. The drop-belt molding treatment, with a "panel-of-color" under the window sills, was back on all the sporty models. Montclairs also had medallions on the front fender moldings, and bright rocker panel accents. As noted above, the Montclair Sport Sedan, with its wide chrome window frames, was replaced by the true four-door Hardtop (called a "Phaeton") early in 1956. This new body style looked especially rich in Montclair trim, which added a wide, multiple-ribbed band of chrome decorating the rear edge of the roof panel, and wrapping over the roof and rear quarter filler panels to the window sill. The drop belt moldings on the Montclair Phaeton's window sill were also slightly different than the two-door Hardtop and Convertible type. They rose upwards at the rear, forming a blade-shaped end plate with a gold "Phaeton" script decorating it. The contrasting color panel below the window sills was also much narrower than those of other models, and didn't drop quite to the door handle level. Montclair list prices were $2,785 to $2,900. Amazingly, this expensive series was the second-

Two-tone vinyl interior with pleated inserts done in off-shoulder pattern was used in Montclair Convertible. (Richard A. Weber)

best-selling 1956 Mercury line, with production of 91,434 units.

The Phaeton models were very heavily promoted in large-format color magazine advertisements. Eighty such cars were given away, at the rate of 10 per week, in television host Ed Sullivan's "$425,000 Mercury Contest" during the summer of 1956. This promotion, which ran through August 6, gave away 345 prizes each week. They were 300 Elgin American Signet cigarette lighters with the winner's initials and Sullivan's autograph; 25 General Electric portable televisions; nine Mercury Monterey Phaetons; and one Mercury Montclair Phaeton, plus an all-expense paid weekend trip to New York City (via American Airlines DC-9) to appear on the "Ed Sullivan Show."

To enter the contest, people had to: 1) Go to a Mercury dealer; 2) Pick up contest rules and an entry blank; 3) Complete the last line of a Mer-

ACCELERATION TESTS around pace cars driven at steady speeds demonstrate THE BIG M's lightning-quick response. There's no lag—no hesitation.

THE BIG M's instant response in pace-car tests proves you save vital seconds when passing

NEW "LIFT" THAT'S REFLEX FAST—Go, stop, climb, turn—THE BIG M's response is quick as a champion athlete's. Shown above, Montclair Phaeton 4-door hardtop.

Two 1956 Mercury Hardtops were used in "pace-car" passing tests. Montclair four-door Phaeton passes a Ford cab-over truck. (Mercury)

Hard to find and expensive today are the four-bar "spinner" hubcaps used on 1956 Montclairs. (Richard A. Weber)

The continental tire kit was a popular accessory with 1956 Mercury owners, and still is today. (Richard A. Weber)

cury Phaeton rhyme; and 4) Mail the official entry blank to Mercury. As special bonus awards, first place winners who bought a new Mercury while visiting their dealer, could take $10,000 in place of the new Montclair Phaeton. If they bought a used car from the Mercury dealer, before they discovered they were a winner, they received $2,000, in addition to the Phaeton.

The 1956 Mercurys came in 15 solid colors: Tuxedo Black; Delta Blue Metallic; Lauderdale Blue; Niagra Blue; London Gray Metallic; Pinewood Green Metallic; Heath Green; Glamour Tan; Grove Green; Verona Green; Saffron Yellow; Cambridge Green; Carousel Red; Classic White; and Persimmon. There were 60 two-tone combinations. This included 28 with new "Flo-Tone" treatments, in which the lower body and top colors are the same, with the mid-section, deck and hood in a contrasting hues. There were 28 cloth-and-vinyl interior trims (14 with monotone colors) and 10 all-vinyl options (four solid colored).

Mercury highlighted 10 "Safety-First Design" features for 1956 models. Some were standard and others were part of a safety options package that all FoMoCo branches were trying to sell in 1956. The features were an impact-absorbing steering wheel with a deeply-recessed hub; new "Triple-Strength" door locks (with child-proof safety-locking device for rear doors available); "Safety-Beam" headlamps; an instrument panel pad; padded sun visors; a full-swivel "Safety Rearview Mirror," nylon safety belts bolted to floor supports; 210- or 225-hp "Safety-Surge" V-8 engines; and improved "Safety-Grip" brakes. The general public did not embrace this early automotive safety campaign. However, in hindsight, Ford Motor Company deserves great credit for its early efforts to push automotive safety.

The new "Safety-Surge" V-8s used in the 1956 Mercurys had a new combustion chamber design, new full-vacuum spark control, and larger four-barrel carburetors. Most advertisements mentioned two options, claiming they could "deliver that extra margin of power where and when you need it -- for split-second pickup, safer passing, easier hill climbing." There were actually three motors. All engines had a 3.80 x 3.44-inch bore and stroke and 312-cubic-inch displacement. They had precision-molded crankshafts; automatic chokes and idling control; gear-type oil pumps; five main bearings; and solid valve lifters. Most cars used a Holley 4000 four-barrel carburetor with a

Rear end detail photo shows fenders, taillamps, and continental tire mounting. (Richard A. Weber)

The 1956 dashboard had a fan-shaped instrument panel with gauges to monitor all systems. (Richard A. Weber)

dashpot provided for cars with automatic transmission or power brakes. However, a Carter WCFB number 2361S four-barrel was also listed for 1956 Mercs.

Cars with three-speed manual or overdrive transmissions had a V-8 with an 8.0:1 compression ratio. It developed 210 hp at 4600 rpm and 312 pounds-feet of torque at 2600 rpm. Cars with Merc-O-Matic had an 8.4:1 compression ratio. They produced 220 hp at 4600 rpm and 320 pounds-feet of torque at 2600 rpm. Optional was a version of the Merc-O-Matic engine with a 9.0:1 compression ratio. It generated 225 hp at 4600 rpm and 324 pounds-feet of torque at 2600 rpm. There was also a 235-hp engine option introduced in the later part of the year. In addition, a dealer-installed M260 engine kit was released in January 1956. It consisted of a new camshaft, cylinder heads and an intake manifold with two four-barrel Holley carburetors. This was used primarily for stock car racing.

All motors were painted gold, but different color valve covers and air cleaners signified different outputs. At the beginning of the year, there were four engines. The two used with standard transmissions had red valve covers and red air cleaners. The compression ratio on these engines was either 8.0:1 or 8.4:1. The remaining pair of engines had 9.0:1 compression. One had a Holley carburetor and one had a Carter carburetor. Late in the year, the 8.4:1 compression engine was dropped. Then the options were 210 hp with 8.0:1 compression (red valve covers and air cleaner); 225 hp with 9.0:1 compression (blue valve covers and air cleaner); and 235 hp with 9.0:1 compression (Argent Silver valve covers and blue air cleaner). The 210-hp engine came only with a Holley carburetor and only in cars with stick shift. Both other V-8s were offered with Holley or Carter carburetors and used only in cars with automatic transmissions.

The powerful Mercury V-8s also had larger piston rings and revised valve train specifications. They were re-timed to five degrees before top-dead-center, versus three degrees in 1955. All had higher cranking pressures of 155 psi, instead of 135 psi. A dual exhaust system was standard on Custom Station Wagons, and all Montereys and Montclairs. They were optional for all other Custom models.

The three-speed manual gear box was standard in all Mercurys. Overdrive was $102 extra. The three-speed Merc-O-Matic, priced at $175.35, was improved with the upshift point raised from just over 30 mph to 40 mph. This gave acceleration just about the same as manu-

Two-toning was seen throughout the Convertible's interior, from door panels, to seats, to dash, and steering wheel. (Richard A. Weber)

Another accessory seen on many 1956 Mercurys is the cowl-mount spotlamp. (Richard A. Weber)

Detailed engine compartment shows how the Mercury "Safety-Surge" V-8 looked. (Richard A. Weber)

ally-shifting the 1955 automatic. Nevertheless, when *Motor Life's* Ken Fermoyle road-tested a Mercury in November 1955, he managed to get a faster 0-to-60 mph time "by starting in low and shifting to high at 40 mph." The technique shaved 0.5 seconds off Ken's first 10.7 second time, which was already a full second faster than the 1955 Mercury achieved. Fermoyle said that a company engineer at the Dearborn Proving Grounds told him, "Just under 11 seconds is about what the car should do."

The 1956 Mercurys switched to a 12-volt, negative-ground electrical system with a big 13HN/4HN/4SN battery. A "Folo-Thru" starter drive was listed as a selling feature. The "Weather-Proof" ignition system had a new inline ballast resistor between the coil and the switch. Other technical aspects of the cars included a ball-joint front suspension; "Safety-Grip" brakes; flat-angle "Sea Leg" shock absorbers; tubeless tires; suspended foot pedals; and a semi-floating rear axle. Size 7.10 x 15 tires were standard equipment, except on Convertibles, Station Wagons and air-conditioned cars, which needed 7.60 x 15 tires.

Auto Age magazine (June 1956) ran a four-car competitive test, featuring the Mercury Monterey and three of its main competitors, the Pontiac Star Chief, the Dodge Coronet and the Studebaker Hawk. The car tested was a Monterey four-door Sedan with the 225-hp Merc-O-Matic engine and 3.15:1 ratio rear axle. "Earlier this year, we tested the Monterey's big brother, the Montclair," advised the magazine. "And while there is something to be said, snob-appeal-wise, for the more expensive car, the Mercury Monterey, especially the two-door Hardtop, is one of the best-looking cars made in the United States, today, regardless of price."

The Monterey interior featured clean, simple materials. Entry and exit was found to be better than with the Montclair two-door Hardtop, because the four-door's roof was two inches higher. The front seat was described as "Ford style," with a low seating position, high cowl, good visibility, and minimum distortion through the compound wraparound windshield. The tester discovered excellent headroom in the front and rear, even with the front power seat fully raised. There was also plenty of hip and leg room. The steering wheel was nicely angled to rise high off the driver's lap. "The dash has all dials neatly and closely grouped in a "V" visible through the steering wheel," noted the magazine. "It has good non-glare properties." The large trunk with a vertical-mounted spare tire was appreciated, too.

The Mercury's ride was good, and not too soft or too harsh. "Bumps sound worse than they feel," said the evaluator. "Traction is maintained, even on rough surfaces." Cornering was described as "tops in the group," but the 1955 Mercury Montclair was still better at cornering. The four-wheel brakes, with 190.9 square inches of effective lining area, gave only "fair" performance, fading badly after six to seven hard stops. The 225-hp Monterey ran from 0-to-60 mph in 11.1 seconds and had a top speed of 105 mph. "If you like a car that really handles, the Mercury is for you," was the final conclusion.

With its new engines, Mercury re-emerged as a force in stock car racing during 1956. The "Big Ms" were ranked fifth in national standings and placed in the top 10 finishers 67 times. They took five checkered flags, 14 second-place finishes, seven third-place awards; seventh fourth-place trophies; and a pair of fifth-place finishes.

A plaid trunk mat was used, and spare tire sat upright in the floor well. Convertibles came with a top boot. (Richard A. Weber)

Continental spare tire moves to the side like this, to allow access to luggage compartment. (Richard A. Weber)

Lots of people who did not race liked 1956 Mercurys, too. Divisional general manager F. C. Reith and his new executive assistant, P.F. Lorenz (formerly comptroller), did an outstanding job reading and reacting to the 1956 marketplace. The new Medalist brought Mercury almost 46,000 extra customers from the low-price field. Also helping to boost production was the January 2 opening of the first auto plant devoted exclusively to Station Wagon production. This factory, in Wayne, Michigan, could build 250 wagons per day. No wonder that model-year production of Station Wagon climbed from 25,102 in 1955 to 31,050 in 1956. Total model-year output of all Mercurys was a healthy 327,943 units.

The nation's 3,100 domestic Mercury dealers did a good job pushing out the 1956 models, even though only about 600 sold Mercurys exclusively. (Approximately 1,000 also sold Fords and 1,500 handled both Lincolns and Mercurys.) Nevertheless, the market slump began to take a firmer grip towards the close of the year. This affected the output of 1957 Mercurys built in the late summer and fall of 1956. As a result, the company's 1956 calendar-year production declined to 246,629 units, 43 percent below the previous year. Mercury managed, however, to remain the seventh-ranked American automaker.

The Studebaker-Packard merger of 1956 benefited both Lincoln and Mercury, as Packard executives, with experience in the luxury car field, went job-hunting. Additional personnel changes at Mercury included the appointment of S.M. Vass to divisional controller. J.E. Bayne, general sales manager in 1955, was replaced by sales manager C.E. Bowie. J.R. Maroni was named market analysis and planning manager (a new title) and R.J. Fisher (formerly advertising department manager) replaced T.J. Henry as national advertising and sales promotion manager.

Turnpike Cruisers 1957-1960

The October 1956 issue of *Motor Trend* predicted that Mercury would be one of the year's most exciting cars. "The most radically changed of the '57 cars will be the new Mercury, which may closely resemble their XM Turnpike Cruiser dream car in appearance," revealed the magazine. "Some details (of the show car), like the pop-up transparent roof sections and the three-piece wraparound rear window, will probably not appear, but it will be the most unusual U.S. car."

The basic 1957 Mercury line entered production in late September 1956, a few months after the magazine hit the newsstands. Showroom introductions were made on November 12. Even the lower-rung Mercury models bore out *Motor Trend*'s crystal ball-gazing. They resembled the show car that Don DeLaRossa and his design staff had readied for 1956 auto shows. All Mercury Station Wagons carried "hardtop" styling. Then, a pair of "Turnpike Cruiser" production models were added to the line on December 8. Both were called Hardtop Phaetons. One had two-doors and the other had four. Mercury is spectacularly different," said the *Popular Mechanics 1957 Car Facts Book.*

"**Beautifully sculptured projectiles give the 'Big M' for '57 a definite 'look of tomorrow,'**" said the 1957 brochure. (Mercury)

"There's not a sign of its younger brother, Ford, in it. It's a car of its own, sharing (body) shells with no other."

"Dream Car" design was a selling point of all 1957 Mercurys. "The first dream car you can own!" said one advertisement. "The Big M for '57." All new models also sported what Mercury called "horizontal plane" styling. Basically, that meant they resembled aircraft carriers, with their flat, long, and wide bodies. The bodies were completely revised in shape, as well as size. The Mercs gained a big three inches of wheelbase (up to 122 inches) and stretched 211.1 inches long, versus just 206.4 inches in 1956.

At 56.5 inches high, loaded, the 1957 Mercury Hardtop was about the same height as last year's "Low-Silhouette" Hardtop. However, because the standard 1956 models were higher, Mercury could advertise the new cars as "four inches lower," since most models *were* lower than their counterparts of the previous year. Five factors contributed to increased overall lowness in the much larger-sized cars. The first was smaller tires, the second was a sharply offset rear pinion, the third was a tapered propeller shaft, the fourth was a longer wheelbase, and the fifth was a flatter roof. Mercury's overall width, at 79.1 inches, was up nearly three inches.

A new concave grille with multiple vertical louvers characterized the front end. A split front bumper, below the grille, had huge "pods" on either side of center. The new hood was front-hinged and flipped forward for engine access. According to the March 1957 issue of *Car Life*, mechanics liked this arrangement because the rear of the engine was much easier to get at and overhead lighting could be used to greater effect. "Along the same work-easing lines, Mercury has relocated the windshield wiper assembly on the firewall, where it is easily reached," said the magazine. "And

The 255-hp "Safety-Surge" V-8 (on left) was standard on Montereys, Montclairs and Wagons. It had 9.75:1 compression. The 290-hp "Turnpike Cruiser" V-8 (on right) had the same compression ratio, but more (368) cubic inches. (Mercury)

(Mercury has) switched the fuse box to the left side of the cowl, which eliminates the need for mechanics to make pretzels of themselves getting at the fuses under the cowl."

"Quadri-Beam" dual headlamps were standard on the Turnpike Cruiser models, and optional on others. Actually, quad headlamps were planned for most American cars in 1957. Initially, eight states refused to change their laws to permit their use. By the time the Turnpike Cruiser appeared, quad headlamps were permitted (and standard) in all states, except Tennessee and South Dakota.

All of the cars had cowl air vents. Long, narrow concave indentations dominated the upper portion of the stylized rear fenders. Ford designers patterned the shape of these indentations after rockets or guided missiles and trade publications labeled them "projectiles." At the rear, canted, v-shaped taillamps mated with the ends of the projectiles. The Mercury's sculptured rear deck lid had a depressed center section. A large, winged ornament decorated the center of the rear deck lid. At the bottom was a twin-pod rear bumper with textured inserts in the center of the pods. The center section finish varied per model.

Montereys were now the base models, as the Customs and Medalists disappeared (the latter for 14 months). Montereys had a front fender model namescript, horizontal-textured panels in their rear bumper pods, and painted headlamp cylinders. (The latter feature changed, as the quad headlamps became more common during 1957.) Body side moldings were of the same width over their

A pair of two-door wagons were offered in 1957. This Commuter has a thinner molding on its front fender than the Voyager edition. (Tom Amendola)

103

COLONY PARK, ONE OF 6 BIG M STATION WAGONS—ALL TRUE HARDTOPS... The most advanced station wagons you can buy. First with a true passenger-car ride. First with true hardtop design. A power-operated back window eliminates the lift gate, provides a unique all-clear loading platform. There's a giant 87.4 cubic feet of cargo space. In addition to the Colony Park shown, there are 2 Voyager models and 3 budget-priced Commuters—the biggest choice in the field.

NEW MONTEREY 4-DOOR SEDAN...PRICED JUST ABOVE LOWEST PRICE CARS... Mercury's lowest price series includes the concealed-pillar sedan shown, and a 2-door sedan, 2-door hardtop, 4-door hardtop, and a convertible. All new Mercurys are more than 17½ feet long, over 6½ feet wide, with new oversized interiors, and exclusive Floating Ride. In this series, 255 hp is standard, 290 and 335 hp is optional. Never before has so much bigness and luxury cost so little.

NEW MONTEREY PHAETON SEDAN, NEW HIGH IN "SEE-ABILITY"...You're surrounded with 28 square feet of glass for excellent all-around vision. And, as in all Mercurys, you can get dream-car features such as Merc-O-Matic Keyboard Control and a power seat that "remembers." And air conditioning is no longer a luxury. Mercury's unique new system combines air conditioning and heating in one low-cost unit. Get the full story today at your Mercury dealer's showroom.

THE BIG MERCURY for '57 with DREAM-CAR DESIGN

MERCURY DIVISION • FORD MOTOR COMPANY

The Colony Park four-door Station Wagon (top) had wood-grained trim and a $3,677 list price. The Monterey four-door Sedan (center) was only $2,645. The Monterey Phaeton Sedan (bottom) went out the door for $2,763. (Mercury)

entire length. There was also no ornament on the rear window ledge. This line of cars included two- and four-door Sedans and Hard-tops, plus a Convertible. They were priced from $2,576 to $3,005. A unique feature offered on some 1957 (and 1958) Mercury Convertibles was a "wraparound" style, plastic rear window. It looked like a three-piece window and increased the driver's rear vision.

Mercury designated all of its pillarless pas-senger cars, whether they were hardtops or rag-tops, with the term "phaeton." Supposedly, this sprang from the fact that the chrome-framed windows looked a lot like those on prewar Con-vertible Sedans. The Mercury Phaeton Hardtops and Phaeton Convertibles were not real pha-etons, of course, and some critics pointed this out. However, what seemed even stranger than using this term, was the fact that Mercury, not Lincoln, employed it. Mercury had offered a Convertible Sedan only once, while Lincoln made many true phaetons, and revived the body style in the early 1960s.

Returning for 1957 was the Montclair. It had an appropriate front fender namescript, chrome-finished headlamp cylinders and an ornament on the rear window ledge. The panels inside the rear bumper pods had a telltale rect-angular-grid design. This car-line offered the same body types as the Monterey series, except for the two-door Sedan. Prices started at $3,188 and went as high as $3,430.

Turnpike Cruisers could be picked out rather easily. They had special nameplates on their rear window pillars; quad chrome-barreled headlamps; streamlined roof air intakes (with built-in decorative antennas); a rear deck orna-ment on the exterior; and a third bumper pod motif with a small, rectangular grid pattern. Most cars received accessory rear bumper pod

"Montclair" was on the front fender. This four-door Sedan listed for $3,188. (Mercury)

Voyager Station Wagons were the coun-terparts of Montclairs. They came in two-door and four-door versions. (Mer-cury)

reflectors instead. The interior of the Turnpike Cruiser was special, too, with a perforated vinyl headliner and chrome-plated roof bows. Turnpike Cruisers also had a "Monitor" control panel with a tachometer and "Average-Speed Computer Clock." In the center section of the owners manual was a map showing all of the turnpikes in the United States in 1957.

For 1957, Mercury offered an amazing array of 136 possible color choices, although not all were available on every model. Solid hues were Tuxedo Black; Classic White; Tahitian Green; Moonmist

List price for this 1957 Mercury Montclair four-door Phaeton Hardtop was $3,317. (Mercury)

The Montclair Convertible sold for $3,430. Only 4,248 were made. Some factory convertible tops were two-toned, with a wide color band around the lower edges of the fabric and the Phaeton name silk-screened on them in script. Naturally, the colors matched those of the body. (Mercury)

Yellow; Regency Gray; Sherwood Green; Pacific Blue; Nantucket Blue; Fiesta Red; Brazilian Bronze; Pastel Peach; Desert Tan; Persimmon; Rosewood; Lexington Green; Sunset Orchid; and Sun Glitter (Pace Car Yellow). There were 59 two-tone combinations of these colors, plus 60 "Flo-Tone" combinations with two colors. Inside, buyers could select from 295 cloth-and-vinyl or 24 all-vinyl interior trim options.

Television host Ed Sullivan did another Mercury giveaway contest in 1957. It took place in the spring, ending on April 20. This time, 15 free Mercurys were awarded each week, as well as 300 Shaeffer "White Dot" snorkel pens (worth $22.75 each) and 50 General Electric "Companion" portable television sets (worth $129.95 each). The cars were given away, each week, as follows: 10 Mercury Monterey four-door Sedans; four Mercury Commuter two-door, six-passenger Station Wagons; and one Mercury Turnpike Cruiser four-door Phaeton as "first Prize." As in 1956, the car winners could get bonus awards of an additional $2,000 if they bought a used car at a Mercury dealership, or $10,000 (instead of the car) if they had purchased a new Mercury from the dealer. First prize winners also got a trip to New York City to appear on Sullivan's television show.

Only two- and four-door Hardtops were available in the Turnpike Cruiser series initially. The first had a $3,758 sticker price; the latter cost about $91 more. The Hardtops had an electrically retractable rear window that provided "Breezeway Ventilation." Ford's "Lifeguard" safety package, with interior padding, a deep-dish steering wheel, and see-from-the-side taillamps was one of the better, and more conventional, standard features of Turnpike Cruisers. The steering wheel had a semi-elliptic, flat-topped design.

Later in the model-year, a Convertible was added to the series. This model was originally created expressly as the Official Pace Car for the 1957 Indianapolis 500-Mile Race. On January 7, 1957 it was announced that the ragtop would become a production model.

The Indianapolis 500-Mile Race was held on May 30, 1957. Francis C. (Jack) Reith, the general manager of Mercury Division, joined entertainer Ed Sullivan to introduce the car to the public. Reith showed up at Indianapolis Motor Speedway behind the wheel of one of the 1957 Cruiser Convertible Official Cars. Another official speedway photograph shows racing legend Sam Hanks posing with the pace car that Jack Reith drove. The queen of the 500 Festival Parade circuited the track in a different car. An unusual accessory, which seems to appear on all of the actual Pace Cars, as well as all of the Official Cars, is a continental tire kit. All 1957

Fully-accessorized 1957 Montclair ragtop sports "cruiser" style skirts and a continental tire kit. (*Old Cars*)

Mercurys were available, direct from the factory, with this so-called "Dream-Car spare carrier" option. The Mercury pace cars were finished in Sun Glitter, a creamy yellow color also known as Pace Car Yellow. Cars seen at Indianapolis Motor Speedway had gold lettering on the doors and rear quarters. This was made available, as a dealer-applied option, on pace car replicas. The lettering was applied at the car owners discretion. The door lettering said, "Mercury Official Pace Car" and the rear quarter was decorated with "May 30, 1957 Indianapolis 500-Mile Race."

FoMoCo gave its Station Wagons different names than other body styles, although they had trim levels that roughly corresponded to certain car-lines. Commuter Station Wagons followed the scheme of Montereys on their exterior and featured woven plastic upholstery. Voyager Station Wagons were the counterparts of Montclairs. The fanciest line of wagons was called Colony Park. These had "wood-look" fiberglass moldings and simulated wood panels on their body sides. There were three Commuter wagons priced from $2,903 to $3,070. One was a two-door model and both others had four doors. The latter pair came in six- and nine-passenger editions. Mid-line Voyager wagons also came in two-door ($3,403) and four-door ($3,577) versions, while the four-door Colony Park, with nine-passenger seating, was offered at $3,677.

A 312-cubic-inch "Safety Surge" V-8 was standard for Montereys, Montclairs and Station Wagons. In the tradition of all previous Mercurys, this engine continued to feature solid valve lifters. They were of the adjustable type, used since 1954. The "312" had 255 horsepower. A new 368-cubic-inch "Turnpike Cruiser" V-8, with 290 hp, was standard on Turnpike Cruisers and optional on other models. It was the first Mercury V-8 to use hydraulic valve lifters. An extra-high-lift camshaft was one new feature, and a paper element air cleaner was another. A triple-carburetor option was offered for the new engine. According to writer Phil Skinner, Bill Stroppe also designed a very rare dual four-barrel induction system. Apparently, it could be ordered through Mercury dealers, although it was difficult to get delivery.

Both engines had 9.75:1 compression ratios and required premium fuel. Mercury promoted a "dual carburetor air intake" system. This system reduced engine warm-up time dramatically. It drew warm air, from the engine compartment,

Turnpike Cruisers could be picked out rather easily by nameplates on the rear window pillars. (Mercury)

Turnpike Cruisers had ribbed, bright metal headlamp "barrels" and the doors over the headlamp lenses were hooded. (*Old Cars*)

The Turnpike Cruiser four-door Hardtop had a $3,849 sticker price. Ford's "Lifeguard" safety package was standard on Turnpike Cruisers. (Mercury)

during the warm-up phase. When normal operating temperature was reached, it began drawing cooler and denser air from outside the engine bay. This was said to reduce choke time by as much as 50 percent in very cold weather. In addition, a clutch-type "Power Booster" was part of the 312-cubic-inch V-8's cooling system. It allowed the fan to free-wheel at speeds over 40 mph. This added to the cars' power and cut engine noise.

A problem incurred by many 1957 Mercury owners was interference and possible grounding between the ignition resistor and the intake manifold. The factory advised bending the ignition resistor mounting bracket in the direction of the coil. This gave more clearance between the lower terminal of the ignition resistor and the manifold.

Cars with manual transmission used a 3.70:1 rear axle. Those with overdrive had an axle with a 3.89:1 ratio.

A new "Keyboard Drive Selector" was provided with the optional ($210) Merc-O-Matic transmission. In addition to changing gears, this push-button control panel started the engine, released the parking brake and locked the transmission for parking. An interesting footnote is the recommended procedure for getting stalled Merc-O-Matic cars going. The factory advised pushing, not

A new combination bumper-grille with multiple concave vertical dividers, plus a parking light in each massive "Jet-Flow" bumper pod, characterized 1958 Mercurys. This is the Monterey two-door Hardtop. (Mercury)

towing the cars, to get started. This entailed turning the ignition on, engaging the neutral-start button and allowing the car to hit 20 mph. At that point, the driver depressed the accelerator slightly and pushed in the low-range or hill-control button to start the vehicle. Towing the car could cause it to speed up, upon starting, and collide with the tow vehicle. A 2.91:1 rear axle ratio was standard with the automatic transmission.

Mercury's engineers claimed to have reworked the suspension to provide a ride that felt comfortable, on straight highways, but firm, when rounding tight corners. Several factors contributed to this. The "Full-Cushion" shock absorbers had three-phase control: Orifice, blow-off and restriction. This prevented the car from bottoming at high speed. Fatter 14-inch tires were another improvement. The "Swept-Back Ball-Joint" front suspension was insulated by rubber bushings. It had as trailing-arm design that rolled, rather than "bumped," over obstructions in the road. Mercurys had a 25 percent stiffer frame with tubular construction. Convertibles used I-beam crossmembers. Body mountings were all-rubber. The ball-and-rack type steering gear was controlled via a "Deep-Dish-Safety" steering wheel.

At the rear, most Mercurys had long leaf springs. On Turnpike Cruisers, Station Wagons and closed models with 368-cubic-inch engines (and optional on other models) was an "Air Cushion" suspension. It absorbed road shocks and provided a softer ride. The forward end of the leaf spring was actually insulated inside a six-inch rubber "tire." It rode on a cushion of air. Mercury said that its engineers had determined that 80 percent of all rear end vibrations were transmitted through the front end of the rear springs. The new air-suspension eliminated such vibrations.

A three-speed manual gear box was still standard on most Mercurys. Overdrive was $120 extra and power steering cost $80. Other options included a "Seat-O-Matic" seat that "remembered" the car owner's favorite adjustment. It was optional in all models. Power brakes, air conditioning, a radio and a heater/defroster were other add-ons. Many options, including the push-button automatic transmission, were specified as standard equipment in Turnpike Cruisers. "Many more dream-car ideas," said the ad copywriters. "The Big M is bigger in every important dimension." In practice, however, most Turnpike Cruisers did not receive options such as power windows and

Released January 1, 1958, this "price leader" was advertised as the "Mercury," although the prototype said "Medalist." (Mercury)

Jack Reith, Mercury general manager, behind the wheel of a 1957 Indy Pace Car. On January 7, 1957 he released the ragtop as production model. (IMSC)

seats. Apparently, the dealers wanted to keep sticker prices lower, to sell more cars in a recession year.

In 1957, Mercury was operated as a separate division of Ford Motor Company, with its headquarters at 6200 West Warren Avenue, in Detroit, Michigan. F.C. "Jack" Reith was a Ford Motor Company vice president, in addition to serving as M-E-L Division's general manager. P.F. Lorenz was his executive assistant. C.E. Bowie was sales manager. H.C. MacDonald was chief engineer, and D.J. Bracken was general manufacturing manager. The division had 3,148 dealers handling its products. A few sold only Mercurys. Most handled Lincolns and Mercurys, some in addition to other car-lines. It was not a good year for mid-priced cars.

During 1957, an economic recession began to take hold in America. It sparked an interest in economy models and imported cars. Both types of cars enjoyed a temporary boom. Big-car buyers started looking at Ford, Chevrolet and Plymouth-sized cars. As a result, Mercury's model-year production fell off by some 40,000 total units. Actually, the company's sales shrunk proportionately to the domestic market, allowing Mercury to keep its seventh-place-in-industry ranking. But, since imports didn't show up in those numbers, Mercury really did have a smaller piece of a smaller pie. The company's output included 157,528 Montereys, 75,762 Montclairs, 16,861 Turnpike Cruisers (including 1,265 Convertibles), and 36,012 Station Wagons.

A new combination bumper-grille with multiple concave vertical dividers, plus a parking light in each massive "Jet-Flow" bumper pod, characterized 1958 Mercurys. They were introduced on November 12, 1957. New hoods and restyled fenders were seen. Dual headlamps were now standard equipment across the board. In addition to a new rear deck lid, V-angle taillamp assemblies appeared. "Torch-shaped" taillight housings were located at the rear of both body side projectiles.

A huge, new, Park Lane was introduced. "Mercury for '58 will move upward, by introducing a new model slated to invade the market occupied by the Buick Super and Roadmaster, and the big DeSoto models," said *Motor Trend* in September 1957. "This new Mercury will be larger overall, will have a wheelbase of at least 124 inches and will be called the Parklane (sic)." Mercury advertisements claimed that this big new car had "Sports car spirit with limousine ride." This was, obviously, a reference to its giant-sized, combined with its powerful V-8. The Park Lane had a 125-inch wheelbase and overall length of 220.2 inches.

Other Mercurys retained a 122 inch wheelbase. Montereys ... initially considered base models ... were longer than in 1957. Like Montclairs, they stretched 213.2 inches bumper-to-bumper. The Turnpike Cruiser Convertible was dropped, although three 1958 versions did exist. All three were

The 1958 Montclair Convertible listed for $3,536. It weighed 4,295 pounds. This one has "Turnpike Cruiser" trim on the right-hand side of the rear deck lid. This model is not listed in the 1958 sales catalog. However, at least three such cars were built as prototypes or executive cars. (Mercury)

The 1958 Mercury Turnpike Cruiser four-door Phaeton had the Breezeway window, rather than the sloped-off rear window of the Montclair counterpart. (Mercury)

Black with Gold rear trim and one had a factory continental kit. These cars may have been prototypes or executive cars. The Cruiser Hardtops were made part of the Montclair series. Mercury Station Wagons were 214.2 inches long. Heights remained low, such as just under 57 inches for a Hardtop Phaeton with a full load. The cars got wider again, too, now measuring 81.1 inches across. A six-foot adult could really stretch out in a 1958 Mercury!

Originally scheduled for January 1 — and arriving about a week later — a Medalist "price leader" series returned to the Mercury line. Its purpose was to shore up big-car sales, which had already started looking disastrous in the fall of 1957. The 1958 Medalist series included a two-door Sedan and a four-door Sedan. Both looked very plain. There was just a single, thin body side molding on them. It ran over the headlight "eyebrow," then down, straight across the front door. Behind the door, it "veed" upwards and downwards, before continuing straight to the rear, to a point below the fender projectile. Medalists had painted headlamp surrounds, no rocker panel moldings and "bottle cap" style hubcaps. The Medalist two-door was $2,547 and the four-door was $70 more.

Montereys had front fender nameplates and painted headlamp doors. Single side moldings stretched under the rear fender projectiles. Dual moldings ran from that point, forward. They had no rocker panel moldings, but full wheelcovers were included. Multiple concave dividers decorated the inside of the rear bumper pods. There was no change in the listing of Monterey body styles. Prices were a bit higher than before, running from $2,652 to $3,081. There were three Monterey-style Mercury Commuter wagons again, and the most expensive one sold for $3,201. They had "Commuter" identification on their front fenders and "breathable" vinyl upholstery.

Montclairs had their name on the front fender, dual full-length side moldings, bright rocker panel accents, full wheelcovers and chrome-accented headlight bezels. The Montclair Turnpike Cruiser Phaeton Hardtops (the official name was almost as long as the cars) had new three-tone paint jobs. Also part of the Station Wagon series was a pair of Montclair-like Voyagers and the Colony Park. The lowest-priced Montclair was the four-door sedan at $2,721. The most expensive was the Colony Park four-door Station Wagon at $3,775. Voyagers had their name on the front fenders and woven plastic upholstery. The Colony Park had simulated wood-grain side trim. Both Turnpike Cruisers cost a little over $3,200. The regular Merc-O-Matic transmission was standard in all Montclair-level cars and wagons.

Three models were incorporated in the Park Lane offerings: Two- and four-door Phaeton Hardtops, and a Convertible. Their prices ranged from $3,867 to $4,118. They had "Park Lane" nameplates on the roof rear quarter panels and the rear deck lid. Ornaments decorated the tops of the front fenders. The headlamp bezels were bright-finished. Four bright-metal-trimmed rectangular "cells" highlighted the inside of the rear bumper pods. There was a single side molding under the rear fender projectile, and a double molding from there forward. A new "Multi-Drive" Merc-O-Matic transmission with "Key Board" control was standard in all Park Lanes. This transmission featured new "hill control," "cruising range," and "high performance" control bars to let the driver pick his or her favorite driving range. Power steering and power brakes were also included.

Mercury ads said the Park Lane had "Sports car spirit with limousine ride." The Convertible was sporty, but not a sports car. (Mercury)

The Colony Park had simulated wood trim. Regular Merc-O-Matic was standard in all upper series cars and wagons. (Mercury)

The 1958 models had new V-angle taillights and torch-shaped taillight housings. (James L. Gwaltney)

The basic colors offered for the exterior of 1958 Mercurys were Tuxedo Black (01); Marble White (07); Parisian Green (15); Emerald Metallic (16); Holley Green Metallic (17); Vineyard Blue (30); Jamaican Blue Metallic (31); Flamingo Red (45); Silver Sheen Metallic (55); Oxford Gray Metallic (56); Autumn Beige (66); Mayfair Yellow (75); Shadow Rose (87); Golden Dust Metallic (92); Twilight Turquoise (97); and Burgundy Metallic (99). Exterior paint codes had a single digit indicating the type of paint scheme. The two-digit number shown here indicate the areas where the paint was applied. This could be the upper body, the lower body or the body side molding area, depending upon whether the paint scheme was solid, two-tone or "Flo-Tone."

Re-introduced for 1958 were optional leather interior trims. There were four of these: White-and-black; two-tone green; two-tone blue; and solid red. Also available were eight all-vinyl options (one solid and the rest two-tone), plus 22 cloth-and-vinyl selections. "It's like lounging in your living room," the 1958 sales catalog boasted about the interior trims and Mercury's optional new "Air Cushion Ride." This was the trade name for an air suspension system with an automatic self-leveling feature. It was optional on all Mercury models, but — like other 1958 air suspensions — was not technically refined, or popular with car-buyers.

Mercury offered a total of four big V-8s for 1958, all with higher 10.5:1 compression ratios. Medalists came with a 312-cubic-inch engine that produced 235 hp. A 383-cubic inch "Marauder" engine was used in Montereys and Commuters. It produced 312 hp. Montclairs, Voyagers and Colony Parks came with a 330 hp version of the 383 cubic-inch engine. The biggest V-8 was the Park Lane's 430-cubic-inch, 360 hp job.

The regular Merc-O-Matic transmission was optional, on models below the Montclair, for $225.80. Multi-Drive Merc-O-Matic was $18.80 extra for Montclair-level models and $244.60 additional for Monterey-level models. Power steering and four power window options were $107.50 apiece. A "4-Way" power seat cost $69.90, while the "Seat-O-Matic" memory seat was $96.80. Other options (and prices) included: Power brakes ($37.70); dual exhausts; ($32.30); power lubricator ($43); "Travel-Tuner" radio with electric antenna ($149.50); push-button radio ($100); rear seat speaker ($16.20); manual heater/defroster ($91.40); "Climate Control" heater/defroster ($109.45);

The Colony Park Station Wagon had vertical slats on its tailgate, like a Chevrolet Nomad or Pontiac Custom Safari. (Mercury)

four-ply rayon 8.00 x 14 white sidewall tires ($41 additional); four-ply nylon 8.00 x 14 white sidewall tires ($67.40 additional); wheelcovers ($12.90); two-tone paint ($17.20); "Flo-Tone" paint ($32.30); tinted glass ($34.40); back-up lamps ($8.10); "Speed-Limit" safety monitor ($12.90); windshield washer ($14); electric clock ($15.10); foam rubber seat cushions ($21.50); air conditioner and heater ($458.75); 360-hp "Marauder" engine ($66.70); padded instrument panel ($21.50); power retracting Station Wagon back window ($32.30); and nine-passenger/three-seat Station Wagon option ($79.60). In March 1958, a 400-hp "Super Marauder" engine with three two-barrel carburetors was made available, as a production option, for an unknown price.

In the middle of January 1958, Ford Motor Company decided to combine the operations of Mercury, Edsel, Lincoln, and the English Ford lines to create a new Mercury-Edsel-Lincoln Division. The group was headquartered at 3000 Schaefer Road, in Dearborn, Michigan, which was formerly Lincoln Division headquarters. The new organization, under the control of general manager James J. Nance (the former president of Packard), was responsible for the engineering, manufacturing, and marketing of Mercury, Edsel, and Lincoln cars, plus the marketing of Anglia, Prefect, Consul, Zephyr, and Zodiac passenger cars, and Thames Van trucks. Each car-line continued to be merchandised, and advertised individually. Dealer franchises were also handled separately. B.D. Mills was assistant general manager, and J.E. Bayne was in charge of Lincoln-Mercury sales.

Mercury's sales were not very good. Business tumbled 55 percent in 1958, as the recession deepened. Car sales were down overall and the trend towards rising imported car sales continued. Thus, in a year when Mercurys were larger than ever, the interest in large cars was smaller than ever! The only American brand that went up in sales was Rambler! The Ford Thunderbird model gained a little popularity, but chiefly because it was changed from a two-seat car to a four-seater. Mercury dropped a full percentage of total domestic-car production. It fell to eighth rank in sales. Total model-year production was a feeble 133,271 cars. That included 18,732 Medalists; 62,312 Montereys; 20,673 Montclairs (including 6,407 Turnpike Cruisers); 9,252 Park Lanes; and 22,302 Station Wagons.

The 1959 Mercurys looked like blown-up 1957 or 1958 models, with all of the styling motifs magnified. The concept behind this transition was to move the Mercury above the Edsel, so that the two cars, which were sold by the same FoMoCo division, would not compete as much against each other. The larger body was seen as a way to upgrade the Mercury and widen the market gap between it and the Edsel. "The 1959 Mercury has been moved to the upper end of the medium-priced field," said *Car Life*. "It's a good-looking car with smoother, simpler lines than in past years. In keeping with its upgrading, Mercury has been enlarged."

Unfortunately, management had decided to emphasize all the Mercury features that weren't selling well in the late-1950s. These elements

S & R Lincoln-Mercury also sold Continentals, Edsels, Simcas, Fiats, Triumphs and Alfas. (Jay Katelle)

included its radically different styling, its immense size, and its very abundant use of chrome. The 1959 cars did get some very positive reviews in contemporary motoring magazines. Viewed in the perspective of their time, they were truly among the best cars in their class. However, they did not catch on with buyers. The Lincoln-Mercury Division had been very sluggish in reacting to the public's growing, but fleeting, demand for small and efficient automobiles in this time period.

For 1959, the Mercury had a diecast cellular grille, sitting above a massive bumper with inset parking lights. The concave projectiles on the rear body sides were longer and wider. New forward-slanting rear window pillars were seen on hardtops. Four inches were added to the wheelbase and overall length of the "smaller" models. There was also a huge, new Park Lane with a 128-inch wheelbase and 222-inch overall length. Wagons gained 4-1/2 inches overall and shared the 126-inch wheelbase. Mercury said that the stretched wheelbases enabled engineers to move the front axle and engine forward and lower the transmission tunnel. The floor was said to be 50 percent flatter.

All Mercurys had new, compound-curved windshields and back windows. The cowl point was also lowered by 2-1/2 inches and the windshield pillars were more vertical. All these changes helped increase the driver's view by 60 percent. Thoughtfully, Mercury also provided 16-inch, two-speed electric, parallel-arm wiper blades that cleaned 43 percent more glass area. The front doors on four-door models were wider, for easier entrance and egress. A new instrument panel was moved six inches forward and helped increase front compartment space, too. Mercury Cruiser Hardtops had a semi-fastback look at the rear, while Sedans featured "overhanging" rear roof lines.

In addition to "Monterey" front fender model nameplates, the cars in the series had three bright metal bands in the side projectiles, just forward of the taillight housings. The back body panel was textured, with horizontal ribbing and painted finish on the lower panel. Full wheel discs were standard, but rocker panel moldings were not. The line included a pair of Sedans, a pair of "Cruisers" (Mercury's new name for its Hardtops) and a Convertible, at prices from $2,768 to $3,150.

Montclairs started with the same features as Montereys and added bright metal trim on the wheel housings and rocker panels A bright metal insert was added to the lower back panel. The Montclair four-door Sedan listed for $3,308, while the four-door Hardtop Cruiser was $3,437.

This 1959 Monterey two-door Sedan from Oak Creek, Wisconsin has two-tone red and white paint and stick shift. (Jerry Lyon)

The 1959 Mercury Commuter Station Wagon was trimmed like a Monterey. Two-and four-door versions were offered. (*Old Cars*)

List price for 1959 Monterey Convertible was $3,150. This one has two-tone treatment and cruiser skirts. (*Old Cars*)

In addition to Montclair equipment, Park Lanes had solid, bright metal taillamp extensions in their rear fender projectiles, plus broad, ribbed aluminum panels behind the rear wheel openings. The bright-accented lower back panel had a "cubed" grid pattern and chrome ornaments decorated the front fender tops. This series included two- and four-door Hardtop Cruisers at $3,955 and $4,031, respectively, plus a $4,206 Convertible.

Station Wagons were now called Country Cruisers. This line included four-door Commuter, Voyager and Colony Park models, as well as a two-door Commuter. The latter was available only in six-passenger configurations and was the only mid-priced two-door wagon left in America.

This year, 16 individual colors were offered on Mercurys. They were: Tuxedo Black; Marble White; Sagebrush Green Metallic; Sherwood Green Metallic; Satellite Blue; Blue Ice Metallic; Canton Red; Silver Green Metallic; Charcoal Metallic; Autumn Smoke; Mederia Yellow; Bermuda Sand; Silver Beige Metallic; Twilight Turquoise; Golden Beige Metallic; and Neptune Turquoise Metallic. Again, the cars came with monotone, two-tone and "Flo-Tone" paint scheme options.

A bright metal back panel was seen on the rear of 1959 Montclairs. The four-door Hardtop was rarest. (Mercury)

The front of 1959 Mercurys featured dual headlamps. (Jerry Lyon)

The 1959 Mercury Park Lane four-door Hardtop featured bright metal trim around the wheel openings and broad, scored aluminum trim behind the rear wheels. (Mercury)

Solid bright metal trim decorated the rear of the Park Lane fender projectiles. The bright metal lower back panel insert had a cubed grid pattern. Larger tail-lamps were mounted in the back panel. (*Old Cars*)

The 1959 Mercury was advertised as a car planned for people who like to put 500 easy miles between dawn and dusk. "Park Lane" nameplates on the front fenders identified the top line. There was no hood ornament. (Mercury)

Inside, the 1959 models could be upholstered in eight all-vinyl trims or 16 cloth-and-vinyl combinations. The leather trims of 1958 proved not to be very popular and they did not reappear for 1959.

All Mercurys were 80.7 inches wide. They rode on a larger and wider "cow-belly" frame, which required a wider 60-inch tread, front and rear, except on Station Wagons. The wagons' tracks were 60 inches in front and 62 inches in the rear. Heights came in around 56 inches (57.8 inches for Station Wagons). Ground clearance was six inches. Standard tire sizes were 8.00 x 14 for Montereys and 8.50 x 14 for Station Wagons and all other cars. A coil spring suspension was used up front, with semi-elliptic leaf springs in the rear.

Mercury offered a total of four big V-8s again for 1959. They were revised to give slightly better fuel efficiency. A special economy engine, with an 8.75:1 compression ratio, was standard in Montereys. It was the two-barrel version of the 312-cubic-inch block, detuned for 210 hp. Mercury ads said it could be operated on regular gas, but *Motor Trend* disagreed. A 383-cubic inch engine, with 10.0:1 compression and a two-barrel carburetor, was standard in Commuters and produced 280 hp. Montclairs, Voyagers and Colony Parks came with a four-barrel, 322 hp version of the 383 cubic-inch engine. The biggest V-8 was the Park Lanes' 430-cubic-inch 345 hp job. It also had a decreased 10.0:1 compression ratio and one four-barrel carburetor. There were rumors of the "triple-carb" engine returning, but apparently this never happened.

Mercurys with three-speed manual transmission came with a 3.56:1 rear axle ratio. Overdrive was optional and mated with a different axle. Once again, two automatics were offered. One was actually a new two-speed (single-range) Merc-O-Matic unit. It had a lightweight aluminum casing and was the "standard " automatic. The three-speed Multi-Drive Merc-O-Matic, used with the big engine, was a bit costlier. Both had hydraulic controls that matched their torque curve and, in both cases, push-button gear selection was discontinued. The selector was back on the steering column again. A 2.71:1 axle was standard with Merc-O-Matic cars.

Automatic transmission was standard in Park Lane, Montclair, Voyager and Colony Park models. Park Lanes also included power brakes and steering at no extra cost. A power rear window was provided with Voyager and Colony Park Station Wagons. Other standard features included self-

The 1959 Colony Park Country Cruiser came as a six- or nine-passenger model. A half-ton of cargo fit in the 101-cubic-foot area behind the driver. (Mercury)

The 1959 Mercury hood was front-hinged. Ford said this gave better accessibility and made it easier to use a trouble light. (Mercury)

Custom Royal four-door sedan. The Mercury got very strong praise in most regards, but was criticized for a cramped instrument panel layout and excessive body lean in any curves taken at above normal speeds. The Montclair did 0-to -0 mph in 10.2 seconds and took 17.6 seconds to cover the quarter-mile at 81 mph. Fuel economy was measured at 12.8 mpg in stop-and-go driving and 15.1 mpg during highway operation. The magazine determined that the self-adjusting brakes, with 205 square-inches of lining area, did a good job stopping this "aircraft carrier." Only slight wheel grab occurred after four good 60 to 20 mph slowdowns.

The 1959 Montclair four-door Hardtop interior offered true six-passenger comfort with six inches more entrance room, and nine inches more front knee room. The transmission hump was 50 percent lower. (Mercury)

adjusting brakes; "Safety-Sweep" tandem windshield wipers; three-phase shock absorbers; ball-joint front suspension; and "Super-Enamel" exterior finish. Other power assists, a radio, a heater/defroster, air conditioning, and more, were optional on all models.

For a huge automobile, the Mercury rode nicely. "Its handling is every bit as good as last year's car," said *Motor Trend*'s Detroit editor, Bill Callahan, in December 1958. "It stays fairly stable on turns, the brakes are efficient, the acceleration is good, the ride is smooth (even over Belgian Blocks at Ford's test track), it takes less steering effort (Mercury claims 50 percent less for parking and 15 percent less on the highway)."

In March 1959, *Motor Trend* did a three-way comparison road test pitting a 322-hp Montclair four-door Hardtop Cruiser against a 260-hp Pontiac Catalina Vista Hardtop and a 305-hp Dodge

BODY FEATURES
Rigidized body construction. Welded steel. Panoramic Skylight Windshield with 1883 sq. in. area. Compound back window with 1850 sq. in. area for 2-door and 4-door Cruiser models. Safety-Sweep electric-powered windshield wipers. Aircraft-type instrument panel. Safety steering wheel. Front-hinged hood. Convertible-type doors for all hardtop models. Cross-flow ventilation. Double-panel hood, doors and rear deck lid. **Curb weights,** 4-door Cruiser models: Monterey—4257 lb.; Montclair—4423 lb.; Park Lane—4591 lb. **Total glass areas,** 4-door Cruiser models: 5041 sq. in. safety glass. **Exterior finish:** Baked Super-Enamel in choice of 16 solid colors and 56 Two-Tone combinations. **Upholstery:** Regular or metallic vinyl and fabrics with 100% nylon face for closed cars. All-vinyl upholstery for Monterey and Park Lane Convertibles.

POWER TRAIN
Engines: Overhead valve V-8 engines in three sizes. 12-volt electrical system. Combination vacuum-centrifugal spark control. Full-flow oil filter. Full-pressure lubrication. Dry-type carburetor air filter. Self-cleaning 18mm spark plugs. The 383- and 430-cubic-inch engines have in-block combustion chambers; 3-stage cooling system; water-jacketed intake manifold; step-top pistons. Capacities: oil—5-quarts (or 6 quarts with filter change); fuel—20 gallons; coolant—20½ to 21 quarts (without heater). Aluminized mufflers. **Merc-O-Matic Transmission:** Combination of fluid torque converter and 3-speed planetary gear train. 5-position selector lever control. Oil capacity—21 pints. Water cooled. **Multi-Drive Merc-O-Matic:** Dual drive ranges with 6-position selector lever control. **Conventional Transmission:** Selective gear type with three forward speeds, one reverse. All gears helical. Constant-mesh second gear. Standard for Monterey and Commuter models.

CHASSIS FEATURES
Ladder-type frame with bowed box-girder side-rails. X-type reinforcement for convertible frame. **Front suspension:** Swept-back ball-joint design with anti-dive. Helical-coil springs. Full-cushion shock absorbers. Link-type front torsion-bar stabilizer. **Steering:** Ball and rack-type with 54 recirculating balls. Steering ratios—29.1 to 1 for Monterey and Commuter; 31.1 to 1 for Montclair, Voyager and Colony Park; 20.5 to 1 with power steering. **Rear suspension:** Splay-mounted leaf-type rear springs—60 inches long and 2½ inches wide. Compression-type rear spring shackles. Full-restricted hydraulic shock absorbers, sea-leg mounted. Hotchkiss drive. **Self-adjusting brakes:** Internal expanding, hydraulic brakes. 11-inch brake drum with full-circle ribs for extra cooling. Self-adjusters keep brakes properly and equally adjusted for life of linings. Brake width—3 in. (f), 2½ in. (r) Total brake lining area—233.1 sq. in. **Tire sizes**—8.00, 8.50, 9.00 x 14.

COUNTRY CRUISER FEATURES
Hardtop design with convertible-type doors. Retracting back window. "Flush-fit" tailgate, concealed package compartment beneath rear floor, vertically-mounted spare tire, 5 wheels and 8.50 x 14 tires with every model, self-storing 3rd seat, optional for 4-door models. **Cargo compartment area:** 39.7 square feet behind front seat with tailgate closed; 46.9 square feet with tailgate open. **Cargo compartment capacity:** 101.1 cubic feet behind front seat: 60.1 cubic feet behind 2nd seat—plus 4 cubic feet in concealed package compartment. **Total glass areas,** Country Cruiser models: Commuter 2-door Country Cruiser—5294 sq. in. safety glass; 4-door Country Cruiser models—5330 sq. in. safety glass.

An extensive list of body, power train, and chassis features for 1959 Mercurys detailed the cars' standard equipment. (Mercury)

FEATURE FACTS AND SPECIFICATIONS ... 1959 MERCURY

MAJOR DIMENSIONS: (4-door hardtop models)	MONTEREY MONTCLAIR	PARK LANE	COUNTRY CRUISERS
Wheelbase	126.0″	128.0″	126.0″
Over-all length	217.8″	222.8″	218.6″
Over-all height	55.8″*	56.1″	57.8″
Over-all width	80.7″	80.7″	80.7″
Wheel tread	60″(f); 60″(r)	60″(f); 62″(r)	60″(f); 60″(r)
*Montclair over-all height—56.1″			

INTERIOR SPACE:

Headroom—effective, front	38.5″	38.5″	39.7″
Headroom—effective, rear	37.0″	37.0″	39.2″
Leg room—effective, front	46.2″	46.2″	45.2″
Leg room—effective, rear	43.1″	43.1″	45.1″
Hip room—front	62.5″	62.5″	62.5″
Hip room—rear	62.8″	62.8″	62.8″
Shoulder room—front	60.5″	60.5″	60.5″
Shoulder room—rear	60.8″	60.8″	60.8″

TRUNK COMPARTMENT:

Max. interior width	75.0″	75.0″	—
Capacity with spare tire	31.5 cu. ft.	34.5 cu. ft.	—
Capacity without spare tire	34.5 cu. ft.	37.5 cu. ft.	—

1959 MERCURY ENGINE-TRANSMISSION COMBINATIONS

SIZE—CARBURETOR	RATINGS	TRANSMISSIONS	MODELS
312 cu. in. displacement Bore—3.80″; Stroke—3.44″ 2-barrel carburetor	210 horsepower 325 foot-pounds torque	3-speed manual; Regular Merc-O-Matic*	Monterey Series
383 cu. in. displacement Bore—4.30″; Stroke—3.30″ 2-barrel carburetor	280 horsepower 400 foot-pounds torque	3-speed manual; Regular Merc-O-Matic*; Multi-Drive Merc-O-Matic*	Monterey Series (opt.); Commuter Country Cruisers
383 cu. in displacement Bore—4.30″; Stroke—3.30″ 4-barrel carburetor	322 horsepower 420 foot-pounds torque	Regular Merc-O-Matic; Multi-Drive Merc-O-Matic*	Montclair Series; Voyager and Colony Park Country Cruisers
430 cu. in. displacement Bore—4.30″; Stroke—3.70″ 4-barrel carburetor	345 horsepower 480 foot-pounds torque	Multi-Drive Merc-O-Matic	Park Lane Series

*Optional at extra cost.

MAJOR OPTIONS*: Merc-O-Matic Transmission†; Multi-Drive Merc-O-Matic‡; power steering‡; power brakes‡; automatic power seat; 4-way power seat; power windows; heater-defroster; air conditioner-heater-defroster with Climate Dial control; tinted windshield and windows; whitewall tires; padded instrument panel†; padded sun visors; seat belts; dual exhaust‡; Safety Speed Monitor.
*At extra cost on certain models.
†Optional at extra cost on Monterey and Commuter models.
‡Standard on Park Lane models, optional other models.

Form No. M-59—104

Litho in U.S.A.

Features, facts and specifications for the 1959 Mercurys included dimensions, interior space, trunk space and engine/transmission combinations. Included in the chart were the major options available that season. (Mercury)

Car Life magazine did a "Consumer Analysis" of the 1959 Mercury line in its February 1959 issue. "I took to the bigger 'M' just like Kentucky bourbon takes to mint and ice," gushed Jim Whipple. "It's a car that a great deal of brain power has been put into." Using a 1-to-5 check-mark rating system, with five checks being the top rating in its price class, the Mercury was given four checks for styling, roadability, serviceability, workmanship, and value per dollar; and five checks for performance, riding comfort, interior design, ease of control, and economy.

Whipple spent several hours in a Park Lane four-door Phaeton Hardtop at Ford's test track in Dearborn, Michigan. His article did not mention fifth-wheel performance tests, but he wrote that the "430" would accelerate a Park Lane to 60 mph in eight seconds and that the car would "leap from 50 to 70 miles per hour in a passing maneuver in just five seconds." Whipple concluded, "The '59 Mercury is an exceptionally well-designed and comfortable car — one that's very easy to drive and a real pleasure to ride in. It's a very good looking car, brilliantly engineered for safe, roadside performance, and beautifully built from the ground up."

An automotive writer who did not wax enthusiastic over the 1959 Mercury was Tom McCahill, who recalled Henry Ford as a "hot rodder" and said he yearned for the days, "When Ed Sullivan would come on the air Sunday nights and announce that Mercurys just finished one, two at Daytona." According to McCahill, the Mercury of the past was "gutsy stuff," far different from FoMoCo's "cream puff approach" of the late 1950s. "A fashion award will never take the place of winning in major competitions," said the scribe. "Glad I don't have to write the copy for that kind of car advertising."

One new Mercury did try racing. It showed up at Daytona, Beach, Florida, in late February, to take part in the Flying Mile competition. The Merc did the distance at 120 mph, fifth behind four 1959 Pontiacs in the Production Stock class. "It is perhaps interesting to note, with regard to the '59 Merc figure, that a 1940 Mercury, running on the same day, registered exactly the same speed," wrote Steve DaCosta in *Motor Trend*.

Perhaps, Tom McCahill was right! The car-buying public, at least, seemed to agree with him. Mercury had its third weak year in a row in 1959. Sales declined by another 10 percent, making Mercury ninth on the domestic sales charts.

Ben D. Mills was made a Ford Motor Company vice president, and general manager of M-E-L Division. Walker A. Williams was his assistant. C.E. Bowie was responsible for sales. D.J. Bracken was still general manufacturing manager. Model-year production peaked at 150,000 units. That total included 89,277 Montereys, 23,602 Montclairs, 12,523 Park Lanes, and 24,598 Station Wagons.

The new line of big Mercurys, announced on October 15, 1959, was the last to come from a separate Mercury Division of Ford Motor Company. In November 1959, effective with the discontinuation of the Edsel, a new Lincoln-Mercury Division was formed. It was charged with the responsibility of marketing Lincoln, Mercury and Comet automobiles. In addition, a number of imports were still under L-M's umbrella. These included Anglia, Prefect, Consul, Zephyr, and Zodiac cars, and Thames trucks, built by Ford of England and the Taunus cars and trucks made by Ford's German branch. Each car line was merchandised and advertised individually and dealer franchises were handled separately. Ben D. Mills, a Ford vice president, was general manager of Lincoln-Mercury Division.

There were 17 Mercury models offered in four series for 1960: Monterey, Montclair, Park Lane and Station Wagon. Overall, the cars had a cleaner, custom-car look and spoke of value. Mercury was abandoning the look of radical styling (as well as hot performance) in favor of an image of conservative luxury. On a model-for-model basis, prices dropped about $200. Mercury advertised, "You'll look a long time before matching Mercury's beauty at such a low price." The sales of these

Front of 1960 Mercury had wide-spaced dual headlamps, and concave vertical-bars in grille. (David G. Eager)

Rear fenders had an abbreviated gull-wing look and vertical taillamps were canted slightly outwards. (David G. Eager)

The 1960 Monterey four-door Sedan was the most popular full-size Mercury, with production of 49,594. (Mercury)

Rear view of David G. Eager's 1960 Monterey Convertible shows styling.

models did improve somewhat, but a new Mercury product, introduced at midyear, was the key to a very successful selling season. This was a compact car called the Comet. It bowed on March 17, which was most fitting. After it got going, Mercury was "wearing the green," or, at least, lots of "green back" dollars were making their way to Mercury dealers. It turned out to be the company's best year since 1957.

The full-size 1960 Mercurys were completely restyled, with a new downward-sloping hood and front fenders, and a new concave grille that enclosed the headlights. The rear fender projectiles were gone. Vertical taillight assemblies, housed in the bumper ends, replaced the triangular design of 1959.

The base line said "Monterey" in script on the rear fenders and had an enamel-finished rear grille. There were five models. Four-door cars included a Sedan and Hardtop. Two-door models were Sedans, Hardtops and Convertibles. Prices began at $2,631 and went to $3,077.

There were three Montclairs. Hardtops came in two- and four-door models. There was also a four-door Sedan. $3,280 to $3,394 was the price range. Identifiers included "Montclair" rear fender namescripts, bright metal lower body and wheelhouse accents, three air foil chevrons ahead of the rear wheel opening, and a bright metal rear grille with a horizontal bar texture.

Park Lanes came in two- and four-door Hardtop Cruiser models, and a Convertible, with $3,794 to $4,018 price tags. They had appropriate rear fender namescripts. Their lower body accents broadened to a butter-knife-shaped applique decorating the rear fender skirts and lower rear body corner. There were five air foil chevrons, ahead of the Park Lane's rear wheels, and the rear grille was bright-finished with a cubed texture.

The sales crew at Brian Lincoln-Mercury used a Monterey Convertible for this promotional postcard photo. It had a $3,077 list price and 6,062 were assembled. (Jay Katelle)

Mercury promised Monterey Convertible buyers "a choice of luxurious interiors that will make you proud each time you lower the top." (David G. Eager)

"First Luxury Compact," said the cover of *Car Life* magazine, in August 1960, below a photo of a red Comet two-door with fancy trim options. Other cover photos showed the grille and rear end of a blue-green car. Jim Whipple described the Comet as a "Compact Deluxe" in the headline to his "Consumer Analysis." Indeed, this small Mercury was the first of the slightly larger, slightly fancier, small cars that were coming down the pike. This "gave it the jump" on a new market niche.

"Just the touch of a button tells the world that Mercury offers more for the money," Mercury bragged about the Monterey ragtop. (*Old Cars*)

The 1960 Comet line included two- and four-door versions of Sedans and Station Wagons. Standard equipment included dual headlamps; a front stabilizer bar; door-operated courtesy lamps; full-width stainless steel windshield and backlight moldings; drip rail moldings; a custom steering wheel; a cigarette lighter; front and rear armrests; and a vinyl headlining. All Comets were available with an extra-cost Fashion Group trim option that included bright exterior window frames; carpeting in Sedans; contour seats; and deluxe, pleated fabric trims. Prices for the four models ranged from $1,998 to $2,365.

All of the large Mercurys now shared a single 126-inch wheelbase, while Comets had two wheelbases, 109.5 inches for wagons and 114 inches for Sedans. Overall lengths were 219.2 inches for the full-size four-door Hardtop, 192 inches for Comet wagons and 195 inches for Comet sedans. The big cars were still around 56 inches high, while Comets were just under 55 inches tall. Width was another big contrast: 81.5 inches for the full-sized Mercs and just 70.4 inches for Comets. Montereys again had 8.00 x 14 tires, while other models had size 8.50 x 14 rubber. Comet Sedans used 6.00 x 13 tires and wagons had 6.50 x 13 tires.

All Mercurys had one of three V-8s offered this season. A new 205-horsepower version of the 312-cubic-inch engine with 8.9:1 compression was standard in Montereys and Commuter wagons. Montclairs, Park Lanes and Colony Parks came with a 430-cubic-inch, 310-hp engine. It had 10.0:1 compression. A 280-hp edition with 8.5:1 compression was optional. The Comet featured a "Thrift Power" inline, overhead valve six with an over-square bore and stroke (3.5 inches x 2.3 inches). It displaced

The Monterey two-door Hardtop was only one-third as popular as the Sedan. It had a list price of $2,781. (Mercury)

The 1960 Mercury Monterey two-door Sedan was the series least expensive model with a $2,631 price tag. (James B. Saxe)

Trimmed like a Monterey, the Commuter Station Wagons also had wider doors, "space-planned" interiors, and a set-back instrument panel with easy-to-read-and-reach controls. (Mercury)

It's an experience you owe yourself. Why not give it a try?

Tucson Turquoise

The scarcest Mercury of 1960 was the Park Lane Convertible. Only 1,525 were built. Prices for the rich ragtop began at $4,018. A metallic all-vinyl interior was featured. (Mercury)

head valve six with an over-square bore and stroke (3.5 inches x 2.3 inches). It displaced 144.3 cubic inches and generated 90 hp. It could deliver up to 28 mpg fuel economy.

In the big-car category, only the Monterey came with standard manual transmission. Overdrive was extra. Merc-O-Matic transmission (plus a padded instrument panel and back-up lights) was standard on Montclairs and Colony Parks. Multi-Drive Merc-O-Matic was standard in Park Lanes, along with a padded dash; back-up lights; power steering and brakes; and windshield washers. Most Comets had three-speed manual "stick shift," but a two-speed "Merc-O-Matic" automatic transmission was optional.

"Road-Tuned" wheels; "3-Speed Safety-Sweep" windshield wipers; chair-high seats; a "Panoramic Skylight" windshield; and a "Jet Stream" defroster were selling features of the 1960 Mercury. The cars also had "Super Enamel" finish; a safety steering wheel; safety glass in every window; "Rigidized" body construction; and a "Safety-Width" box-girder frame.

ng power

All full-size Mercurys used V-8s. Options included 205-, 280- and 310-hp engines. (Mercury)

Selling points for the economical Comet included an engine said to be 32 percent lighter than standard sixes and a transmission that was 45 percent lighter than usual. It offered "Big Car Ride" with a longer wheelbase than other compacts and butyl-lined rear leaf springs. The body and frame were a single unit, which provided more room, greater strength, enhanced safety, and a quieter

Javelin Bronze Metallic

"When the wonderful fun of faraway places beckons, picture yourself behind the wheel of this dazzling automobile," said Mercury of the 1960 Montclair two-door Sedan (coupe). (Mercury)

The Country Cruiser rear window retracted into the tailgate, doing away with the inconvenience of a liftgate. (Mercury)

minized muffler; 131 square inches of total brake area (151 square inches for wagons); and a 14-gallon gasoline tank.

Motor Life magazine reviewed the 1960 Mercury in its May 1960 issue, noting that the test car was a Montclair Sedan "that had the biggest V-8 of any current automobile, 430 cubic inches." The big V-8 was "lightly stressed to produce 310 hp with a two-barrel carburetor and 10-to-1 compression ratio," the review said. "Its Multi-Drive transmission followed the familiar pattern of a torque converter and three-speed gear box." The car had the 2.71:1 rear axle ratio.

Performance-wise, the magazine managed a 0-to-60 mph time of 11.5 seconds, and found that the Montclair delivered between 11 and 16 mpg. It was pointed out that the Merc's forward-mounted power team and shallow dash design provided outstanding seating comfort for six passengers, and that the engine's location did

The 1960 Colony Park Country Cruiser Station Wagon had "four-door hardtop" styling, plus "Super-Enamel" finish and simulated wood-grained side paneling. It was trimmed much like a Park Lane, without fender skirts. (Mercury)

Mercury described the 1960 four-door Hardtop Cruiser as "the peak of Park Lane elegance." (Mercury)

not have a negative effect on handling. "The front springs were stiffened to support the added weight so that even cornering behavior was up to reasonable standards, though understeer was pronounced," *Motor Life* reported, adding. "The steering itself was a power system that combined the virtues of quickness and road feel." The Mercury exhibited a soft ride quality, without floating or swaying at high speeds and was comfortably quiet inside.

Car Life's review of the Comet (April 1960), included a drive trial by Jim Whipple at a test strip in Arizona. Interestingly, Whipple made a comparison between the dimensions of this new-sized compact and those of 1952-1954 FoMoCo cars, which were just a few inches larger in wheelbase, overall length and width. Some auto writers of the day who criticized the super-big Mercs of 1957 to 1959, had made reference to the higher popularity of the marque's mid-1950s models. They had suggested that smaller, hotter-performing Mercs had more appeal. The Comet's ultimate success went to prove that they had a legitimate argument, as far as size went, though early Comets were not high-performance cars.

With a 144.4-cubic-inch six, a one-barrel carburetor, and a 3.10:1 rear axle ratio, the Comet was promoted as a car that could go as far as possible on each gallon of gasoline. "The new Thrift Power Six delivers up to 28 mpg of regular gas," said one advertisement. "You'll save with every tankful." However, as Jim Whipple noted, "This engine is smooth and well-balanced, and, in the Falcon, more economical than any other compact — with the possible exception of the overdrive Lark and Rambler. However, in the Comet, the 140-cubic-inch (sic) six-cylinder engine with the same 8.7 to 1 compression ratio just doesn't have the moxie to haul the mail."

The Comet was 14 inches longer than the Falcon, with the extra inches devoted to more trunk room. However, due to a sloping trunk lid, the Merc actually had only 2.1 more cubic feet of trunk space than the Ford. The Comet's advantage was in styling. It did have a design relationship to the big Mercury, the Lincoln and the Thunderbird, which made it seem like a great value. Its longer rear springs also contributed to a more comfortable ride. "From a handling and roadability standpoint," said Jim Whipple, "The Comet is more than acceptably good." Whipple did not, however, like the slow 27-to-1 ratio recirculating ball gear steering. He noted that the car's unit-body frame structure made it quiet-riding and rattle-proof. The suspension blotted up vibrations fairly well, but there was some sense of excessive brake dive. Whipple mentioned this, but added that it was, "within today's acceptable limits." In general, other than its low performance, Whipple liked the compact Mercury.

As mentioned earlier, it was a good model-year for Mercury. General sales manager C.E. Bowie did an especially good job finding buyers for the new Comet. Increased showroom traffic also lifted Mercury's production and sales totals. Model-year production rose to 155,000 units (up from 150,000), but gave Mercury a slightly lower 2.6 percent market share. In all, 271,331 cars were produced. This figure included 116,331 Comets; 102,539 Montereys; 19,814 Montclairs; 10,287 Park Lanes; and 22,360 Station Wagons. Mercury zoomed up to fifth spot in American car sales.

1960 MERCURY FEATURE FACTS AND SPECIFICATIONS

STANDARD EQUIPMENT ON ALL 1960 MERCURYS

- Self-Adjusting Brakes • Directional Signals • Back-Up Lights • Safety Steering Wheel
- Padded Garnish Mouldings • 3-Speed Electric Wipers • Safety Glass in Every Window
- Foam Front-Seat Cushion • Disposable Carburetor Air Cleaner • Disposable Fuel Filter
- Full-Flow Oil Filter • 8.00 x 14 or 8.50 x 14 Tyrex Cord Tires • Dual Fender Ornaments
- Aluminized Muffler • Teflon Bearings in Ball-Joint Front Suspension • Super-Enamel

MAJOR SPECIFICATIONS (4-Door Hardtop Models)

Over-all Dimensions

Wheelbase	126.0″
Wheel tread, front and rear	60.0″
Over-all length	219.2″
Over-all width	81.5″
Over-all height (design load)	55.8″/56.1″

Trunk Compartment

Capacity with spare tire	31.5 cu. ft.
Capacity without spare tire	34.5 cu. ft.

Passenger Space

Front head room*	38.5″
Rear head room*	37.1″
Front leg room*	46.2″
Rear leg room*	43.0″
Front hip room	62.5″
Rear hip room	62.8″
Front shoulder room	60.5″
Rear shoulder room	60.8″

*Effective Dimension

1960 MERCURY ENGINE-TRANSMISSION COMBINATIONS

Series	Displacement Bore & Stroke	Horsepower Torque	Compression Ratio	Transmission
MONTEREY & COMMUTER	312 cu in. 3.8″ x 3.44″	205-hp 328 ft-lbs	8.9 to 1	3-speed manual Merc-O-Matic†
MONTEREY & COMMUTER (Opt.)	383 cu in. 4.30″ x 3.30″	280-hp 405 ft-lbs	8.5 to 1	Merc-O-Matic† Multi-Drive†
MONTCLAIR & COLONY PARK	430 cu in. 4.30″ x 3.70″	310-hp 460 ft-lbs	10.0 to 1	Merc-O-Matic Multi-Drive†
PARK LANE	430 cu in. 4.30″ x 3.70″	310-hp 460 ft-lbs	10.0 to 1	Multi-Drive

†Optional at extra cost

BODY FEATURES: Rigidized body construction—with double-panel hood, deck lid and doors. Compound windshield. Safety-Sweep windshield wipers. Cross-flow ventilation. Safety steering wheel. **Exterior finish**—baked Super-Enamel in 15 colors; 36 two-tones.

POWER TRAIN: Overhead valve V-8 engines in three sizes. 12-volt electrical system. Combination vacuum-centrifugal spark control. Full-pressure lubrication. Gas-saving 2-bbl carburetors. Self-cleaning 18mm spark plugs. The 383- and 430-cu in. engines have in-block combustion chambers; 3-stage cooling; water-jacketed intake manifold; hydraulic valve lifters; step-top pistons. **Merc-O-Matic:** Combination of fluid torque converter and 3-speed planetary gear set. 5-position selector lever. Multi-Drive Merc-O-Matic with 6-position selector lever and dual drive ranges. **Conventional transmission:** Selective gear type with 3 forward speeds. High-economy rear axles with 2.71 to 1 or 2.91 to 1 ratios with 383- or 430-cu in. engines.

CHASSIS FEATURES: Ladder-type frame — with bowed box-girder side-rails. X-type center reinforcement for convertible frame. Front suspension: Swept-back ball-joint design with anti-dive. Helical-coil springs. Full-cushion shock aborbers. Link-type front torsion-bar stabilizer. Steering: Ball and rack-type with 54 recirculating balls. Over-all steering ratios—29.1 to 1 for Monterey and Commuter; 31.1 to 1 for Montclair and Colony Park; 20.5 to 1 with power steering. Rear Suspension: Splay-mounted leaf-type rear springs—60″ long, 6-leave springs, except station wagons (7). Compression-type rear spring shackles. Hotchkiss drive. Self-adjusting Brakes: 11-inch brake drums with full-circle ribs for extra cooling. Brake width 3″ (f), 2½″ (r). Total lining area—233.1 sq in.

MAJOR OPTIONS: Air-blending heater-defroster; combination air conditioner-heater with Climate Dial Control; independent air conditioner; power steering; power brakes; 4-way power seat; power window lifts; transistorized radio; belt-driven windshield washer; trunk compartment lock release; tinted windshield and windows; padded instrument panel; floor-anchored safety belts.

(Merc-O-Matic transmission and padded instrument panel standard for Montclair and Colony Park Models. Merc-O-Matic, power brakes, windshield washer, padded panel and Multi-Drive Merc-O-Matic standard for Park Lane Series.)

Mercury Division of Ford Motor Company, Dearborn, Michigan reserves the right to discontinue or change, at any time, specifications or design without incurring any obligation.

QUALITY HEADQUARTERS ...YOUR MERCURY DEALER'S

DON'T BUY ANY CAR UNTIL YOU'VE DRIVEN THE ROAD-TUNED 1960 MERCURY

The 1960 Mercury specifications described a large, heavy, powerful car with a wide array of standard equipment features. The engines available this year were all V-8s of 312-, 383- and 430-cubic-inches. (Mercury)

HERE'S WHAT'S IN COMET FOR YOU!

WHEELBASE
SEDAN........................114.0"
STATION WAGON...........109.5"

OVER-ALL LENGTH
SEDAN........................194.9"
STATION WAGON...........191.8"

TREAD
FRONT........................ 55.0"
REAR......................... 54.5"

OVER-ALL HEIGHT
SEDAN........................ 54.5"
STATION WAGON........... 55.1"

CHASSIS
UNITIZED BODY: Extra strong, extra solid with zinc-coated underbody box-section members.

FRONT SUSPENSION: Ball-joint front suspension with anti-dive feature. Coil front springs. Internally mounted hydraulic shock absorbers.

REAR SUSPENSION: Alloy steel, leaf-type rear springs for greater stability. Hotchkiss Drive. Direct-acting, angle-mounted hydraulic shock absorbers.

STEERING: Recirculating ball-and-nut type steering gear. Over-all steering ratio: 27.0:1.

BRAKES: Hydraulic, internal-expanding type. Total brake lining area: 114.3 square inches (station wagons: 137.2). Brake drum diameter: 9 inches.

PARKING BRAKE: Independent mechanical; operating on the rear wheels. Brake application and release controlled by handle located beneath the instrument panel, to the left of the steering wheel.

WHEELS AND TIRES: Stamped steel disc wheels. 13-inch diameter. Tire size: 6.00 x 13, 4-ply rating except station wagons which are 6.50 x 13, 4-ply rating. White sidewall tires optional at extra cost on all models.

POWER PLANT
THRIFT-POWER 6: High-economy, inline 6-cylinder block. Overhead valves. Displacement: 144.3 cubic inches; horsepower: 90 @ 4200 rpm; maximum torque: 138 @ 2000 rpm; compression ratio: 8.7:1; recommended fuel: regular grade.

ENGINE LUBRICATION: Full-pressure lubrication system. Rotor-type oil pump with nonfloating screened inlet. Oil capacity (with filter change): 4.5 quarts.

ENGINE COOLING: Downflow, pressurized radiator. Full-length water jackets around all cylinders. Capacity without heater: 8.7 quarts; capacity with heater: 9.7 quarts.

FUEL SYSTEM: Carburetor: 1 venturi, downdraft type. Mechanical diaphragm fuel pump with vacuum-booster feature as standard equipment. Dry-type air cleaner with replaceable element. Fuel filter locations: fuel tank; fuel line between pump and carburetor. Fuel tank capacity: 14 gallons.

ELECTRICAL: 12-volt system, 54-plate battery. Centrifugal vacuum spark control. Positive engagement starter. 18mm anti-fouling spark plugs.

TRANSMISSIONS AND REAR AXLE
COMET DRIVE AUTOMATIC TRANSMISSION: 5 position selector lever. Selector positions: P(Park), R(Reverse), N(Neutral), D(Drive), L(Low). Fully automatic air-cooled fluid torque converter with 2-speed planetary gearset. Air cooled. Oil capacity (refill): 7.25 quarts.

THREE-SPEED MANUAL SHIFT TRANSMISSION: Selective gear type with three forward speeds. Gear ratios: First gear: 3.29:1; Second gear: 1.75:1; Third gear: 1.00:1; Reverse gear: 4.46:1. Oil capacity: 3¼ pints.

CLUTCH: Semi-floating, single dry-plate type. Outside diameter: 8½ inches.

REAR AXLE: Semi-floating type with hypoid gears. Two-pinion differential, tapered roller bearings. All axle ratios have been carefully selected to provide maximum economy and peak performance under all driving conditions.

"Here's what's in Comet for you!" said a chart listing the dimensions, chassis features, power plant offerings and drive train options for the new 1960 Comets. (Mercury)

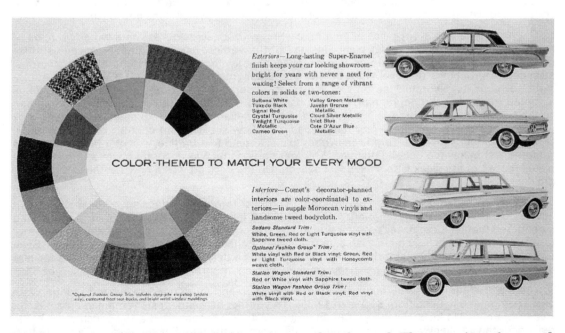

Inside and outside, the 1960 Comets were color-themed. The exteriors featured long-lasting "Super Enamel" finish with a choice of 11 colors. The decorator-planned interiors were color-coordinated. (Mercury)

125

All that glitters 1961-1965

The 1961 Mercurys and Comets were introduced on October 6, 1960. The Comet was mostly unchanged, but air conditioning was added to the options list. The Mercurys had substantial refinements for a new venture into the low-priced automobile market. Shorter by four-and-one-half inches, and narrower by one-and-one-half-inch, the 1961 model offered a Ford-like body with more headroom, a wider rear seat, and more trunk space, despite its smaller exterior. As the year began, industry observers were predicting another banner year for the Comet and keener competition for the Mercury, in its new market niche.

A new rust-proof aluminum grille, the addition of three vertical chrome "hash marks" to the front fenders, and emblems on the roof pillars were the main styling differences between 1961 Comets and the previous year's models.

This Eastlack Mercury postcard dates from 1961. In the early 1960s, about 2,500 dealers sold Mercurys. (Jay Katelle)

Engineering-wise, the compact sold by Mercury dealers (the Comet still did not have Mercury model identification) got a much-needed engine option. Also, some drive train upgrades were added to go with the new motor, and an improved suspension system was introduced.

The new grille was a one-piece aluminum casting with a new texture. There were five rows of horizontal bars arranged in a flat plane, instead of the vertical bars and double-concave surface used in 1960. The dual headlamps were moved slightly forward. The front fender chevrons, arranged in groupings of three, were behind the headlights on the body sides. Chrome "bomb-sight" ornaments decorated the tops of the front fenders. On the sides, bright metal moldings accented the body belt line, running straight back from the fender tips to behind the doors, then curving upwards to trace the tailfin contours. Canted taillamps with a "Siamese cat's-eye" look were another styling trait. Each rear fender had a shallow scooped-out contour on its side and a chrome "Comet" signature. On the rear body panel's main feature line, a center-fill gas cap was centered just below the deck lid opening. The rear body panel was decorated with a Comet name-plate, instead of the block letters used last season. On the deck lid was a new handle with an integral lock.

Mercury considered Comet a "family-sized" compact. *Motor Trend* called it "over-sized," but gave a positive ring to the description. Ads bragged that it had a "spirited sense of proportion" and highlighted that the Comet was roomier and longer than its competitors. "Overall, the Comet story for the coming year is little more than a variation on the theme for 1960," said *Motor Trend*. "Such a development is hardly a surprise, considering the basic design has been in production for less than a year. The existing styling has been credited with an important share of the car's success."

There were four models in the base Comet series, two-and four-door Sedans and Station Wagons. They ranged in price from $1,998 to $2,353. The Comet passenger cars remained on an exclusive-to-Mercury 114-inch wheelbase. Comet Station Wagons, though, had a 109.5-inch stance. The reason for the smaller wagon is that it was the same size as the Ford Falcon Station Wagon. In fact, at the rear, the Comet Station Wagon had Falcon styling. The body sides had straight-line sculpturing with a straight, full-length upper belt molding. The wagon's taillamps were larger, and wedge-shaped, with chrome divider moldings on the lenses. The tailgate had double moldings that

126

See the new COMET S-22...and

"The niftiest interior under the smartest roof in the compact field," described the 1961 Comet S-22. In 1960 and 1961, the Comet was not officially a "Mercury." (Mercury)

with the taillamp moldings. The name "Comet," in large, block letters, was spelled out in the center of the tailgate.

With 76 cubic feet of cargo-carrying space inside the Falcon-sized Station Wagon body, FoMoCo saw no marketing need to tool up different sheet metal for the Comet series. When *Motor Trend* compared compact wagons in June 1961, it agreed. "Outside measurements have little to do with the basic purpose of a station wagon, and the most important question is how good is overall design," said the magazine. "In this category, both the Falcon and Comet score high; in fact, no other compact wagon can quite equal them for practical or utilitarian purposes."

Inside, too, Comets had just a few minor changes. The dome lamp was relocated from just above the windshield to the center of the roof. A new emblem highlighted the glove box door. New standard and optional trim fabrics were offered to better harmonize with revised exterior colors. Three deluxe cloth trims (black; blue and green) were offered in combination with white. Another deluxe two-tone cloth trim was red-and-black. Solid red, in combination with a red and gray cloth, was one of the standard two-tones. In addition, three colors (white, blue or green) could be had in combination with a blue-green cloth standard trim. The same eight trim options were offered in vinyl, plus additional deluxe two-tones of red-and-white and black-and-white. Overall lengths were 191.8 inches for wagons and 194.8 inches for passenger cars. The cars used their extra length to provide Mercury buyers with a 28 cubic-foot trunk, which had exceptional sales appeal. The unit-body had a zinc coating applied to minimize corrosion.

A new S-22 coupe was introduced, as a midyear addition, during the 1961 New York Automobile Show. Apparently, the alpha-numerical designation had no significant meaning. The S-22 was a dressed-up Comet two-door Sedan with a $2,282 price tag. It was designed to cash-in on the growing popularity of sporty compacts. Standard features included T-bird-style contoured front bucket seats that were lifted from Ford's Falcon Futura. The bucket seat-backs folded flat forward and had a convenient, manually adjustable seat-back angle. There was a storage console, also pirated from the Futura, between the seats. It had a ribbed, diecast metal top and a plastic liner. The lid popped up when a button was pressed. *Motor Life* called it a "central glove compartment," saying. "It can't really be called a console," because of its short size. Mercury called it a console, though.

Comet S-22s also had a full-width, foam-padded rear seat. The rear seat upholstery was pleated in a fashion that gave a bucket seat-like look to it. Special carpeting and side panel trim were used. The steering wheel had a sports car appearance, with vinyl hand grips, but the instrument panel was the same as in other Comets. Standard equipment included chrome wheel discs; color-coordinated deep-loop yarn carpeting; front and rear armrests; a custom horn-ring steering wheel; and rear roof pillar badges. Compass-style rear fender medallions were placed just ahead of the "Comet" signatures, about 50 pounds of extra insulation were used inside, and the S-22s had factory applied undercoating. White sidewall tires were standard, too.

Base engine in all Comets was again a 144.3-cubic-inch six with 85 hp. It had an 8.7:1 compression ratio and a one-barrel carburetor. The larger, new optional power plant was a 170-cubic-inch six that was essentially an enlarged version of the "144." Both had the same 3.5-inch bore, but the "170's" stroke grew, from the smaller engine's 2.5 inches up to 2.94 inches. This change was accomplished with a new "long throw" crankshaft, shorter connecting rods and special lightweight pistons. To maintain the 8.7:1 compression ratio, the pistons had a lower compression height and the cylinder head's shape was modified. Though only two percent heavier than the base six, the new engine was 18 percent larger.

Several engine and drive train components had to be modified to tolerate the big six's higher horsepower and torque ratings. A larger 15-inch fan and a heavier-duty radiator were used. The manual transmission was beefed-up. It also had a larger one-barrel carburetor, intake manifold, and intake valves, plus a recalibrated distributor. The bigger engine was supposed to be 11 percent faster in passing acceleration and 22 percent better at climbing hills. Mercury said that the 101-hp Comet could pass a car doing 50 mph in 11.7 seconds, opposed to 13 seconds with the 85-hp engine. Accelerating from 35 mph to 60 mph was claimed to take 8.7 seconds with the "big six," a 3.2-second (27 percent) improvement.

Three-speed manual transmission was standard. A two-speed Merc-O-Matic was optional. This transmission used a single-stage, three-element converter with a two-speed planetary gear train. With the gear-shift selector in drive, the 1-2 shift took place at 10 to 15 mph. The transmission automatically down-shifted to low between five and 15 mph with a closed throttle. It was interesting that the two-speed automatic was labeled a "Merc-O-Matic," although the Comet was, technically, not a "Mercury" this year. "Comet-O-Matic" just didn't come off the tongue as easily. Cars with the two-speed Merc-O-Matic got a water-cooling system for the transmission.

A heavier ring-and-pinion gear was also installed in the rear axle. Other technical upgrades involved giving the Comet the Ford Falcon's front coil springs and semi-elliptic rear springs. Also, Comets had "permanent" lubrication, with a pre-lubricated, threaded metal bushing in each front upper A-arm. This replaced a rubber bushing and slowed front suspension rebound action, giving the cars a less jarring ride. Rear spring rates had to be lowered a bit and a thinner stabilizer bar was used.

Motor Life magazine tried out a 1961 Comet S-22 with the 170-cubic-inch, 101 hp engine and two-speed Merc-O-Matic, and concluded that it "bogs down in performance." The car needed 22 seconds to go from 0-to-60 mph and an additional 1.6 seconds to cover the quarter-mile, with a 62 mph terminal speed. However, the car did provide 16 mpg in around-town driving and 20-plus mpg out on the highway.

The Mercury for 1961 was smaller, lower-priced and offered an optional six-cylinder engine. It was the first six ever offered in a Mercury, since the Comet was not officially a Mercury until 1962. Cars in the base series and one-step-up series were called Meteor 600s and Meteor 800s, while top-of-the-line cars used the Monterey name. Many people associate the Meteor name with the new-for-1962 mid-size Mercury Meteor. However, the 1961 edition was a full-size car. The Monterey name, of course, had a "full-size" connotation. It had appeared on a variety of different type Mercurys since 1950. The one thing they had in common was their large size. While the first Monterey had been a Lincoln-like Mercury, this new one was more like a Ford. It shared its 120-inch wheelbase, 214.6-inch overall length (214.8 inches for Station Wagons) and width of 79.9 inches with the 1961 Meteor. Both cars were 4.6 inches shorter than 1960 Mercury models. At a mere 55 inches high, they were built much closer to the ground than the "Low Silhouette" models of the middle 1950s.

These down-sized cars marked a complete change in Mercury's game plan ... a move away from the huge cars of 1957 to 1960. This about-face was not due to a wild mood swing by Mercury's management. There were market factors and corporate influences that dictated using the smaller "Ford" platform for the Mercury. Outside influences were the same ones that inspired GM and Chrysler to shrink their early 1960s models. The Dodge Dart started this trend and many other cars followed. It takes three or more years to design an automobile, and the 1961 models were designed around 1958, when the public wanted smaller, more economical cars. When work started on these cars, smaller seemed like the way to go. Unfortunately, the public's taste swung back to big cars by the time the smaller ones hit the showrooms. The 1961 Meteors and Montereys were not a huge success.

Within the Ford "family" of cars, the 1957 to 1959 Mercurys had been moved to a higher market niche, to keep them from competing with Edsels. Now, with the Edsel gone, FoMoCo had a gap to fill further down the market. The smaller new Mercurys, with their lower price tags, were targeted to fill this niche. "Granted, the Merc will lose some of its large proportions," predicted *Motor Trend's* September 1960 issue. "But, it will remain a car with a distinct personality. Based on the Ford shell, it will have many styling features of past Mercurys and, surprisingly, Lincolns. Most of the Ford engine options will be available, including the high performance 'police' special."

Meteors had a full-width, concave grille with thin, segmented vertical bars. The center grille section was stamped from heavy gauge sheet metal, while the outer section was made of diecast metal. The front end was dominated by a large, simple bumper that incorporated rectangular parking lights at its outer ends. The lip of the plain, rounded hood was slightly "veed" towards the center of the car. It was trimmed with a center ornament. Four circular, chromed headlight rims were mounted horizontally, with wide spacing between each pair. The front fenders looked massive, but not aggressive. There was a crisp, squared-off roof line, patterned after the "T-bird look." Short, outward-canted tailfins characterized the rear of the cars, which had many styling traits of late-1950s Lincoln-Continentals. Oval taillights, with three protruding circular lenses, were set well out in an oval-shaped rear "beauty panel." This panel resembled a grille at the rear of the car.

"The Mercury has gained in stature as it shrunk in size," *Motor Trend's* December 1960 styling analysis editorialized. "The new Ford-based version is notably improved in styling.

The 1961 Meteor 800 two-door Hardtop came with all the bright metal accents seen here. (Mercury)

Perhaps this is because the new package is better within the grasp of Mercury stylists; in any case they have done a good job for 1961." Another observer noted that styling devices used on the 1961 Mercurys had been seen before at Ford Motor Company. "On the four-door Hardtop models, the rear doors have the chrome triangle that the 1959 Ford four-door Hardtops had," he noted. "At the rear, you have to look twice to see if it is a 1961 Mercury or a 1958 Continental, as they both have about the same taillights and the same fin treatment. Station Wagons have taillights like those of the 1960 Comet Station Wagon."

Meteor 600s had chrome body side moldings running from behind the front wheel openings to the rear fenders. There was a decorative ornament on top of each front fender. Sedans in this series featured thin roof lines with sloping, compound-curve "fastback" rear windows. This base Meteor line included a two-door Sedan and a four-door Sedan priced at $2,533 and $2,587 respectively.

Cars in the slightly upscale Meteor 800 series had three horizontal chrome bars on their front fenders, bright rocker panel accents, chrome tailfin tips, and more trim on the roof rear quarters. The hood lip had a chrome molding that extended around the body corners. It ran down the fenders, and onto the door, before ending. Back-up lights and an electric clock were part of the standard equipment. The Meteor 800s also had a flat rear window, similar to the 1960 Lincoln's. There were four Meteor 800 models. Both Sedans and Hardtops came in two- and four-door models. Prices ranged from $2,711 to $2,837.

Mercury's top-of-the-line offering was the Monterey series. These cars could be identified by their chrome rear fender stone guards and full-length body side moldings. This molding incorporated something new. It was a rubber cushion that protected the metal molding against parking lot door "dings." The Monterey series consisted of a four-door Sedan, two-and four-door Hardtops and a Convertible. They were priced between $2,869 and $3,126.

Mercury also marketed four-door Commuter and Colony Park Station Wagons. The Commuter, priced at $2,922, looked like a Meteor. The Colony Park had imitation wood-grain trim and a power tailgate window. It shared the same standard features as the Monterey.

Inside, the Mercurys had a new cowl and dashboard. The crash pad was no longer deeply recessed away from the passengers in front. As a result, the cars offered more under-dash leg room and deeper glove compartments. The steering wheel had a spoke-less upper section, making the wide, sweep-hand speedometer easier to read.

Lincoln-Mercury Division offered 25 solid paint colors in 1961. Mercurys came with a choice of 10 cloth upholstery options. Solid trim colors included blue, gold, turquoise and green. Two-tones were white-and-black, turquoise-and-brown and blue with either turquoise or a gray-white blend. There were 17 different vinyl options, six in solid colors and the rest in two-tones.

The new six (the first six ever offered in a big Mercury) was a 223-cubic-inch inline engine with 8.4:1 compression, a one-barrel carburetor, and 135 hp. Standard in Montereys and available at

This Meteor "800" two-door Hardtop offered a 12,000-mile/12-month "extended" warranty. (Mercury)

extra cost for other Mercs, was a 292-cubic-inch 175-hp V-8 with a two-barrel carburetor, an 8.8:1 compression ratio, and solid valve lifters. Also optional in all models was a 352-cubic-inch 220-hp V-8 with hydraulic lifters and a two-barrel carburetor. In addition, a 390-cubic-inch V-8 with a 9.6:1 compression ratio; four-barrel carburetor; dual valve springs; and dish-dome "slipper" type pistons, was available for all models except Meteor 600s. This motor had 300 advertised horsepower and 220 net horsepower. This was enough to move a Merc along at a 113 mph top speed.

The powerful "390" was Ford's "Police Interceptor" engine. It was derived from the "352." Late in the year, this big-block engine was offered in a 330-hp edition, with a single four-barrel carburetor. It also came in a 375-hp version, with three two-barrels. However, these were options only in Meteors, which meant they were intended for racing. In a move that revealed growing environmental concerns, Mercury made an "Emission Reduction System" standard on "390" engines and optional on other power plants. It was basically a positive crankcase ventilation system that piped unburned combustion gases back to the intake manifold. They were then re-introduced into the combustion chamber and burned more completely.

Transmissions offered in 1961 Mercury Meteors and Montereys included three-speed manual; two- or three-speed Merc-O-Matic; and Multi-Range Merc-O-Matic.

The frame, though changed in size to match the new wheelbase, was similar to the 1960 design, with bowed-out, box-sectional construction. The full-size 1961 Mercurys had Ford's new 30,000-mile chassis lubrication system. The suspension ball-joints and the steering linkage were pre-lubricated and sealed. However, grease could be added, via a sealed recess that accepted a regular lube fitting, whenever needed. The new suspension layout used coil springs and unequal control arms up front and semi-elliptic rear leaf springs. Rubber torsioners were added at critical pivot points. Shackles, instead of bushings, were used to attach the front lower suspension arms. Both ends of the rear springs were also shackled. This permitted the wheels to "move" over road obstructions.

In March 1961, *Motor Trend* gave two 1961 Mercury four-doors, a Sedan and a Hardtop, one of its "Full-Range" road tests. Under the hood of the second car was a 292-cubic-inch V-8. The Sedan had a 390-cubic-inch 300 hp big-block. Both had Multi-Range Merc-O-Matic transmissions and 3.00:1 rear axle ratios. The smaller engine took the Hardtop from 0-to-60 mph in 14.5 seconds. It gave 12 to 16 mpg in normal driving and up to 18 mpg on the highway. Car number two did 0-to-60 mph in 10.2 seconds and averaged 10 to 14 mpg around town. The "390" was also noticeably noisier.

During the test, the new suspension helped deliver a smooth, quiet ride. The extra wheel movement did not adversely affect handling, either. There was acceptable body sway, but the quick steering (3.9 turns lock-to-lock) was not precise. Tight turns were easy to negotiate, however, and all handling aspects were improved from 1960. Overall, *Motor Trend* liked just about everything Mercury offered. The magazine praised the clearly marked power window controls, the blinking "parking-brake-on" lamp, and the soundness of the overall design. However, the 16-cubic-foot trunk was criticized as "poorly designed" because it was too shallow.

Mercury competed in the 1961 Mobilgas Economy Run. It covered 2,500 miles from Los Angeles, California to Chicago, Illinois. Two Comets placed fourth and fifth in the class for compacts with manual transmission, averaging 28.64 and 27.83 mpg, respectively. A Falcon took the class with 32.68 mpg. Comets placed seventh and eighth in the automatic transmission compact car class with 26.06 and 25.82 mpg averages. A Corvair Monza won with 29.35 mpg. Larger Mercurys placed in three other categories. A Meteor was third in the class for sixes with automatic transmission. It managed 22.56 mpg. Another Meteor was fifth in the class for low-priced V-8s with automatics. It went 20.85 miles per gallon of gas. In the medium-priced V-8 with automatic class, an 18.43-mpg Monterey was eighth.

There was some shuffling of personalities in the Lincoln-Mercury Division during 1961. Chase Morsey, Jr. replaced Walker A. Williams as assistant to general manager Ben D. Mills. C.R. Paulson became public relations manager early in the year. Blaine Cook took over as manager of marketing research. Jack Dekker was the new programming department manager.

The Comet made 1961 a good year, with model-year production of 197,263 units. This included 78,100 standard Comets, 92,800 with the deluxe trim kit or S-22 option, and 26,300 Station Wagons. The compact now accounted for 54.6 percent of Lincoln-Mercury's calendar year sales. Production of 120,088 Mercurys brought the grand total to 317,351 cars. The 120,088 included 18,117 Meteor 600 models; 35,005 Meteor 800 models; 50,128 Montereys; and 16,838 Station Wagons.

The 1962 Comets and Mercurys were introduced on September 21, 1961. The Comet had significant rear end styling changes and a new aluminum grille. It officially became a Mercury. There was "Mercury" lettering on the hood lip and other locations. The new grille had a slotted outline around distinct, vertical bars. Quad headlamps were mounted in individual, round bezels. The sides of the fenders had chrome "Comet" signatures. Cars with custom trim had bar-like badges below the chrome signatures.

Mercury's 1961 Monterey line offered a Convertible for $3,126. (Lowell E. Eisenhour)

Chrome "bombsight" ornaments still decorated the front fenders. The front bumper was of simple design, with rectangular parking lamps at its far outer ends. In the center, the bumper face bar flared up above the license plate indentation. The 1962 wheelcovers had concentric rings around their outer edges and a smooth, pointed center. Body side trim consisted of a molding that traced the shape of the upper feature line from front to rear, widening slightly as it neared the taillamps.

The canted-fins-and-cat's-eyes rear end treatment was discontinued. In its place, on passenger cars, were smaller, Ford-like tailfins and separate taillamps. The rear deck was higher, flatter, and squared-off. The deck lid was wider and deeper, for easier access. Four taillamps were standard on regular models and six on S-22s. Half of the lenses were placed on each side of the car, in a sunken rear body panel with rounded upper corners. On S-22s, the standard white back-up lenses were positioned in the center of the two red taillamp lenses. If back-up lights were ordered for other Comets, the white lenses were mounted towards the center of the car, with the red lenses in the outer two positions. A chrome molding traced the side and upper feature lines of the rear body panel. In the center of the panel was a round gas filler cap. The rear bumper was a simple, straight unit, with a center license plate indentation.

Station wagons had no tailfins. The upper portion of each rear fender was rounded-over to meet the body side feature lines. The curved chrome trim at the back of the feature lines intersected a straight molding running across the tailgate. On Custom models, this was a double-wide molding. The tailgate had a circular lock and ornament in its center and a "Mercury" script on the upper right-hand side. For tail lighting, the Station Wagon had small chrome ovals housing two round lenses. Wagons without back-up lights got two red lenses on each side. If back-up lights were ordered, the white lens replaced the red inner lens.

The standard equipment list for Comets now read: tubeless tires; front armrests; dual sun visors; oil filter; front foam seat cushions; heater and defroster; turn signals; fuel filter; dual horns; and factory undercoating. Comet Customs had all of this, plus a Convenience Group; contoured front bucket seats; carpets; a glove compartment lock; and deluxe upholstery. The Comet series offered a total of nine models at the start of the year and 11 by year's end. However, there were only four body styles. The two- and four-door Sedans, plus the two-and four-door Station Wagons, all came in the Comet series ($2,084 to $2,439) and Comet Custom series ($2,171 to $2,526). The ninth model was the S-22 two-door Sedan with bucket seats and a console. It was priced at $2,368, which also included all-vinyl upholstery; back-up lights;

The 1962 Comet Custom Hardtop's 29.8-cubic-foot trunk held six extra grocery bags. (Mercury)

The 1962 Mercury Meteor had a new grille. (Lowell E. Eisenhour)

rear foam seat cushions; and white sidewall tires. The midyear additions were both fancy four-door "Villager" Station Wagons. One Villager had bucket seats, and both had simulated wood trim.

Exterior paint colors for 1962 Comets, Meteors and Mercurys were Presidential Black; Ocean Turquoise Metallic; Pacific Blue Metallic; Sea Blue; Blue Satin Metallic; Castilian Red; Sultana White; Scotch Green; Sheffield Gray Metallic; Jamaica Yellow; Champagne; Chestnut; Black Cherry Metallic; and Desert Frost Metallic.

Comets had a restyled instrument cluster. The Convenience Group package included matching chrome-and-white finish for the steering wheel, turn signal switch, shift lever, and door hardware; a bright horn ring; rear seat armrests and ashtrays; automatic dome light switches; and a cigarette lighter. Custom interiors had bright trim moldings; carpeting; upgraded pleated upholstery; contoured front seat backs; and a locking glove box. The five cloth interior trims came in beige, blue and turquoise solid colors and two-tones of white-and-black or red-and-black. Besides the same five choices in simulated leather, the 12 vinyl trim options included black, and red solids; different beiges, blues and turquoises, plus a distinctive white-and-red two-tone and a second black-and-white combination.

The 1962 Comet engine options were exactly the same as in 1961, with the most minor changes in specifications. There was a new 30,000-mile fuel filter with a replaceable element and a new oil filter good for 6,000 miles between service calls. The crankshaft and main bearings were improved and Mercury claimed the engines were quieter. This was said to be due to an improved rear engine mounting. It consisted of a small three-leaf spring, a dual rubber insulator, and a special bracket to attach it to the frame of the car.

The Comet again featured unitized construction with a 114-inch wheelbase and 194.8-inch overall length. The front tread was 55 inches and the rear tread was 54.5 inches. The S-22 tipped the scales at 2,711 pounds. The front independent suspension had a single lower arm, coil springs, a stabilizer bar and direct-acting shock absorbers. Five-leaf semi-elliptic springs were used at the rear, in conjunction with a rigid axle and direct-acting shock absorbers. Steering was by way of recirculating ball-and-nut, with a 39.9-foot turning diameter and 4.64 turns lock-to-lock. The Comet's chassis did not include a 30,000 mile lubrication system. The dual-servo, self-adjusting hydraulic brakes had an effective lining area of 114.3 square inches. The brake cylinders were improved, with baffles, to eliminate "clunking" noises.

In its May 1962 test of three Mercurys, *Motor Trend* included a Comet S-22 Coupe with the "big six," automatic, an optional 4.09:1 ratio rear axle, and air conditioning. The car went from 0-to-60 mph in 22.2 seconds. The quarter-mile took 24.1 seconds at 61 mph. The car got 15.7 to 16.3 mpg in combined city/highway use, averaging 16.2 mpg for 1,000 miles under all conditions. The magazine found the car grossly under-powered, and criticized its lack of rear seat roominess and its large 17-inch steering wheel (for cramping the driver.) However, the Comet was recognized as a well-built vehicle. "Performance is not, and never has been, synonymous with quality," said technical editor Jim Wright.

Must reading for Comet restorers and collectors should include an article that ran in the July 1962 edition of *Mechanix Illustrated*. Written by Frederick C. Russell, a member of the Society of Automotive Engineers, it was titled, "Car Care: Your New Comet." The 4-1/2-page long article gave a very detailed, illustrated account of the 1962 Comet's technical features and carefully outlined the maintenance requirements that pertained to cars driven in differently. It gave a very common sense description of how to take great care of a 1962 Mercury Comet.

Extras (and their retail prices) for 1962 Comets were listed as: Air conditioning ($270.90); Convenience Group ($25.80); "big six" ($45.10); back-up lights ($10.70); Station Wagon luggage rack ($39); padded instrument panel ($16.40); padded sun visors ($4.50); two-tone paint ($19.40); push-button radio ($58.80); smog reduction system ($5.70); electric power tailgate window ($29.75); tinted glass ($30.90); tinted windshield ($12.95); two-speed Merc-O-Matic ($171.70); wheel discs ($16); windshield washers ($13.70); and two-speed electric windshield wipers ($9.65)

"This neat little performer is designed to fill the gap between the Comet and the Mercury," Tom McCahill wrote of the Mercury Meteor in the June 1962 issue of *Mechanix Illustrated*. This car was the last of the '62s to make its debut. Based on the Ford Fairlane, which had arrived a bit earlier, the new Meteor's styling made it pretty clear what the car represented. It had a one-inch longer wheelbase than the Fairlane. In the front, it resembled the Comet. The grille had similar convex, vertical blades, but with a narrow, concave center section running between two full-width horizontal bars. Quad headlamps were set into round bezels, with two on either side of the car. At the rear, the Meteor clearly resembled a full-size Mercury. It had the same kind of protruding taillamps "tunneled" into scoops at the ends of the rear fenders and a Mercury-like rear beauty panel with a vertically textured, full-width trim plate. The roof had a Thunderbird shape to it and a flat rear window.

Mounted on a 116.5-inch wheelbase, the Meteor's unitized body was not exactly small. "This little job (It had an overall length of 203.8 inches and a width of 71.3 inches) was handy and neat," said McCahill. "But, certainly not gaudy." However, by today's standards, the Meteor — at least the fancier editions — had quite a bit of gaudiness. The word "Mercury" was spelled out, in block letters, on the hood lip. The front fender tops had bombsight ornaments. There was a full-length body side molding that drooped slightly at the rear. Chrome

A turn radius of 19-3/4-feet gave the 1962 Mercury Meteor four-door Sedan compact-car handling. (Mercury)

windshield moldings and window frames were seen. The roof rear quarters had horizontally ribbed trim plates. There were three "windsplit" moldings ahead of the rear wheel openings on Customs. Above these, there was a molding that ran towards the rear, widening into a horizontally ribbed, lower rear quarter panel trim plate. "Meteor" was written, low on the front fender, above a bar-like badge. There was also a wide rocker panel molding, and chrome taillamp trim. The full wheel discs were similar to, but not the same as, the Mercury units.

Unit-bodies were costly to tool, so the first Meteor came only as a two- or four-door Sedan. Both featured new, self-centering, double-toggle door latches. Both were available with standard or Custom trim, the Customs constituting their own series. There was also a midyear S-33 two-door Sedan with features comparable to the S-22 Comet. Seven cloth interior options (five solid colors and two two-tones) were offered, plus two vinyl (imitation leather) trims, and six genuine leather trims. "The imitation leather upholstery will undoubtedly prove very serviceable," wrote Tom McCahill. "Though it was as chintzy, in appearance, as knotted shoe strings." Uncle Tom did admit that the seats were comfortable. He also liked that the Coupe's front seats folded forward and across, in one movement, to permit rear passengers to enter. And he raved because the Meteor had a neat dashboard layout and complete gauges, instead of "idiot" lights. This was an exclusive feature among FoMoCo products.

Meteors started the model-year with a choice of the 170-cubic-inch 101-hp "big six" or a new 221-cubic-inch 143-hp engine. This small-block V-8 was tuned for regular gas. It had an 8.5:1 compression ratio and two-barrel carburetor. Its lightweight cast iron block was only 75 pounds heavier than the six. Other features included stud-mounted, ball-joint type rocker arms molded of iron alloy, and a water heat spacer, below the carburetor, to improve the fuel-to-air mixture. *Motor Trend*'s May 1962 issue tested the Meteor Coupe with the "221" V-8, registering 15.2 seconds for 0-to-60 mph and 21.5 seconds (70 mph) for the quarter-mile. Top speed was 95 mph. Gas mileage was in the 11.3 to 14.8 mpg range in combined city and highway driving. In freeway-only use, it went as high as 17.7 mpg, bringing average consumption up to 14.8 mpg. The magazine mentioned that a set-back engine position gave better weight distribution. It also mentioned a soon-to-be-released 260-cubic-inch V-8 option.

The 1962 Comet series offered two- and four-door models in both passenger car and wagon series. (Mercury)

Tom McCahill's Meteor had the "260" V-8. "I'd been touted that this was a real rocket ... so I was anxious to get it out on the speedway (Daytona) where deeds tell a lot more than promotion yaks," he joked. "This test car was as new as tomorrow's fresh eggs and was not what you would call in full-running performance tune. In fact, it was still so stiff that I had to make my high-speed runs one or two laps at a time and then allow time for a cool-off. On the big two-and-a-half mile course I clocked this job on three separate laps at 107.1; 107.4 and 106.8 mph." McCahill also averaged 0-to-60 mph in 10.4 seconds and 0-to-30 in 3.4. "Very fast for a barge of this size," he stressed. "The car, as bare as Yul Brynner's scalp, sells for just over $2,400," McCahill warned his readers. "But my

62 Mercury Monterey

The 1962 Monterey had "candle holder" taillamps and a Lincoln-like rear "grille" with a segmented vertical texture. (Mercury)

test car, which I didn't notice being particularly lush with extras, sells for $3,111." He suggested that the higher price for the larger V-8, a heater, a radio and whitewalls seemed on the high end. "Maybe they counted the roof as an extra," he chided. "Anyhow, that under $2,500 tag is attractive, but the $3,111 deal takes some of the crease out of the pants. But, admittedly, you can buy some so-called compacts with price tags that push hell out of $4,000 when loaded like a Bronx bum at a distillery picnic."

Other than size and V-8 options, specifications for Meteors were very similar to those of Comets. The front and rear suspensions were completely unique among all Ford products. Meteors had the soft-riding, Ford "Cushion-Link" suspension system. A 3.00:1 ratio rear axle was standard with automatic (an optional 3.5:1 axle was installed on *Motor Trend's* test car). Front and rear suspensions were about the same. Steering was of the Comet type, but with a 39.5-foot radius and 4.3 turns lock-to-lock. Brakes were a bit heftier, with 6.2 more square inches of lining area than Comets. The Meteors had a 57-inch front tread and 56-inch rear tread.

Senior Mercurys were again based on the Ford, although the Mercurys had a longer wheelbase. The exterior had considerable face-lifting. The new grille had slender, vertical bars with a convex surface, instead of concave. There were again quad headlamps inside individual round, chrome-plated bezels. The outer bezels resembled shiny cans. A horizontal bar with a crest emblem at its center ran between the inner headlamp bezels. The hood no longer had a "pinched" center section. Instead, there were parallel chrome moldings bordering the top and the bottom. The upper molding had a slight drop in width at its center, with "Mercury" spelled out above the narrowed section in block letters. The molding continued around the front body corners, mating with the body side molding. A plain, massive front bumper with rectangular parking lamps was seen. On all models, except Convertibles, the roof extended further forward than in the past, to shade the front passenger compartment. This resulted in 176 square inches less glass area, with no decrease in forward vision.

Low, wide and slab-sided, but rounded on top of the fenders, the Mercury body looked trim and purposeful. Side trim consisted of a body side molding, extending from the hood molding, and running almost straight back to the door-break line. It then curved slightly downward to intersect a second molding that ran, along the middle of the rear fenders, to the "grille" on the back of the car. One writer described the trim as "resembling the shape of the fenders of '49-'51 Mercs," but it really looked more like a tree branch. The rear grille or beauty panel had multiple groupings of three chrome stripes against a flat black background, with wedge-shaped white plastic back-up light lenses tucked in either end. It was surrounded by a wide, loop-shaped chrome molding, and had a winged crest in its center. The tubular taillamps were blended into "scoops" on the tips of the rear fenders, with chrome trim moldings adding a bright touch.

Monterey and Monterey Custom models both came as two-door Hardtops, four-door Sedans, four-door Hardtops, and four-door Station Wagons (six- or nine-passenger). The Monterey line also offered a two-door Sedan. The Monterey Custom line added a Convertible. Monterey Station Wagons were called Commuters. Monterey Custom Station Wagons had simulated wood-grain side trim. They were called Colony Parks. Monterey sixes were priced from $2,672 to $2,920, while V-8s ran from $2,781 to $3,029. Monterey customs were $2,965 to $3,222. Very late in the year, a Monterey S-55 series was added. It incorporated a two-door Hardtop and a Convertible. The S-55 Convertible with a 406-cubic-inch, 405-hp V-8 (triple carburetion); four-speed manual transmission with floor shift; radio; power windows; electric windshield wipers and washers; seat belts; a 70-ampere battery; a padded dashboard and padded sun visors; a Courtesy Lamp option group; 7.10 x 15 tires; and an outside rear view mirror sold for $4.634.65.

Standard equipment on Monterey sixes, Monterey eights, and Commuter Station Wagons was listed as: 7.50 x 14 tubeless tires (8.00 x 14 for Station Wagons); directional signals; oil filter; armrests; cigarette lighter; fender ornament; fuel filter; carpets; heater and defroster; front courtesy lights; front foam seat cushions; windshield moldings; rear panel moldings; body sill moldings; and rocker panel moldings. Monterey Customs and Colony Parks also had an electric clock; back-up lights; rear courtesy lights; and lower rear quarter panel and drip rail moldings. Colony Park wagons included a power rear tailgate window, and Convertibles featured all-vinyl trim. Mercury offered five cloth trim options (four with solid colors) and 10 vinyl trim options (seven in solid colors).

Other options (and retail prices) for Mercurys included the Courtesy Light Group ($14.80); air conditioning and heater for V-8s only ($360.90); electric clock ($14.60); back-up lights ($10.70); Station Wagon luggage rack ($39); padded instrument panel ($21.30); padded sun visors ($5.80); two-tone paint, except convertible ($22); power brakes ($43.20); power rear window, in Commuters ($32.30); 4-Way power seat ($63.80); power steering ($81.70); Power Transfer rear axle ($38.60); power windows ($102.10); push-button radio ($58.80); Smog Reduction system ($5.70; all tinted glass ($43); tinted windshield ($21.55); Station Wagon third seat ($70.20); Merc-O-Matic, with six-cylinder ($179.80) or with V-8 ($189.60); Multi-Drive Merc-O-Matic ($220.90); trim option ($27.20); full wheel discs ($19.20); windshield washer ($13.70); and two-speed windshield wipers ($7.75)

While many sources show one six-cylinder and three V-8 engines for Mercurys, there were nine possibilities in 1962, although two were for export only. The seven engines available in the United States were: the 223-cubic-inch six with 138 hp at 4200 rpm, 203 pounds-feet of torque at 2200 rpm, 8.4:1 compression and a one-barrel carburetor; the 292-cubic-inch V-8 with 170 hp at 4200 rpm, 279 pounds-feet of torque at 2200 rpm, 8.8:1 compression and a two-barrel carburetor; the 352-cubic-inch V-8 with 220 hp at 4300 rpm, 336 pounds-feet of torque at 2600 rpm, 8.9:1 compression and a

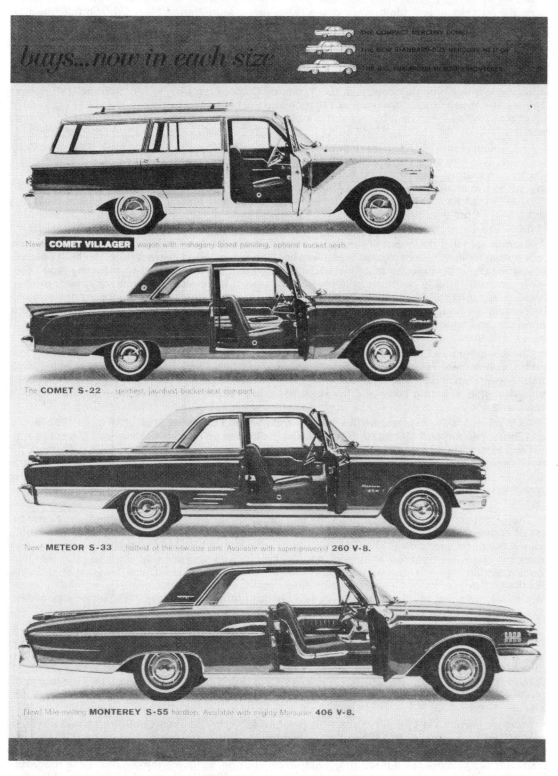

Bucket seats came in these 1962 Mercs (top-to-bottom): Comet Villager wagon; Comet S-22 Coupe; Meteor S-33 Coupe; and Monterey S-55 Hardtop. (Mercury)

two-barrel carburetor; the 390-cubic-inch V-8 with 300 hp at 4600 rpm, 427 pounds-feet of torque at 2800 rpm, 9.6:1 compression and a four-barrel carburetor; the 390-cubic-inch V-8 with 330 hp at 4600 rpm, 9.6:1 compression and a four-barrel carburetor; the 406-cubic-inch V-8 with 385 hp at 4800 rpm, 9.6:1 compression and a four-barrel carburetor; and the 406-cubic-inch V-8 with 405 hp at 5000 rpm, 10.9:1 compression and a three-two-barrel carburetors. The 352-cubic-inch engine cost $51.50 to add to Mercury eights. The 390-cubic-inch, 300-hp option was $137.60 for Mercury eights. The other V-8s were special-order items, however, the extra cost of the 406-cubic-inch, 405-hp V-8 was reported as $379.90. Cars equipped with this motor could not have power steering, power brakes, air conditioning, or automatic transmission.

Motor Trend (May 1962) again got hold of a Monterey Custom Convertible with the 390-cubic-inch, 300-hp "Marauder" big-block V-8, the three-speed Multi-Range Merc-O-Matic transmission, and the 3.00:1 rear axle ratio. This car moved from 0-to-60 mph in 10.5 seconds. It was going 81 mph by the time it passed a quarter-mile (from a standing start) in 18.9 seconds. Its top speed was 114 mph. Stopping from 60 mph required 158.5 feet. At the time, the magazine felt that this was the best Mercury it had tested, from the standpoint of performance. In combined city and highway driving it managed 8.9 to 11.3 mpg. On the highway, it could hit 15.5 mpg. Coming off the straightaway at Riverside International Raceway, in the Monterey Custom ragtop, the *Motor Trend* staff noticed their electric speedometer was reading 110 mph and the tachometer was pegged at 4300 rpm. "The big Merc didn't seem to be laboring at this point," they wrote. "And no doubt (it) had a few more mph left."

In an unusual move, *Motor Trend* published a road test of the midyear Mercury S-55 in its October issue. This was after some of the 1963 cars (including the Comet) had already been featured in articles. This story was probably held over from an earlier edition and considered important enough to run after deadline. Wayne Thomas did the analysis of a Convertible with the "406/405" V-8, four-speed floor shift, high-performance suspension and brakes, and bucket seats. This racy ragtop went from 0-to-60 mph in a scant 7.65 seconds and did the quarter-mile in 16.5 seconds at 94 mph. Top speed was 120 mph.

Thomas said that the quarter-mile figures were impressive, but not indicative of the car's "competition capabilities." He explained that it had been tested in "honest street trim," without as much as straight pipes or a factory tachometer. This hinted that those planning to seriously race "406" Fords would be able to do much in the way of improving their already outstanding performance. "Where we found the Merc to be magnificently strong, was in the mid- and upper-speed ranges," Thomas added for those interested in a big-block for regular driving. The car got 10.1 mpg in combined city and highway operation (9.6 mpg while "cruising" in Los Angeles) and stopped from 60 mph in 161 feet.

Chassis differences associated with the big Mercs included the "Cushion-Link" type front coil spring arrangement; larger 8.00 x 14 tires (compared to 6.00 x 13 for Comets and 6.50 x 14 for Meteors); bigger 11-inch diameter front and rear brakes with 180 square inches of effective lining area; and, of course, separate body and frame construction. The full-sized Mercurys had an "X" type frame and body

All in all, magazine road testers like the ride and handling characteristics of all three 1962 Mercurys (Comet, Meteor and Monterey), They praised the brakes on the full-sized model. Mercury's interior and exterior quality and workmanship were also universally regarded as excellent. Mercury put much thought into all of its products, down to safety details such as interior door panel lights, in Hardtops and Convertibles, that came on at night when the doors were opened. These alerted motorists approaching from the rear, that the Mercury was stopped to take on or dispense passengers.

The biggest criticisms seemed to be the lack of adequate engine power in the Comet (and the use of under-powered base engines in other lines); a long reach to work floor-mounted gear-shifts; poorly designed snaps on Convertible top boots; the Monterey's long and shallow trunk, which made the spare tire hard to get at; and the fact that the folding front seat stops used in two-door models tended to punch holes in the factory seat belts. And, of course, Uncle Tom McCahill did not like the knit vinyl seats or the price tags on fully-optioned cars. He was, also, against the extended service intervals that all of Detroit was so heavily promoting at this time. "It's just a sales promotion gimmick at best," he stated with characteristic bluntness.

Ben D. Mills continued at the helm of Lincoln-Mercury Division during model-year 1962. The division had a new comptroller (W.M. Caldwell) and programming manager (J.P. Neville), but very few other personnel changes. Slightly over 2,500 dealers operated Monterey-Meteor-Comet franchises (of these, 83 were signed up for Montereys only). Model-year production included 165,305 Comets, 69,052 Meteors, and 107,009 Mercurys for a grand total of 341,366 units. That was a 5.1 percent share of total industry output, down from 5.8 percent in 1961, although total production was up.

Mercury introduced its 1963 models on October 4, 1962. The 1963 Comet remained the same type of "senior compact" that it had been since the start of the marque. *Motor Trend* (September 1962) explained why the early 1963 Comets had the same engines. "Ford isn't anxious to rock the boat with the Comets selling hot and giving excellent operating economy," noted the magazine. The new models had some modest styling changes from 1962. However, the big news of the year was saved until midyear, when Mercury shot down *Motor Trend's* theory with a new V-8-powered Comet Sportster model.

The base Comet line offered two- and four-door Sedans, plus two- and four-door Station Wagons at prices from $2,084 to $2,483. All models had a new grille with horizontal bars and three vertical dividers between the headlamps. Quad headlamps, in wide-spaced chrome bezels, made another return appearance. There was a "Mercury" script on the left edge of the hood. "Comet" scripts appeared on the sides of the front fenders. On passenger cars, thinner, continuous body side moldings accented both the upper and lower feature lines, making a loop at the rear of the car. Four taillamps appeared on the rear. The Station Wagon rear end was cleaned up somewhat, with moldings extending across the tailgate from the top and bottom of the 1962-like taillamp housings. Comets had four-bolt wheels with 6.00 x 13 tires as standard equipment.

Comet Customs had new hubcaps and three "wind-split" moldings added to the extreme rear body sides. The interior sported a color-keyed headliner and steering wheel column. New materials used on the seats and the doors included "Aristocrat" cloth and crushed-grain vinyls. They were more luxurious and matched the exterior colors. The rear body panel had a full-width "grille" with 10 horizontal ribs and four taillamps. The Custom series included all the same body styles found in the base Comet series, plus a two-door Hardtop, a Convertible and a Villager Station Wagon with simulated Mahogany-grain paneling. Even bucket seats were optional in the Villager. On Custom Station Wagons, the area between the tailgate moldings was filled with an "electric shaver" textured trim panel. There was also "Mercury" block lettering and a "Comet" script on the right-hand side of the tailgate. List prices began at $2,171 and climbed as high as $2,754.

In the Comet S-22 series, a convertible was added. It featured a fully unitized body. Heavy-gauge supports strengthened the structure and gave it good resistance to torsional stresses. Galvanized body panels and zinc-rich primers were used to help keep down corrosion on the Comet unit body. All S-22s had small, round medallions on the body side moldings, behind the front wheel openings, and S-22 interior badging. There were also three "wind-split" moldings at the extreme rear body sides. Unique to the 1963 model were six taillamps lighting up the rear end. The rear body panel had a textured beauty panel and "turbine" style hubcaps were featured. As in the past, T-bird style semi-bucket seats and a mini-console gave the S-22 a sporty feeling. There were three models, a two-door Sedan, a two-door Hardtop and the Convertible, with list prices from $2,368 to $2,710.

The 1963-1/2 Comet Sportster was Mercury's version of the Falcon Sprint. Both were two-door Hardtops with a special, semi-fastback roof line. This roof not only looked good; it also added 200 extra square inches of glass area, for improved visibility. The heart of the car was a Ford small-block V-8 of 260 cubic inches. The body and chassis components were beefed-up in 14 places to handle the V-8. They also had five-bolt wheels with 7.00 x 13 tires. Bigger 10-inch drum brakes were used, too. The rear axle was pirated from the Econoline truck parts bin and both the manual and

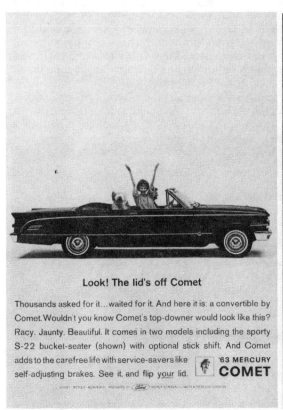

Look! The lid's off Comet

Thousands asked for it...waited for it. And here it is: a convertible by Comet. Wouldn't you know Comet's top-downer would look like this? Racy. Jaunty. Beautiful. It comes in two models including the sporty S-22 bucket-seater (shown) with optional stick shift. And Comet adds to the carefree life with service-savers like self-adjusting brakes. See it, and flip your lid. **'63 MERCURY COMET**

Quick as a bunny...new Comet V-8!

COMET

A Comet Convertible was added to the line for model-year 1963. This is the sporty S-22. (Mercury)

New-for-1963 Comets was a bunny-fast 260-cubic-inch V-8. Here's the semi-fastback Hardtop. (Mercury)

Bucket seats were included with the 1963 Meteor S-33 models. (William L. Opfer, Jr.)

power steering systems were beefed-up. Said *Car Life* (July 1963), "As a mid-1963 model, the Mercury people 'Meteorized' the Comet." The magazine also referred to the S-22 Sportster as the "Mercury Sprint" The Sportster carried a $2,594 base price.

Colors offered by Mercury in 1963 were: Presidential Black; Peacock Turquoise; Ocean Turquoise Metallic; Pacific Blue Metallic; Sea Blue; Cardinal Red; Light Aqua; Blue Satin Metallic; Castilian Gold; Sultana White; Scotch Green; Sheffield Gray Metallic; Jamaica Yellow; Champagne; Pink Frost; Black Cherry Metallic; Cascade Blue; and Desert Frost Metallic. At this time, the auto industry was leaning more towards the use of vinyl trimmed interiors and solid-color upholstery. Comets followed the general trend, offering five cloth upholstery options (three in solid colors) and 13 vinyl interiors (including only five two-tone combinations).

Until the Sportster arrived, the 1963 Comets had the same engines as 1962, with new 6,000-mile extended service intervals for oil changes and 30,000-mile chassis lubrication. Both engines now had hydraulic valve lifters. Also, there was a smoother-operating, more economical carburetor, an improved distributor, and a positive crankcase ventilation (PCV) system. After the Comet V-8 was introduced, the smaller 144.3-cubic-inch six was dropped. The 170-cubic-inch motor then became the standard engine.

"The new '260' came from the Fairlane/Meteor '221' V-8," advised *Car Life*. "It's a tough, relatively light power plant, by virtue of the Ford developed thin-wall casting techniques." It had a 3.80 x 2.87 bore and stroke, an 8.7:1 compression ratio, and a two-barrel carburetor. Advertised horsepower was 164 at 4000 rpm. It produced 258 pounds-feet of torque at 2200 rpm. This gave it 62 percent more power than the 170-cubic-inch six, according to *Car Life*. Comets with the "170" had 27 pounds per horsepower, versus 20.2 pounds with the V-8. The V-8 was *not* as fast as the six from 0-to-30 mph. It needed 5.0 seconds, as opposed to the sixes' 4.7. However, in all other regards, except fuel economy, the V-8 was tops. It went from 0-to-60 in 14.5 seconds, as opposed to 15.2 for the "big six." The V-8 did the quarter-mile in 19.3 seconds at 72.6 mph, against 20.2 seconds and 67.4 mph for the six. Top speed was 85 mph for the six and 103 mph for the V-8. These comparisons are based on *Car Life*'s results with a Sportster having the two-speed Merc-O-Matic and 3,25:1 ratio rear axle. It got 14-16 mpg overall economy. It also had a radio; white sidewall tires; seat belts; an outside rear view mirror; power steering, power brakes, and a $3,182 price tag.

Motor Trend also got its hands on a Sportster, of course. As usual, it was different from the other magazine's test car. This one had a four-speed manual gear box; a radio; white sidewall tires; power

The Meteor S-33 offered a choice of a Hardtop or Convertible with bucket seats and floor-shifter. (Mercury)

steering; heater; electric tachometer; padded dashboard and sun visor; and seat belts. That gave it a slightly higher $3,356.95 price tag. This car did 0-to-30 mph in 3.7 seconds and 0-to-60 mph in 11.5 seconds. The quarter-mile took 19 seconds at 75 mph. *Motor Trend* liked everything about the car, except its 17-inch steering wheel and its uncomfortable back seat.

The standard transmission was a three-speed manual gear box with synchronized second and third gear ranges. A four-speed manual transmission was added to the list of extras. Used in conjunction with both six-cylinder engines was a four-speed unit that came from Great Britain, where it was used in English Fords. It cost just $90. The V-8 models used a beefier, American-built, four-speed transmission. It added $188 to the price of the cars. The optional two-speed Merc-O-Matic had a higher-ratio low gear range for quicker take offs. Other technical upgrades were self-adjusting brakes with thicker linings, and extended-life light bulbs in all lamps.

In the 1963 Mobilgas Economy Run, a Comet driven by Mary Faulkner placed third, behind the smaller Falcon and Valiant, in Class B. That was the category for medium-engined compacts 169 to 170 cubic inches. The Merc averaged 25.75 miles on each gallon of fuel it consumed. That was not bad in the mid-1960s.

The Meteor was Mercury's "in-between sized" car. Minor styling changes included a heavier-looking front end sporting a grille with eight vertical-louver-segments running across

The 1963 Meteor Country Cruiser was advertised as the "Low-price wagon with a white-tie look." (Mercury)

it. There were also double body side moldings on the main feature line; new "bird's beak" taillamps (except Station Wagons); and new scripts, badges and trim plates. The options list continued to grow, offering a tachometer, a Citizen's Band (CB) radio, a rear speaker "reverb" unit, and air conditioning. The reverb feature gave an "echo" to music played on the radio and was very popular with young buyers at this time. The base series offered two- and four-door Sedans as in 1962, plus a new four-door Station Wagon. All Meteor Station Wagons had 1962-style taillamps. Prices ranged from $2,278 to $2,631 for base series models.

A new Hardtop Coupe and two Station Wagons were added to the Meteor Custom series. Customs had bright rocker panel accents and roof pillar trim plates. The fanciest wagon was a four-door Country Cruiser with simulated wood-grain paneling. This model's tailgate had a loop-shaped, full-width rear beauty panel, with an "electric shaver" texture and round back up lamps at the outer edges. Options included a rear-facing third seat and a power tailgate window. Prices for the five Custom models ran from a low of $2,366 to a high of $2,886.

The Meteor S-33 was a two-door Hardtop. The inside had the same full-length bucket-seat-and-console layout as the Mercury S-22 and the Ford Fairlane The S-33 also had unique three-tone vinyl upholstery. On the exterior, there were three horizontal chrome bars on the front fenders. Thunderbird-like badges were mounted high on the roof's rear quarters and "S-33" scripts appeared on the trailing edges of the rear quarter panels. The same wheelcovers used on the S-55 were also seen. The S-33 had a $2,628 sticker price.

At first, Meteor engine choices were the same as in 1962, with some minor improvements. For instance, "Twice A Year" servicing was advertised. During the model-year, changes were made. The 170-cubic-inch six was made standard equipment and a 200-cubic-inch 116-hp engine became the "big six." Finally, a 289-cubic-inch high-performance V-8 is mentioned in some sources, although no production has been documented. It featured a 10.5:1 compression ratio and a four-barrel carburetor, which was enough to generate 271 horsepower.

Mercury Montereys were marketed in four series for 1963. There were seven body styles and 16 distinct models. The car-lines were the same as late-1962: Monterey, Monterey Custom, S-55 and Colony Park. Big Mercurys had the most radical styling changes of the year in the FoMoCo lines. The new design included a revised front silhouette and a different grille. The body looked more slab-sided, but not flat. The "slabs" were contoured in-and-out-and-in. The body side moldings accenting the upper feature lines ran towards the modified tailfins, then back along the lower feature lines, "hopping" over the rear wheel openings. There was a rear beauty panel with segmented vertical louvers and three taillamps per side. The rear panel had a wide, horizontal chrome molding stretching across its center. All the big Mercs again had a 120-inch wheelbase. The cars were 215 inches long and had 7.50 x 15 tires. Station Wagons were shorter, at 212.1 inches long, but had larger 8.00 x 14 tires.

Bucket seats, a console and console gear-shift were standard in big 1963 Mercury S-55s. (Mercury)

Mercury reintroduced the reverse-slanting "Breezeway" rear window in 1963. (Mercury)

Among styling news of the year was Mercury's re-introduction of the reverse-slanting "Breezeway" rear window. This traced back to a Mercury show car of the 1950s and had been used on mid-century production models, too. It had practical aspects. *Motor Trend*'s Wayne Thomas (March 1963) noted three advantages as: 1) More headroom; 2) Shading of rear seat passengers; and 3) Aids ventilation. "We found the ideal way to keep a supply of fresh air flowing through the Mercury was to open one or both of the dash-controlled cowl vents with the rear window part way down," he revealed. Thomas found no added noise from this procedure, but warned that putting the window all the way down, at highway speeds, caused a swirling, uncomfortable draft.

Another new model, also based on a Mercury show car, was the midyear Fastback model. One example of this body style was added to each car-line. Conceptually, they were inspired by the Marauder Convertible. This was a "dream car" that was seen on the auto show circuit early in 1963 and pictured in *Motor Trend*'s (January 1963) "Spotlight on Detroit" column. By March 1963, *Motor Trend* had a bright red Fastback on its cover. A month later, Mercury was running full-page ads for the "Marauder" Hardtop. Most showed the fancy S-55 version.

Motor Trend **said three advantages of Breezeway styling were: 1) More headroom; 2) Shading of rear seat passengers; and 3) Aids ventilation. (Mercury)**

The base Monterey series started out with two- and four-door Sedans, and two- and a four-door Hardtops, at prices from $2,834 to $2,995. Fastbacks were added in the spring. The Monterey Custom version came with a $3,083 price, same as the regular two-door Hardtop. There was also a new Custom Convertible at $3,333. Other Customs were priced between $3,075 and $3,148. The Monterey S-55 line had a two-door Sedan, two- and four-door Hardtops, and the two-door Marauder Fastback. Low and high prices for S-55s were $3,650 and $3,900. The full-sized Colony Park Station Wagon came in six-passenger ($3,295) and nine-passenger ($3,365) formats. Both had wood-grained side trim and Monterey Custom decorations.

The option list for full-size 1963 Mercurys also got more full-sized. New additions were an AM-FM radio, an electronic tachometer, a "Swing-Away" steering wheel, a "6-Way" power seat, and speed control. The latter, called "Cruise Control," was manufactured by the Perfect Circle company, a firm best known for its piston rings. It was a dealer-installed item made available, late in the 1963 model-year, for $90 to $110. Prices for other extras were $102 for power windows; $221 for Merc-O-Matic; and $360 for air conditioning. Six cloth interiors and 14 vinyl interiors, all in solid colors, were offered.

With American big-car buyers no longer on an economy kick, Mercury pulled out all stops under the hood of Montereys. Besides no longer offering a six, the 292- and 352-cubic-inch V-8s were gone, too. The base engine was the 390-cubic-inch motor (4.050 x 3.784 inches bore x stroke) with an 8.9:1 compression ratio, a two-barrel carburetor and 250 hp at 4400 rpm. It produced 378 pounds-feet of torque at 2400 rpm. Transmission options were basically the same in 1963 as they were in 1962. Small cars could be had with three-speed manual transmission, the English-built four-speed manual or Merc-O-Matic. The three-speed manual transmission was synchronized on second and third gears. Transmissions used in the big Mercs were three-speed manual, three-speed manual with overdrive, and Warner four-speed with any engine, and automatic with any 390 engine up to 340 hp.

Motor Trend (March 1963) road tested a 1963 Monterey Custom four-door Hardtop with the 390-cubic-inch, 250-hp V-8, Merc-O-Matic, air conditioning, power windows, 6-Way electric seat, power brakes, power steering, radio, whitewalls and seat belts. It went out the showroom door for $3,075. The magazine pointed out that the Merc was two inches longer than a Lincoln Continental and had enormous 80-inch-wide seats. Still, it moved from 0-to-30 mph in four seconds and from 0-to-60 mph in 11.3 seconds. The quarter-mile required 18.5 seconds and got the Monterey moving at 75.5 mph. Its top speed was 102 mph. The brakes stopped the car in 148 feet, which was good for the time. "If the performance we recorded with the least powerful mill is any indication, these new (427-cubic-inch) engines should make the Monterey a terror," hinted Wayne Thomas about two new motors Mercury had just announced.

The four-door Hardtop had soft, but excellent ride characteristics. "Handling was "not as good as we would like," said Thomas, who also admitted that body roll was "not as bad as it felt." The steering system had 3.9 turns lock-to-lock and a 41.6-foot turning circle. Thomas discovered excessive under-steer in tight turns. He liked the idea of full gauges on the dash, but found the horn rim easy to "honk" without trying. In addition, the brakes were criticized for heating up fast.

After the mildest Mercury engine option, things got very exciting. Standard in Monterey S-55 models was a more powerful version of the "390." It had a four-barrel carburetor and 10.8:1 compression. The advertised horsepower was 300 at 4600 rpm. Torque was 427 pounds-feet at 2800 rpm. Also back, early in the year, was the "Police Special" V-8. It had a four-barrel and 10.5:1 compression. Output was 330 hp at 5000 rpm and torque was 427 pounds-feet at 3200 rpm.

Motor Trend (December 1962) had said, "As this is written, all 1963 Ford and Mercury high-performance V-8 engines are unchanged from 1962 in all particulars that affect performance." This proved to be the understatement of the month, if not the year. The first of several very significant additions to the engine line up came out at the same time. It was based on the "390" block with 10.8:1 compression, three two-barrel carburetors, and a big-port aluminum manifold. It gave 340 hp at 5000 rpm and replaced the 330 hp V-8. This option came only with three-speed Cruise-O-Matic transmission and a 3.0:1 rear axle. A new, clutch-type Equa-Lock axle was optional. This was a simplified, "Dual-Drive," torque-dividing differential that cost less to produce than its predecessor. Test drivers said that it worked on ice or snow, but not at the drag strip. The 340 hp option required heavy-duty suspension and brakes.

The 385 hp and 405 hp editions of the "406" (both with 11.5:1 compression) were also available at the start of model-year 1963. Several new speed parts were offered for them, including a new, aluminum dual four-barrel intake manifold, new heads, improved pistons, a new camshaft and a beefier block casting. The 406s survived until late 1963. In the spring, two new engines were added to the top of the list. These were the monster 427-cubic-inch "Super

Breezeway Styling was available for Monterey S-55 two-door Hardtops, as seen here kicking-up dust. (Mercury)

The 406 V-8, seen here, lasted until late 1963. Two 427-cubic-inch "Super Marauder" V-8s bowed in the spring. (Kirk Dillery)

The new-for-1963 Mercurys sported a revised front silhouette and a different grille. The body looked more slab-sided, but not flat. (Kirk Dillery)

The Monterey S-55 line had a two-door Marauder Fastback priced from $3,650 to $3,900. (Kirk Dillery)

Marauder" V-8s. They had a 4.2346 x 3.874 bore and stroke and represented a further development of the "406" big-block. Both had 11.5:1 compression ratios and mechanical valve lifters. The first, with a single four-barrel, generated 410 hp. The second, with two four-barrels, cranked up 425 hp at 6000 rpm and 480 pounds-feet of torque at 3700 rpm.

Ford had a 428-cubic-inch V-8 at Bonneville, the previous summer, in a 1962 Galaxie that ran 172 mph on the salt flats. The "428" was based on the "406," with an over-bore, longer stroke, larger ports, experimental cam, and two four-barrel carburetors. It produced over 500 hp. This engine was being prepared for 1963 factory Super/Stock lightweight racing cars. Then, NASCAR and NHRA announced a 7-liter (427-cubic-inch) limit on engine displacement and it made no sense to release the motor.

While there would be no 428-cubic-inch production engine for 1963, the "427 Super Marauder" V-8s became a production reality. "Shift to Mercury's newest sizzler ... the Marauder," said a color ad that appeared in car enthusiast magazines that May. The 427-cubic-inch V-8s were available in all Montereys, except Station Wagons. The price for the more powerful version, described on the invoice as the "427 8V Hi-Perf," was $461.60. Both versions could be had with three-speed manual, overdrive, or four-speed manual transmissions. Instead of the normal 24-month/24,000-mile Ford warranty, the 427s came with a three-month or 4,000-mile power train warranty.

In April 1963, *Car Life* road tested a Mercury "427 Super Marauder" S-55 Hardtop. The car cost $4,201 as tested. This price included the 427 V-8 package with suspension and steering upgrades and a four-speed transmission with floor-shifter. It also had 8.10 x 14 white sidewall tires, tinted glass, a radio, courtesy lamps, a positive crankcase ventilation system, and windshield washers. The term Marauder referred to the engine, in this case. It had no relationship to the body type, since the test car was a notch-back model. The car did 0-to-60 mph in seven seconds and covered the quarter-mile in 15.1 seconds at 87 mph. It gave respectable open road performance, but felt too stiff to steer in town. It had high-quality finish, but the stainless steel trim looked a bit gaudy. The 8.00 x 14 tires did not grip very well on full-throttle acceleration. Also, back-pressure developed after several high rpm runs. It blew the mufflers right off the header pipes. The tester said the car felt respectable on open roads, but that the steering felt stiff in town.

The March 1963 *Motor Trend*, with the red Fastback and a 427-cubic-inch "Super Marauder" engine on its cover, had a cover blurb reading, "Mercury Goes Racing." The Fastback body was aerodynamically attractive to professional stock car racers, and that was the reason it was added as a production model. Offering it to the public made it "legal" for stock car builders to use the sleeker roof style.

Mercury wanted to buffer itself from direct sponsorship of stock racing cars, but became heavily involved through "indirect" factory participation. A contract was inked with Bill Stroppe (the old Mexican road racer and economy run wizard) to organize a Mercury racing team. Then 27 major NASCAR and USAC events were put on the schedule. Stroppe initially signed drivers Troy Ruttman, Rodger Ward, Parnelli Jones, Chuck Daigh, Darel Dieringer, and Whitey Gerkin to pilot his cars. Louie Unser was also contracted to slide behind the wheel of a Merc at the Pike's Peak Hill Climb on July 4. Parnelli Jones drove there, too. Later, Joe Ruttman (Troy's brother), and independent driver John Rostick, also raced Mercurys. According to *Motor Trend*, Rostick bought one of the "Super Marauder" Fastbacks, from Stroppe, for a price between $8,000 and $10,000.

Elmer Larson has owned this 1963-1/2 Monterey Marauder "390" since 1965. It has gone over 345,000 miles. (E. Larson)

The Super Marauder 427-cubic-inch V-8s were used in the race cars. The number 2, 3 and 4 main bearings were held firmly by cross-bolted rod caps. For stock car races, a single four-barrel carburetor was mounted on a special, lightweight aluminum manifold. With 11.5:1 compression, the four-barrel motor cranked out 410 hp. It had special water-cooled head gaskets; extra ribbing added to the engine block bulkheads; and a lot more "goodies." The fan belt even featured a Dacron inner liner that shrunk when it was heated up, giving a tighter fit at high speeds. The red-white-and-blue race cars weighed only about 4,000 pounds, even with their big 22-gallon fuel tanks. Heftier Lincoln brakes were employed to stop them. Three months after *Motor Trend*'s race car story, *Car Life* (June 1963) did almost the same article. The title "Mercury Goes Racing" was used again.

Fran Fernandez, who had been on Lincoln's famous Mexican Road Race team, with Bill Stroppe, in the early 1950s, was appointed "performance and evaluation director" of Lincoln-Mercury Division in mid-1963. He had also been on Ford's NASCAR racing crew in 1956 and 1957. His new role showed how "serious" Mercury was about not being involved in motorsports. Divisional manager Ben Mills made statements that linked Mercury racing with safety, much like the company's 1955 promotion of larger "Safety-Surge" V-8s. "The race track is a logical extension of our engineering programs," Mills emphasized. "Cars with 110 hp or less have two to three times as many accidents, per mile, as cars with 300 hp."

This 1963-1/2 Monterey S-55 Marauder belongs to Kirk Dillery, of Battle Creek, Michigan. It has the "Super Marauder 406" and four-speed gear box. Kirk says a handful of 1964 Mercurys, built in 1963, had this engine. (Kirk Dillery)

One of the sportiest 1963 Mercurys was the Monterey S-55 Convertible. The option list got bigger. New were an AM-FM radio, electronic tachometer, "Swing-Away" steering wheel, "6-Way" power seat and speed control. (Mercury)

Production totals for Monterey Convertibles were 3,783 Customs, and 1,379 of the S-55s. (Lowell E. Eisenhour)

Did racing really sell Mercurys? In 1963, the answer seemed to be yes. Model-year production of the big-cars rose to 121,048 units, which was the highest it had been since 1960. The factories also turned out 134,623 Comets, and 50,775 Meteors. The grand total for all three lines was 306,446 cars, a drop from 1962. It was clear that racing was helping sell cars. The Comet had to move in more of a high-performance direction. Calendar-year production totaled 292,086 units, including 150,694 Comets, 22,577 Meteors and 118,815 Mercurys.

When Mercury introduced the Marauder and hired Bill Stroppe to build stock car racing versions, sales of big Mercs shot upwards for the first time in four years. At the same time, the smaller Mercs — Meteors and Comets — continued to stress economy over power. They did not even offer real high-performance engines in 1963. The closest thing was the Comet Sportster with a small "260" V-8. This put Mercury in a bind. The era of the muscle car or "factory hot rod" was dawning rapidly. At the same time, the last remnants of America's post-1958 economy binge were vanishing. Economy-of-operation and a slightly larger size were not enough to keep Comet and Meteor sales on an even keel. A major image change was needed for the smaller cars to compete. Their move towards a new role in the marketplace began in 1964.

For beginners, Ford product planners decided that a slight enlargement and upgrade of the fanciest Comet would allow one series to do the job of two. The Meteor was discontinued. With that decision made, Mercury had to decide whether to take the Comet racing. Motorsports had become the second largest spectator activity in the United States. Racing fans — both those at trackside and watching on television — bought cars that looked like the ones they saw winning. Since Marauder sales seemed to be benefiting from exposure in racing (even though the cars took only one 1963 NASCAR win), Mercury chose to make the Comet not only a competitor, but a winner.

Starting on September 21, 1963, five new Comet Calientes did an over-100,000-miles-at-105-mph run at Daytona International Speedway in Florida. The original goal was to establish a new Class C endurance record by traveling at least 50,000 miles at an average speed of 100 mph (including refueling and maintenance). During the six-week-long trial, the Comets hit speeds as high as 112 mph, continuing to circle the speedway in sunshine and rain. The cars were prepped by Andy Hotton, of Dearborn Steel Tubing Company, who did the famous Ford Fairlane "Thunderbolt" drag cars.

The cars had 289-cubic-inch V-8s with mechanical valve lifters, special camshafts, 10.5:1 compression ratios, and larger-than-stock oil pans. They were linked to three-speed manual transmissions and 2.70:1 rear axles. Hotton built the Comets up to NASCAR specs, which included the addition of a full roll cage, heavy-duty wheel rims, heavy-duty shock absorbers, and the addition of one leaf to each rear spring. They originally had special, lightweight tailpipes, but these melted very early in the run and, after that, the exhaust gases came out right in back of the stock mufflers. The tires were 8.00 x 14 Firestones made to police specifications. The cars had two-way radios for communications.

At 40,000 miles into the run, Mercury reported a complete lack of major repairs. Anti-roll bar bushings had been replaced and the spark plugs were switched at 27,000 miles. One car also needed a rear axle seal. The endurance run cars broke over 100 world records and generated much publicity for the 1964 Comets. "The sales success of the 1964 Comet following the Comet Durability Run at the Daytona International Speedway last fall presents graphic proof that performance does help sell cars," Lincoln-Mercury vice president and general manager Ben D. Mills told *Car Life* in September 1964. "Before the Durability Run became public knowledge, Comet sales trailed the year-before period by six percent, but in the second 10-day period, the situation reversed as the run began to be publicized and advertised. Sales were 12 percent ahead. In the third 10-day period of October, sales were up 28 percent. After that, sales continued to gain momentum, reaching a high of 187 percent ahead in the final 100-day period of January." Mills mentioned that positive responses to the run also showed up on a national survey and in public awareness studies. In addi-

Between September 21 and October 30, 1963, a fleet of 1964 Mercury Comets covered 100,000 miles at speeds above 105 mph at Daytona International Speedway. They broke over 100 world endurance records. (Mercury)

The Comet Custom evolved into the Comet Caliente. A two-door Hardtop was in the fancy line. (Mercury)

tion, Caliente two-door Hardtops, like those used in the 100,000-mile reliability run, displaced the low-priced Comet four-door Sedan as the marque's most popular model.

Between March 26 and March 30, 1964, five new Comets competed in the grueling "East African Safari." *Car Life* covered this in a detailed article, titled "Comets over Africa," in its April issue. This was a "figure 8" rally in which 94 vehicles set out to cover 3,188 miles. Only 21 vehicles finished the five-day rally. The rally cars were a combined effort of Bill Stroppe and Ford of England. They were equipped with 289-cubic-inch, 271-hp "Super Cyclone" V-8s. Solid valve lifters; 10.5:1 compression ratios; four-barrel carburetors; high-performance cam-

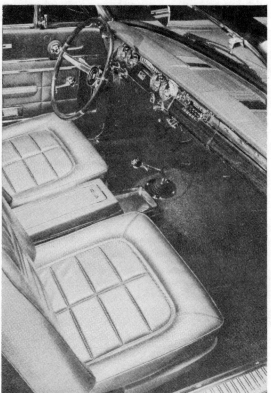

Wood-grain dash inserts and bucket seats, embossed with textured panels in an oblong design, were standard in 1964 Calientes. (Mercury)

shafts; four-speed manual transmissions; 4.57:1 ratio rear axles; skid plates; fog lamps; heavy-duty suspensions; oil coolers; metallic brake linings; and 7.60 x 15 tires were features of these cars. Inside, there was a single seat, a roll bar, and a water tank. Extra spare tires were stored where the rear seat was usually located. On the outside, the Comets had fog lights. Among the finishers of the rally was a pair of the Comets.

Besides endurance run cars and rally cars, Fran Fernandez supervised a factory-dealer-backed Comet drag racing program that chalked up one record win after another. A fleet of about 50 Factory Experimental (FX) vehicles was built. They included B/FX cars with modified "289s" and A/FX cars with 427-cubic-inch Ford engines. Even Comet Station Wagons were drag raced. The Comets were very successful on the drag strip, since they were lighter than Fairlane Thunderbolts and had more of their weight near the rear wheels. At the National Hot Rod Association (NHRA) "Winternationals," one Comet did a wheelstand coming off the line at 6,000 rpm. In the same event, a Mercury Comet Hardtop driven by Ronnie Sox won "Top Eliminator" honors in the Factory Stock racing class with a 123.45 mph run that took 11.49 seconds to cover the quarter-mile.

Another big-name drag racer, Don Nicholson, ran in the low 11s, at above 125 mph, at the American Hot Rod Association (AHRA) "Winternationals" in Scottsdale, Arizona. During the event, however, there was a disagreement between the promoters and the Mercury drag racing team over the legality of using Ford's 427-cubic-inch engine in cars like Nicholson's Comet Station Wagon. The Mercury team pulled out and went home.

Nevertheless, the Comets were winners in event after event. A Mercury advertisement promoting the accomplishments of the "Comet Boss Dragsters" listed: 1) A pair of track records set at Emporia, Virginia on January 5, 1964 (with a top run of 11.3 seconds at 123.11 mph); 2) a record run of 11.33 seconds at 121.62 mph on February 9, 1964 at Long Beach, California; and 3) a track record of 123 mph (11.72 seconds) set at Fontana, California, also on March 9.

New drag racing records were also set by the fire-breathing, "factory lightweight," A/FX-class Comets at Pamona and Bakersfield, California. These special cars generated so much excitement that, in September 1964, *Car Life* magazine actually printed a "road test" of the Chrisman-Shrewsberry A/FX Comet that Mercury's Jack Chrisman and Bill Shrewsberry competed with on the West Coast. The magazine noted that "the non-dealer-connected enthusiast" could not get such a car. The Chrisman-Shrewsberry car operated as a factory-dealer-sponsored racer out of Sachs & Son Lincoln-Mercury, of Downey, California. It had the full drag racing package that Mercury made available around the first of the year. "This is not the 7,000 rpm NASCAR kit," said *Car Life*. "But it uses the NASCAR kit's valves, though with modified hollow valve stems and a ram air intake."

Other features of the A/FX Comets included "nostril" type hood scoops (mounted at the front edge of the hood); fiberglass front fenders, bumpers, hood, doors, and trunk lid; no padding or

The mid-priced 1964 Mercury Montclair "Marauder" four-door Fastback had a base price of $3,170. (Mercury)

sound deadening material; big mufflers; and aluminum inner body panels. The suspension was specially designed and the cars carried a 72-pound battery and spare tire in the trunk, at the extreme rear, to give them a 49 percent rear weight bias. They had blown, nitro-burning 427-cubic-inch V-8s and 4.56:1 axles. Special wheels held 9.00 x 15 M & H slicks at the rear and fatter-than-stock front tires. *Car Life* put quarter-mile performance at 11.02 seconds with a 128.04 mph terminal speed. In less than one-year, Mercury's over-sized compact had changed from having no racing heritage at all, into an international champion that beat the best thrown at it by other automakers, as well as by Ford Division.

For the general public, Mercury upgraded the 1964 Comet and marketed it in three series. The bottom Comet 202 car-line included two- and four-door Sedans and a four-door, six-passenger Station Wagon at prices from $2,084 to $2,483. The mid-range cars were Comet 404s. The same body types were offered in the 404 series, at prices from $2,171 to $2,570.

The Comet Custom evolved into the Caliente, with bench seats. The S-22 became the Cyclone, with bucket seats. Comets were available with sixes or V-8s. There was a two-door Hardtop, four-door Sedan and Convertible in the fancy line. This upgraded version of the Mercury compact was more of a car than the Custom had ever been. It really filled the market niche vacated by the Meteor.

Mercury's top-of-the-line 1964 Park Lane Marauder two-door Hardtop listed for $3,348. Park Lanes had wide lower body side moldings. (John J. Muller)

The rear of the 1964 Park Lane Marauder had a glittery look with a "grille" and triple taillamps. (John J. Muller)

There were five solid color cloth trims; and 15 vinyl upholstery selections for 1964. (John J. Muller)

Car Life (November 1963) said that it "moves the Comet up to what it originally should have been."

All Comets had a more massive, Lincoln Continental-like front end treatment. The look was square and slab-sided, with a wedge-shape to the car's profile. Up front, a-rectangular grille with rounded-off corners had two headlamps in connected round bezels that resembled eyeglasses on either side. Between the headlamps was a grid with eight rectangles (arranged as two rows of four) with cross-hatched patterns inside each rectangular opening. Parking lamps were notched into the vertical, "knife-edge" front fender tips, with "egg-slicer" ornaments decorating them. The bumper was more massive, too, with a larger license plate indentation in the center and rectangular parking lamps at each end, but not quite as far out as in the past. A "Comet" script was seen on the left-hand side of the hood lip.

The body sides looked high and crisply tailored, with a narrow, full-length horizontal "V"sculpted along the body. This "V" had (shades of the '50s) guided missile-shaped trim at its rear. On Calientes, this had "C-O-M-E-T" block letters and a red, white and blue bar-badge. The back of the cars had a beauty panel filled with a cross-hatched texture and three round taillamps at either side. The center taillamp lenses were white.

All 1964 Comets shared a 114-inch wheelbase and 195.1-inch overall length. The front track was 55 inches; the rear was 56 inches. The cars stood 54.9 inches high and were 71.4 inches wide. Base Comets had 212 square inches of effective brake lining and 6.50 x 14 tires. The Caliente models featured larger brakes with 261 square inches of lining area. They also wore 7.00 x 14 tires.

The Caliente could be had with the 170-cubic-inch, 101-hp six or a 200-cubic-inch "big six" with 116 hp. The latter came with two-speed Merc-O-Matic transmission only. Fans of V-8 power could get the 260-cubic-inch 164-hp engine for starters. However, the real heart of the Caliente's "Total Performance" tie-in was the new 289-cubic-inch V-8. This engine had the same relatively mild compression ratio used in the other Comet power plants. Buff magazines listed its compression at 8.7:1 initially, but later corrected the ratio to 9.0:1. It also shared a single exhaust system and hydraulic valve lifters with other Comet V-8s, but added light-weight rocker arms, a front-mounted distributor, larger connecting rods, a fat six-inch muffler, and larger valves and seats. It used a single, four-barrel carburetor. The 210 hp it produced was a new high for the nameplate.

Car Life (January 1964) road tested a Caliente with the standard 289-cubic-inch V-8 and three-speed Merc-O-Matic (Cruise-O-Matic) transmission. The test drivers had some trouble with the car's air conditioner affecting the transmission, but noted handling improvements over earlier models and better roadability. The under-steer normally expected with a nose-heavy car like the Comet (it had 56.6/43.4 percent front-to-rear weight distribution) changed to a comfortable, "neutral" feeling at high speeds, but the car exhibited brake shudder and lock-up in 80-mph panic stops. It also had poor-fitting body panels, and a balky door latch. The Comet, an early edition V-8, did 0-to-60 mph in 11.8 seconds and covered the quarter-mile in 16.5 seconds at 73.8 mph. It got 12 to 15 mpg in normal driving.

In October 1963, *Car Life* had hinted at a way to "warm up" the small-block V-8. "With the soon-available Shelby-Cobra parts, most of which will readily fit, the Caliente will be the first Comet to really go like one," said the magazine. By January 1994, *Car Life* referred to an optional "HP" (also called "H.O.") version of the "289," with mechanical lifters and 271 hp at 6000 rpm. This had 10.5:1 compression (some sources say 11.6:1) and, initially, came only with the standard three-speed manual transmission or optional Warner T-10 four-speed. However, by July, it could be ordered with Mercury's version of the Ford "Cruise-O-Matic" transmission.

This new three-speed torque converter Merc-O-Matic transmission was also available with other V-8-powered Comets. It was lighter in weight and smaller than the two-speed Merc-O-Matic used with small sixes. There was even a difference in the standard transmission used with different Comets, as six-cylinder cars used a gear box pirated from Ford of England with a 3.16 first gear,

Convertibles were part of the 1964 Monterey Marauder and Park Lane Marauder sub-series. This is the Park Lane. (*Old Cars*)

2.21 second gear and 1.41 third gear. Comet V-8s switched to an American Ford three-speed with gear ratios of 2.78, 1.93 and 1.36, respectively. (Full-sized Mercurys offered two other three-speeds, as well.)

In midyear, a new Comet Cyclone high-performance model arrived. It featured less chrome than other Comets. There were thin moldings over the wheel wells, and under the doors, and "C-O-M-E-T" lettering only on the rear fins. Marauder-like "Cyclone" front fender badges sat low on the fenders. Standard in the Cyclone was the four-barrel, 210-hp version of the "289" with 9.0:1 compression. It also featured 14-inch stainless steel wheelcovers that gave the appearance of chrome wheel trims. Camera-case-grained black vinyl replaced wood trim on the instrument panel. It came with new, pleated black bucket seats and a console with color-keyed vinyl in special colors. A special option was a "convertible" style vinyl roof. Cyclones offered a three- or four-speed manual transmission, plus Merc-O-Matic. Promotions for the car were tied into the 100,000-mile endurance run at Daytona.

As tested in *Car Life* (April 1964), the Cyclone priced-out at $3,027 with options. The magazine listed 0-to-60 mph times of 11.8 seconds with automatic transmission and 10.2 seconds with a four-speed. The 1/4-mile was covered in 16.5 seconds at 73.8 mph by the Merc-O-Matic-equipped Cyclone and 16.4 seconds at 77 mph by the four-speed Cyclone. The car with automatic averaged 12-15 mpg in normal driving, while the stick-shift car did a bit better at 13-16 mpg. Top speed was listed as 109 mph.

There was also a fastback Comet "Super Cyclone" concept car that debuted at the New York Automobile Show. It had a special body with a Plymouth Barracuda-like glass back window. Also featured were chrome racing wheels; Cibie rectangular headlamps; through-the-rear-fender exhausts,; "Rally-Pak" instrumentation with a vacuum gauge, a tachometer, and an elapsed time clock; a walnut steering wheel with flat aluminum spokes; a "radar" warning device (for fog); and a vertical bar grille with a horizontal center molding.

Comets offered eight cloth trims, including one two-tone (in black-and-red). There were 21 vinyl upholstery options, including the black-and-red combination, plus blue, red, black, turquoise or Palomino with white. Bucket seats,

The 1964 Colony Park Station Wagon listed for $3,423 with two seats and $3,493 with three seats. (Chris Dunn/ Lincoln Land, Inc.)

Parnelli Jones won the Pikes Peak Hill Climb in 1963 and 1964 driving Bill Stroppe-built Mercurys. (Leroy Byers)

embossed with textured panels in an oblong design, were standard in Calientes. Their interiors followed the trend towards luxury, featuring simulated wood trim on the instrument panel, dashboard, door inserts; and steering wheel.

A sturdier under-body structure, made necessary by the offering of V-8s, was used throughout the Comet car-line. It featured stronger front spring towers (still lighter than the Fairlane's), and heftier tower-to-dash brace, reinforced front side rails, beefier fender aprons; and torque boxes welded between the frame side rails and rocker panels. The rocker panels were also fashioned of heavier-gauge steel.

Suspension refinements included improved front ball-joints; new upper pivot arm bushings; double thickness shock insulators; needle bearings in the steering gear sector; longer and wider four-leaf rear springs; wider and more stable rear spring shackles and bushings (for a softer ride and improved handling); and rear shock absorbers with better valving and all-weather fluid. The rear tread was widened to 56 inches. Power brakes were added to the option list and a new 20-gallon fuel tank was specified.

Some options available for the 1964 Comets included Merc-O-Matic transmission for $182; Multi-Drive Merc-O-Matic for $190; power steering for $86; a four-speed manual transmission for $188; and air conditioning for $232.

Big Mercurys were restyled, with a front end reminiscent of the 1963 Thunderbird. There was a "veed," electric shaver look to the grille. The fenders were also "veed" at the front and had an almost "upholstered" look, with their rolled-edge contours. A "Mercury" script decorated the left-hand hood lip. Chrome signatures on the rear fender identified the series. There were three "wind-split" moldings on the front fenders. Marauders also had special checkered flag fender emblems ahead of the front wheel openings. Taillamps were more rectangular and flatter. There were three taillamps on each side. The inner taillamp lenses had back-up lamps in their center. A rear body "beauty panel" had seven segments with short, horizontal grooves. The center segment was the gas filler door. There were short, pointed tailfins. Overall, the rear end looked like a 1958 to 1960 Lincoln rear end.

Advertising copywriters sorted 1964 Mercurys — which were offered in Monterey, Montclair, and Park Lane series — into separate Marauder and Breezeway sub-series. Marauders were the pillarless models or Convertibles and Breezeways were pillared models. Marauder buyers could choose from nine models. There were two-door Hardtops or Fastbacks in all three trim levels, plus four-door Hardtops or Fastbacks in Montclair and Park Lane formats. Convertibles were included in the Monterey Marauder and Park Lane Marauder sub-series. There was a two-door Sedan in the standard Monterey line and four-door Sedans in all three (non-Marauder) lines. Station Wagons came in Commuter or Colony Park editions. List prices for the big Mercs started at $2,834 and ran to $3,365.

"The price is medium ... the action maximum ... the car is Mercury," said an advertisement in *Car Life* in September 1963. This is the newest of all Marauders — a 4-door hardtop in the luxurious top-line Park Lane series." The advertisement associated the new Park Lane four-door Fastback with Mercurys racing at Pikes Peak and Daytona. It said that "staying power and response ... have made the Mercury the new performance champion of the medium-priced field."

Car Life (June 1964) "tested" a 1939 Mercury in the same issue that it reviewed the 1964 Park Lane. This was done to mark Mercury's 25th anniversary. The older car was described by Dean Batchelor, who wrote some personal recollections about his Mercury hot rodding days. Road performance figures for the '39 were extracted from a contemporary edition of *The MoToR*, an English magazine that tested the first Merc when it was new.

The late-model car came with the Multi-Drive (or Cruise-O-Matic) type transmission. *Car Life* was not crazy about it, describing it as a warmed-over Ford on the outside and a gaudy car on the inside. The car had pleasant road manners on smooth highways, but "bounced on back roads like it had worn shocks," said the magazine. "Poor human engineering" was cited as another Mercury drawback. The reviewer noted that the speed control mechanism was a "long reach" away from the driver, with its dash-top location. The projecting dashboard also limited knee room and the air conditioning outlets had dangerously sharp-edged corners.

Car Life liked the Breezeway window, noting that it did not get as dirty as a conventional backlight. The brakes (346.5 square inches of lining standard and 381.2 square inches with the heavy-duty option) were very good. The Park Lane moved from 0-to-60 mph in 9.3 seconds and did the quarter-mile in 16.9 seconds at 83 mph. It also managed 12 to 15 mpg and a top speed of 112 mph. In short, we think the Mercury is a pretty good automobile as a deluxe Ford," said the writer. "But it fails to meet its heritage of 25 years as a luxury performance car."

Mercury colors for 1964 were: Onyx Black; Peacock; Silver Turquoise; Pacific Blue; Palomino; Aztec Gold; Carnival Red; Anniversary Silver; Bittersweet; Polar White; Pecan Frost; Yellow Mist; Fawn; Maize; Pink Frost; Burgundy; Glacier Blue; and Platinum Beige. There were five solid color cloth trims; and 15 vinyl upholstery selections. Models with bucket seats had a new, thin-shell type. Convertibles had a new, five-layer fabric top.

In Marauders, the 390-cubic-inch V-8 was standard. A new 266-hp version for automatic transmission was added. The Police type "390" with 330 hp and a police-special solid lifter camshaft, was now on the regular options list. Also available, again, were the standard 250-hp engine, plus a 300-hp edition of the "390" and 410- and 425-hp versions of the 427-cubic-inch "7-Liter" engine. Mercury ads referred to the "427" as "the engine that set a new world's stock-car record in the most recent Pikes Peak Climb." The all-synchro three-speed transmission that was added in 1963 was now standard. Other mechanical changes for 1964 Mercs included a heavier anti-roll bar; new universal joints; "piloted" wheels with true concentricity; and a "vacuum-piston" automatic choke with water-warmed control mechanism.

Cars with 390-cubic-inch V-8s had a standard Ford (U.S.) three-speed manual transmission with gear ratios of 2.36, 1.78 and 1.41. When the "427" V-8 was ordered, the three-speed used had 2.32, 1.69 and 1.29 gearing. Transmission options included a four-speed manual gear box and a three-speed Merc-O-Matic. Multi-Drive Merc-O-Matic (Mercury's name for the Cruise-O-Matic type transmission) was a $232 extra. Other Mercury options and prices included power steering ($106); four-speed manual transmission ($232); air conditioning ($402); Sports package ($370); and 390-cubic-inch four-barrel engine ($52 over standard V-8).

Like the Comet, the big Mercury was seen in a factory "dream car" rendition for 1964. The "Super Marauder" concept vehicle had Lucas headlamps; side-mounted exhaust pipes; through-the-hood carburetors; a low, racing-style windscreen; and "TV antenna" style headrests. There was also a "Cougar II" show car on the circuit. This was a coupe designed by Ford styling chief Eugene Bordinat. It had a Corvette-like image with its pop-up headlamps, but the roof line resembled that of the early 1970s "boattail" Buick Riviera. While the concept vehicle was considered a Ford, the production Cougar would become a Mercury sports/personal car.

The Bill Stroppe-built big Mercury stockers assaulted the NASCAR ovals again in 1964, with drivers such as Billy Wade (car number 6); Darel Dieringer (car number 7) and Dave MacDonald (car number 10) piloting for the factory dealer-backed team. "Johnny Rutherford set some kind of record, as he slid his Mercury, upside down, along the back chute for 300 yards," said *Car Life* in its 1964 Daytona 500 coverage. While they were not extremely successful, an interesting thing about these cars was their longevity. At least as late as 1966, several of the 1964 Mercurys were still competing.

Louis J. Unser drove a Marauder in the 1964 Pikes Peak Hill Climb. By 1964, 11 Unsers had raced there and Louis was a two-time winner. (Leroy Byers)

Ben D. Mills was Mercury's "boss" again in 1964. Paul F. Lorenz took over as his assistant and S.A. Skillman became general sales manager. R.L. Peters became Lincoln-Mercury product planning manager, with H.I. Miller in charge of Mercury planning and R.E. Kimball in charge of Comet planning. Finally, Dr. Seymour Marshak was named manager of marketing research. Model-year production totaled 110,342 Mercurys, and 189,936 Comets. This left Mercury with a total of 300,278 assemblies, some 6,000 less than the previous season. Its share of industry output dropped from 4.2 percent to 3.8 percent. However, Comet sales (determined on a calendar-year basis) marked a 12 percent increase over 1963 and Mercury sales rose 11.6 percent, with both figures reflecting the popularity of new models ... which were the 1964 Comet, plus the 1965 Mercury (released in the fall of 1964).

Both the 1965 Comets and Mercurys were introduced on September 25, 1964. The 1965 Comet had a front end restyling. The flat-topped fenders now rose up above the plane of the hood. Vertically positioned dual headlamps were mounted in them. A new grille had four groups of multiple, horizontal blades and a red, white and blue vertical center ornament. There was a "Comet" script on the left-hand lip of the hood. Three "portholes" decorated the front fender sides with small crests behind the front wheel openings.

Inside, the 1965 Comets had a new steering wheel and hub ornament, plus a redesigned horn bar. The rear end was revised from a finned treatment with a Lincoln-look, to a wedge-shaped Mercury-like appearance with horizontal wraparound taillamps and full-width horizontal "grille" bars hiding the taillights on the Caliente and Cyclone models. In the area of technical improvements, there was a new battery with greater electrolyte capacity, a 38-ampere alternator, a redesign of both manual and power steering gears, and wider tires. Offerings continued with the 202, 404, Caliente and Cyclone series.

Standard equipment on Comet 202s included front and rear armrests; a heater and defroster; turn signals; front seat belts; and five 6.95 x 14 tires. There were 202 emblems on the rear fenders. Base interiors were trimmed in Milieu fabric upholstery. There were two-door and four-door Sedan models and a four-door Station Wagon priced from $2,154 to $2,491.

Comet 404s had all the above features, plus carpets, and chrome window frames. This series had the same basic body types, but there were two Station Wagons, the Villager being the fanciest. The four-door Villager Station Wagon also came simulated wood-grain side trim and a power tailgate window. Prices were between $2,297 and $2,762 for cars in this line.

The Caliente series was back with a four-door Sedan, a two-door Hardtop and a Convertible priced from $2,378 to $2,664. Calientes added a padded instrument panel, door courtesy lamps, wheel lip moldings, and ribbed rocker panel moldings to the standard equipment list. There was a "Caliente" script and red, white and blue bar-badge at the upper rear fenders. The Convertible had a power top. Convertibles with the optional V-8 and air conditioning had 7.35 x 14 tires.

The Cyclone series consisted of a single two-door Hardtop priced at $2,683, making it the second most expensive Comet after the Villager Station Wagon. It had a special grille with only two groups of horizontal blades and black-out finish around the perimeter. Cyclones had all the equipment that came on Calientes, plus bucket seats in front, a center console, a tachometer, unique deluxe wheelcovers, curb moldings, and a 289-cubic-inch "Cyclone" V-8 engine with a two-barrel carburetor. A distinctive twin-air-scoop fiberglass hood was optional.

In May 1965, *Motor Trend* printed a road test titled "2 Comets: Hot & Cool" that compared the Caliente and Cyclone two-door Hardtops. The Caliente had the 289-cubic-inch, 200 hp engine and Merc-O-Matic. It did 0-to-60 mph in 11 seconds and ran down the drag strip in 18.1 seconds with a 76 mph terminal speed. Its top speed was 96 mph. The Cyclone had the 225-hp version of the "289" and a four-speed gear box. It trimmed 2.2 seconds off the other car's 0-to-60 mph time and the quarter-mile took 17.1 seconds at 82 mph. Top speed was 108 mph. The magazine liked the restyled Comet front end, the higher horsepower, its handling and its large trunk. The brakes (the Caliente had power assist and the Cyclone did not) were both good. Stopping distance from 60 mph was 158 feet with assist and 161 feet without assist. The major criticisms of technical editor John Ethridge were the Cyclone's wheelspin and rear axle hop (which hurt acceleration times) and that the Caliente's "hang-under-dash" air conditioner interfered with the driver's right leg.

The 195-hp "Cyclone V-8" engine was a $108 option for non-Cyclone models. It had a 9.3:1 compression ratio. In addition, there was a 220-hp "Super Cyclone 289" with a 10.0:1 compression ratio and a four-barrel carburetor. This engine cost $45.20 extra in Cyclones and $153.20 additional in other models. The Comet's base engine was upgraded from a 170-cubic-inch inline six to a 200-cubic-inch, 120-hp inline six. A 260-cubic-inch V-8 was no longer offered.

A three-speed manual gear box was standard with all engines. A four-speed manual transmission was $188 extra, and Multi-Drive

Completely restored 1965 Comet Convertible is one of 1,280 made with bucket seats. It has a 289-cubic-inch V-8 and automatic transmission. (Jim Nelson)

Merc-O-Matic ran $189.60 additional. This was, again, a three-speed automatic, comparable to the Ford Cruise-O-Matic.

The Comet cars used a 114-inch wheelbase and 195.3-inch overall length. They were 72.9 inches wide and 55.1 inches high. The front track was 55 inches; the rear track was an inch wider. They had a 40-foot turning circle and 13.5 cubic feet of luggage space inside the trunk.

An endurance trial called "Journey from the Bottom to the Top of the World" was the focus of Comet promotional efforts this season. This 40-day-long, 24-hour-per-day durability run started on September 12, 1964. The Cape Horn-to-Fairbanks (Alaska) challenge covered a distance of 16,247 miles. It put a trio of light green 1965 Comets to the test. On October 22, the three cars reached their destination in a blizzard.

The first leg of the run took the cars across an icy route over the Andes Mountains, where they traversed foot-deep ruts. They also endured mud, mire, and jungle rains in other locales. Fresh drivers were airlifted ahead of the cars to keep them rolling night and day. Traveling through Canada, to Alaska, on the final leg, the Comets pushed through ice and snow to make it to Fairbanks. Mercury offered buyers a 16-page booklet tracing the Comets' historic run through 14 countries. *Motor Trend* (February 1965) carried eight pages of the booklet as an informative "advertorial."

The full-sized 1965 Mercurys were completely restyled, with a three-inch increase in overall length and more luxurious appointments than last year's models. Styling consisted of a squared-fender profile, similar to that of the Lincoln Continental. All four corners were punctuated with slim, well-shaped lamps. "Mercury" lettering was widely spaced across the hood lip. The extruded aluminum grille had horizontal bars, plus a center panel that protruded slightly to resemble a Mercedes-like "radiator-grille." Body side panels had two horizontal "ribs" and full-length, parallel, body creases. There was a large wind-split decoration on the front fenders, but the overall look remained clean since the wind-split moldings were quite thin. There was a broad selection of 15 models in three series, with six different roof lines. They included the distinctive Breezeway four-door Sedan.

Besides having completely revised looks, the Mercs had a new "rigid" body straddling a torque-box perimeter frame. This gave a quieter, more comfortable ride. The front suspension featured a drag-strut design, with independent coil springs and tubular shocks inside the coils. A drag strut extended, from each lower suspension arm, forward to the frame. A front anti-roll bar was provided. Three links located the coil-spring rear axle and a rear sway bar (Panhard rod) was incorporated in the suspension design. It helped to control side sway in the big cars. There was a new flow-through ventilation system for the four-door Hardtops, a redesigned power steering system, low-profile tires and totally new interiors. A vertically mounted gas tank allowed more useable trunk space.

Jack Chrisman was the driver of the super-charged 1965 Comet Cyclone drag car of Moriarty Brothers Lincoln-Mercury. (Jon Graves)

153

The 1965 Monterey series included a Convertible base-priced at $3,000. (Mercury)

Park Lanes were priced from $3,267 to $3,599. This Park Lane Marauder four-door Hardtop came with a padded dash, padded sun visors, visor-vanity mirror, trip odometer, courtesy lamps, and "Super Marauder 390" V-8. (Mercury)

The Monterey series, with prices from $2,767 to $3,230, consisted of six models. There were two- and four-door Sedans and Hardtops, plus the Breezeway and the Convertible. Monterey equipment included a heater and defroster, front seat belts, directional signals, carpets, and five 8.15 x 15 black sidewall tires. The Convertible added all-vinyl upholstery.

The Montclair line included three models, which were two- and four-door Hardtops and a Breezeway Sedan. Their prices started as low as $3,135 and rose as high as $3,210. They came with all Monterey features, plus an electric clock, full wheelcovers, and interval selector windshield wipers. The Commuter Station Wagon, priced at $3,235, was somewhat comparable to a Montclair.

Park Lanes came in the same body styles as Montclairs, plus a Convertible. They were tagged from $3,267 to $3,599. Along with the Montclair equipment, they had a padded instrument panel, padded sun visors, a visor-vanity mirror, a trip odometer, courtesy lamps, and the "Super Marauder 390" V-8. Especially nice were the Park Lane's deluxe wheelcovers with a handsome rim section that cleanly framed the coupling-shaped center casting. The wood-grained Colony Park Station Wagon was "related" to the Park Lane series.

Standard engine in Mercurys was the two-barrel 390-cubic-inch V-8 with 9.4:1 compression and 250 hp at 4400 rpm. It was used with the three-speed manual gear box. When Multi-Drive Merc-O-Matic was added, a 266-hp engine was listed with the same basic hardware. A third version of the "390" had 10.1:1 compression and 300 hp at 4600 rpm. It had a single four-barrel carburetor and was standard in Park Lanes and optional in other models at $51.50 additional. A 330-hp "Police Special" version of the "390" with an 10.1:1 compression ratio and single four-barrel was $105 extra for Park Lanes and $153.10 extra for other full-size Mercurys. Also available, right on the standard factory options list, was a 427-cubic-inch 410-hp high-performance engine. It was $340.90 additional for Park Lanes, and $388.70 for other models. The "427s" had 11.5:1 compression ratios and this "mild" version featured a single four-barrel carburetor. Also available was a 425-hp version of the big "big-block" with dual-quad carburetion.

Mercurys continued to use a different three-speed manual transmission than the six-cylinder Comets and the small-block V-8s. Transmission options included four-speed manual (except in Station Wagons and cars with "4-Way" power Seats), and Multi-Drive Merc-O-Matic. Both were $231.70 extra. A 3.00:1 ratio rear axle was used with the "390" V-8s and automatic transmission. Three-speed stick-shifted cars had 3.00:1 or 3.50:1 rear axles. A 3.50:1 axle was standard with the four-speed manual gear box, which was mandatory with the "427" engines. The 3.50:1 axle, plus a 3.25:1 unit, were on the option list for certain drive teams.

New this year was a Sports package option with a $423 price tag. It more or less replaced the S-55 model. The package included bucket seats; a center console; Multi-Drive or four-speed transmission; a column-mounted gear shift lever; an elapsed time clock; and a console-mounted tachometer. Buyers could also get leather bench seats in Park Lanes, for $98.80 extra, and (late in the year) a small Philco television that hooked over the front seat back.

Paul F. Lorenz took over as general manager of Lincoln-Mercury Division in 1965. S.A. Skillman remained general sales manager. He had an easy job this season. Sales-wise, the nation's 303 Mercury dealers and 2,522 Ford-Lincoln-Mercury dealers delivered 177,008 big Mercs in 1966, a whopping 38 percent increase. Comet deliveries for the same period were 154,312 units, down from the record year 1964, but up from 1962 and 1963.

Production also took a positive trend, zooming to 181,699 Mercurys and 165,052 Comets in the model-year. That totaled 346,751 cars, which was an all-time record for Mercury products. However, the company's 3.9 percent share of industry output was only slightly up from 1964. The auto business, as a whole, was growing faster than Mercury's production. A milestone in marque history was also honored on January 14, 1965, when the 11-millionth Mercury built since 1938 left the assembly line.

About an hour before the road was closed for 1965's Pikes Peak Hill Climb, a 1965 Mercury Monterey Convertible took Smokey Bear to remind people to be careful with matches to avoid starting a forest fire. (Leroy Byers)

Dave Kunz is the owner of this restored 1965 Mercury "Boss Comet" B/FX drag racing car that appeared at the 1992 "Supercar Showdown." (John Gunnell)

The sign of the cat 1966-1969

All Mercury models had new safety glass, with a thicker vinyl inter-layer. Windshields were now attached using a new butyl tape system. The "bear hug" door latches were redesigned, and a padded dash became standard equipment. Front and rear seat belts were installed in all cars, unless buyers specifically deleted them from the equipment list. They were not yet a federally mandated item. Also found in many cars were other safety items, which would soon be required by federal law, including padded sun visors; an outside rearview mirror; windshield washers; two-speed windshield wipers; courtesy lamps; back-up lights; and four-way flashers. All cars sold in California came with a Thermactor emission control kit on their engines.

The 1966 Comets had fully unitized bodies. The feature lines were softer and more rounded. The front cowl and torque box structure was beefed-up for added sturdiness. Comets grew from compact cars into intermediates. They had two-inch longer wheelbases. The dual, stacked headlight arrangement was continued. The grille had two narrow, full-width horizontal slots. They were stacked in a twin-tier configuration. The grille inserts had criss-crossed moldings, with slightly wider vertical moldings in the center. "Comet" was lettered in the left-hand corner of the upper grille slot. Curved side glass was new. The rear quarters of the body had the "Coke bottle" shape, which was very popular in the 1960s. The rear body panel had a full-width, slot-shaped indentation. Horizontal taillamps were mounted at either end. There was "Comet" lettering on the edge of the trunk lid, just above the right-hand taillamp. Some cars had rear moldings, or beauty panel appliques, with the model name spelled out across them in block letters.

Three bent vertical bars decorated the front fenders of Comet 202 models, and the rear fenders had nomenclature bars. The base six-cylinder models were two- and four-door Sedans. Prices for both were slightly above $2,200. A heater, and defroster, were standard. These cars used the same wheelbase as other Comets, but had a 195.9 overall length. That made them 7.1 inches shorter than Capris, Calientes, and Cyclones. Different rear quarter panels were used. The new size allowed them to be priced with the least expensive competitors in the mid-size field. No wonder this was the best selling Comet series. Production was over 55,000 units. The Capri series was a new Comet line. Capris had rocker panel moldings, horizontal "star" front fender medallions, chrome-trimmed side windows, "Capri" rear fender scripts, and a rear body panel molding. The interiors featured

A 1966 Comet Cyclone GT served as Official Pace Car for the 1966 Indy 500. This car is still in the Indianapolis Motor Speedway's possession. (IMSC)

The Indy 500 Official Cars had Indiana 150th Anniversary state license plates. (IMSC)

In base form, the 1966 Comet Caliente Convertible sold for $2,841. (Mercury)

all-vinyl or parquet cloth-and-vinyl upholstery, and carpeting. The Capri series also offered two models. The four-door Sedan sold for $2,378, and the two-door Hardtop was $2,400. There was a "Custom Sport Coupe" version of the Capri Hardtop that came with a number of options at a special price. The extras included white sidewall tires; deluxe wheelcovers; a vinyl interior; wall-to-wall carpeting; a heater, and defroster; front, and rear seat belts; and emergency flashers. Almost 32,000 Capris were produced.

Comet Calientes were sporty models. They had the same trim basics as Capris, except the rocker panel moldings were thinner. "Caliente" scripts decorated the rear fenders. In addition, the rear body panel had a bright applique. The Cranbrook cloth, and "crinkled" vinyl interiors were a bit plusher than those of other Comets. There was wood-grain trim inside the cars, too. This series included a four-door Sedan, two-door Hardtop, and Convertible at prices between $2,453 and $2,735. Production of Calientes was more than 45,000 units. This included the one millionth Comet made ... a four-door Sedan with a vinyl roof.

At the top of the Comet lineup was the Cyclone series. It offered two body styles, but both came in standard and optional GT formats. Cyclones had a front fender bar with a checkered flag emblem, lower body perimeter racing stripe, and a different grille. Bucket seats and chromed wheels were standard. Prices for the Cyclones ranged from $2,700 to $3,152. Nearly 25,000 were built. The Cyclone GT was a new-for-1966 version. Both the GT Hardtop and Convertible were powered by the warmed-up 390-cubic-inch, 335-hp V-8, linked to a standard three-speed manual transmission. The new "SportShift" automatic transmission was optional. Cars with automatics were designated GTAs. Also offered was a four-speed manual gear box. Buyers could add a fiberglass hood with simulated air scoops, and a special handling package. The latter included beefier springs, heavier stabilizers, fatter wheel rims, and high-performance tires. *Car Life* gave the Cyclone GT Hardtop a somewhat critical review, in April 1966, summarizing it as a follower, rather than a leader, in the high-performance marketplace. This test car was equipped with a number of options, including the Sport-Shift automatic transmission; a clock; power steering; power brakes; AM-FM radio; and seat belts. These added $500 to its $2,891 base price. It also had a 3.25:1 rear axle ratio. The road test suggested that the GT's "390" engine, even with its higher valve lift, did not deliver really top performance. This was borne out with a 0-to-60 mph time of 6.6 seconds, and a 15.2-second quarter-mile at 90 mph. "The Comet times are median for the big-engine/small-car group; good, but not outstanding," said the reviewer. Other criticisms included poor-fitting body panels; a "tachometer-less" instrument panel; imprecise steering (due to poor weight distribution); sloppy handling; and a long gas filler tube that snaked almost half way across the trunk, and looked "vulnerable" to damage.

Despite this appraisal, *Super Stock & Drag* magazine named the Cyclone GT its "Performance Car of the Year," and the GT Convertible

Wide, English-pleat vinyl seats and a business-like instrument panel were seen in 1966 Comet Calientes. (Mercury)

The 1966 Cyclone continued the high-performance model's clean, but purposeful personality. (Mercury)

Comfort, style and performance were promised in the 1966 Mercury S-55 Convertible. (Mercury)

was picked to be Official Pace Car for the 1966 Indianapolis 500-Mile Race. Not too long ago, the author was shown one of the actual 1966 Comet Pace Cars in the basement storage facility at Indianapolis Motor Speedway's "Hall of Fame" Museum.

There were two Comet Station Wagons, too. The Voyager version was based on the Capri trim level. It listed for $2,553. The Villager was the upscale edition, related to the Caliente, with simulated wood-grain side trim. About 11,500 Comet wagons were made.

Inside the Comets was a new instrument panel with "swept away" styling on the passenger side, and integrated air conditioning outlets. Twenty-nine different interior trims were available. Six used cloth-and-vinyl combinations. The rest were all-vinyl. Colors used included silver; black; blue; red; aqua; gold; Emberglow; Parchment; burgundy; white; and Palomino. Colors offered for the outside of 1966 Comets and Mercurys included: Black; Dark Executive Metallic Gray; Light Blue; Light Beige; Dark Metallic Blue; White; Medium Metallic Palomino; Dark Metallic Green; Red; Medium Metallic Turquoise; Emberglow Metallic; Metallic Maroon; Metallic Light Blue; Metallic Sage Gold; Metallic Dark Turquoise; Medium Metallic Silver; Red; and Yellow. The 200-cubic-inch six was standard in Comets. It developed 120 hp, the same as 1965. A 200-hp version of the Ford

289-cubic-inch "small-block" V-8 was standard in Cyclones. Power plant options included three versions of the Ford 390-cubic-inch "big-block" V-8. While not new to the Ford family, this engine now fit in the enlarged Comet engine bay. It was equipped with new cylinder heads and "narrow-passage" intake manifolds. Lighter piston assemblies, and a higher lift/longer overlap camshaft were used, too. The "390s" offered up 265, and 335 hp. The least powerful version had a two-barrel carburetor, 9.5:1 compression ratio, and single exhausts. A four-barrel carburetor, 10.5:1 compression, and dual exhausts came with the big motor, which was offered only in GTs.

There was also a new "XPL" or "SportShift" three-speed torque converter type automatic transmission. This was a modified version of the Ford C-6 transmission, with added hydraulic

Base-priced at $3,144 was the 1966 Montclair Fastback. Breezeway roof was not offered in this line. (Mercury)

People with famous names starred in some 1966 Mercury ads. Chris Columbus "sailed" along in a Park Lane Hardtop. (Mercury)

Mercury's top series included a Park Lane four-door Hardtop with a $3,460 sticker price. (Mercury)

The 1966 Park Lane Fastback had wide, full-length lower body moldings and a rear "grille." (*Old Cars*)

controls that permitted "manual" gear shifting. With this transmission, drivers could select, and hold, first or second gear, either for up-shifting or down-shifting, or keep the selector in "D" position for normal automatic shifting. It also featured a lightweight, leak-resistant, one-piece aluminum alloy case.

All Comet cars had a 116-inch wheelbase, and all but Comet 202s had a 203-inch overall length. Station Wagons were still based on Ford wagons, with a 113-inch stance, and 199.9-inch length. Most cars used 6.95 x 14 tires, but Convertibles, Station Wagons, and GTs used size 7.75 x 14. Brakes for V-8s were upgraded to 10-inch drums, while the sixes stayed with nine-inch drums. The former had 251 square inches of effective lining area; the latter had 212 square inches. Front and rear track were both 58 inches, on most models, and 58.3 inches on Cyclones. Overall width was 73.8 inches. Hardtops stood 5.13 inches tall Sedans were 55.4 inches high. There were no radical changes in the Comet suspension, which continued to use coil springs in front, above a stamped A arm. The single, stamped, lower arm was again located by a drag strut attached to the front frame rail with a rubber bushing. There were changes to camber adjustment procedures, plus a higher roll center and wider track. The front geometry also had more jounce travel and a link-type stabilizer bar. The torque boxes on the Comets' new platform were fully isolated from the toe board. This transferred road vibration, and harshness, to the under-body side rails, and enhanced the cars' ride quality. In the rear was a Hotchkiss suspension with 58-inch-long leaf springs. Comets also had longer steering arms, and new equal-length tie rod ends. Steering gear ratios were increased.

Comet options and prices included: Air conditioning ($363); automatic transmission ($184); four-speed manual transmission ($183); limited-slip differential ($37); power drum brakes ($42); power steering ($84); power windows ($99); power seats ($62; and AM-FM radio ($126). Mercurys were largely unchanged under the skin, for 1966, although the exterior was extensively revised. A new horizontal-bars grille, with a thin, vertical center molding, characterized full-size 1966 Mercurys. The grille moldings curved to a peak at their center. There were new "razor edge" front fenders, and a down-sloping hood. Smaller parking lamps wrapped around the front body corners. "Mercury" appeared on the hood, and the deck lid. "Mercury stylists have rediscovered the chrome room and ornamentation has proliferated," said *Car Life*'s initial new models review. A large, "ice cube tray" ornament decorated the front fenders. Buyers could, however, order new, optional cornering lights to replace the large, glittery ornaments. Two-door hardtops had a new roof line with a concave back window. Large side view taillamps, segmented by three thin, chrome moldings, slanted upwards at the large of the rear fenders. There was thin rear "grille" with thin, horizontal ribs. The Mercury lineup consisted of 15 models in four series, with Breezeway lowerable rear windows available for Monterey, and Park Lane, four-door Sedans. A new "Dual-Action" tailgate was standard for Commuter and Colony Park Station Wagons.

This 1966 Park Lane Convertible with the 410-cubic-inch V-8 has gone 90,000 miles since new. It has bucket seats and a console, which is a relatively rare extra in a Park Lane. (Dick Garstang)

FOREGROUND: MERCURY COLONY PARK; REAR: MERCURY COMET VILLAGER

Luxury Station Wagons featuring simulated wood-grain exterior paneling in the 1966 Mercury model line-up were the Comet Villager and Colony Park. (Mercury)

Montereys had cloth-and-vinyl upholstery (all-vinyl in Convertibles), and carpeting. There were seven models: Two- and four-door Sedans and Hardtops, the four-door "Breezeway" Sedan, a two-door Hardtop, and a Convertible. Prices started at $2,783, and climbed to $3,237. The factory produced 65,688 Montereys.

Mercury's middle-priced full-size line was the Montclair series. These cars had full-length body side moldings, and chrome-accented rocker panels. An electric clock; interval-type windshield wipers; a deluxe steering wheel; and full wheelcovers were standard. There was a pair of four-door Montclairs (Sedan, and Hardtop), and a two-door Hardtop. Base prices started at $3,087, and ran to $3,217. Model-year output of Montclairs came to 41,871 units.

Four cars made up the 1966 Park Lane series. Two door entries were a two-door Hardtop and a Convertible. Four-door lovers could get a Hardtop Sedan or a Breezeway Sedan. Park Lane window stickers ran from $3,389 to $3,608. Park Lanes had full-length body side moldings, and rear deck lid trim. Mercury built 38,800 Park Lanes.

The sporty Mercury S-55 models had full-length body side moldings, chrome rocker panel moldings, and rear fender medallions. Both two-door Hardtops, and Convertibles were offered. Bucket seats, a center console, and dual exhausts were standard. Also standard was the 428 cubic-inch engine. This was Mercury's rarest line, with only 3,585 produced.

Motor Trend magazine did a road test of the 1966 Mercury S-55 two-door Hardtop in its August 1966 issue, summing it up with the words, "Comfort, style, performance come at no extra charge in Mercury's sportiest model." The car had just about every option, except air conditioning. The list included a remote deck lid release, automatic headlamp dimmer, and cruise control. The extras drove the price of the car to $4,735.94. They also brought the curb weight up to 4,260 pounds. Even at that, the standard "428" took the beast from 0-to-60 mph in 8.9 seconds, and down the quarter-mile in 16.9 seconds at 85 mph.

The magazine had the opportunity to drive its S-55 in all types of weather, and encountered no adverse steering or handling characteristics. It turned out to be "surprisingly agile" and made hill climbing, and mountain road driving an easy job. "The S-55 wasn't built to corner with a Grand Prix racer," said MT's Steve Kelly. "But it rates 'exceptional,' considering its size and weight handicap." Kelly also liked the Merc's easy-to-clean vinyl seat materials, the roominess of the huge trunk, clean-lined styling, easy to-get-at engine components, and trailer-hitch-friendly rear bumper. Coming in for criticism were the square edges of the steering wheel (for tiring his hands), the unpadded and uncarpeted luggage compartment, and the optional disc brakes, which needed 169 feet to stop the car from 60 mph. There was no comment about the S-55's average fuel economy of 12 mpg, but it was the '60s and gasoline was less than 45-cents-a-gallon!

The Mercury Station Wagon line included a four-door, six-passenger Commuter with Montclair-like trim. It had prices starting at $3,240. There was also a four-door, six-passenger Colony Park with simulated wood-grain trim, and full wheel discs. The latter had an advertised price of $3,502. The wagons contributed 25,741 assemblies to a successful season.

In the Monterey, the Montclair and Mercury Station Wagons, the base engine was a regular fuel 265-hp rendition of the 390-cubic-inch V-8. It was also available with dual exhausts, and 275 hp. These ratings were up from last season's 250 hp, and 266 hp, due to a redesigned induction system, and a hotter camshaft. Oil capacity was reduced to four quarts. Park Lanes had a 410 cubic-inch V-8, with 330 hp. This was a Mercury-only motor, derived from the "390" with a 0.2-inch stroke. Interestingly, it came with a 2.8:1 "economy" rear axle. The Park Lane engine was optional for Montereys, Montclairs, and Station Wagons. All could also be had with a 428-cubic-inch, 345-hp four-barrel V-8. A limited-production option was a 428-cubic-inch "Police Interceptor" engine. This version had the same 10.5:1 compression ratio, and single four-barrel carburetor, as other 400-plus cube engines, but it generated 360 hp at 5400 rpm, and 459 pounds-feet of torque at 3200 rpm. Supposedly, only law enforcement agencies could order it. Mercury introduced a new fuel delivery system, including a 25-gallon gas tank, and nylon fuel lines. A column-shifted three-speed manual transmission was standard in Mercurys, and a floor-shifted four-speed manual gear box was an extra. Ford's new C-6 was the automatic transmission used with most over-400-cubic-inch engines, but Multi-Drive Merc-0-Matic was required with the police car engine. Power front disc brakes were added to the options list. Like Comets, the Mercurys offered different wheelbases for cars (123 inches) and wagons (119 inches). Overall lengths were 220.4 inches and 215 inches, respectively. This made the cars an inch *shorter* for 1966, which was interesting. In 1965, Mercurys had grown almost two inches longer than Lincolns. This must have upset the folks at Lincoln. In 1966, the Lincoln was stretched four-and-one-half inches, which made it one-half-inch longer than the Mercury! Front and rear track were 62 inches. Overall width was 79.4 inches for "Mercurys" and 79.6 inches for Park Lanes. At 55.1 inches, the Park Lane was .09-inch lower than other models. Standard tires were size 8.15 x 15.

Mercury options and prices included: Air conditioning ($421.28); automatic transmission ($226.79); four-speed manual transmission ($226.79); limited-slip differential ($46.80); heavy-duty suspension ($14.29); power disc brakes ($97.20); power drum brakes ($42.29); power steering ($103.95); power side windows ($103.95); power side and vent windows ($155.63); 6-Way power seats ($94); 6-Way power left bucket seat ($84.20); tilt steering wheel ($42.19); AM-FM radio with "Studio-Sonic" sound ($141.34); AM-FM radio without "Studio-Sonic" sound ($145.93); 8.15 x 15 whitewall tires ($39.85 additional); tinted glass ($42.09); bucket seats (standard in S-55); tachometer ($52.95); automatic headlamp dimmer ($41.60); automatic "Cruise Control" speed regulator ($90.74); and vinyl roof cover ($88.99). First seen on the options list in 1965, and back again for 1966, was a nine-inch Philco television set designed to hang over the front seat

Several Mercurys competed in stock car races in 1966. Early in the season, drivers Ron Hornaday, John Steele, John Wynn, and Daryl Dieringer were racing, but rarely placing very high with old 1964 Mercurys. Later in the year, several drivers, including Dieringer, started running 1966 Comets. In drag racing, a well-known competitor was "Dyno" Don Nicholson in the Mercury Comet "Eliminator I." This match race car had a 427-cubic-inch single overhead cam V-8 that put out 900 hp. With a flip-up-front fiberglass body, its total weight was 1,800 pounds. It could do the quarter-mile in 8.7 seconds with a terminal speed above 160 mph. Other Comet Cyclone GTs with the standard 335-hp V-8 were running in C/Stock drag racing classes, and hitting up to 110 mph. One advertisement urged enthusiasts to write Frank E. Zimmerman, Jr., Mercury's general marketing manager, for copies of a booklet entitled *What Makes Drag Racing*? During 1966, rumors about a new "Mercury Mustang" began circulating. "Dubbed the S-7, the car will be an expanded version of the present Mustang," reported *Car Life* in February. The magazine predicted the sports/compact model would have a 111-inch wheelbase, 190-inch length, body styling that looked like a cross between the Mustang and Thunderbird, and a choice of 289- or 390-cubic-inch V-8s. "Target date is September or October 1966," writer Ed Janicki noted. "There will be only one model, a two-door Hardtop." By May, the buff magazines were calling the new model by the name "Cougar," and describing it as, "one of the sexiest styling projects since the American Underslung."

Lincoln-Mercury general manager E.F. Laux saw Mercury's share of industry output drop from 2.1 percent to 1.8 percent during 1966. However, this wasn't a reflection of any weakness in general sales manager F.E. Zimmerman's efforts to move new cars out of the nation's 253 Mercury, and 2,293 Lincoln-Mercury dealerships. Model-year production totals listed assemblies of 158,254 Comets. This included some 51,800 Comet 202s; 26,200 Capris; 44,900 Calientes; 16,000 Cyclone GTs; and 11,100 Comet Station Wagons. Big Mercurys had a run of 165,466 units, including about 65,700 Montereys; 37,500 Montclairs; 33,800 Park Lanes; 3,600 S-55s; and 24,900 Station Wagons.

The big news for 1967 was the Cougar. This Mercury product was a dressed-up Mustang. It featured disappearing headlights, wraparound front and rear fenders, and triple taillights with sequential turn signals. The front and rear end styling were similar. Cougars came equipped with all-vinyl bucket seats; a three-spoke, Sports-style steering wheel; deep-loop carpeting; deluxe seat belts; and a floor-mounted three-speed manual transmission. A fancier Cougar XR-7 was introduced in mid-model year. Except for a medallion on the roof's quarter panel, it looked like the standard Cougar. However, the XR-7 came with a wood-grained dashboard insert, a fancier interior, different gauges, and a "handling" suspension. The base model had a list price of $2,851 and the XR-7 pricing started at $3,081. The 289-cubic-inch, 200 hp V-8 was standard in the Cougar.

For 1967, the Mercury Comet had a horizontal grille, with a vertical piece in the center. It was framed by stacks of two headlights on each fender. The sides were clean, except for a "202" nameplate on the front fenders. The vertical taillights were on the ends of the rear fenders. About the

This publicity photo for the all-new 1967 Mercury Cougar was taken at Red Rocks Park in Morrison, Colorado. The like-new 1939 Mercury Convertible then belonged to professional photographer Leroy Byers. (Leroy Byers)

only extras not optional on the Comet 202 were a dome light and a cigarette lighter. The Comet 202 Series offered only two models, a two-door Sedan and a four-Door Sedan. The standard engine was the 200-cubic-inch six with 120 hp at 4400 rpm.

Comet Capris had nearly full-length, mid-body side moldings and nameplates on the rear quarter panel. Vinyl and fabric or all-vinyl upholstery, deep-loop carpeting and rear armrests were among standard features. This Series offered the four-door Sedan at $2,436 and the two-door Hardtop at $2,459. The Voyager wagon ($2,604) had a distinctive elongated U-shaped chrome piece on its front fenders.

The Comet Caliente was back again in 1967. Bright fender ornaments, rocker panel and wheel opening moldings set the sporty model apart from the pack. It also had full-length upper-body pin stripes. Its interior featured wood-grained dash and door panels, luxury armrests and paddle-type door handles. The models were the same as in the Capri series, plus a convertible. The Villager featured wood-grained side and tailgate panels. It came with crinkle vinyl upholstery and a dual-action tailgate. Calientes and Villagers were priced from $2,535 to $2,841.

The Comet Cyclone looked about the same as the Caliente, less the fender ornaments. Its grille had fewer horizontal pieces. The rear deck panel was blacked-out and the word "Cyclone" was spelled out on it. Bucket seats and all-vinyl upholstery were standard. The two-door Hardtop was $2,737 up and prices for the Cyclone convertible started at $2,997. Base engine in the Cyclone was the 289 cubic-inch V-8 with 9.30:1 compression, a two-barrel carburetor and 200 hp at 4400 rpm.

The Monterey name was used on the basic full-size Mercury. The center section of the horizontal bar grille protruded slightly and the signal lights were now located in the front bumpers. Wheel well openings had chrome moldings. The only additional side trim on the Monterey was a front fender criss-cross pattern trim piece and the Monterey name on the rear fenders. Regular equipment included: Carpeting; padded dash and visors; two-speed windshield wipers; windshield

It's hard to tell whether this is a posed or actual breakdown. The men seem to be striking a pose, but the women do not. The first Cougar Hardtop had a $2,851 base price. (Leroy Byers)

Mercury Cougar Dan Gurney Special

Specially priced for a limited time! At your Mercury dealer's.

It's Motor Trend Magazine's "Car of the Year"...with special extras inspired by racing champ Dan Gurney. Plus the unique set of persuasions that put Cougar in a league by itself to start with. Drive something special, Mercury Cougar Dan Gurney Special.

Specially equipped with:
- Turbine wheel covers
- F70 x 14 wide-oval nylon cord whitewall tires
- Chromed engine dress-up kit
- Dan Gurney signature decal
- Cougar 289 cu. in. V-8

Plus these fine Cougar features:
- Concealed headlamps that open, cat-like, at night

- Sequential rear turn signals
- Foam-padded front buckets
- Simulated wood-grain steering wheel
- Choice of 16 colors
- Pleated vinyl upholstery
- Wall-to-wall carpeting
- Sound insulation package
- Ford Motor Company Lifeguard Design safety features

Race driver Dan Gurney was depicted in an advertisement for a Cougar model named after him. The ad listed the "Dan Gurney Special" equipment. (Mercury)

washers; emergency flasher; courtesy light group; and remote-control outside rearview mirror. A fabric and vinyl interior was standard, except in the Convertible, which had all-vinyl upholstery. There were five Montereys in all, priced from $2,904 to $3,311. Four-door models included a Sedan, a Hardtop and a Breezeway Sedan. The Breezeway sedan had a slanting and retractable rear window. Two-door models were a Hardtop and Convertible. An S-55 sports package was optional on the Monterey Convertible and two-door Hardtop.

Mercury Montclairs had all the Monterey features, plus full-length upper body moldings. A nameplate was located on the rear fenders. Standard features included deluxe wheelcovers, electric clock, deluxe steering wheel and deluxe front and rear seat belts with a reminder light. The Montclair series offered the same trio of four-door models and the two-door Hardtop (but not the Convertible). They were priced from $3,187 to $3,316.

163

The Cougar interior featured bucket seats, a console and a console gearshifter. (Mercury)

The Cougar's headlamps hid by day (top) and opened automatically at night (center). Sequential turn lamps (bottom) were used. (Mercury)

Mercury Park Lanes featured full-length, tire level body moldings. Wheel well chrome trim and front fender emblems were other trim features of the Park Lane. Standard equipment included an automatic parking brake release, rear seat armrests, vanity mirror, spare tire cover, and power front disc brakes. This series offered the conventional and Breezeway Hardtops with four doors and the Sport Coupe and Convertible with two-doors. Prices spanned $3,736 to $3,984.

Broughams were similar to the Park Lane models, but slightly fancier. Extra body insulation, unique interior and exterior ornamentation, and wood-grain steering wheel and trim were standard features. The four-door Breezeway Sedan ($3,896) and the conventional four-door Sedan ($3,986) were available in this car-line.

Two noticeable features of the new Marquis two-door Hardtop were a vinyl roof and five, full-length, lower body pinstripes. Power front disc brakes; wood-grain interior trim; deluxe body insulation; electric clock; courtesy light group; spare tire cover; and plush, fabric and vinyl upholstery were among the many standard items in the Marquis. The front seats had individual fold-down armrests. The Marquis had a list price of $3,989. Only 6,510 were made.

A pair of Station Wagons was available to full-size Merc fans. The Commuter Station Wagon had full-length upper body moldings. The Colony Park had wood-grain panels outlined by chrome trim.

A total of 3,797 Comet Cyclone GTs was built in model-year 1967. This total included 3,419 Hardtops like this one, plus 378 Convertibles. (Mercury)

Base-priced at $2,818, the 1967 Comet Caliente Convertible was a relatively rare car. Only 1,539 of these cars were assembled. (Mercury)

Both wagons had a heater and defroster and dual-action tailgate. In addition, the Colony Park came with an electric clock; deluxe wheelcovers; deluxe steering wheel; power rear tailgate window; power front disc brakes; and all-vinyl or parchment Mosaic fabric interiors. Prices for these models were $3,289 and $3,657 respectively.

Standard in the Monterey was a 390-cubic-inch V-8, with a four-barrel carburetor, a 10.5:1 compression ratio, and 270 hp at 4400 rpm. The Park Lane, Brougham, and Marquis came with a 410-cubic-inch 330 hp engine. Wheelbase: (passenger cars) 116 inches; (Station wagons) 113 inches. Overall Length: (four-doors and Convertibles) 203.5; (two-doors) 196 inches; (Station wagons) 199.9 inches. Tires: (passenger cars) 7.35 x 14; (Station wagons and Cyclone GT) 7.75 x 14.

Prominent horizontal grille bars were one trait of the 1967 Comet Cyclone models. (Mercury)

Mercury said the mid-priced 1967 Marquis two-door Hardtop had seven "better ideas" from the Lincoln Continental. It was advertised as "Mercury, the Man's Car," which would be very "politically incorrect" today. (Mercury)

The 1967 Mercury Colony Park Station Wagon featured a Dual-Action tailgate and "yacht deck" walnut paneling. A rook rack was extra. (Mercury)

Mercury general manager E.F. Laux was happy to see his Cougar win *Motor Trend*'s "Car of the Year" award for 1967. General sales manager F.E. Zimmerman, Jr., did his best to get the company's 253 Mercury dealers, and 2,293 Lincoln-Mercury dealers to use the award as a selling tool. It must have worked, as Mercury counted production of 150,893 Cougars. In addition, the assembly lines cranked out 81,133 Comets, and 122,894 full-size cars. That was a total of 354,920 units, and 4.6 percent of industry output (compared to 323,730 cars and 3.8 percent the previous season).

If you liked the 1967 Cougar, you probably liked the 1968. The biggest change was the addition of side marker lights. Standard equipment included; a dual hydraulic brake system with warning light; front and rear seat belts; outside rearview mirror; padded dash; padded sun visors; two-speed windshield wipers and washers; four-way emergency flasher; and back-up lights. The Cougar two-door Hardtop listed for $2,933.

Cars in the XR-7 series added bright rocker panel moldings, special wheelcovers, deck lid medallions, and XR-7 plaques on the rear roof pillars. Standard equipment included; an overhead console (with map and warning lights); deep loop carpeting; tachometer; trip odometer; gauges; leather-trimmed vinyl seats; and walnut tone instrument-panel. At $3,232, the XR-7 seemed an attractive buy.

The Comet was restyled for 1968. It looked like a full-size Mercury that went on a diet. There was a new horizontal grille, rocker panel moldings, side marker lights, and chrome-encased, vertical taillights. Among the standard features were an energy-absorbing steering column and steering wheel; front and rear seat belts; shoulder belts; padded dash; padded sun visors; dual brakes with warning light; and two-speed windshield wipers and washers. Only one model was left in the base series. It was the two-door Hardtop with a base price of $2,477.

Mercury added an exciting 7.0-liter Cougar GT-E high-performance model to the line-up. (Mercury)

Dressed-up version of the Montego two-door Hardtop was the MX. It listed for $2,831. (Mercury)

166

Although based on the Ford Mustang, the 1968 Cougar Coupe had a totally different image, combining European elegance with American power. "America's best equipped luxury sports car," it was called. (Mercury)

The new Montego looked about the same as the Comet. It had all the same standard features, plus curb moldings, a cigar lighter, and a glove box lock. There were two variations. The four-door Sedan prices started at $2,504 and the two-door Hardtop sold for $2,552.

Full-length upper and lower body trim, chrome wheel well trim, and a vinyl top were styling features of the Montego MX. It also had bright metal upper door frames, simulated wood-grain inserts in the lower body molding, wood-grain door trim panels inserts, and carpeting. The Montego MX line offered a four-door Sedan, two-door Hardtop, Convertible and Station Wagon at $2,657 to $2,935.

Cyclones had a mid-tire level tape stripe. Those with the GT option had an upper body level racing stripe; bucket seats; wide tread whitewalls; special wheelcovers; all-vinyl interior; and special handling package. Cyclones were offered in two-door Hardtop and two-door Fastback models and both had a base price of $2,768.

For full-size Merc fans, the Monterey had a new, equal-size horizontal bar grille that protruded at the center. The vertical signal lights wrapped around the front fenders. The rear end treatment

This 1968 Montego MX Convertible features the "390 GT" engine, AM/FM radio, and power steering, brakes and top. (Robert L. Brown)

Mercury replaced the Comet with the Montego in 1968. This is the two-door Hardtop. (Mercury)

The 1968 Cougar XR-7 G included fog lamps, hood-locking pins, a simulated hood air scoop, racing-style rearview mirrors, and GT exhaust extensions. An electric sunroof was optional. (Mercury)

In 1968, Mercury made just 962 Montego MX Convertibles with bucket seats, plus 2,286 with bench seats. The base sticker price for the ragtop was $3,040. (Mercury)

After the Mustang 2+2 proved a popular model, Ford added a "kammback" body style to many of its car-lines. This is the 1968 Mercury Cyclone. (Mercury)

Mercury's got it.
A "Competitive Edge" Sale.

Mercury Premiere Coupe. Specially equipped, specially priced for a nice competitive edge.

Includes a big 390 V-8, deluxe interior trim, wall-to-wall carpeting, and an AM radio. (Also in a 4-door sedan.) You expect a good deal. And you'll get it: white sidewall tires, deluxe wheel covers with medallion, and all.

A competitive edge for all kinds of people.

Everybody's different. So we make different cars for everybody. Get the Mercury that's exactly right for your pocketbook and personality now.

First hardtop with yacht-deck vinyl paneling.

It's the paneling made famous by our Colony Park wagon. You see it here on our Park Lane sweptback. This paneling is tougher, longer-lasting than real wood. And every bit as beautiful. Also available on our Park Lane convertible. At your Mercury dealer's.

Your competitive edge on the tee: Arnold Palmer Golf Balls. 3 for $1.95.

The same quality Arnie uses. Regularly $3.75. Available for a limited time at participating Mercury dealers.

MERCURY LINCOLN

The Fine Car Touch inspired by the Continental.

Dan Gurney Cougar. Limited edition. Specially priced.

With deluxe interior, remote control mirror, wide tread whitewalls, Gurney decal, special turbine wheel covers, plus concealed headlamps, buckets, 302 V-8 engine, sequential rear turn signals, etc. And remember we said specially priced.

MERCURY

Ford

The Mercury Premiere Coupe, the Park Lane Sweptback with "yacht-deck" paneling, and the Cougar "Dan Gurney Special" were promoted by an ad offering Arnold Palmer golf balls at a low price. (Mercury)

Upper and lower tape stripe treatment characterized the 1968 Mercury Cyclone GT model. The Fastback model had a list price of $3,207. (Mercury)

resembled last year's. As before, the back window on cars with the Breezeway option could be lowered. Standard features included: Dual brakes with warning light; energy-absorbing steering column and steering wheel; seat belts; padded dash; padded sun visors; outside rearview mirror; side marker lights; heater/defroster; ashtray light; trunk light; four-way emergency flasher; glove box light; and shoulder belts. There were four Montereys — four-door Sedan, Convertible, two-door Hardtop, and four-door Hardtop at $3,052 to $3,858.

Deluxe wheelcovers and full-length, tire level moldings were two exterior differences between the Montclair and the lower-priced Monterey. An electric clock was among the many standard Montclair features. Montclair models (with window stickers between $3,331 and $3,459) were the four-door Sedan, two-door Hardtop, and four-door Hardtop.

Park Lanes had full-length, tire level moldings that looked like two thin parallel strips with a narrow band of chrome between them. The wheel opening lips were also chromed and there were three slanted trim pieces on the roof quarter panels. Like all full-size Mercurys for 1968, the Park Lane had a redesigned, clustered dash with the instruments placed in proximity to the driver. The electrical system was improved as well. A seldom-ordered Park Lane option was "yacht paneling." This was a fancy name for exterior wood-grained appliques used to dress up the Park Lane passenger cars. A four-door Sedan, Convertible, two-door Hardtop and four-door Hardtop were marketed at $3,575 to $3,647.

The Marquis was trimmed similar to the Montclair, except it came with a vinyl-covered roof. Its interior was also plusher. The sole model was a two-door Hardtop at $3,685. Only 3,965 were built.

Both Station Wagons had full-length, tire level moldings, and chrome-trimmed wheel openings. Both were four-door models. Prices for Commuters started at $3,441. The Colony Park ($3,760) had plank style wood-grain appliques on its sides. A dual-action tailgate was standard on both. A total of 5,191 Commuter and 15,505 Colony Park wagons came with either rear-facing or dual-center-facing rear seats.

In January 1968, at the Detroit Automobile Show, Mercury introduced simulated wood-grain exterior trim for three models other than the Colony Park Station Wagon. Advertisements and sales

After the Mustang 2+2 proved a popular model, Ford added a "kammback" body style to many of its car-lines. This is the 1968 Mercury Cyclone. (Mercury)

The 1968 Monterey Convertible had 123-inch wheelbase and 220-inch over-all length. (Dave Scott)

Mercury's 1968 Model 63A Monterey two-door Hardtop was the Fastback model. (Mercury)

folders used a number of names to describe this unusual option. In the four-page folder, it was called "wood-tone paneling." A 1968 *Mercury Salesman's News Flash* newsletter (released in December 1967) refers to it as "Colony Park Paneling." One 1968 advertisement called it "yacht-deck vinyl paneling." A different, two-page advertisement, printed in March 1968, describes it as "walnut-grained vinyl paneling" and "Colony Park paneling."

According to Mercury expert John Adamek, the wood-look trim was supplied by the 3M Company. It is technically known as a "DI-NOC wood-grain transfer." All ads and factory literature indicate that the option could be added to Park Lane Convertibles and two-door Hardtops (the Fastback or Sweptback version), and Mercury Brougham two-door Hardtops. However, Adamek owns an original, unrestored Monterey Fastback that has the simulated wood-grain trim, as well as a Park Lane Convertible and Colony Park.

Original, unrestored 1968 Mercury Monterey two-door Hardtop with the simulated wood-grain paneling is a rarity. This option was not officially offered for this model. Mercury used a variety of names for this extra. (John Adamek)

This 1968 Mercury Monterey Convertible, one of just 1,515 produced, was built on April 25, 1968, at the St. Louis assembly plant. It has the 390-cubic-inch, 280-hp engine and SelectShift Merc-O-Matic transmission. (Dave Scott)

Adamek has done extensive research on the simulated wood-grain option. In 1968, the price of this extra was $129.55. He has documented the existence, today, of 15 Park Lane Convertibles, one Park Lane Fastback, and one Monterey Fastback with the option. Adamek estimates that no more than 200 cars were delivered with the special trim. He has seen asking prices as high as $25,000 asked for such cars in collector magazines.

Mercury engines varied by series. The Comet, Montego and Montego MX offered the 200-cubic-inch, 115 hp six. Cyclone, Cougar and Cougar XR-7 models came standard with a V-8. This was a 302-cubic-inch, 210-hp job with a bore and stroke of 4 x 3 inches, 9.0:1 compres-

The 1968 Park Lane Fastback listed for $3,575. A new Park Lane Brougham line had a Hardtop, but not a Fastback. (Mercury)

Not any more!
Now Mercury convertibles and 2-door hardtops have it too!

Wood-tone paneling has always been a good idea, but until now it could only be found on luxury station wagons. (Like our best-selling Mercury Colony Park.)

At Lincoln-Mercury, this good idea has been expanded into an even better idea.

Now, the extra fine-car touch of simulated walnut-tone paneling is available on our Mercury Park Lane convertible and 2-door hardtop, and our Mercury Brougham 2-door hardtop. It's the same paneling that's used on our Colony Park; incomparably rich looking, handsome and durable.

And this fine-car touch is just as practical as it is beautiful. Its gleaming hard surface protects your door edges and body sides from accidental bangs and scratches, and minimizes unsightly paint chips.

Wood-tone paneling is available with all exterior paint color choices except two-tone combinations. And only Mercury's got it!

Stop in today, and see what the fine-car touch from the makers of Lincoln Continental is all about.

This folder promoted a "wood-tone paneling" option for Park Lane Convertibles and two-door Hardtops, and Mercury Brougham two-door Hardtops. This option was introduced at the Detroit Auto Show in January 1968. (Robert L. Brown)

The Fastback was also advertised as the "Sweptback" model. This is the only Monterey version built with wood-look trim. (John Adamek)

Will the "real" 1968 Colony Park please stand? The dressed-up wagon had a base price of $3,888. (John Adamek)

sion, and a two-barrel carburetor. Montereys and Mercury wagons got a little more power from a 390-cubic-inch V-8 with 265 hp. Standard in Park Lanes and Marquis was a 315-hp version of the "390."

Mercury built a total of 6,105 Cyclone Fastbacks and 334 two-door Cyclone Hardtops with the Cyclone GT option. Mercurys won seven NASCAR Grand National races in 1968.

In 1968, M.S. McLaughlin became general manager of Lincoln-Mercury. He was also a Ford Motor Company vice-president. General sales manager F.E. Zimmerman, Jr. was back again. This season, there were only 213 Mercury dealers, but the number of Lincoln-Mercury dealers rose to 2,395. That gave a higher total of 2,605 franchises, which bucked an industry-wide trend towards a decline in dealer counts. The assembly lines cranked out 113,700 Cougars, 123,100 Comets, and

In option-less form, the 1968 Park Lane Convertible was advertised for $3,822. This one has the standard 390-cubic-inch, 315-hp V-8. (Robert L. Brown)

Only 15 of the 1968 Mercury Park Lane Convertibles with Colony Park paneling have been documented to survive today. The original production total for this option is unknown to date. (John Adamek)

117,500 full-size cars. That was a total of 354,330 units, and 4.2 percent of industry output (compared to 354,920 cars and 4.6 percent the previous season).

The 1969 Cougar's grille had horizontal pieces that protruded slightly at the center. Bucket seats were standard equipment, but 1,615 Cougar Hardtops were ordered with optional front bench seats. Retractable headlights were used again. Rocker panel strips, wheel opening moldings, and two parallel full-length upper body pinstripes decorated the Cougar's sides. The back-up lights wrapped around the rear fenders, and the taillights were trimmed with concave vertical chrome pieces. A vinyl interior with foam-padded bucket seats and carpeting was standard. The Cougar came in a two-door Hardtop ($2,999) and a Convertible ($3,365). A GT appearance group option for Cougars included: "Comfortweave" vinyl bucket seats; a rim-blow steering wheel; a remote-control left-hand racing mirror; turbine design wheelcovers; GT decals; a GT dash nameplate; and F70 x 14 fiberglass belted tires for $168.40.

The XR-7 looked about the same as the basic Cougar from the outside. Its standard extras included: a rim-blow steering wheel; courtesy light group; visual check panel; left-hand remote-control racing mirror; electric clock; deluxe armrests; walnut-toned instrument panel with tachometer and trip odometer; leather with vinyl upholstery; vinyl door trim panels; and special wheelcovers. The same two body styles were offered in the fancier series with prices of $3,298 and $3,578 respectively.

Besides standard Cougar engine options, the 302-cubic-inch V-8 was standard in an "Eliminator" performance package. It featured a two-speed street rear axle; a blacked-out grille; a ram-air hood scoop; special side body stripes; and front and rear spoilers. The 290 hp 351-cubic-inch V-8 was standard in a "351 Performance Package." This option included: A competition handling package, dual body stripes, and a "Power-dome" hood. The "Ram-Air Induction" option came with a 428 V-8, a hood scoop, and F70 x 14 tires. High-performance rear axles and heavy-duty Traction-Lok differentials were optional. At least two Cougars were produced with "Boss 429" big-block engines.

Base price on the 1969 Cougar XR-7 Convertible was $3,578. (Mercury)

The new Comet had a framed horizontal-bars grille. It protruded slightly in the center section, where a Comet emblem was housed. The side marker lights were now at bumper level. Teakwood-toned appliques were used on the instrument panel. The upholstery was cloth-and-vinyl. The base model was a two-door Hardtop priced from $2,515.

Standard 1969 Montegos had moldings above the rocker panels and trunk lid. There were fender-to-fender upper body twin pin stripes. Carpeting and cloth-and-vinyl, or all-vinyl upholstery were standard. There were two Montego models. The four-door Sedan was $2,538 and the two-door Hardtop was $2,588.

Full-length lower body moldings, chromed wheel lip openings, fender-to-fender upper-body chrome trim, trunk lid appliques, and wood-tone appliques on the lower dash panel were features of the Montego MX. An MX Brougham option package for the Montego MX Hardtop or Sedan included: A Comfort Stream ventilation system; a remote-control mirror; rear roof pillar Brougham

High-performance was the center of Mercury's attention in 1969. It was highlighted by models like the Cougar Eliminator two-door Hardtop. (Phil Hall)

identification; luxury-level cloth/vinyl interiors; vinyl-covered door pull handles; a Brougham dash panel nameplate; and a rim-blow steering wheel. The MX Station Wagon was $2,962, the four-door Sedan was $2,701, the two-door Hardtop was $2,719, and the Convertible was $2,979. Convertibles had an all-vinyl interior, and a power top with glass rear window. Yacht deck paneling was a $149 option for MX wagons. Figures show that 3,621 Montego MX Station Wagons came with wood-grain side trim. Also, 1,590 four-door Sedans and 1,226 two-door Hardtops had a Brougham option package, and only 363 Convertibles were sold with bucket seats.

The sporty Cyclone Fastback, priced from $2,754, had rocker panel and wheel lip opening moldings. It also featured twin racing stripes. They ran from the front bumper and across the sides to the end of the rear fenders. Standard items included: Carpeting; all-vinyl upholstery; ventless windows; tinted rear window; and wood-tone appliques on the instrument cluster and lower dash. Only 5,882 of these cars were built in 1969. Mercury also built the Cyclone Spoiler II in 1969. It was the company's equivalent to Ford's NASCAR racer called the Torino Talladega.

There was also a new Cyclone CJ model. It included a black-out grille framed in chrome. There was a single chrome piece in the middle, running from each end of the grille. There was also a Cyclone emblem in the center, highlighting the front of the Cyclone CJ. Additional features included wheel opening moldings; dual exhausts; a 3.50:1 rear axle; an engine dress-up kit; a hood tape stripe; and competition handling package. A Sports appearance group including bucket seats; a remote-control left-hand racing mirror; turbine wheelcovers; and a rim-blow steering wheel was optional for the Cyclone CJ at $149 extra. This car had a list price of $3,207 and a mere 3,261 were assembled.

The 1969 Monterey had a new, horizontal-bars grille with a vertical piece in the center. Signal lights wrapped around the front fenders. The concave, rectangular taillights were clustered in the rear deck panel, which was heavily trimmed with vertical chrome pieces. The wheel opening openings, trunk lid and roof quarter

The 1969 Montego Convertibles had all-vinyl upholstery, power tops and glass rear windows. (Mercury)

Another new model for the drag racing set was the 1969 Cyclone Spoiler II Fastback. (*Old Cars*)

The 1969 Mercury Marquis Convertible had a production run of 2,319 cars. (*Old Cars*)

Nick Sanborn raced a 1969 Mercury Cyclone Spoiler II up Pikes Peak from 1969 to 1972. He won the time trials in 1970. Sanborn was a five-time winner in the Stock Car Division in the annual hill climb. (Leroy Byers)

175

A unique two-tone paint scheme was offered on the new-for-1969 Mercury Marauder and Marauder X-100. Standard in this X-100 two-door Hardtop was a 429-cubic-inch V-8 with 360 hp. (Phil Hall)

panels had moldings. Standard features included: ventless side windows; nylon carpeting; wood-toned dash and door panels; heater and defroster; and dome light. The Convertible had an all-vinyl interior, while other body types had cloth-and-vinyl trims. The Monterey line offered five models this year — four-door Sedan, Convertible, two-door Hardtop, four-door Hardtop, and Station Wagon — at prices from $3,141 to $3,523.

Cars in the Monterey Custom Series had rocker panel moldings and deluxe wheelcovers. The Customs also had a deluxe steering wheel; leather door pulls; wood-grained vinyl appliques; a front seat center armrest; bright seat side shields; and rear door courtesy lights. There were four models — four-door Sedan, two-door Hardtop, four-door Hardtop, and Station Wagon — priced from $2,442 to $3,740.

The attractive front-end styling of the Marquis was influenced by the Lincoln Continental Mark III. The integrated bumper-grille had a horizontal-bars theme and a prominent center section. Hidden headlight covers blended into the grille. Dual lower body pin stripes ran above the full-length bright curb moldings. Except for two back-up lights, the rear deck panel was a solid row of concave, rectangular, chrome-accented taillights. The interior featured deep-pile nylon carpeting; burled-walnut vinyl paneling on the dash and doors; front door courtesy lights; an electric clock; and a steering wheel with wood-toning on the spokes and rim. The Marquis series had the same five models as the Monterey line, with higher list prices of $3,840 to $4,380. The most expensive entry was the Colony Park Station Wagon and 18,003 Colony Park Station Wagons came with an optional third seat.

The Marauder had a Marquis front end, a special "tunneled" rear window treatment, and twin upper body pin stripes. There was a unique sculptured section, with five short, horizontal, chrome pieces just behind the doors. The six taillamps and two back-up lamps were embedded in the rear deck panel. Set between them was a blacked-out section with the "Marauder" name written in chrome. A cloth-and-vinyl interior was standard. This sports-luxury-level two-door Hardtop listed for $3,351.

The 1969 Marauder X-100 featured styled aluminum wheels, leather-and-vinyl seats, and fender skirts. (Mercury)

The extra-high-performance Marauder X-100 featured a two-tone paint job; fender skirts; leather-with-vinyl interior; rim-blow steering wheel; electric clock; glass-belted wide-tread tires; and styled aluminum wheels. It also came only in two-door Hardtop format, with window stickers starting at $4,074. Mercury built 5,635 of them.

The 1969 Comet, Montegos and MXs offered a 250-cubic-inch six with 155 hp at 4000 rpm. A 302-cubic-inch V-8 was standard in the Cyclone series. It featured a four-barrel carburetor, a 9.5:1. compression ratio and 220 hp at 4400 rpm. A larger V-8 was standard equipment in Cougar, XR-7, and Cyclone Spoiler models. All three used the 351-cubic-inch block. The

Cyclone Spoiler version had 10.7:1 compression and 290 hp at 5200 rpm. Cougar buyers had to settle for 9.5:1 compression and 250 hp, at least as standard equipment. The Cyclone CJ's V-8 was the 428-cubic-inch "big-block" with 10.6:1 compression ratio: 10.60:1, a single four-barrel and 335 hp at 5200 rpm. A wide range of engine options were available for the compact and mid-sized Mercurys, including a 320-hp 390-cubic-inch V-8 with a four-barrel carburetor; a 360-hp 429-cubic-inch V-8 with a four-barrel carburetor; and a 390-hp 427-cubic-inch V-8 with a four-barrel carburetor. A three-speed manual transmission was standard except in the Cyclone CJ, which came with a four-speed manual gearbox. Four-speed and Select shift automatic transmissions were optional in the other Series.

The 1969 Marquis Brougham Hardtop was $4,175. This one, with 27,000 miles, is for sale at $4,000 today. ("Red" May/ May Motors)

Big-car power plants started with the 390-cubic-inch, 265-hp V-8 on the Monterey, Monterey Custom and Marauder standard equipment list. Marquis, and Marquis Broughams featured a 429-cubic-inch, 320-hp V-8. The Marauder X-100 V-8 was also the 429-cubic-inch block, but with 10.5:1 compression and 360 hp at 4600 rpm. Also optionally available were a 280-hp 390-cubic-inch V-8 with a two-barrel carburetor; and a 335-hp 428-cubic-inch V-8 with a four-barrel carburetor. A three-speed manual transmission was standard, except in the Marquis and X-100, both of which came with Select-Shift automatic. The automatic was optional in the other models. A competition handling package, which included heavy-duty shocks and larger stabilizer bar, was a $31.10 option on the Marauder and X-100. High-performance and power transfer axles were also offered.

Cougars had a 111-inch wheelbase and overall length of 193.8 inches. They rode on E78 x 14 tires. The Comet/Montego chassis featured a 116-inch wheelbase (113-inches for Station Wagons) and overall lengths of 206.2 inches for cars and 193.8 inches for wagons (Cyclone/Cyclone CJ 203.2 inches). Tire sizes were 7.75 x 14 for the Cyclone and 7.35 x 14 for other models. Mercury Station Wagons and Marauders had a 121 inch wheelbase, while other models had a 124-inch stance. Overall lengths were 224.3 inches for Marquis; 221.8 inches for Montereys and Customs; 219.1 inches for Marauders and X-100s; 220,5 inches for Colony Parks; and 218 inches for Monterey and Custom Station wagons. Tire sizes were: (Marquis and Station wagons) 8.55 x 15; (X100) H70 x 15; (other models) 8.25 x 15.

In 1969, M.S. McLaughlin served his second year as general manager of Lincoln-Mercury and Ford Motor Company vice-president. General sales manager F.E. Zimmerman, Jr. returned, too. This season, there were only 188 Mercury dealers, but the number of Lincoln-Mercury dealers rose again, to 2,440. This represented another increase to 2,628 franchises, which continued to buck the industry trend towards declining dealer counts. The assembly lines cranked out 100,069 Cougars, 117,421 Comets and Montegos, and 140,516 full-size cars. That was a total of 358,006 units, and 4.2 percent of industry output (compared to 354,330 cars and 4.2 percent the previous season).

Mercury's list price for the 1969 Marquis Convertible was $4,107. This model was not available in the top-of-the-line Brougham series. Wire-spoke wheelcovers were a popular option. (Mercury)

Mercury in the '70s 1970-1979

Refinements in styling, and engineering characterized the 19 Mercury models that were marketed for 1970. New freon-filled shock absorbers were promoted as an important advance in ride control. They were standard on all models.

A completely redesigned Montego was lower, and wider. It offered concealed headlamps, bias-belted tires, and an oval-shaped steering wheel. Two new 351-cubic-inch power plants, plus a 429-cubic-inch V-8 were added to the list of engine options.

The protruding hood Mercury had been using for the past few years was carried to extremes on the new Montego. Its grille looked like the front end of a coffin. It had horizontal bars on it, and an emblem in the center. The signal lights were placed in the front fenders. wheel opening , and roof drip moldings were used. There were four hooded taillights. Each was evenly divided into four sections by chrome trim pieces. Standard equipment included: Concealed windshield wipers; front, and rear side markers; cloth-and-vinyl or all-vinyl interior; a wood-tone applique on the dashboard; and front, and rear armrests. The base series included a two-door Hardtop, and a four-door Sedan for $2,473, and $2,560, respectively.

The Montego MX had mid-body side moldings, and chrome trim around the trunk lid on all models. The window frames of four-door models were also chrome-framed. The interior featured loop carpeting; pleated cloth-and-vinyl (or all-vinyl) upholstery; and a teakwood applique on the steering wheel. The MX line included the two base models, plus a four-door Station Wagon, at prices between $2,563, and $2,996.

The Montego MX Broughams featured concealed headlights; chrome rocker panels; wheel opening moldings; dual upper body pin stripes; six-pod taillights; and silver or black appliques

The high-performance 1970 Cougar Eliminator had a standard 351-cubic-inch four-barrel V-8. (*Old Cars*)

Only 1,977 of the 1970 Mercury Cougar XR-7 Convertibles were built. The Cougar Convertible of the same year saw just 2,322 assemblies. (Mercury)

on the rear deck panel. Standard equipment included a cloth-and-vinyl interior; nylon loop carpeting; and a wood-grain vinyl insert in the steering wheel. This line consisted of three four-doors (Sedan, Hardtop, and Villager Station Wagon), plus a two-door Hardtop. List prices were in the $2,712 to $3,090 range.

The protruding center section of the Mercury Cyclone's distinctive grille was outlined by a chrome square. It was equally divided into four pieces, with a chrome circle in the center. Rectangular running lights were embedded in the grille. The lower back panel was finished in either silver or black. Loop carpeting, an all-vinyl interior and a competition handling package were standard. There was one model, a two-door Hardtop, with a $3,037 price tag.

Concealed headlights; a non-functional scooped "performance" hood; full-length lower body side moldings; left-hand remote-control; and right-hand manual racing mirrors; high-back "Comfortweave" vinyl bucket seats; special door panel trim; and a three-spoke sports style steering wheel were standard GT features. The single Hardtop model was $3,025. Only 10,170 were built.

The Cyclone Spoiler was aptly named. It had front, and rear spoilers; exposed headlights; mid-body side stripes; traction belted tires; scooped hood; dual racing mirrors; competition handling package; and full instrumentation. Prices started at $3,540. Production was a mere 1,631 cars.

The five-model Cougar line offered a base 351-cubic-inch, two-barrel V-8 engine. The high-performance Eliminator had four engine options, including the "Boss 429" four-barrel V-8. Evolutionary design changes included a new vertical grille, and a forward-thrusting front end. Promoted as "America's most completely equipped sports car," the 1970 Cougar's grille had a center hood extension, and an "electric shaver" style insert. Its design was reminiscent of the 1967, and 1968 models' grilles. Basic trim included upper body pin stripes; wheel opening, and roof moldings; and windshield, and rear window chrome accents. The interior featured high-back bucket seats; courtesy lights; carpeted door trim panels; a vinyl headliner; and a rosewood-toned dash panel. The Convertible had a "Comfortweave" vinyl interior; door-mounted courtesy lights; three-spoke steering wheel; and power top with folding rear glass window. There was a two-door Hardtop, plus a Convertible, for $2,917, and $3,264, respectively. Only 2,322 of the ragtops were made.

The Cougar XR-7 had distinct wheelcovers; rocker panel moldings; a remote-control racing mirror; and an emblem on the rear roof pillar. Interior features included vinyl high-back bucket seats with leather accents; map pockets on the seat backs; a tachometer; a trip odometer; a rocker switch display; a burled walnut vinyl applique on the instrument panel; rear seat armrests; map and courtesy lights; a visual check panel; loop yarn nylon carpeting; and an electric clock with elapsed-time indicator. The XR-7s came in the same body styles as the base Cougar, at $3,201, and $3,465, respectively. The XR-7 ragtop had a run of just 1,977 units.

Highlighting the 1970 Mercury Monterey line were a new grille, new taillamps, and an oval-shaped steering wheel. The Monterey grille had thin, bi-level horizontal bars. They were outlined in heavier chrome. There was a slender vertical emblem in the middle; four recessed chrome rimmed headlights; and large, wraparound signal lights. There were bright moldings on the wheel opening openings, rear roof pillar base, and windows. Two large, narrow, rectangular, deck panel taillights

A scooped hood identified the 1970 Mercury Cyclone GT. A Cyclone Spoiler with more muscle was available, too. (Mercury)

Total output of big 1970 Mercury Convertibles was 1,814 and 1,233 were Marquis models, such as this one. Note the "pinstripe" whitewall tires. (Mercury)

were centrally divided by back-up lamps. The interior featured nylon carpeting; dark teakwood vinyl instrument panel appliques; a color-keyed steering wheel; adjustable head restraints; a steering column lock; pleated design cloth-and-vinyl upholstery (all-vinyl in the Convertible); and heavy sound insulation. The line included a four-door Sedan, two- and four-door Hardtops, a Station Wagon, and a very rare Convertible (only 581 built). Prices started at $3,029, and stopped at $3,440.

Monterey Customs had full-length; mid-body side chrome spears (with vinyl inserts); deluxe wheelcovers; and curb moldings. On the inside was the cloth-and-vinyl (or all-vinyl) upholstery; a front seat arm rest; teakwood-toned inserts in the steering wheel; vinyl-covered door pull handles; and rear courtesy light switches. The Custom line had no ragtop or Station Wagon. Prices were in the $3,288 to $3,436 bracket.

Mercury Marquis models received a modest face-lift for 1970. Vertical pieces were added to the bumper-integrated grille, and to the signal lights. Dual pin stripes ran from fender to fender, at tire level, and above the wheel opening openings, outlining them. There were bright, and black curb moldings, and chrome trim on the lower front fenders. A luxury "Rim-Blow" steering wheel; front door courtesy lights; and wood-toned door panel inserts graced the Marquis' interior. This line included all five body types, and there were two Station Wagons. The Villager version had wood-grain exterior panels. Prices ran from $3,793 to $4,123. Only 1,233 Convertibles were produced, and only 1,429 Station Wagons had an optional third seat.

Instead of pin stripes, the Marquis Brougham used upper body moldings. They ran from the face of the front fenders to the rear. Also seen on these luxury models were chromed wheel openings and vinyl roofs. The interior featured individually-adjustable, twin comfort lounge seats (with two folding armrests.) The door trim panels were wood-toned, and the door-pull handles were covered with vinyl. This had the same three models as the Monterey Custom line, with $4.02 to $4,219 price tags.

Except for its name spelled out in chrome on the face of the hood, the big-but-sporty Mercury Marauder looked the same as the Marquis in front. Side trim consisted of twin upper body pin stripes; window moldings; and a sculptured section with five short horizontal chrome pieces behind the doors. A "tunneled" rear window remained a Marauder styling high point. The same distinctive taillight treatment used last year, was on the 1970 model. The Marauder two-door Hardtop sold for $3,271, and just 3,397 was made.

Things did not end with the Marauder models, though. There was a special Marauder X-100 Series. Cars in this series featured fender skirts; wheel opening moldings; and special wheelcovers Other differences included high-back, all-vinyl bucket seats with center console (or twin "Comfort-lounge") seats; luxury steering wheel; and bright seat side shields. The X-100 two-door Hardtop sold upwards from $3,873. Production was 2,626.

Standard engine in the Montego/Montego MX/Montego Brougham models was a 250-cubic-inch overhead valve six producing 155 hp. Standard in Cyclones, and Marauder X-100 was the 429-cubic-inch V-8 with 360 hp at 4600 rpm. Cyclone GTs, Cougars, and XR-7s used the 351-cubic-inch V-8 with 250 hp. In the Cyclone Spoiler, standard engine was the 429-cubic-inch, 370 hp V-8. Monterey, and Monterey Custom models used a 390-cubic-inch, 265 hp V-8 as standard equipment. The Marquis/Marquis Brougham/Marauder engine was the 429-cubic-inch with 320 hp.

Montego, and Cyclone passenger cars had a 117-inch wheelbase; Station wagons had 114 inches. Overall lengths were 209.9 inches for cars, and 209 inches for Station Wagons. Tires used were: (Cyclone Series) G70-14; (other models) E78-14. The Cougar chassis featured a 111.1-inch wheelbase. Overall length: was 196.1 inches. Tires were size E78-14. Mercury wagons, Marauders, and X-100s had 121-inch wheelbases. Other models had a 124-inch stance. Overall lengths were: (Marquis, and Brougham) 224.3 inches; (Marquis wagons) 220.5 inches; (Monterey, and Custom) 221.8 inches; (Monterey wagons) 218 inches; (Marauder, and X-100) 219.1 inches. Standard tires also varied by car-line, as follows: (Monterey, and Custom) G78-15; (Marquis, Brougham, Marauder) H78-15; (Monterey wagons) H70-15.

180

A full-length upper belt molding identifies the 1970 Mercury Monterey Custom Convertible. (Lowell E. Eisenhour)

Bennett E. Bidwell led Mercury into the 1970s. F.E. Zimmerman, Jr. Was general sales manager. W.E. Carbett was in charge of doing development work with the company's 112 exclusive Mercury dealers, and 2,585 multi-line dealers. Model-year output included: 103,873 Montegos; 72,363 Cougars, and 129,080 full-sized Mercs. This added up to 305,316 automobiles, which was the lowest total that the company had realized since 1964. Mercury's share of overall industry output stood at four percent, the lowest since its 3.8 percent share of 1966. Generally, 1970 was not a good year for the company, as the nation's motorists were beginning to focus on smaller, more fuel-efficient automobiles.

Mercury entered the sub-compact car market on September 18, 1970, when it introduced its new-for-1971 models. The new product was a dressed-up version of Ford's Maverick. It revived the Comet name. The two-door Sedan, selling for $2,217, had a 103-inch wheelbase. The four-door Sedan, selling for $2,276, had a 109-inch stance. Four engines were offered. A "170" inline six with 105 hp was standard. Options included 200- (120 hp), and 250-cubic-inch (155 hp) sixes, and a "302" V-8 with 220 hp. Transmission choices were three-speed manual or three-speed automatic. The small six came only with stick shift, and the big one came only with the automatic. The sub-compact model of most interest to car collectors is the Comet GT. It came with racing stripes, a blacked-out grille, and a simulated hood air scoop. Most Comets had more options, and bigger engines, than Mavericks. Otherwise, both cars are about the same. They are not seen often today, due to attacks of the dreaded "tin worm."

The intermediate-size Montego continued. The 1971 model was again based on the mid-sized Ford (Falcon-Torino)/Mercury (Comet/Montego) series first launched in 1968. Base Montego; Montego MX; Montego MX Brougham; Cyclone; Cyclone GT; and Cyclone Spoiler series were offered. There were 12 models with list prices from $2,772 to $3,801. All Cyclones were two-door Hardtops. Two-door Hardtops, four-door Sedans, four-door Station Wagons, and four-door Hardtops were included

The 1971 Mercury Comet was offered in three models, with a 302-cubic-inch V-8 as one option. (Mercury)

in the Montego offerings, but not all models came in all series. The two-door Hardtops are favorites with collectors. Some prefer the fancy MX Brougham, while others like the Cyclones. With these cars, the longer their model names, the better their collector-car potential is. The Montegos, and Cyclones were tough cars with good reliability. It was the final year for the Cyclone name in 1971. Cyclones had a distinct grille, a hood scoop, and running lights. GTs added high-back bucket seats, and full instrumentation. With Cyclone Spoilers you got front and rear spoilers. Cyclones came standard with a 351-cubic-inch, 285-horsepower V-8. GTs included a 240-hp version of the "302." Other models used a 250-cubic-inch inline six as base engine, and offered a 302-cubic-inch, 210 hp V-8 option. A 429-cubic-inch "Super Cobra Jet" V-8, with 370 hp, was standard in Cyclone Spoilers and available in some models as an option. In terms of fuel economy, the "427" went less than 10 mpg, but it had some real muscle. Mandatory with this engine was a new "Competition Suspension" with stiff springs, and shocks, and a fat anti-roll bar.

Cougars had the most dramatic changes seen, since the marque's 1967 introduction. There was a longer wheelbase, a lower silhouette, interior refinements, and a new GT model. Inspiration for the thinner roof, and windshield pillars was said to have come from Europe. The 1971 models were "horse-sized" ponies, based on the big, new Mustangs. They were four inches longer (113 inches) in wheelbase, and seven inches longer (197 inches) in overall length. With a radiator-style grille, they looked even heftier than that. The Cougars had better

Comet four-door Sedans had a 110-inch wheelbase, seven inches longer than two-door models. (Mercury)

The most popular 1971 Montego MX model was the sporty-looking two-door Hardtop. (Mercury)

Mercury's flagship, the Marquis Brougham, was more luxurious than ever. It had two new V-8s. (Mercury)

manners than the Mustang, with more sound deadening materials, and nicer appointments. Only big V-8s went under the hood. They included a "351" with 240 hp (two-barrel) or 285 hp (four-barrel), plus a "429" with 370 hp. There were two Cougar series, each with a Hardtop, and a Convertible. The XR-7 was the sporty version with bucket seats, full instrumentation, and a vinyl half-roof. Cougar list prices started at $3,289, and went to $3,877. The Convertible had a very distinctive look. It has been picked, by some observers, as a good prospect for future collectability. Survivors are scarce, though. In 1971, Mercury built only 1,723 base ragtops, and 1,717 XR-7 Convertibles. So far, these series of Cougar Convertibles seem to be rare, but affordable cars.

Rounding out the 1971 Mercury model line up was the "big M" itself. All 1971 Mercury models received all-new sheet metal, trim, and ornamentation. Changes were seen in front end treatments, rear bumpers, and taillamps. Some innovations included one-piece door windows, flush door handles, and concealed wipers. Monterey, Monterey Custom, Marquis, and Marquis Brougham series were offered. Each had four-door Sedans, and Hardtops and a two-door Hardtop. All except the Monterey Custom series had a pair of four-door Station Wagons; one with two seats, and one with three seats. The Marquis Brougham wagons used the traditional Colony Park name to signify their simulated wood-grain side paneling. Mercury's wide range of full-sized models allowed it to fill the wide price spectrum from $3,858 to $5,033. These were durable "land yachts," which were based on Ford LTDs. They had much luxury in the upper model ranges. A Lincoln-like ride was soft, but not taut. The powerful Mercury V-8s have very little trouble passing anything (but gas stations).

Mercs shared a 124-inch wheelbase (121-inches for Station Wagons), and a 224.7-inch length (220.4 inches for Station wagons). Engine choices started with the 351-cubic-inch, 240-hp motor. A 400-cubic-inch, 260-hp V-8 was available. Marquis, and Marquis Broughams came with a 429-cubic-inch engine with 320 (standard) or 360 optional horsepower. These cars were not often recommended to used car buyers, but they do have the large-size, V-8, rear-drive appeal that some old car collectors still drool over. High-trim-level examples, in near-mint condition with many extra-cost goodies, can deliver plenty of old-fashioned "Turnpike Cruiser" appeal. They are also great for towing that trailer with your antique or classic car riding inside. In addition, they can be a tremendous buy in today's "gas-crunch-conscious" marketplace. Often, they sell for $1,000, or less. Many people mistakenly believe that nobody wants them.

This is the 1971 Mercury Cougar XR-7 Convertible, of which 1,717 copies were made. There was a standard ragtop, of which 1,723 were built. (Duffy's)

Another new product available from about one-third of America's Lincoln-Mercury dealers (990 to be exact), was the West German-built Capri. It was sold, starting in May 1970, as a 1971 model. This four-passenger GT "Super" Sport Coupe was known as the "European Mustang." It became something of an import sensation in the United States. It had a 100.8-inch wheelbase, a 67-inch width, and an overall length of 168 inches. Size 165 x 13 tires were mounted. The British-made 97.6-cubic-inch four-cylinder engine below its hood had a 3.188 x 3.056 bore and stroke. It developed 75 hp. A 122-cubic-inch, 86 hp four was optional. Standard equipment included a four-speed manual transmission, power front disc brakes, styled steel wheels, and rack-and-pinion steering. A larger 155.7-cubic-inch V-6, made in Germany,

A wrap-over Landau roof treatment was an option for the 1971 Mercury Cougar XR-7 Hardtop. (Mercury)

was a running change in December 1971 (for 1972 models). It could be had with optional automatic transmission. Port of Entry prices for Capris started at $2,445.

The Lincoln-Mercury Division quietly, and methodically, went about its business. It sold cars through 2,874 franchised dealers in 1971. Of these, 2,782 sold Mercurys, and other Ford products, while 92 were exclusive Mercury dealers. Bennett E. Bidwell remained at the helm of the division. Replacing F.E. Zimmerman, Jr., as the general sales manager, was W.P. Benton, the former general marketing manager. (However, by the end of the year, Benton moved "up the ladder" and Lee Whiteman became general sales manager.) A.B. Connors took over Benton's old title. Interestingly, the company controller's name was J.G. Buick. Other high-placed Lincoln-Mercury executives having names the same as vintage automobiles were W. Chase (Southern regional manager), R.F. Lewis (Central regional manager), and T. Daniels (sales operations manager). Model-year production of cars built in United States factories included 83,000 Comets; 62,864 Cougars; 57,094 Montegos; and 128,099 Mercurys. For the calendar-year, 56,118 Capris were sold. This was besides the 17,258 cars retailed in the last nine months of 1970.

Introductions of 1972 Mercury models were scheduled for September 17, 1971, a day earlier than the previous season. A major restyling of the Montego, and face-lifts of other models paced the new-car news of the year. Innovations included an anti-skid braking option, which was the first offering of this feature on a medium-priced Mercury. The Capri was available with the new V-6.

The 1972 Comet had virtually no changes, except for some modifications of engine output ratings to reflect net, rather than gross, horsepower. The "170" engine carried an 82 hp rating; the "200" had 91 hp; the "250" was rated for 98 hp; and the "302" V-8 listed 143 hp. Comet's biggest styling change for 1972 was its dual, full-length upper body pin stripes. Besides that, it looked the same as last year's model. Standard features included: A locking steering column; two-speed windshield wipers, and washers; a left-hand outside rearview mirror; a padded dashboard; door-operated courtesy lights; carpeting; and a heater. Prices dropped approximately $40 on both models.

Leroy Byer's 1972 Mercury Capri has 27,000 original miles on its German-made 2.8-liter V-6. It is finished in Silver Metallic paint. (Leroy Byers)

Mercury built 53,267 Comet two-door Sedans in 1972. This one sports a vinyl top. (Mercury)

An "egg-crate" grille graced the front end of the 1972 Mercury Monterey Custom two-door Hardtop. (Mercury)

The GT package was $173 extra. It again included a huge hood scoop, and "Comet GT" lettering on the sides of the cowl, replacing the normal Comet script behind the front wheel opening. A Select-Shift automatic transmission was available with any optional engine, and could be ordered with a floor-mounted selector lever in the GT. Factory air conditioning was $360. Comet dimensions, and chassis specifications, were the same as 1971. However, there was a change to standard 6.45-14 size tires.

In the mid-size Mercury offerings, the Cyclones had "stormed" out of the model listings. Base, MX, Brougham, and GT models were entirely revised. The new bodies, and sheet metal were mounted on a redesigned chassis featuring a perimeter frame, and four-coil suspension. Other new features included one-piece windows; recessed door handles; and the center-type grille. The Montegos were marketed in nine models, with prices from $2,843 to $3,438. Four-door cars gained one inch (118 inches) in wheelbase. Two-door models had the same 114-inch wheelbase formerly reserved just for Station Wagons. Base Montegos had wheel opening moldings. The new grille, with criss-cross patterning, carried over to the headlights. MXs had pin stripes on the upper body, and bright-accented rocker panels. Deluxe sound insulation, carpeting and, on the wagon a three-way tailgate, were standard features for the MX line. Wheel well opening moldings were found on all upper car-lines. The four large, rectangular taillights were bumper-integrated. Interiors were trimmed in either cloth, and vinyl or all-vinyl. MX Broughams had more chrome moldings, a "Flightbench" armrest seat, deluxe wheelcovers, and wood-grain interior trim. The Villager Station Wagon also had exterior wood-grain paneling. MX Brougham body styles were the same as those in the MX series. GTs substituted a "waffle" pattern grille; full-length tire-level side moldings; a performance hood with twin air scoops; racing mirrors; behind-the-door louvers; a tachometer; and full gauges in a black-finished instrument panel.

The base Montego series had a four-door Sedan, and a two-door Hardtop. The MX series had the same models, plus a four-door Station Wagon. One six-cylinder power plant was offered in 1972. This was the 250-cubic-inch engine with a 95 hp (net) rating. One version of the 302-cubic-inch V-8 was still around, too. It used a two-barrel carburetor, and generated 140 hp. Optional engines started with two versions of the "351" V-8 offering 161 or 248 hp. A 400-cubic-inch V-8 with a two-barrel carburetor, and 168 hp, was listed, too, plus a "429" with 205 hp. Montegos had a one-inch longer wheelbase, but a one-inch shorter length this season.

The fine, criss-cross pattern on the wraparound front signal lights was replaced by horizontal lines. Otherwise, 1972 Cougars looked virtually the same as last year's models. Among the standard features were: High-back bucket seats; sequential turn signals; a locking steering column; back-up lights; a consolette with illuminated ashtray; concealed two-speed windshield wipers; dual racing mirrors; a two-spoke steering wheel; Deluxe wheelcovers; instrument panel courtesy lights; a glove box light; and flow-through ventilation. The XR-7 came with an emblem in the center of the grille; a half-vinyl roof; bucket seats with leather seating surfaces; a tachometer; a "sissy" bar; an

The 1972 Mercury Montegos had one-piece door glass. This is the Brougham four-door Sedan. (Mercury)

The 1972 Cougar came as a Hardtop or a Convertible. The "351 CJ" was one of two new V-8s. (Mercury)

alternator gauge; an oil pressure gauge; and nylon carpeting. Both series offered a two-door Hardtop, and a Convertible. Prices were $3,016 to $3,547. Base engine for the Cougar, and Cougar XR-7, was the 351-cubic-inch, 164 hp V-8. There were two options, based on the same size block. The first, with 262 hp, featured a special "quiet exhaust" system. The second, with 266 hp, was the Cobra-Jet version. Both had four-barrel carburetors. There were no size or chassis specification changes in the Cougar line.

A "waffle" pattern grille was the biggest Monterey styling change for 1972. The plain Monterey series had two- and four-door Sedans, a two-door Hardtop, and a four-door Station Wagon. Standard features included: Power steering; a simulated Cherrywood instrument cluster; a color-keyed two-spoke steering wheel; power front disc brakes; nylon loop carpeting; and cloth-and-vinyl upholstery. Cars in the Monterey Custom series included four-door Sedans, and Hardtops, plus a two-door Hardtop. They had full-length mid-body side moldings. Deluxe wheelcovers, and chrome rocker panels also helped distinguish Customs from basic Montereys. The Custom's cloth-and-vinyl interior was more luxurious, too. A new ice-cube-tray-pattern grille, and a similar treatment in the center section of the rear deck panel, were the main styling changes for 1972 Marquis. This line offered all four body styles. Standard equipment included: Power front disc brakes; power steering; deluxe sound insulation; power ventilation; 100 percent nylon-loop carpeting; deluxe wheelcovers; a wood-grain instrument panel; an electric clock; a map light; a luggage compartment light; twin ashtrays; and courtesy lights. Marquis Broughams had fender-to-fender upper body moldings. In addition to standard Marquis features, they came with a vinyl robe cord; cut-pile nylon carpeting; front door courtesy lights; a vanity mirror on the right-hand sun visor; power windows; a vinyl roof; color-keyed wheelcovers; interior pillar lights; and ashtrays, and lighters, in the rear seat armrests. Models were the same as Marquis. List prices for the big cars started at $3,793 for the Montereys, and climbed to $5,034 for the Marquis Brougham four-door Hardtop. Base engine in Monterey was the 351-cubic-inch, 163 hp V-8. Monterey Station Wagons, and Monterey Custom passenger cars came with a 400-cubic-inch, 172 hp V-8. In addition, a 429-cubic-inch, 208 hp V-8 was standard in Marquis, and Marquis Broughams. Wheelbase, length, width, and tire sizes for the big Mercurys were unaltered from 1971. New options included a "Sure-Track" anti-lock braking system (formerly available only on Lincolns), and larger steel-belted radial tires.

Also back in Lincoln-Mercury showrooms was the Capri. The addition of the V-6, and automatic transmission, pushed the German-built Sport Coupe into the largest sales increase of any imported brand for the year. The V-6, also made in Germany, had a 3.54 x 2.63-inch and stroke. It developed 107 hp.

Future collector cars in the crop of 1972 Mercury products most likely include the "big-block" Cougars, and the Capri. With the loss of the Cyclone name, the Montegos lost a share of their appeal to enthusiasts (and later muscle car collectors). The big, full-size cars are also seen in the hands of collectors who appreciate their "classic" styling, and their high level of luxury appointments, not to mention their huge, powerful (but gas-guzzling) V-8s.

William P. Benton was Ford Motor Company's new vice president, and general manager of Lincoln-Mercury Division. It was a terrific year for sales, as the nation's 2,844 Lincoln-Mercury dealers (78 exclusives) realized a 30 percent increase over 1971's record. "Despite serious challenges to many areas of our business, sales have never been better, and the future has never been brighter," Benton reported at the start of 1973. "It's especially so at Lincoln-Mercury, which recorded the greatest increase in sales, over a year ago, of any division in the industry." Model-year production totals listed 82,359 Comets; 135,087 Montegos; 53,702 Cougars; and 174,154 Mercurys. Imports of

Rare again in 1972, the Cougar Convertible had a total run of 3,169 units, of which 1,929 were of the XR-7 style shown here. (Mercury)

185

Mercury built 53,267 Comet two-door Sedans in 1972. This one sports a vinyl top. (Mercury)

tem; blend-air heater; wheel lip moldings; rocker panel moldings; carpeting; front, and rear ashtrays; and cloth-and-vinyl upholstery. The four-door Sedan listed for $2,389, and the two-door Sedan was $2,432. Base engine in the 1973 Comets was a 200-cubic-inch six with 94 hp at 3800 rpm. Chassis specifications included: Wheelbase: (two-doors) 103 inches; (four-doors) 109.9 inches. Overall length: (two-doors) 185.4 inches; (four-doors) 192.3 inches. Tires: 6.45 x 14.

Larger, energy-absorbing bumpers were the most noticeable change made to Montegos for 1973. The standard interior was cloth-and-vinyl. The base series featured a two-door Hardtop, and a four-door Sedan. Like last year, rocker panel moldings and dual upper body pinstripes helped set the MXs apart from the basic Mont-

the Capri also soared to 91,995 units, for a 5.7 percent share of "captive import" sales. This was up from 3.6 percent in 1971.

The 1973 Mercurys were introduced on September 22, 1972. Coming off a record-breaking business year, there was little time to plan major revisions. Instead, most Mercurys featured appearance, and engineering refinements. There were some changes in base power plants, and standard equipment. Some new options were released for various models.

The 1973 Comet received a new, criss-cross pattern grille, and energy-absorbing bumpers. However, basic styling remained the same as it had since 1971. Standard features included: Dual hydraulic brakes with warning light sys-

Base engine in the 1973 Comet Coupe was a 200-cubic-inch six with 94 hp at 3800 rpm. (Mercury)

egos. They also had deluxe sound insulation, and color-keyed deep loop carpeting. This series had a Station Wagon as a third body style. Bright upper body moldings, and deluxe wheelcovers were two distinguishing exterior features of the Montego MX Broughams. They came with Flightbench seats. These were bench seats with backs that resembled buckets, and a folding armrest between them. This car-line also had three models, but the wagon was a Villager with wood-grain trim on the outside. The steering wheel had a wood-grain insert. In the Montego GT models, new energy-absorbing bumpers, and placing the "G" over the "T" on the front fender nameplate, were the styling changes made for 1973. The only body type offered was a two-door Fastback. Standard features included: Deluxe sound insulation; deluxe wheelcovers; a sports-type three-spoke steering wheel; deep-loop carpeting; dual racing mirrors; and a performance hood with non-functional dual

Rocker panel moldings, and dual, upper body pinstripes helped set the MXs apart from the basic Montegos. They had deluxe sound insulation. (Mercury)

The last year for the Mercury Cougar Convertible was 1973. A total of 3,165 Cougar XR-7 ragtops were assembled that year. (Duffy's)

scoops. Base power plant for cars in all Montego series was changed to a 250-cubic-inch six with 92 hp. The only V-8 option was a 302-cubic-inch block with 137 hp. Montego chassis features included: Wheelbase: (two-door) 114 inches; (four-doors, and Station Wagons) 118 inches. Overall length: (two-doors) 211.3 inches; (four-door) 215.3 inches; (Station Wagons) 218.5 inches. Tires: (Station Wagons) F78 x 14 GT or G78 x 14; (other models) E78 x 14. Prices for the mid-size Mercs ranged from $2,843 to $3,438.

Cougar styling changes for 1973 consisted mainly of vertical chrome pieces in the headlight panels, a more refined radiator-look grille, and vertical trim pieces on the taillights. Standard equipment included: Sequential turn signals; high-back bucket seats; wheel lip moldings; a two-spoke color-keyed steering wheel; a consolette with ashtray; and power front disc brakes. Chrome rocker panels, and the XR-7 emblem on top of the grille were two ways to tell the top-of-the-line Cougar from the standard one. In addition to the features offered on the basic Cougar line, XR-7 buyers received special wheelcovers; toggle switches; a remote-control mirror; a vinyl roof; a tachometer; a trip odometer; an alternator gauge; an oil pressure gauge; and a map light. The high-back bucket seats had leather seating surfaces. Both Cougar lines offered the two-door Hardtop, and the Convertible. Prices were $3,372 to $3,903. Cougars, and XR-7s were powered by a 351-cubic-inch, 168 hp V-8. The Cobra-Jet version of the "351" was available at extra cost. Cougars had a 112.1 inch wheelbase, and 199.5 inch overall length. The standard tires were size E78 x 14.

The 1973 Monterey was about two inches shorter than last year's model, but nobody mistook it for a Comet. Its ice-cube-tray grille was outlined in chrome. The horizontal bars on the recessed headlight panels carried over to the large wraparound signal lights. A full-length, mid-body side chrome spear, chrome wheel well openings, and chrome rocker panels graced the Monterey's sides. Six square, chrome trimmed taillights, and two back-up lights were located on the rear deck panel. Between them was trim that matched the grille's pattern. All 1973 Montereys came equipped with power steering; nylon loop carpeting; front bumper guards; an automatic parking brake release; energy-absorbing bumpers; and power front disc brakes. A cloth-and-vinyl interior was standard. The Monterey Custom was a standard Monterey with a plusher interior, and a more powerful engine. Changes in the Mercury Marquis, for 1973, included energy-absorbing bumpers; "finger" grille squares; wraparound signal lights; a free standing hood ornament; and full-length lower body, and wheel well opening moldings. An automatic parking brake release; fender skirts; an electric clock; an inside hood latch release; power front disc brakes; and power steering were among its many standard features. The Marquis Broughams had fender-to-fender upper-body side moldings; power windows; halo vinyl roofs; shag cut-pile carpeting; a vanity mirror on the right-hand sun visor; rear pillar, and luggage compartment lights; and deluxe wheel covers with inserts. The Colony Park Station Wagon came with a three-way tailgate, power rear window, and Cherry woodgrain yacht deck exterior paneling. Window stickers ranged from $3,793 for the lowest-

The 1973 Cougar XR-7 Hardtop featured a three-quarter vinyl roof, leather seats, and full gauges. (Mercury)

187

Big 1973 Mercurys had a more formal front end appearance and thinner windshield pillars. (Mercury)

priced Monterey, to $5,034 for the Marquis Brougham four-door Hardtop. The "351" (with a 159 hp rating) was the standard big-car engine. Standard in Marquis Brougham Wagons, and optional in other Marquis was a 400-cubic-inch, 171 hp V-8. Another option was a 429-cubic-inch, 198 hp V-8. Mercury chassis specifications were: Wheelbase: (Passenger cars) 124 inches; (Station Wagons) 121 inches. Overall length: (passenger cars) 222.5 inches; (Station Wagons) 223.4 inches. Tires: (Passenger cars) HR78 x 15 steel-belted radials; (Station Wagons) JR78 x 15 steel-belted radials.

The 1973 Capri had an almost $500 price increase, and it now listed for $2,983. It also grew seven inches longer overall, and measured 175 inches bumper-to-bumper. The body was also two inches wider, at 67 inches. There was a new, larger four-cylinder engine, too. It had a 3.575 x 3.029-inch bore-and-stroke for 122 cubic inches, and 86 hp. The 155.70-cubic-inch V-6, introduced in model-year 1972, continued to be available.

One of the Mercurys the author owned was a 1973 Monterey Custom four-door Sedan with a 400-cubic-inch, two-barrel V-8. It was a well-built machine, with many interesting features, such as the brocade-pattern upholstery, the automatic emergency brake, and the best air conditioner he has ever seen. It ran like a tank, although the body was quite rusty by the time he got it. Naturally, the infamous seat-belt-interlock system was a pain in the neck. A similar car, in mint condition, would definitely have a permanent home in John Gunnell's garage. Other good bets for 1973 are Montego MX Brougham two-door Hardtops, Cougar XR-7s, and (because it makes a great tow car) the Colony Park Station Wagon. Sports car enthusiasts will also savor that certain Capri with a well-maintained V-6, and a like-new body. Unfortunately, that is a rare combination.

The best 1973 Mercury models to collect are the Cougar XR-7, the Marquis Brougham, the Grand Marquis, the Colony Park, and the Capri. Some younger auto enthusiasts also take a shine to Comets with the GT package, although the appeal of this car is limited in the overall marketplace. The fancier Montegos, in two-door Hardtop style, do have their fans, as well. Big engines seem to add to the investment potential, even though they sponge up the petrol.

William P. Benton steered Lincoln-Mercury through 1973, with total model-year output of Mercurys (not including Capris) rising from 421,626 units, in the previous season, to 462,674 units. However, the company's share of total industry production declined from 4.9 percent to 4.7 percent. Model-year assemblies of 1973 Mercurys built in the United States included 94,691 Comets; 156,805 Montegos; 60,628 Cougars; and 150,550 Mercurys. Model-year sales by dealers here were: 77,434 Comets; 136,826 Montegos; 52,860 Cougars; 163,793 Mercurys; and 111,953 Capris.

New front, and rear bumpers, and slightly different upper, and lower body moldings were the biggest Comet styling changes for 1974. Standard features included dual hydraulic brakes with warning light system: Blend-Air heater; windshield washers; locking steering column; cigar lighter; energy-absorbing steering wheel; and two-speed windshield wipers. The Comet line again consisted of a two-door Sedan ($2,432), and a four-door Sedan ($2,489). The six-cylinder engine had the same 200-cubic-inches, but a new rating of 84 hp at 3800 rpm. The wheelbase was 114 inches, overall length was 214.2 inches, and tires were size HR78 x 14.

The slightly protruding, chrome-outlined Montego grille had a criss-cross pattern. The four headlights were nestled in chrome panels. Wheel well openings, and center mid body moldings were seen on the sides. The taillamps were located on the rear deck panel, and wrapped around the fenders. Standard features included front disc brakes; impact-resistant bumpers; a locking steering column; concealed windshield wipers; an inside hood release, and color-keyed deep-loop carpeting. Models in the base series were the same: two-door Hardtop, and four-door Sedan. Rocker panel moldings, and nameplates on the lower front fenders, were two identifying traits of the MX. Along with a slightly plusher interior than the base Montego, the MX had deluxe sound insulation. This series consisted of the two-door Hardtop, four-door Sedan, and four-door Station Wagon. Upper body, and lower rear quarter panel moldings, plus a super sound-insulation package, and wood-grain applique on the instrument panel, were Montego MX Brougham features. This series was composed of the same three body styles found in the MX line, but the Villager Station Wagon had simulated wood-grain body side, and tailgate panels, plus a power tailgate window. There was a Flight-bench seat with center armrest inside, plus imi-

The last year for early style German-built Capris was 1974. A larger V-6 was available. (Old Cars)

tation Cherry wood instrument panel, and dash panel appliques. The Montego engine was a 302-cubic-inch, 140 hp V-8. Chassis specifications for Montegos were: Wheelbase: (two-doors) 114 inches; (four-doors, and Station Wagons) 118 inches. Overall length: (two-doors) 215.5 inches; (four-doors) 219.5 inches; (Station Wagons) 223.1 inches. Tires: (Station Wagons) H78 x 14; (other models) G78 x 14. Montego prices ranged from $2,842 to $3,438.

Cougar XR-7 front end styling was similar to last year's model, except the grille was wider, and it had the previous emblem replaced by a hood ornament. Side trim consisted of upper body chrome running from the tip of the fenders to the rear roof pillars, where it connected with a chrome band that went across the roof.

New front, and rear bumpers, and upper, and lower body moldings were the Comet's 1974 changes. (Mercury)

There was also full-length, upper-tire-level moldings, and an opera window. The rear deck panel taillights wrapped around the fenders. Standard features included: Soft, vinyl bucket seats or twin "Comfort Lounge" seats; steel-belted radial tires; power steering; performance instrumentation; a luxury steering wheel; cut-pile carpeting; and an inside hood release. The Cougar listed for $4,706 with a standard 351-cubic-inch, 168 hp V-8. The only power option was a 400-cubic-inch, 220 hp V-8. Chassis details included a 114-inch wheelbase, a 216-inch overall length, and HR78 x 14 tires.

The Mercury Monterey had a "squares-within-squares" chrome-framed grille. This pattern was carried over to the headlight panels. Signal lights wrapped around the front fenders. Rear quarter roof pillar nameplates, and trim, full-length mid-body spears, and wheel opening, and rocker panel moldings, were seen on the sides. Among the standard features were: Nylon carpeting; a glove box light; power steering; an automatic parking brake release; solid state ignition; and cloth-and-vinyl upholstery. This line had the two-door Hardtop, four-door Sedan, and four-door Station Wagon in it. A "Custom" series script on the rear roof quarter panel, deluxe wheelcovers, a deluxe steering wheel, and an all-vinyl interior were standard features of the Monterey Customs. The Station Wagon was not included in this series. The Marquis grille had rectangular vertical pieces with finer bars within them. The hidden headlight doors had horizontal bars, which extended around the wraparound signal lights. "Mercury" was spelled out in chrome, above the grille. Side trim consisted of full-length, lower body moldings. The six square taillights, and two back-up lights were located in the rear deck panel. Standard features on Marquis included: Power front disc brakes; power steering; a deluxe sound insulation; loop-pile carpeting; courtesy lights; fender skirts; and power ventilation. The interior was cloth-and-vinyl. The Marquis included a four-door Sedan, two- and four-door Hardtops, and a four-door Station Wagon. Full-length upper body moldings; a halo vinyl roof; power windows; door pull straps; a left-hand remote-control mirror; Deluxe wheelcovers

For 1974, the Cougar XR-7 became a new, mid-size luxury car. A 351-cubic-inch V-8 was featured. (Mercury)

The chrome-outlined Montego front end had a criss-cross pattern grille and four headlights. (Mercury)

The 1974 Marquis grille had rectangular vertical pieces with finer bars within them. (Mercury)

with inserts; pillar lights; and lights under the instrument panel were Brougham features. The Brougham series had the same body styles as the Marquis line, but the Station Wagon featured Villager trim. Prices for the full-sized Mercurys ran from $4,367 to $5,519. Big-car power plant was the 460-cubic-inch, 195 hp V-8. Chassis specifications included: Wheelbase: (Passenger cars) 124 inches; (Station Wagons) 121 inches. Overall length: (Passenger cars) 226.7 inches; (Station Wagons) 225.6 inches. Tires: (Passenger cars) HR78 x 15; (Station Wagons) JR78 x 15.

This was the last year for the original Capri, which is sometimes called the "Capri I," to distinguish it from its replacement. (The new car was officially named the Capri II.) A larger V-6 was introduced, to replace the original option, since the 155.7-cubic-inch engine proved to be troublesome, and exhibit reliability problems. The new motor had a 170.8-cubic-inch displacement.

The sportier Montegos, the Cougars (especially the XR-7s), and the big, ultra-luxurious Marquis, again seem like good picks as future collector cars. Keep in mind that people who collect such late-model cars are not interested in restoring them. They are looking for those well maintained, low-mileage originals, loaded with big V-8s, and oodles of options. Especially appreciated are cars of this description which sell at low prices, because their used-car value is low. Such cars ARE around, and collectors do have a way of finding them. The 1974 Capri is also a car to watch. It is the last, and most refined of the series, and the larger V-6 was an improvement.

William P. Benton was in his last year as the "head honcho" at Lincoln-Mercury Division. In mid-1975, Walter S. Walla took over at Mercury. Benton then became vice president, and general manager of Ford Division. L-M's general sales manager, A.B. Connors, had a tough job in 1974. Total model-year output went from 462,674 Mercurys in 1974, to 398,682 in 1975. The year saw 125,695 Comets leave Mercury factories, as this model benefited from the nation's economy-car kick. In addition, the Cougar line had an increase to 91,670 assemblies. However, Montego output dropped nearly 60,000 units to 91,670 cars, and the production of large Mercurys declined almost 70,000 units to 83,298. That was painful for America's 61 Mercury, and 2,843 Lincoln-Mercury dealers, as the full-sized, option-loaded cars accounted for substantial profits. The imported Capri had United States dealer sales of 82,057 units in model-year 1974.

The new Bobcat brought Lincoln-Mercury into the sub-compact car market. This was quite an image change. The Bobcat was based on Ford's Pinto. It had an attractive, chrome-framed, "Lincoln-like" grille with vertical bars. The word "Mercury" spelled out above it. Both headlights were recessed into bright moldings. The long, rectangular vertical taillights were placed on the rear deck panel. Standard equipment included a luxury interior with low-back bucket seats; cut-pile carpeting; a sound insulation package; disc brakes; and a four-speed transmission. Bobcat models included a three-door hatchback called the Runabout ($3,189), and a two-door station wagon called the Villager ($3,481). Bobcats were powered by an overhead camshaft four-cylinder engine with a cast iron block. Piston displacement was 140-cubic-inches. It had a 3.78 x 3.13 inch bore and stroke, 8.40:1 compression ratio; and a one-barrel carburetor. The output was 83 hp at 4800 rpm. Chassis features were: Wheelbase (Runabout) 94.5 inches; (Villager) 94.8 inches. Overall length: (Runabout) 169 inches; (Villager) 179 inches. Tires: B78 x 13.

The Comet was originally scheduled for deletion in 1975, but the sales spurt it experienced the previous season saved it. As a result, it looked virtually the same as last year's model. Standard features included: A locking steering column; a deluxe sound insulation package; a deluxe steering wheel; a color-keyed instrument panel with lighted dash; pleated cloth-and-vinyl seats; pleated door trim panels with simulated wood accents; a deluxe steering wheel; a trunk liner; a sound insulation package; a dual hydraulic-brake system with warning light; and cut-pile carpeting. Buyers had their choice of four colors of upholstery. The models offered were, again, the two-door Sedan ($3,236), and the four-door Sedan ($3,270). There was a GT package, too. Standard under the hood was a 200-cubic-inch six, now with 75 hp. Chassis features included: Wheelbase: (Four-door) 109 inches; (two-door) 103 inches. Overall length: (Four-door) 196.9 inches;

(two-door) 190 inches. Tires: (Four-door) CR78 x 14; (two-door) BR78 x 14.

Mercury called its all-new Monarchs "precision-size luxury cars." In overall size, they were compared to the Mercedes 280. Monarchs also had a Lincoln-style, chrome-framed grille. It had vertical bars, and "Mercury" spelled out above it. The two headlamps were enclosed in square "boxes," and large, vertical parking lamps wrapped around the front fenders. Full-length trim moldings on the rear of the car, the wheel lips, and the windows, plus chrome-accented rocker panels, were seen. The wraparound rectangular taillights were located on the rear deck panel. The word "Mercury" was printed in a chrome-framed section, between the taillights. Standard equipment included: Individually reclining bucket seats; front disc brakes; foot-

The Comet was scheduled to be dropped in 1975, but a sales spurt saved it for one year in without changes. (Mercury)

operated parking brake; solid-state ignition; a locking glove box; and an inside hood release. Wide, full-length upper tire level moldings, and upper body pin stripes made it easy to distinguish the Ghia from the basic Monarch. It came with a deluxe sound insulation package; a left-hand remote-control outside mirror; an Odense-grain vinyl roof; unique wire spoke wheelcovers; a carpeted luggage compartment; a digital clock, and a luxury steering wheel. Prices for Monarchs began at $3,764, and rose to $4,349 for the Ghia four-door. Standard engine for Monarchs was a 3.68 x 3.126 inches bore and stroke, 200-cubic-inch six. It had 8.0:1 compression, a one-barrel carburetor, and 105 hp at 4000 rpm. A second cast iron block, overhead valve six was optional. It had the same 3.68-inch bore, but a longer 3.91-inch stroke. It displaced 250 cubic inches. With a one-barrel carburetor, and an 8.0:1 compression ratio, SAE net horsepower was rated 72 at 2900 rpm. Monarch buyers could also add a pair of V-8s. The first was the "302" with 129 hp, and the second was the "351" with 154 hp. A three-speed, column-mounted transmission was standard. Optional were "three-on-the-floor," and an automatic. The latter was available with a choice of column- or floor-mounted gear shifter. Chassis-wise, the Monarch had a 109.9-inch wheelbase 109.9 inches, and overall length of 200 inches. Tires were size DR78 x 14.

Twin slots in the center of the lower front bumper were the main changes to Mercury Montego styling for 1975. Standard features included power brakes; power steering; solid state ignition; a locking steering column; and cut-pile carpeting; concealed windshield wipers; and front bumper guards. Buyers could choose from a cloth-and-vinyl or all-vinyl interiors in black, tan, or blue. The base Montego line consisted of a $4,092 two-door Hardtop, and a $4,128 four-door Sedan. Upper body pin stripes, and rocker panel moldings were seen on the Montego MXs. They also had extra sound insulation, and slightly fancier interiors. Models in this line included the four-door Sedan, and Station Wagon, and the two-door Hardtop. Montego MX Broughams had upper body moldings; door-pull straps; a super sound-insulation package; vinyl roofs; wood-grain appliques on their steering wheels; and wiper-mounted windshield washer jets. The Villager Station Wagon had wood-grain vinyl paneling on its sides, and tailgate. It also included a power tailgate window; a deluxe steering wheel; and a "Flightbench" seat with folding center armrest. Montego prices ranged from $4,092 to $4,909. Power came from a "351" rated for 148 hp at 3800 rpm. A 400-cubic-inch two-barrel V-8, and a 460-cubic-inch four-barrel V-8 were options. Montego chassis features included: Wheelbase (two-door) 114 inches, (four-door, and Station Wagons) 118 inches. Overall length (two-door) 215.5 inches; (four-door) 219.5 inches; (Station Wagons) 224.4 inches. Tires: HR78 x 14.

The addition of two rectangular openings, between the front bumper guards, on the lower bumper, was the extent of styling changes made to 1975 Cougar XR-7s. They came with power steering; bucket seats with a console (or "Twin Comfort Lounge" seats); a luxury steering wheel; deep cut-pile carpeting; a passenger assist handle; an inside hood release; a locking steering column; and power front disc brakes. The Cougar XR-7 was priced $5,218. It came with the same base V-8 used in Montegos, plus the same two V-8 options. Cougar chassis features included a 114 inch wheelbase, and an overall length of 215.5 inches. The tires were size HR78 x 14.

Twin slots in the center of the front bumper were the main changes to Mercury Montegos in 1975. (Mercury)

The 1975 Cougar XR-7 was priced at $5,218. It featured the same V-8 used in Montegos, plus the same two options. A real cat was not included. (Mercury)

The 1975 Marquis' chrome framed-grille consisted of six rectangular chrome pieces, each containing five vertical bars. A single vertical bar evenly divided the grille in two. Concealed headlamps were standard on all Marquis. They looked like music boxes, and both had an emblem in the center. The wraparound signal lights were circled by four thin chrome bands. Side trim consisted of full-length lower-body moldings, and upper body pin stripes. "Mercury" was lettered on the center rear deck panel, between the wraparound, rectangular taillights. Standard features included power steering; power front disc brakes; wood-grain appliques on instrument panel; a left-hand remote-control mirror; a power ventilation system; deluxe wheelcovers; and cut-pile carpeting. This series was composed of a pair of four-door models, the Sedan, and the Station Wagon, plus a two-door Hardtop. The 1975 Mercury Marquis Broughams had full-length upper body moldings; a vinyl roof; deep cut-pile carpeting; an electric clock; power windows; fender skirts; Brougham wheelcovers; and a visor-mounted vanity mirror. The Colony Park Station Wagons also featured simulated Rosewood paneling on their sides, and tailgate; a Flightbench seat with center armrest; door-pull and seat back assist straps; Brougham wheelcovers; deluxe seat, and shoulder belts; a visor-mounted vanity mirror; and a three-way tailgate. This was a three-model series with a two-door Hardtop, a four-door Sedan, and the Colony Park. A wide, upper-tire-level band of molding, running across the body sides, set the Grand Marquis apart from cars in other full-size Mercury series. They came with deep, shag cut-pile carpeting; dual map-reading lamps; left-hand remote-control mirrors; vinyl roofs; carpeted luggage compartments; hood, and deck lid paint stripes; and passenger assist straps. Prices started at $5,049, and went up to $6,469. Marquis, and Marquis Brougham Station Wagons had a 460-cubic-inch displacement, and 158 hp. Optional in Broughams, and standard in Grand Marquis, was a 218-hp version of the "460." Mercury chassis features were: Wheelbase (passenger car) 124 inches; (Station Wagon) 121 inches. Overall length: (passenger car) 229 inches; (Station Wagon) 227 inches. Tires: (passenger cars) JR78 x 15; (Marquis) HR78 x 15.

There was no "1975 Capri," but the all-new Capri II was introduced at midyear. Officially, it was a "1976" model, but over 60,000 were sold in calendar-year 1975. It came in standard, and Ghia lux-

The 1975 Monarch had a Lincoln-style vertical bars grille and "Mercury" lettering above it. (Mercury)

The West German-built Capri got a redesigned Hatchback body at midyear. It was renamed the Capri II. (Mercury)

Concealed headlamps were standard on all 1975 Marquis. This is the Grand Marquis four-door Sedan. (Mercury)

ury editions. The glass area was increased by 40 percent, and the rear seats were designed to fold down, for extra storage space.

Continuing to appeal most to collectors are the sportier Montegos, the high-performance Cougar XR-7s (especially those with "460" V-8s), and the big, ultra-luxurious Marquis, and Colony Parks.

Walter S. Walla was appointed corporate vice president, and general manager of Lincoln-Mercury Division. A.B. Connors continued as general sales manager. E.S. Gorman took over from O.W. Bombard as public relations manager. G.B. Ellis moved from sales administration manager to administrative assistant to the general manager, a brand new corporate title.

Three factors helped Mercury's 1975 production. They were the midyear introduction of the Bobcat, the release of the all-new 1976 Capri II, and the addition of the luxurious Grand Monarch Ghia. Model-year production included 38,650 Bobcats; 53,848 Comets; 103,936 Monarchs; 65,180 Montegos; 62,989 Cougars; and 84,465 full-size Mercurys, for a total of 409,068 cars. United States dealer sales for the same period were 63,494 Capris; 23,018 Bobcats; 51,093 Comets; 77,409 Monarchs; 50,624 Montegos; 49,211 Cougars; and 67,005 Mercury Marquis.

Following a year which saw the most extensive running changes in its entire history, Lincoln-Mercury Division's general manager, Walter S. Walla, announced that 1976 would be a marked by engineering improvements designed to gain further fuel economy.

Mercury's entry into the low-priced economy race was the "MPG" version of the Bobcat, which was carried over from the previous year. A new hood and grille, on the standard "Pinto" body and, chassis, the car came standard with a 140-cubic-inch (2.3-liter) four-cylinder engine and, a 94.5-inch wheelbase. Also standard was a plusher interior, than found in the Ford counterpart. It had new high-back bucket seats. Wood-grain body side panels were standard on the Station Wagon, but optional on the Runabout for the first time. A 170-cubic-inch (2.8-liter), 100-hp V-6 engine was also available. Base prices for the two models were $3,338, and $3,643.

The Comet series carried over, in 1976, with minor changes in the grille area, plus new options packages. The revised front end appearance consisted of black-out paint on the vertical bars of the grille, and around the headlamp doors, and parking lamps. The GT model was replaced with a "Sports Accent" group offering new colors, and a revised Custom interior. This package also included extra moldings, "Tu-Tone" paint, styled wheels, white sidewall tires, and dual racing mirrors. Standard engine for the 103-inch wheelbase two-door, and 109.9-inch four-door was a 200-cubic-inch (3.3-liter), 81-hp inline six. Options included a 250-cubic-inch (4.1-liter), 90-hp six, and a 302-cubic-inch (5.0-liter), 138-hp V-8. The two-door listed for $3,398, and the four-door was $3,465.

Mercury's Monarch continued, basically unchanged, as a 1976 offering. Both the base, and Ghia lines included two- and four-door Sedans, at prices between $3,927, and $4,510. A new luxury four-door model-option, called the Grand Monarch Ghia, was added to the lineup. A "Monarch S" model was also introduced at midyear. It featured styled wheels; wheel trim rings; gold trim accents; a landau vinyl roof; bucket seats; a floor shift; and more. Engineering revisions were said to enhance ride quality, and lower interior noise levels. Standard power plants were the 200-cubic-inch six in base models, and the 250-cubic-inch six in Ghias. Options included the 302-cubic-inch V-8, plus the 351-cubic-inch (5.8-liter), 152-hp V-8.

The intermediate-size Montegos were unchanged in 1976, which was the final year for this popular nameplate. There were six "passenger car" models available in three series: Montego, Montego MX, and Montego MX Brougham. Each had a two-door Hardtop (114-inch wheelbase), and a

Simulated wood-grain paneling was an option available for 1976 Bobcat "Run-about" Hatchbacks. (Mercury)

Mercury's entry into the low-priced economy race was the "MPG" version of the Bobcat. (Mercury)

The 1976 Comet front end had black-out paint on the vertical grille bars and around the headlamp doors. (Mercury)

The 1976 Cougar XR-7 was dressed up a bit for the personal/luxury market. A "Flightbench" seat was new. (Mercury)

A half-vinyl Landau top option looked neat on the 1976 Mercury Marquis Brougham Hardtop. (Mercury)

four-door Pillared Hardtop (118-inch wheelbase). The two upper series also included one Station Wagon each. The Brougham-level wagon had Villager trim. In February 1976, luxury editions of both passenger cars were added. Base prices spanned the $4,299 to $5,065 range. Five new exterior colors were introduced. The 351-cubic-inch V-8 was the standard motor. Both 400-cubic-inch (6.6-liter), 180-hp, and 460-cubic-inch (7.5-liter), 202-hp V-8s were optional.

The 1976 Monarch and Monarch Ghia lines included two- and four-door Sedans priced between $3,927, and $4,510. (Mercury)

The Cougar XR-7 was also considered an intermediate. It continued to be based on the 114-inch wheelbase Montego two-door Hardtop. It was dressed up a bit and aimed at the personal/luxury car market. New was a standard "Flightbench" seat. Several items that were previously standard, were made options. They included a luxury steering wheel, wheel trim rings, and bucket seats with a console. Other new interior options included reclining "Twin Comfort Lounge" seats, and new upholstery materials. Base price for the XR-7 was $5,125. This included the 351-cubic-inch V-8. The 400- and 460-cubic-inch V-8s were optional.

The full-size Mercury standard bearer continued to be the Marquis series. The line offered a two-door Hardtop, and a four-door Pillared Hardtop in Marquis, Marquis Brougham, and Grand Marquis trim levels, plus a Station Wagon, and Colony Park wagon in a separate series. Prices began as low as $5,063, and climbed as high as $6,528. The Colony Park had simulated wood-grain exterior paneling. New options included a "Tu-Tone" color group, with "Glamour" paints, and a landau-style half-roof for two-door Hardtops. The Station Wagons had a 121-inch wheelbase, and other models featured a 124-inch stance. For the big cars, the 400-cubic-inch engine was standard, and the "460" could be added.

The most changed "1976 Mercury" was introduced in March 1975, and was not made by Mercury at all. The West German-built Capri got a redesigned body, with Hatchback styling, in mid-model-year. It was renamed the Capri II, and was introduced as a 1976 model. Also new was its larger base engine. It was the same motor used in Ford Pintos, and Mercury Bobcats. This engine displaced 2.3-liters, and generated 92 hp. A 170.8-cubic-inch (2.8-liter) German-built V-6 was optional. The Hatchback had the same 100.9-inch wheelbase as the previous Capri, and the same 174.8-inch overall length. It sold for $4,117, about $600 more than the Capri I. A Ghia Sport Hatchback was also offered for $4,585.

The 1976 Colony Park had simulated wood-grain exterior paneling and a 121-inch wheelbase. (Mercury)

Mercury opened model-year 1976 on a strong note. General sales manager A.B. Connors reported initial sales for Lincolns, and Mercurys at the 5.8 percent of market level, versus 5.2 percent for the same period a year earlier. The Monarchs, Cougars, and Marquis lead the opening rally, as Mercury's 2,847 dealers (55 exclusives) moved their sales efforts into high gear. The program held steady, as model-year output for the full season leaped upwards by almost 85,000 cars (a 16.9 percent increase). Model-year production included 49,989 Bobcats; 36,074 Comets; 145,823 Monarchs; 51,095 Montegos; 83,765 Cougars; and 92,924 Mercurys. Mercury dealers also sold 32,114 Capri IIs in the 1976 model-year.

The 1977 Mercury Bobcat looked like the 1976 model, but with slightly enlarged front parking lamps. It was powered by 2.3- (89-hp), and 2.8-liter (93-hp) engines that featured a second-generation electronic ignition system. There was a reduced maintenance schedule, which included 10,000-mile oil change intervals. A new aluminum front bumper, plus several equipment deletions, were used to help improve fuel economy. The base Runabout model had 142 pounds removed (152 pounds in California). The base, and Villager, Station Wagons lost 108 pounds (114 in California). A new 2.73:1 rear axle ratio, standard in the Runabout, also contributed to better fuel economy. The Runabout was $3,438; the Station Wagon was $3,629.

The 1977 Mercury Comet was again offered as two-door, and four-door Sedans. They were priced at $3,544, and $3,617, respectively. A new interior decor group included seat trim in cloth-and-vinyl or all-vinyl. There was also a high-level sound package, a deluxe steering wheel, and color-keyed lap, and shoulder belts. An optional driver's bucket seat, that manually adjusted up, and down, as well as forward, and backward, was available for the first time. The 1977 Comet

For 1977, the Mercury Bobcat offered an optional, all-glass third door, which is shown here. (Mercury)

The 1977 Comet Coupe was available with the same 3.3-, 4.1- and 5.0-liter engines. (Mercury)

engine lineup included the same 3.3-, 4.1- and 5.0-liter engines. They had slightly revised outputs of 96-, 98-, and 137-hp.

New for the 1977 Monarch was a standard four-speed, manual overdrive transmission. The new transmission included a 0.81:1 fourth-gear ratio that reduced the engine's work load once cruising speed was reached. The transmission accompanied the base 3.3-liter six, the optional 4.1-liter six (standard in Ghia models), and the 5.0-liter V-8. Some mid-1976 appearance options included a landau-style half-vinyl top, dual racing mirrors, and styled steel wheels. The Monarch offered two- and four-door Sedans in base, and Ghia trim, at $4,076 to $4,812.

In 1977, the Montego name disappeared, and the former Montegos became Cougars. The previously available Cougar XR-7 was marketed, too. Cougars had vertical taillights. XR-7s had wraparound-style, horizontal taillamps, and a "spare tire" rear deck lid. All this created some unusual situations. For instance, this was one of only two years that Cougar Station Wagons were offered. One such model was the plain four-door wagon. The other was the Villager model with wood-grain exterior trim. There were also two-door Hardtops, and four-door Pillared Hardtops in the Cougar and Cougar Brougham series. The XR-7 two-door Hardtop was the top-of-the-line model. Prices ran from $4,700 to $5,274. All the 1977 Cougars featured new exterior sheet metal. The front end was highlighted by vertical "swing-away" grilles, and dual rectangular headlamps. The 5.0-liter V-8 was standard in the XR-7, and all Cougar Hardtops, and Sedans. In Station Wagons, the 5.8-liter V-8 was the base engine.

The 1977 Marquis was again offered in three series: Marquis, Marquis Brougham, and Grand Marquis. Seven new exterior body colors, and three new vinyl roof colors were available. A landau-style half-roof became standard on the Marquis Brougham, and the Grand Marquis two-door models. Both the 6.6-liter V-8 (standard on Marquis and Marquis Broughams), and the 7.5-liter V-8 (standard on Grand Marquis, except in California) featured FoMoCo's improved electronic ignition. They were slightly de-tuned, and produced 173 hp, and 197 hp. Each line included a two-door Hardtop, and a four-door Pillared Hardtop. The base series also had a four-door Station Wagon. Wood trim for wagons was part of a $351 Colony Park option package.

For the first time, the 1977 Cougar series included four-door Sedan and Station Wagon models. This is the four-door Brougham model. (Mercury)

196

The completely new Cougar XR-7, which is seen above, featured bold styling, and a more efficient and comfortable interior. (Mercury)

A 7.5-liter V-8 was standard on the Grand Marquis four-door Sedan, except those sold in California. (Mercury)

A new mid-1976 Monarch appearance option included a landau-style half-vinyl top. (Mercury)

The Capri II was back again. It came in three-door Sport, and three-door Ghia Sport versions at $4,373, and $4,585, respectively. Imported from West Germany, the Sport Coupe had a 100.9-inch wheelbase; a 173-inch overall length; and a 67-inch width. It rode on 165 SR x 15 tires. Base engine was a 140-cubic-inch four. The optional V-6 was 170.8 cubic inches, with 103 hp.

The 1977 model-year started with Walter S. Walla in charge of Lincoln-Mercury Division. At midyear, Walter J. Oben took over as general manager, after Walla became general manager of Ford Division. Other personnel changes included a move, by T.G. Daniels, from general marketing manager to general sales manager, along with R.L. Rewey's appointment to Daniel's old slot. C.D. May also replaced W. Chase as southern regional manager. The nation's 46 Mercury dealers, and 2,897 Lincoln-Mercury dealers enjoyed another good year, in 1977. Leading the way was the full-size Marquis, which gained 22,000 model-year sales. The Cougar name also boosted sales of intermediates, while the XR-7 gained nearly 41,500 new buyers. Model-year output included 34,724 Bobcats; 21,545 Comets; 127,680 Monarchs; 194,823 Cougars, and XR-7s; and 147,969 Mercurys. That totaled 526,751 cars or 5.79 percent of total industry output, compared to 459,670 cars, and a 5.67 percent share in 1976. In addition, model-year sales of the imported Capri hit 25,000 units.

Mercury lost a Comet in 1978, but gained a Zephyr. It weighed 300 pounds less than the Comet, and held 48 percent more luggage. This new car was a clone of Ford's Fairmont. Zephyr styling trademarks were its vertical grille, dual rectangular headlamps; and large, horizontal taillamps. Boxy, and conventional, it turned out to be a dependable, mid-size, front-engined, rear-wheel-drive machine. The Zephyr four- and six-cylinder series offered two- and four-door Sedans, a four-door Station Wagon, and a two-door Sport Coupe named the Z-7. Four-cylinder model prices began at just $2,572, and the highest-priced six listed for $4,336. A Villager wood-grain trim option was offered for the wagon. All models were on a 105.5-inch wheelbase. The Z-7 was 196 inches long, and the rest were 194 inches long. All models were 72 inches wide. The engines offered were a 2.3-liter, 88-hp four; a 3.3-liter, 85 hp V-6; and a 5.0-liter, 139 hp V-8. Also standard were a four-speed manual transmission, strut-type front suspension; and four-link coil-spring rear suspension. A choice of 13 exterior paints, plus Euro-style trim was offered.

Other than one less four-cylinder horsepower, and three less V-8 horsepower (a reflection of the movement towards higher economy) the 1978 Bobcats looked like 1977 models. Engineering refinements helped boost their efficiency. The carburetor venturi size was reduced for improved fuel and air mixing with the standard 2.3-liter engine. A three-way catalyst, with an electronically controlled carburetor, was standard on cars, sold with that engine, in California. A revised torque converter upgraded the engine and transmission efficiency of the optional 2.8-liter engine. The series offered a three-door Runabout, a standard two-door Station Wagon, and the Villager Station Wagon at prices between $3,830, and $4,244. A new option was variable-ratio rack-and-pinion steering.

The Monarch came in six-cylinder, and V-8 series, with two- and four-door Sedans in each. List prices were in the $4,366 to $4,662 range. There were no special trim levels, but a Ghia option package was $426 extra. Even more expensive was the $524 Monarch "ESS" option. It was a Euro-styled sporty model, with a blacked-out grille. A 4.1-liter six (97 hp) became the base engine. It came standard with a four-speed manual transmission. A 5.0-liter V-8 (139 hp) was available. Other specifications were unchanged. New styling features included a revised front end, with a smooth-topped vertical radiator grille; square headlamps (with rectangular parking lamps below them); new front fender caps (with slit-style side marker lamps);

The Bobcat series offered a Villager Station Wagon that listed for $4,244. (Mercury)

and a slightly revised bumper with no center slot. A front bumper spoiler, and hood-to-grille opening seal added aerodynamic improvements. Also new were restyled taillamps, and a reflectorized lower back panel. Two-door models had split opera windows. This compact model was again on a 109.9-inch wheelbase.

Cougar styling was the same as in 1977. Aerodynamic improvements were realized with a new low-restriction fresh-air intake system, plus a reduced back-pressure exhaust system. The base

Boxy, and conventional, the new-for-1978 Mercury Zephyr turned out to be a dependable, mid-size, front-engined, rear-wheel-drive machine. (Mercury)

Cougar series had a two-door Hardtop, and a four-door Pillared Hardtop. A Brougham option was offered. These cars were, again, basically Montegos. There were no 1978 Cougar Station Wagons, since the new Zephyr wagons filled the same market niche. At the top-of-the-line was the Cougar XR-7 two-door Hardtop, which was a clone of the contemporary Thunderbird. It was more stylized than the standard models, and offered a new Midnight/Chamois decor interior, plus four new exterior paint colors. Prices ranged from $5,052 to $5,720. Specifications were the same as in 1977, except for the horsepower ratings. The base 5.0-liter V-8 came with four more (134) horsepower. The 5.8-liter V-8 offered 144 hp, and 152 hp options (with single or dual exhausts), compared to 161 hp in 1977. The 6.6-liter V-8 was rated at 166 hp, down from 173 hp.

The 1978 Monarch came in six-cylinder and V-8 series, with two- and four-door Sedans in each. (Mercury)

Mercury Marquis body styling was untouched from 1977, but some mechanical improvements, and some new equipment options appeared. A new engine starter was designed to combat overheating problems. There were also new controls on the automatic, driver-adjustable air conditioning temperature control mechanism. Four new exterior colors, plus new interior, hood, and trim hues, were available. Full-size Marquis, Marquis Broughams, and Grand Marquis came in two-door Hardtop, and four-door Pillared Hardtop models. A Station Wagon was offered in the base series. All models had a standard 5.8-liter,

The top-of-the-line Cougar was the XR-7 two-door Hardtop, which was based on the Ford Thunderbird. (Mercury)

145-hp V-8. The 6.6- (160 hp), and 7.5-liter (202 hp) engines were available, for all models, at extra cost.

The Capri was not imported in 1978, but was still promoted (as a 1978 model) at events like the New York Auto Show. The show's program noted the addition of four new, metallic clear coat enamel paint colors. Another 1978 Capri feature was the bold "Le Cat Black" option. It offered a dramatic appearance with Black (or White) exterior finish, gold exterior stripe accents, black-out

There were new controls on the 1978 Marquis' automatic, driver-adjustable air conditioning controls. (Mercury)

moldings; and a special black interior with gold cloth seat inserts.

Walter J. Oben continued as Mercury's general manager in 1978. Thomas G. Daniels was back as general sales manager, and Robert L. Rewey was again general marketing manager. In a major move, the company changed advertising agencies, moving from its long-time association with Kenyon & Eckhardt, Incorporated, to a new one with Young & Rubican. Model-year sales of all Lincoln-Mercury products zoomed 15 percent, for a total of 764,331 units. The new Zephyr realized a 453.4 percent increase over the Comet that it replaced.

Model-year production included 36,745 Bobcats; 87,439 Zephyrs; 91,714 Monarchs; 213,270 Cougars, and Cougar XR-7s; and 145,627 big Mercurys. That was a total of 574,795 cars, and 6.43 percent of industry output, compared to 526,751 cars, and 5.79 percent in 1977. In addition, 8,914 Capri IIs were sold in model-year 1978 by the 2,962 dealers that sold Mercurys. Of these, only 43 handled the Mercury nameplate exclusively. Most of the rest were Lincoln-Mercury dealers. The Capri was handled by only 1,069 dealership franchises.

A new "shovel-nose" front end characterized the 1979 Bobcats. The headlamps, and parking lamps were rectangular. The grille had thin, vertical blades in eight individual rectangular segments. The bumper was straighter, and had black, rubber bumper guards. It showed the gravel pan below it. A rear end restyling featured a bright rear bumper, with black end caps, and horizontal taillamps on the three-door model. Also new were a rectangular instrument cluster; longer-wearing electronic voltage regulator; and five new choices of body paint. Wheelbases, lengths, widths, tire sizes, and the base engine (2.3-liter/88 hp four) were unchanged from 1978. The optional, 2.98-liter V-6 had 12 more horsepower. Prices for the Runabout, Station Wagon, and Villager Station Wagon started at $4,104, and went to $4,523.

The 1979 Mercury Capri was an all-new, American-made car. It was a Mustang clone, except that no notch back body style was offered by Mercury. Only the three-door Hatchback came from Mercury. Styling characteristics included dual rectangular headlamps in bright frames; upper body side paint stripes; color-keyed simulated hood louvers; and a low hood line for a slightly wedge-shaped profile. The Sport Coupe sold for $4,872, and the Ghia Coupe was $5,237. A zippy RS package was a $249 option, and there was an RS Turbo option for the base four-cylinder model, at $1,186. Built on a 100.4-inch wheelbase platform, the Capri stretched only 179.1 inches end-to-end. Manual or automatic transmissions were available. The base engine was a 2.3-liter four. Optional were a 2.8-liter V-6, and a 5.0-liter V-8. Capris had a 77.2-foot turning circle, and weighed about 2,700 pounds.

The Zephyr came in four models (four-door Sedan, two-door Coupe, two-door Z-7 Hardtop, and four-door Station Wagon), in four-cylinder, and V-6 series. Prices started at $4,253, and climbed to $4,888. All specifications were the same as in 1978, except that the drive train was upgraded with a new four-speed overdrive manual transmission as standard equipment on the 3.3-liter six, and the 5.0-liter V-8. It featured a single-rail shift, with an enclosed linkage, that eliminated scheduled adjustments. The 5.0-liter engine was down-rated to 137 hp, instead of last year's 139 hp. Use of the 3.3-liter motor was extended to Station Wagons. New options included speed control, a tilt steering wheel, performance instrumentation, and eight fresh exterior hues.

The news about the 1979 Mercury Monarch was mainly in the area of trim. However, a lighter weight, aluminum single-rail shift design also was new on the standard four-speed manual overdrive transmission. The Monarch was considered a compact specialty car, and it was offered in

A new "shovel-nose" front end characterized the 1979 Bobcat three-door. Its 2.8-liter V-6 was improved. (Mercury)

The 1979 Zephyr teamed a standard four-speed overdrive manual transmission with a 3.3-liter six or 5.0-liter V-8.

The 1979 Mercury Capri was an all-new American car based on the year's Mustang Coupe. This is the sportier RS model. A Turbo RS was offered, too. (Mercury)

The 1979 Cougar XR-7 offered a new black-bright accent grille, horizontal rear end styling and new color combinations for the Chamois Decor Group. (Mercury)

The 1979 Zephyr teamed a standard four-speed overdrive manual transmission with a 3.3-liter six or 5.0-liter V-8.

two- and four-door Sedan models. A 4.1-liter six was the standard power plant, and a 5.0-liter V-8 was optional. Monarchs came in three trim levels: ESS, Ghia, and Decor. All were upgraded with new front door trim panels featuring large armrests. A choice of a bench seat or reclining bucket seats was available. Monarch prices were $5,018 for the two-door Sedan, and $5,124 for the four-door Sedan.

The Cougar series was down to two models (two-door Hardtop and four-door Pillared Hardtop), and the Cougar XR-7 line had only one two-door Hardtop. There was a new radiator style grille with fine, criss-cross moldings in each of four, individual segments. The XR-7 was revamped with a new black-bright accent grille, a horizontal rear end styling theme, and new color fabric treatments for the Chamois Decor Group. Prices for Cougars ranged from $5,379 to $6,430. Engine choices were cut back somewhat, with a 5.0-liter, 133-hp V-8 as standard Cougar equipment, and a pair of 5.8-liter V-8s available. A 135-hp version of the bigger motor was standard in XR-7s, while a 151-hp version was optional in all Cougars. New in Cougars was an electronic voltage regulator, carburetor modifications, and revised interior trims.

Big Mercurys were all-new for 1979, and they reflected the trend towards down-sizing. They shared a new 114.3-inch wheelbase chassis with Ford's redesigned LTD. They were 17 inches shorter, and 800 pounds lighter than their 1978 counterparts. Better road manners, and enhanced fuel economy were benefits of the new styling. The overall design theme was similar to before, but on a smaller size scale, and more refined. For example, the grille still had vertical blades inside six vertical segments, but now each segment was framed in bright metal. The fenders had less of the "razor edge" look, and the parking lamps were shorter, and smoother. Engineering highlights

The 1979 Marquis Brougham Coupe was all new. It shared a down-sized 114.3-inch wheelbase chassis with Ford's redesigned LTD. (Mercury)

The 5.0-liter V-8 was standard in all full-size Mercurys, including this Grand Marquis Coupe. (Mercury)

The 1979 Monarch was a compact specialty car offered in two- and four-door Sedans. (Mercury)

included a redesigned frame; new front, and rear suspension systems; larger areas of glass; and adaptation of mini spare tires. The Mercurys also sported thinner doors; more compact armrests; and thin-shell front seats that allowed more rear seat leg room. There were three car-lines, each with a two-door Hardtop, and a four-door Pillared Sedan. They were called Marquis, Marquis Brougham, and Grand Marquis. There was also a Station Wagon series with a pair of regular wagons, and a pair of Colony Parks. One in each pair had two seats, and the other had three. The 5.0-liter V-8 was standard in all full-size Mercurys. The only engine option was a 5.8-liter V-8 for Marquis Station Wagons, and Colony Parks. A new EEC II (electronic engine control) system was standard. Also new was an all-electronic radio. Prices for the big Mercurys started at $6,292, and stopped at $7,909.

Mercury personalities again included Walter J. Oben, Thomas G. Daniels, and Robert L. Rewey. Mercury's model-year production increased to 621,717 units, for a 6.75 percent share of total industry output. This compared to 574,795 cars, and 6.43 percent in 1978. The total included 50,266 Bobcats; 110,144 American-made Capris; 72,476 Zephyrs; 75,879 Monarchs; 172,152 Cougars, and XR-7s; and 140,800 Mercurys.

Mercury in the '80s
1980-1989

The 1980 Mercury Bobcat was upgraded with a three miles-per-gallon improvement in fuel economy on its base 2.3-liter four. Standard equipment included styled steel wheels, rack-and-pinion steering, a front stabilizer bar, and steel-belted radial tires. The standard tires were of a new BR78 x 13B size. The subcompact was available as a three-door Hatchback (called the Runabout), as a base Station Wagon, and as a Villager Station Wagon. Prices climbed an average of $666, and ran from $4,764 to $5,070. New was a revamped interior, and a modified exterior that was one inch shorter in overall length due to a bumper redesign. The Runabout model's Sports Option ($206 extra) received a front air dam, a rear deck lid spoiler, and black-accented trim. Tinted glass; a rear window defroster; and an AM radio were standard equipment. The engine used was the 2.3-liter, 88 hp four, with no options offered.

The Capri competed in the subcompact specialty-car market. New standard equipment included halogen headlamps; P-metric radial tires; and many new trim and comfort options. Styling was carried over, except for a new, slotted gravel pan. An automatic transmission was made available on the turbocharged version of the base 2.3-liter four. Also offered were the 3.3-liter six, and a new, lighter, more efficient 4.2-liter (255-cubic-inch) V-8. Capri's stylish Ghia package received an optional roof-top luggage carrier with a cover. Capri RS, Turbo RS, and GS sporty versions were offered again. The RS models featured a dummy hood scoop, a rear spoiler, and a simulated engine-turned dash. The RS Turbo added "Turbo" plaques on its hood scoop, three-spoke wheels, and "Turbo RS" tape graphics. The GS had Euro-style headrests, luxury cloth seats, and a wood-accented

Styling for the 1980 Capri was carried over, except for a new, slotted gravel pan. (Mercury)

steering wheel. Another package, priced at $644, was the "Black Magic" option. It included Black or White paint with gold accents, aluminum wheels with special gold finish, black vinyl seats, and more. In midyear, a five-speed overdrive manual gear box was released, as an option, for the four-cylinder model. Base prices were $5,672 for the three-door, and $5,968 for the Ghia three-door.

The Zephyr had new power plant options. A turbocharger and automatic transmission drive train was an option for the base 2.3-liter four, except in Station Wagons. The new 4.2-liter V-8 was available, too. The Zephyr's fuel efficiency was also enhanced by new steel-belted radial tires as standard equipment. Aerodynamic improvements, plus the use of new high-strength steel components, was also noted in

The Cougar XR-7 Hardtop was completely re-engineered for 1980 and lost 700 pounds. (Mercury)

The 1980 Zephyr Hardtop The Zephyr had a turbocharger and automatic transmission option. (Mercury)

Mercury press releases. Dual rectangular sealed-beam halogen headlamps, and a fluidic windshield washer system were other added features, along with fresh new interior decors. Zephyrs were built in two-, and four-door Sedan models, four-door Station Wagons, and a sporty Z-7 two-door Sedan. All were available with optional Ghia appointments. Standard engine was the 2.3-liter four with 88 hp. No horsepower figure for the turbocharged engine was given. Other options included the 3.3-liter six with 91 hp; and the 4.2-liter V-8 with 119 hp.

The Mercury Monarch entered its sixth year with several new trim choices, plus a variety of electronic stereo, and tape player options. There was a new criss-cross grille texture. The specialty compact was available in two- or four-door Sedan models, with numerous standard, and optional equipment refinements. Its Ghia "designer" package ($476), and sporty "ESS" option group ($516) offered a choice of bench or bucket seats. Pleasant-sounding electronic chimes replaced the tiresome buzzer warning system. The 5.0-liter, 134-hp V-8 was the only engine available in California, while the 4.1-liter, 90-hp inline six remained the standard federal power plant. Some reference sources also list availability of the new-for-1980 4.2-liter, 119-hp V-8. Base prices were $5,628 for the two-door Sedan, and $5,751 for the four-door Sedan.

Base Cougar two- and four-door models were dropped. For the Cougar XR-7, everything was brand new, from a 700-pound weight loss, and shorter wheelbase, to halogen headlamps. The redesigned sports/luxury car had a 108.4-inch wheelbase, 201-inch overall length, and 75-inch width. It had a $7,045 base price. Cougar's new, unitized two-door Sedan body came equipped with the fuel-efficient 4.2-liter, 115-hp V-8; rack-and-pinion steering; strut suspension; coil-spring rear suspension; and metric radial-ply tires. A new four-speed manual overdrive transmission was offered with the optional 5.0-liter, 131-hp V-8. A keyless door lock system, electronic instrument panel, and electronic sound equipment headed the list of new options. Luxury, comfort or performance were available through the GS, LS, Decor, Luxury, and Sport Group packages. The GS option cost $320 to $371, and the LS equipment was $715 to $972. Leather seat trim was $303 extra.

Big Mercurys had the look introduced in 1979. New appearance touches included taillamps, and lower back moldings; "dark-on-top" paint combinations; halogen headlamps; and front bumper guards. They also changed to P-radial tires. Both the 5.0-liter, and 5.8-liter V-8s were back, each with two more horsepower. All federal models of the "medium-full-size" car, could be ordered with automatic overdrive transmission (AOD) on the 5.8-liter engine or on base 5.0-liter Sedans. Ford's improved electronic engine control (EEC) system was standard on all 5.8-liter engines, and on Marquis with the 5.0-liter engine sold in California. There were 10 model choices, composed of two- and four-door Sedans in the Marquis, Marquis Brougham, and Grand Marquis series, plus four Station Wagons. The Marquis, and wood-trimmed Colony Park wagons were both offered with either two- or three-seat setups. Leather seats were $303 extra. A Grand Marquis Decor package was $581 extra, and a Formal Coach Roof option was $500.

Walter J. Oben began the 1980 calendar-year as Mercury general manager, but Gordon B. Mackenzie took over that position during the year. Robert L. Rewey continued as general sales manager, and Joseph E. Cappy (who had started his Ford career in the Edsel era) was general marketing manager. The nation's 22 Mercury dealers, and 2,693 Lincoln-Mercury dealers saw their model-year sales tumble. They fell from 690,243 cars in 1979 to 432,579 cars in 1980. Model-year production totals included 24,650 Bobcats; 79,984 Capris; 70,068 Zephyrs; 30,518 Monarchs; 58,028 Cougar XR-7s; and 54,328 Mercurys. That represented a total output of 317,576 units, and a 4.89 percent share of the entire industry's assemblies.

Mercury debuted its new LN7 in April 1981, as a 1982 model. This two-seater was based on the new Lynx. It combined a 1.6-liter (97.6-cubic-inch) overhead cam four with a four-speed manual overdrive transaxle to give fuel economy of 29 city/46 highway miles per gallon. The sporty little Mercury was offered in a single, highly-equipped model with a long list of standard features including, power-assisted front disc brakes; electric rear window defroster; steel-belted radial-ply tires; an electric, remote-control liftgate release; a console with full-instru-

From one model, the 1981 Cougar offerings were expanded to include two- and four-door Sedans like this GS model. (Mercury)

An 1981 Capri option, priced at $644, was the "Black Magic" package. It included Black or White paint with gold accents and more. (Mercury)

mentation; a padded sport steering wheel; and an AM radio with dual front speakers. A "bubble-back" rear window distinguished the LN7 from the counterpart Ford EXP.

The "missing Lynx" in Mercury's car-lines was a subcompact with a 1.3-liter, four-cylinder "hemi" engine that came with a long list of options, and trim levels. The base model came only as a Hatchback with a low, low $5,199 price. Four other levels named L, GL, GS, and RS offered that body style, plus a Liftgate Wagon. The top-of-the-line LS came as a Hatchback. Even L models had high-back front bucket seats, carpets, and bright moldings. GLs added things like reclining seats, moldings with silver stripes, and a consolette. GS models also had body side accent stripes, low-back bucket seats, and full-instrumentation. The RS had tape stripes, and decals, plus a black-out grille, and styled wheels. LS trim added "Tu-Toning," and pleated velour seat trim. Prices ranged from the low entry-level sticker mentioned above, to $7,382.

The Zephyr series was the same as 1980, except that an "S" model with equipment deletions was added to lower the price to $5,769. Other models listed for as much as $6,790. There were no obvious styling differences. The Turbo option was dropped. Engines were the same as last season, with some minor horsepower revisions.

Capris were offered in the same series, and models, as 1980. Prices ranged from $6,869 to $7,261. The Turbo RS option was $1,191 (the engine alone was over $600). Minor styling changes were made to the lower front fascia, and the "power bulge" on the hood. Specifications, and engines were all the same, except horsepower ratings changed slightly, according to vehicle weights.

From one model in 1980, the Cougar offerings were expanded. They now included two- and four-door Sedans in four- and six-cylinder formats, plus XR-7 two-door Hardtops in six-cylinder or V-8 series. Prices ranged from $6,635 to $8,231. A Carriage Roof option was $823 extra. The same V-8s were carried over, but the base engine (except XR-7s) was now a 2.3-liter four. The 3.3-liter six was extra in base models, and the 4.2-liter V-8 was standard in XR-7s, but optional in other Cougars. The 5.0-liter V-8 was no longer available.

Full-size Mercurys dropped to nine models, as the base Marquis series lost its two-door Sedan. All other model offerings were unchanged. Prices started as low as $8,110, but could run as high as $9,821. Then you could add a Formal Coach roof for $601, a CB radio for $305, leather trim for $383, and a Grand Marquis Decor option for $521. A number of engine changes took effect. The 4.2-liter, 120-hp V-8 was standard in most models. Grand Marquis four-door Sedans, and all Station Wagons, had a 5.0-liter, 130-hp V-8 as standard equipment. The 5.8-liter V-8 was optional. It generated 143 hp with single exhausts, and 165 hp with dual exhausts.

During 1981, Gordon B. Mackenzie completed his first full year at the helm of Lincoln-Mercury Division. Robert L. Rewey continued as general sales manager, but Bud J. Coughlin took over the title of general marketing manager, after Joe Cappy moved to American Motors Corporation. The total number of dealers handling Mercurys fell by 30, to 2,663, and only 21 were exclusive Mercury dealers. This drop reflected a continued decline in model-year sales, which wound up at 429,917 vehicles (including 13,954 of the 1982 LN7s, and 90,961 Lynx models). United States model-year production included 22,716 LN7s; 111,978 Lynx models; 58,946 Capris; 52,276 Zephyrs; 53,653 Cougars; 37,275 Cougar XR-7s; and 61,638 Marquis. This totaled 375,756 units, up from 317,576 in 1980. Mercury's share of total domestic industry production rose to 5.63 percent, from 4.69 percent. In addition, about 14,200 Zephyrs were manufactured in Canada.

Introduced as the auto industry's first 1982 model, the Mercury LN7 two-seater, sporty Coupe failed to meet sales expectations, despite its high fuel efficiency. An optional, higher, final gear ratio of 4.05:1 was offered in midyear, along with a new, close-ratio manual transaxle. The front-wheel-drive subcompact came in a single model base-priced at $7,787. The standard engine was the 1.6-liter, 70-hp four. Optional was an H.O. version of this engine.

For 1982, Mercury added a five-door Hatchback model to the Lynx three-door Hatchback, and four-door Station Wagon. It was aimed at buyers who wanted a sporty Hatchback, with the convenience of rear passenger doors. The front-wheel-drive Lynx was Lincoln-Mercury's best selling car, and delivered 31 city/47 highway mpg ratings with the base 1.6-liter four. A larger 11.3-gallon fuel tank was made standard to increase its cruising range. There were three- and five-door Hatchbacks in the base series, and all three body styles in the L, GL, GS, and LS series. The RS came only as a three-door model. Window stickers started at $5,502, and went as high as $8,256.

Performance was an integral part of the Capri's appeal. A 5.0-liter H.O. V-8, a Sport suspension package, and four-speed manual overdrive transmission were made available. The standard power plant was a 2.3-liter four. Other options included the 3.3-liter six, and 4.2-liter V-8. Larger engines incorporated a new SelectShift transmission, with a lock-up torque converter. It was designed to improve fuel economy by eliminating gear slippage. The Capri was merchandised according to engine type. The four-cylinder series included three-door Hatchbacks in base, L, and GS trim levels. Only the L, and GS models were offered with a six, and the RS was the only V-8. Aluminum wheels added $348, and genuine leather seats were $409 extra.

Mercury combined the Zephyr's base model, and Z-7 deluxe package to give the 1982 model wider market appeal. Two-door Sedans, and Station Wagons were dropped. This left only two-door Hardtops, and four-door Sedans available. New features included six added paint colors; a deep-well trunk; and an optional 20-gallon gas tank. The 105-inch wheelbase Zephyr was powered by a 2.3-liter, 86-hp four. The 3.3-liter, 87-hp inline six was optional.

For only the second time, Station Wagon models had Cougar nameplates in 1982. The GS-level wagon featured 74 cubic feet of cargo capacity, and an optional two-way liftgate for loading, and unloading ease. It had a 3.3-liter, 87-hp inline six as its standard engine. The Cougar cars were unchanged, except for adopting the 2.3-liter four as their base power plant. The series included two- and four-door Sedans in GS, and LS trim. Overall Cougar prices started at $7,983, and went to $8,587. A 3.8-liter V-6 was optional. Both sixes could be had with "SelectShift" transmission. A strut-type front suspension, and rack-and-pinion steering was also standard.

The Cougar XR-7 had the 3.3-liter six as base engine. A new option was the 3.8-liter V-6. Equipped with an aluminum head, plastic valve covers, and other lightweight materials, it was designed to keep poundage low. This motor, as well as the optional 4.2-liter V-8, could be teamed with a new "SelectShift" automatic transmission featuring the lock-up torque converter. The Cou-

Grand Marquis four-door Sedans had a 5.0-liter, 130-hp V-8 as standard equipment. (Mercury)

A five-door Hatchback model was added to the 1982 Mercury Lynx offerings. (Mercury)

The 1982 Cougars were unchanged, except for adopting the 2.3-liter four as base engine. (Mercury)

Performance was an integral part of the 1982 Capri's appeal. A 5.0-liter H.O. V-8 was available. (Mercury)

gar XR-7 offered base, and LS level two-door Sedans in six, and V-8 series. Prices started at $9,094, and peaked at $9,847.

Full-size Marquis featured design refinements, more standard equipment, and an optional dashboard data panel. A "Tripminder" helped drivers plan their fuel stops, and predict arrival times with optimal fuel efficiency. The Brougham and upgraded Grand Marquis models were equipped with an electric analog clock, and a new, two-speaker AM radio. The 5.0-liter, 132-hp V-8 with electronic fuel-injection was standard for four-door Sedans, and Station Wagons. The 4.2-liter, 122-hp V-8 was standard in Coupes.

Gordon B. Mackenzie guided Lincoln-Mercury Division through 1982. Robert L. Rewey continued as general sales manager, and Bud J. Coughlin remained general marketing manager. The total number of dealers fell to 2,581, although the same 21 were still exclusive Mercury dealers. The overall drop reflected a continued decline in model-year sales, which wound up at 401,350. United States model-year production included 2,448 LN7s; 100,578 Lynx models; 36,134 Capris; 39,092 Zephyrs; 56,950 Cougars; 16,867 Cougar XR-7s; and 77,157 Marquis. About 17,400 additional Lynx models were manufactured outside the United States.

An aerodynamic nose, Euro-inspired wraparound taillamps, and a high-swirl-combustion engine characterized the Topaz, which was released, in the spring of 1983, as a 1984 model. The Topaz replaced the Zephyr. It was available in three- and five-door notch back styles. Both models were offered in base, GS, and LS trim levels at prices between $7,200 and $7,756. A computer-controlled 2.3-liter, 90-hp four was standard under the hood. The Topaz had a 99.9-inch wheelbase, 176.5-inch overall length, 52.7-inch height, and 68.3-inch width. They weighed just under 2,500 pounds.

Lynx, the top Lincoln-Mercury sales-grabber for 1982, was revved-up, and redecorated for 1983. It had new striping, and a new grille treatment, plus greater engine options, and revised cloth seats. Buyers could opt for a base 1.6-liter, 70-hp engine with a two-barrel carburetor hooked to a four-speed manual, or three-speed automatic transmission. An electronically fuel-injected version of the same engine, with 82 hp, was standard in the Lynx RS three-door model, and optional in others. Also available was a 1.6-liter H.O. engine with a two-barrel carburetor.

For 1983, the LN7 received optional multi-port fuel-injection, which provided precise control of the fuel mixture. This increased its driveability, idling smoothness, and low-end torque. The engine choices were the same as those for Lynx models, except the RS. Prices started at $7,787.

Refined aerodynamic styling characterized the 105.6-inch wheelbase 1983 Mercury Marquis. (Mercury)

A new "bubble back" rear window design; revisions to the grille, and taillamps; and greater engine options characterized the rear-wheel-drive, Capri subcompact. The 2.3-liter, 90-hp overhead cam four returned as base engine. It had new long-reach spark plugs. In midyear, a turbocharger was released for it. Other engine choices were the 3.8-liter inline six, and the 5.0-liter V-8. The latter engine had a higher (177 hp) new rating. All Capris had the same body, but there were three different base trim levels, plus various options. The four-cylinder line included base, GS, and LS models. The six-cylinder series had L, and GS models. The V-8 powered RS was the top of the line. Prices were $7,156 to $9,241.

Priced to suit the lower-middle segment of automobile buyers, the 1983 Mercury Zephyr retained the same lines. The rear-wheel-drive compact was available in a four-door Sedan, and a sporty Z-7 two-door Hardtop. The 2.3-liter four was standard, and the 3.3-liter six was optional. Not seen again was the 4.2-liter V-8. The Zephyr came in base four-door Sedan, Z-7 Sport Coupe, GS four-door Sedan, and Z-7 GS Sport Coupe Models, and in four- and six-cylinder series. Prices started at $6,442, and rose to $7,550.

The 1983 Mercury Cougar sported a very distinct, "chopped-off" rear roof treatment, plus a reverse-curve quarter window to distinguish it from the new 1983 Thunderbird, with which it shared a platform. It had a 103.8-inch wheelbase, a width of 71 inches, a height of 53.4 inches, and an overall length of 197.6 inches. There was no Cougar XR-7, but the car came in base two-door Hardtop, and LS two-door Hardtop models, and in V-6, and V-8 series. Prices ranged from $9,521 to $11,138. Cougars came

The 1983 Mercury Colony Park Station Wagon was now an official member of the Grand Marquis series. (Mercury)

standard with a 3.8-liter, 112-hp V-6. There were no engine options at first, but a 5.0-liter, 130-hp EFI V-8 was made available, at extra cost, as a running production change. An optional "Voice Alert" system was added at midyear.

Crisp, clean styling was seen on an all-new, down-sized, rear-wheel-drive Marquis. It was now a totally different machine than the Grand Marquis. Its features included a 105.6-inch wheelbase, a width of 71 inches, a height of 53.6 inches, and an overall length of 197 inches. Marquis came with nitrogen-pressurized shock absorbers; a luxury sound package; individual reclining seats; and an optional trip odometer. Available four-cylinder models included a four-door Sedan, and a four-door Brougham Sedan. The six-cylinder series had both, plus a Station Wagon, and a Brougham Station Wagon. Prices were $7.893 to $8,974.

Rumors suggesting that the full-size Grand Marquis was doomed proved to be unfounded. It was bag with a new grille, and new taillamp treatment. The big six-passenger, full-size models included two- and four-door Sedans in base, and LS trims, plus a Colony Park Station Wagon. The latter was also available in nine-passenger format, with three seats. Prices spanned the $10,654 to $11,273 bracket. Leather seats were a $418 option. A 5.0-liter, fuel-injected, 130-hp V-8 was the sole engine choice.

Gordon B. Mackenzie guided Lincoln-Mercury Division through 1983, before moving on to become Ford of Europe's vice president of sales in 1984. Robert L. Rewey (general sales manager), and Bud J. Coughlin (general marketing manager) also stayed put. Model-year sales at domestic dealerships hit 484,688 cars, including 21,745 of the 1984 Topaz models. United States model-year

The 1983 Cougar was an all-new, mid-size, aerodynamic automobile. It offered the elegant sophistication of a personal luxury car at an affordable price. Its new design included a formal roof line and limousine type doors. (Mercury)

production included only 4,206 LN7s (699 U.S. factories); 75,108 Lynx models (69,497 U.S.); 25,119 Capris; 17,596 Topaz (14,008 U.S.); 22,703 Zephyrs; 69,876 Cougars; 69,876 Marquis; and 90,844 Grand Marquis.

The 1984 Lynx featured a new instrument panel, a new diesel engine option, and a more simplified product lineup for 1984. The new two-liter, four-cylinder diesel came with a five-speed manual transaxle, which boosted EPA fuel economy ratings. A 1.6-liter, four-cylinder turbocharged engine was made available at midyear. The L, GS, and RS trim levels were offered, along with a new top-of-the-line LTS option. Prices started at $5,758.

The sporty Capri offered two performance-oriented models for 1984, including the RS, and the Turbo RS. Both had front, and rear gas-pressurized shock absorbers, a rear quad-shocks configuration, tubular exhaust headers, dual exhausts, and a higher-lift camshaft. The RS had a base 5.0-liter V-8 with a four-barrel carburetor, while the basic GS had a four-cylinder motor. Prices started at $7,758.

Virtually unchanged from its mid-1983 introductory appearance, the five-passenger Topaz front-wheel-drive had a base 2.3-liter four with high-swirl combustion chambers. Its operation was precisely controlled by an EEC-IV onboard computer. Optionally available was a 2.0-liter, four-cylinder diesel engine with an aluminum cylinder head. A tachometer was standard equipment. Topaz prices started at $7,477.

The 1984 Mercury Topaz was created quickly as the result of extensive computer-aided designing. (Mercury)

For 1984, the Cougar came in V-6, V-8, and XR-7 series. The first two offered base, and LS two-door Hardtops, and the third offered only one two-door Hardtop. The XR-7 badge returned on this upscale, "Turbo Four" version of Mercury's sports-luxury car. A 2.3-liter four, plus three-speed automatic or five-speed manual transmissions were standard in the XR-7. The Turbo generated 145 hp. It also had special performance shock absorbers, like the counterpart Ford Thunderbird Turbo Coupe. The Cougar and Cougar LS standard 3.8-liter V-6 engine was upgraded with electronic fuel-injection. It generated 120 hp. Prices ran the gamut from $9,978 to $11,648.

The Marquis continued to be offered as a mid-size, rear-drive car. The 1984 model featured a new front bench seat, which upped its passenger capacity to six people. Ride, and handling were enhanced by gas-pressurized shocks, and struts, combined with a front stabilizer bar. Automatic transmission and power steering were standard, along with a 2.3-liter,

The 1984 Cougar and Cougar LS standard 3.8-liter V-6 was upgraded with electronic fuel-injection. (Mercury)

The 1984 Mercury Marquis continued to be offered as a mid-size, rear-drive car. (Mercury)

The 1984 Cougar and Cougar LS standard 3.8-liter V-6 was upgraded with electronic fuel-injection. (Mercury)

The 1984 Mercury Marquis continued to be offered as a mid-size, rear-drive car. (Mercury)

88-hp base four-cylinder engine. Marquis Station Wagons came standard with the 3.8-liter, 120-hp six, which was optional in cars. A propane-fueled 2.3-liter four was another option for Sedans. Prices started at $8,727.

A revitalized market for full-size cars brought the Grand Marquis additional attention in 1984. It was again powered by a 5.0-liter, fuel-injected V-8, matched with a four-speed automatic overdrive transmission. Prices started at $11,576 for the base, and Brougham lines of two- and four-door Sedans, and four-door Colony Park Station Wagons.

Robert L. Rewey, Jr. took over as Ford vice president, and general manager of Lincoln-Mer-

The 1984 Mercury Topaz was created quickly as the result of extensive computer-aided designing. (Mercury)

cury Division. Bud J. Coughlin became general sales manager. Ross H. Roberts was named general marketing manager. Model-year sales at domestic dealerships hit 644,308 models. United States model-year production included 64,483 Lynx models; 17,114 Capris; 89,102 Topaz; 124,491 Cougars; 97,472 Marquis; and 139,345 Grand Marquis.

The Lynx was available in a simplified series lineup for 1985. Offerings included the low-line base model, the slightly enriched L, and the fancier GS trim level. All three were offered in three- and five-door Hatchbacks, plus a four-door Station Wagon. Prices started at $5,753, and stopped at $7,341. Gear shift patterns for both the four- and five-speed transmissions were revised to help prevent confusion between first gear, and reverse. Lynx entertainment systems were upgraded to include flat-face designs that blended into the instrument panel. Increased corrosion protection was also added. All models came standard with 1.6-liter four-cylinder engines, but there were three versions. The base two-barrel generated 70 hp. The GS version, with MPFI (multi-point fuel-injection, with one injector per cylinder), cranked up 84 hp. Then came the 120 hp turbocharged engine, which also had the MPFI technology. A 2.0-liter diesel with IDI (indirect injection — a pre-combustion chamber type, used on diesels — with one injector per cylinder) was available, too.

The 1985 Mercury Topaz was available in two- and four-door models. They came in GS, and LS trim levels, for a total of four models priced from $7,767 to $8,980. The standard 2.3-liter HSC (high-swirl-combustion) four-cylinder engine received electronic single-point fuel-injection, and a standard five-speed manual transmission featuring a new gear shift pattern. A GS Sport Option group was $439 extra. It included an H.O. high-performance version of the 2.3-liter engine with new cylinder heads, and a better-breathing intake manifold. Also new for 1985 were child-proof rear door locks, an all-new instrument panel, and a new seat belt system. A 2.0-liter four-cylinder IDI diesel was another option.

The Capri had revisions to the body side moldings, plus a new bumper system. A number of items that were optional in 1984 became standard equipment. The sporty, rear-drive compact came only as a three-door Hatchback in four-, six-, and eight-cylinder series. The six came only with GS trim, and the other versions were offered in GS or RS models. Sticker prices ranged from $7,758 to $11,212. A 2.3-liter, two-barrel four with 88 hp was standard in the GS models, along with a five-speed manual transmission. A three-speed automatic was extra with the four. For GS Capris, an SDFI (single-point dual-injector) 3.8-liter V-6 with 120 hp was optional. It could be had with a choice

Available only as a two-door Coupe, the 1985 Cougar came in six-cylinder, V-8, and XR-7 lines. (Mercury)

of five-speed manual or four-speed automatic transmissions. RS versions of the Capri came standard with a 5.0-liter, four-barrel V-8. They also offered five-speed manual or four-speed automatic transmissions. An SDFI 5.0-liter V-8 with 140 hp could be added to the RS.

Available only as a two-door Coupe, the Cougar came in six-cylinder, V-8, and XR-7 lines, with base or LS models in the first two. The price ladder had five rungs, from $10,650 to $13,599. New grilles, taillamps, and wheelcovers emphasized model-year distinctions. The grille had a "Mercedes-Benz" look with a vertical center bar, and two horizontal bars dividing it into six rectangular segments. The gravel pan, below the front bumper, was smoother. Also new were 15-inch wheels, and a redesigned instrument panel featuring side window defoggers, and "shut-off" air conditioning registers. Base Cougars came standard with the 3.8-liter SDFI V-6. The 5.0-liter SDFI H.O. V-8 with 140 hp was optional. XR-7s included the 2.3-liter MPFI Turbo Four with 145-hp, and-155 hp ratings.

The Marquis had a new grille with bright vertical bars creating six slot-shaped segments on either side of a slightly wider, bright center bar. New, wide body side moldings, and redesigned tail-lamps were also seen. Other revisions included new trim colors, and fabrics, and upgraded AM/FM stereo cassette players. The four-cylinder series offered a four-door Sedan, and a four-door Brougham Sedan. The V-6 series offered both Sedans, plus standard, and Brougham Station Wagons. Prices were listed from $8,996 to $9,805. The low series used the 2.3-liter, 88-hp carbureted four, which had new low-friction piston rings, and a higher compression ratio. Automatic transmission was standard. Station Wagons had the 3.8-liter SDFI V-6 (optional in base models) as standard equipment, along with a different automatic transmission.

Mercury's top-of-the-line, full-size car was the Grand Marquis. It was offered in two- and four-door Sedans, as well as a four-door Station Wagon. The Sedans came in base or LS trim, and the wagons came as a two-seat or three-seat Colony Park. Prices spanned the $12,305 to $12,854 bracket. Leather seats were a $418 option. Standard power train was the 5.0-liter SDFI V-8 with 140 hp, linked to a four-speed automatic transmission. New for 1985 were nitrogen gas-pressurized shock absorbers; improved exterior trim; single-key door and ignition locking; improved corrosion

This 1985 Mercury Capri Convertible is a limited-edition model made by ASC/ McLaren. It is number 241 of 350 such cars built. (Mercury)

protection; and upgraded entertainment systems. A urethane coating was applied to protect against nicking from road debris.

A new car available at Mercury dealerships in 1985, was the Merkur XR4Ti, a sporty version of a European model called the Sierra. It was built at the Ford Werke AG factory in Cologne, Germany. A two-door Hatchback, the Merkur had a 102.7-inch wheelbase, and measured 178.4 inches long overall. It was 68 inches wide. Power was supplied by a Brazilian-built 2.3-liter MPFI Turbo Four. Priced at $16,361, the Merkur was expected to compete with products from Audi, BMW, and Volvo. Although coming under

Mercury's top-of-the-line, full-size car for 1985 was the Grand Marquis. (Mercury)

the auspices of the Lincoln-Mercury Division, the Merkur was treated as a separate franchise. This suggested that additional models were planned for the marque as it established a foothold in the United States.

In mid-1985, Thomas J. Wagner took over as Ford vice president, and general manager of Lincoln-Mercury. Another new name was that of general sales manager T.D. Mignanelli. A somewhat more familiar name, though new in a sense, was Edsel B. Ford II. He was now working as L-M's general marketing manager. Lincoln-Mercury Division now had a total of 2,748 dealerships in the United States, of which 835 were solely dedicated to Mercury sales. Model-year sales by dealers in the United States included 84,870 Lynx models; 16,829 Capris; 79,899 Topaz; 98,166 Marquis; 130,015 Cougars; 145,242 Grand Marquis; and 6,384. Model-year production (domestic factories only) included 80,551 Lynx models; 18,657 Capris; 62,091 Topaz; 104,198 Marquis; 117,274 Cougars, and XR-7s; and 37,101 Grand Marquis.

For 1986, the Lynx front-wheel-drive subcompact was available as a three- or five-door Hatchback or a Station Wagon. The standard power train was a 1.9-liter two-barrel four, with 86 hp, and a four-speed manual transmission. A 2.0-liter, four-cylinder IDI diesel was available with a five-speed manual transaxle. New was the XR3 model, featuring a 108 hp H.O. type 1.9-liter MFI four, and standard five-speed manual transaxle. Prices started at $6,182, and climbed to $8,193 for the XR3.

Topaz, Mercury's front-wheel-drive "family" compact was offered as a two- or four-door Sedan for 1986. Two trim levels, GS and LS, were available. The standard engine was a 2.3-liter TBI four with 86 hp, and a manual five-speed transaxle. The 2.0-liter, four-cylinder IDI diesel power plant was optional. It came with a five-speed manual transaxle only. Also available was the 2.3-liter H.O. New aero headlamps, and a new grille, highlighted a restyled front end. Prices began at $8,085, and spanned the gap to $9,494.

Capri was Mercury's sporty, rear-wheel-drive, Mustang three-door clone. It came in GS, and 5.0-liter models for 1986. The standard power train was a 2.3-liter four with a one-barrel carburetor, and 88 hp. It came with four-speed automatic transmission. An optional 3.8-liter TBI V-6, with 120 hp, came with a three-speed automatic transmission. Standard on the 5.0-liter model was the "small-block" SFI, 150 hp V-8, and a five-speed manual transmission. Prices began at $8,331, and ran as high as $10,950.

The Cougar was available only as a two-door Coupe again. It was Mercury's intermediate-size, rear-drive, personal-luxury car. The standard power train was a 3.8-liter TBI V-6 (120 hp) with three-speed automatic transmission. XR-7 models came standard with a 2.3-liter Turbo Four, and five-speed manual transmission. The Turbo Cougar generated 145 hp with single exhausts, and 155 hp

New in 1986 was the Lynx XR3 with a 108 hp H.O. type 1.9-liter MFI four and a five-speed transaxle. (Mercury)

213

The 1986 Cougar LS was Mercury's intermediate-size, rear-drive, personal-luxury car. (Mercury)

with dual exhausts. A 5.0-liter SFI V-8 was available on all models, except the XR-7. It was teamed with a four-speed automatic transmission. Prices started at $11,421, jumping up to as much as $14,377 for the XR-7.

Also available to intermediate-size car buyers was the Marquis. It was offered in base, and Brougham Sedans, and Station Wagons. Its engine was the 3.8-liter V-6 fitted with a new TBI (throttle-body-injected) fuel delivery system. There were no engine options for Marquis. Prices started at $8,996, and ran to $9,805. Wood-grain exterior paneling for the Station Wagons was a $282 option.

Grand Marquis were standard-size cars. They came with a 5.0-liter SFI V-8 that generated 150 hp. The standard transmission was a four-speed automatic. There were no power train options. Grand Marquis were available as two- or four-door Sedans, or two- or three-seat Colony Park Station Wagons. They came in two trim levels, base and LS. The 1986 models got new 15-inch wheels, and a single-key door and ignition lock system. Prices started at $13,480. The two-door LS was the most expensive offering, with a base price of $13,929.

The all-new Mercury Sable was a standard-size, front-wheel-drive clone of the Ford Taurus, with aerodynamic styling. Perched on a 106-inch wheelbase, it stretched 190.9 inches long (191.9 inches for Station Wagons), and was 70.7 inches wide, and 54.4 inches high. The Sable was offered only in one series, with GS or LS trim levels. Prices started at $11,331, and went to $13,068. The Sable GS Sedan's standard power team consisted of a 2.5-liter TBI four, with 88 hp, attached to a three-speed automatic transaxle. The Sable GS Station Wagon, and LS Sedan used a 3.0-liter MFI V-6 that produced 140 hp. It was mated to a four-speed automatic transaxle.

The all-new 1986 Mercury Sable was a standard-size, front-wheel-drive clone of the Ford Taurus. (Mercury)

The Merkur was again imported, from West Germany, to Lincoln-Mercury dealers in the United States. It returned in a single-model series for 1986. Mercury said that sales of the car had been slower than expected, and blamed an improper model mix that was weighted too heavily with five-speeds, and cloth interiors. Still, the company believed the Merkur could be competitive with Audis, BMWs, Saabs, and Volvos. Promised for late in the year, but not arriving until 1988, was a larger Scorpio model. The Turbo XR4Ti three-door Hatchback had the same $16,361 price tag. Two power trains were offered, both using the Brazilian-built 2.3-liter MFI Turbo Four as their engine. However, the transmissions (and horsepower ratings) varied. Five-speed manual cars had a 175 hp rating. Cars with automatic transmission had a 145 hp rating.

The "head honchos" at Lincoln-Mercury Division were mostly the same in 1986, except that Bobby G. Jenkins replaced Frank H. Gibbs as dealer service manager. DeWayne Lancaster took over from Richard L. Fenstermacher as market representation manager. Model-year sales of Mercurys, and Mekurs fell from 1985. The totals for individual models were 71,753 Lynx models; 13,358 Capris 62,089 Topaz models; 72,652 Marquis; 70,563 Sables; 121,972 Cougars; 112,225 Grand Marquis; and 14,509 Merkurs.

Capri, the Mustang "clone" with a Mercury badge, dropped out of the lineup for 1987. The name would later return, but on a different type of car sourced from Ford's Australian branch. In March 1987, a new sub-compact Mercury, called the Tracer, was introduced as a 1988 model. Tracers were counted among Mercury's 1987 model-year production, but were *not* included in domestic dealer sales totals for 1987 models.

Lincoln-Mercury dealers did sell the Merkur XR4Ti. It was a high-tech, high-performance model imported from Germany. *Motor Trend* described this front-engined, rear-wheel-drive car as "one of the nicest sporty cars around, but misunderstood by the public." Dealers did not quite know what to do with it, either. It had a three-door Hatchback body with a weird-looking "bi-plane" spoiler. The engine was a 2.3-liter, overhead cam, inline for with a turbocharger, and 145 hp at 4400 rpm. Optional was 175 hp at 5000 rpm. Along with the high-performance of the car, came a steep-sounding $17,832 price tag.

The biggest news for Mercury's Lynx subcompact was the addition of standard fuel-injection, to replace the carburetors on the 1.9-liter four-cylinder engine. This would be the Lynx's final year, as the Tracer replaced it. The diesel engine was still available, at no extra charge, except on the sporty XR3. The Lynx came in base, and GS three-door Hatchback editions, a five-door GS Hatchback, a four-door GS Wagon, and a three-door XR3 Hatchback, at prices between $5,569, and $8,808.

The front-engined, front-wheel-drive (or all-wheel-drive) Mercury Topaz had just a few engine changes for 1987. The HO engine lost six horsepower, and the diesel was dropped. Nitrogen-filled shock absorbers went into the Topaz suspension for 1987, to help ride, and handling a bit. Two notable options joined the list: A new three-speed automatic with fluid-linked torque converter, and a part-time four-wheel-drive system. Four-wheel-drive was available only with automatic transmission, and an optional high-output engine. A driver's side air bag, available only in limited quantities in 1986, became a regular production option this year. A pair of Topaz two-door models, both with GS-level trim, included the Sedan, and Sport Sedan. Both of these also came as four-door Sedans, along with a top-of-the line LS edition. Prices spanned the gap from $8,562 to $10,213.

Air conditioning became standard on top-rung LS models. Ford's four-cylinder engine was not offered on Sable, though it continued as a Taurus staple. Instead, Sables had a 3.0-liter V-6 with four-speed overdrive automatic transmission. There were two lines in the Sable series. Both lines included a four-door Sedan, and a four-door Station Wagon. They had list prices from $12,240 to $15,054.

Grand Marquis had "a level of luxury only a traditional full-size automobile can deliver," said Mercury's 1987 catalog. (Mercury)

Mercury's mid-size Cougar, a cousin to the Thunderbird, was restyled for 1987. It included a new greenhouse profile, aero headlamps, flush-fit glass, and full-width taillamps. The sporty XR-7 switched from the former turbo-charged four to a 5.0-liter V-8. All models now came with standard four-speed overdrive automatic transmission, and manual gear shifts dropped out of the lineup. The base GS model also disappeared. Both Cougar models came with standard air conditioning, and tinted glass. Late in the year, *Motor Trend* tested a special 20th Anniversary edition. The Cougar LS Coupe sold for $13,595 with a V-6 or $14,234 with a V-8. The V-8-powered XR-7 was $15,832.

Except for the addition of air conditioning as standard equipment, the full-size Mercury Grand Marquis (close kin to Ford's LTD Crown Victoria) changed little for 1987. New standard equipment included an electronic-tuning radio, replacing the former manual version. The LS version of the Grand Marquis came in two- and four-door Sedans, while the lower-priced GS came only with four-doors. There was also a Colony Park Station Wagon listing at $15,462 in GS trim, and $16,010 with LS appointments.

Merkur's engine options have already been described. The base 1.9-liter Lynx four came in 113 hp, and 115 hp versions. The 2.0-liter diesel had a 58-hp rating. The standard Topaz engine was a 2.3-liter, 86-hp four with throttle-body-injection (TBI), and high-swirl combustion (HSC) design. A high-output version with 94 hp was offered, too. A 3.0-liter, 140-hp V-6 was standard in Sables. The Cougar used a larger 3.8-liter, 120-hp V-6, and the 5.0-liter, 150-hp V-8 was standard in XR-7s, and optional in other models. This V-8 was also used in Grand Marquis, and Colony Parks.

Wheelbase measurements were: (Merkur) 102.7 inches; (Lynx) 94.2 inches; (Topaz) 99.9 inches; (Sable) 106.0 inches; (Cougar) 104.2 inches; (Grand Marquis) 114.3 inches. Overall lengths were: (Merkur) 178.4 inches; (Lynx) 166.9 inches; (Lynx Wagon) 168.0 in; (Topaz) 177.0 inches; (Sable) 190.0 inches; (Sable Wagon) 191.9 inches; (Cougar) 200.8 inches; (Grand Marquis) 214.0 inches; (Grand Marquis Wagon); 218.0 inches.

A four-speed manual transmission was standard on Lynx, with five-speed manual or three-speed automatic transmissions optional. A five-speed manual gear box was standard on Topaz, and a three-speed automatic was optional. Four-speed overdrive automatic was standard on Sable, Cougar, and Grand Marquis models.

The Grand Marquis had a recirculating ball steering system, but other models used rack, and pinion. Lynx and Topaz models had a MacPherson strut-mounted, coil spring front suspension with lower control arms, and a stabilizer bar. Cougars featured a modified MacPherson strut suspension with lower control arms, coil springs, and an anti-sway bar. Sables had MacPherson struts with control arms, coil springs, and an anti-sway bar. The Grand Marquis used coil springs with long and short A arms, and an anti-sway bar. Rear suspension for the Lynx was independent trailing arms with modified MacPherson struts, and coil springs on the lower control arms. The Topaz had an independent quadra-link MacPherson strut rear suspension. Sables used MacPherson struts with coil springs, parallel suspension arms, and an anti-sway bar. A four-link setup with coil springs was found at the rear of Cougars, and Grand Marquis. All models had front disc, rear drum brakes.

Ross H. Roberts was General Manager of Lincoln-Mercury Division in 1987, and Edsel B. Ford II was general sales manager. There were 2,752 Lincoln-Mercury dealer franchises in the United States, but only 853 were exclusives in a single marque. The 1987 Mercury line was introduced on October 2, 1986. It met some success in the marketplace, with combined Lincoln-Mercury dealer sales for the model-year totaling 665,557 cars, versus 648,441 in 1986. However, the Mercury-only dealer sales figure for 1987 was 470,644 units, down from 474,612 in 1986. Model-year production totaled 494,502 units. This included 14,201 Merkurs (9,968 XR4Tis, and 4,233 Scorpios imported from West Germany); 40,026 Lynx models; 27,478 Tracers; 72,861 Topaz models, 109,801 Sables; 100,447 Cougars; and 122, 732 Grand Marquis. The Scorpios, and Tracers, although included in 1987 U.S. dealer model-year sales figures, were 1988 models.

For car collectors, the 1987 model with the most appeal seems to be the Cougar XR-7. When we put announcements in *Old Cars* magazine, asking for Mercury photographs to fill this book, a number of serious collectors mailed in pictures of mid- to late-1980s Cougars. A rarity built for the last time this year was the Grand Marquis with a 351-cubic-inch (5.8-liter) V-8. It had an advertised 180-hp rating. Ford Motor Company built only 15,906 of the 5.8-liter V-8s for installation in 1987 cars. They were available in only the LTD Crown Victoria, and the Mercury Grand Marquis, so the number of "351" Mercs must be quite low. Another model with an outside shot at becoming a special-interest car is the Merkur XR4Ti.

The Lynx subcompact bit the dust this year, while the full-size Grand Marquis, and compact Topaz enjoyed a restyling. The aero-look Sable added a larger, more potent power plant option.

The imported-from-Germany Merkur line offered the new Scorpio model. This was a five-door Hatchback that Mercury management perceived as competition for Mercedes-Benz, Saab, and Volvo. In Europe, it earned "Car of the Year" honors in 1987, and industry observers raved about it here. However, it never caught on with American buyers. The Scorpio shared a front-engined, rear-wheel-drive layout with the XR4Ti. It had a V-6, a larger wheelbase, and length, around the same performance, and a $5,000 steeper price tag ($23,248). The Merkur XR4Ti, which had all the same styling, and specs, but a new single-wing spoiler, was back with a steeper list price of $19,065.

Mercury's Tracer entered the marketplace in March 1987, as a 1988 model. It replaced the Lynx. The Tracer was based on the Mazda 323. It was a "world car," combining Mazda Motor Corporation's design, and engineering with production at a Ford factory in Hermosillo, Mexico. Labor problems at the factory, late in 1987, disrupted supplies of the Tracer, but sales projections for the first year proved accurate, nevertheless. The front-wheel-drive sub-compact Tracer was marketed in two-door Hatchback ($7,926), four-door Hatchback ($8,364), and four-door Station Wagon ($8,727) models. Standard equipment included a 1.6-liter electronically-fuel-injected four, five-speed manual transaxle, power front disc brakes, and P175/70R13 black sidewall tires. A Sport Package including two-tone paint, styled aluminum wheels, and stripes was about $250 extra, and not available for wagons.

Both Topaz four-cylinder engines added power this year, as four-door versions of Mercury's compact took on new sheet metal. Two sporty models were added. The XR5 two-door, and LTS (Luxury Touring Sedan) Sport four-door replaced the former GS Sport edition. The Topaz grille had a vertical-bars pattern, quite different from the related Ford Tempo with its twin-slot grille. Bumpers were now integrated into the body. Wraparound signal and side-marker lamps flanked aero headlamps. At the rear were full-width wraparound taillamps. Under Topaz hoods, multi-point fuel injection replaced the former single-point system. Both the XR5, and the LTS were powered by a high-output version of the standard engine. A new analog instrument cluster contained a tachometer. Motorized automatic front shoulder belts became standard. Front-drive models came standard with a five-speed manual gear shift (automatic optional), but the four-wheel-drive version could only have automatic. The Topaz came in the GS, and XR5 two-door Sedan models, plus GS, LS, and LTS four-door Sedans. Base prices were $9,166 to $11,541.

Performance fans could order their 1988 Sables with a new 3.8-liter V-6 option. It was teamed with the four-speed automatic that was also used with the standard 3.0-liter V-6. That engine had a counter-rotating balance shaft for smoother running, as well as multi-point fuel injection. Both engines produced 140 horsepower, but the 3.8 delivered considerably more torque. Air conditioning, and tinted glass became standard in all Sables, but could be deleted on the GS. The GS added other formerly optional items as standard this year: intermittent wipers, separate front seats, digital clock, and a cargo net. Whitewall tires were optional only with the standard steel wheels, not the optional cast-aluminum or poly-cast wheels. Both the four-door Sedan, and four-door Wagon were offered in GS, and LS formats at $14,145 to $15,683.

Engine modifications gave Cougar's base 3.8-liter V-6 engine an extra 20 hp for 1988. A new balance shaft made it smoother-running. Multi-port fuel-injection replaced the former throttle-body (single-point) system. Dual exhausts, and a higher axle ratio became standard with the optional "XR-7" 5.0-liter V-8, while blackwall tires went on the base LS model. The sporty XR-7 (V-8 engine only) added body-colored bumpers on both ends. It also got a body-color grille, body side moldings, and mirrors, for a monochromatic look. The new monochromatic color schemes were Black, White, and Scarlet. New 16-spoke cast aluminum wheels came in either Argent Silver or body color. Analog instruments replaced the former electronic cluster in the XR-7 dashboard (but the electronic version remained optional). The XR-7 final drive ratio switched from 2.73:1 to 3.08:1 to boost acceleration. Aluminum wheels held 225/60VR15 tires. The standard Cougar had a list price of $14,134 with a V-6, and $14,855 with a V-8. The V-8-only XR-7 Coupe was $16,266.

Revised front and rear styling gave the full-size, rear-drive Mercury Grand Marquis a new look, as the lineup dropped to four-door Sedans, and Station Wagons only. The two-door model was gone. This year's bumpers had an integrated appearance, while wraparound taillamps highlighted the rear. Wide lower body side moldings were standard on both the GS, and LS models. Sedans added a half-vinyl roof (rear only). Whitewall P215/75R15 tires became standard on all models. An automatic headlamp on and off warning system also was standard. Joining the option list was an Insta-Clear heated windshield. The four-door Sedan, and four-door Colony Park both came in GS, and LS trim levels. Prices started at $16,100, and peaked at $16,926.

Only one engine was offered in the new Merkur Scorpio. It was a 2.9-liter V-6 that developed 144 hp at 5500 rpm. The Merkur XR4Ti had the same turbo four. The new Tracer came standard with the 1.9-liter, 88-hp four, which was sourced from Ford, and had been used in the Lynx. The LTS model came with a Mazda 1.8-liter, 127 hp four. Most other models offered the same power teams as in 1987. However, the base 2.3-liter four in the Topaz was upped to 98 hp, and the high-output version (standard in XR-7, LTS, and four-wheel-drive models) was tuned for a higher 100 hp rating. As mentioned, the Cougar V-6 gained 20 hp, and the V-8 gained five. The Sable had its new, "torquier" 140 hp optional V-6. Grand Marquis had no changes, except that the optional 5.8-liter (351-cubic-inch) V-8 of 1987 was no more.

A 108.7-inch wheelbase was used for the Scorpio, which was 186.4 inches in overall length. It had a 69.5-inch overall width, 54.6-inch overall height, and front, and rear track was 58.1 inches. The new Tracer had a half-inch longer (94.7 inches) wheelbase than the Lynx, but a five-inch shorter (162 inches) overall length. The Tracer Station Wagon, however, at 170 inches, was longer than the Lynx Station Wagon had been. Width was the same 66 inches that the Lynx had. The various body styles were 53- to 53.7 inches tall. Other 1988 Mercurys had no changes in chassis or basic dimensions from their 1987 counterparts.

The 1988 Tracer was introduced in March 1987. Most other models bowed in the showrooms on October 1, 1987, but introduction of the Topaz was delayed until November. Lincoln-Mercury Division had a new marketing plans manager named David E. Breedlove, but few other top-level personnel changes occurred. Total model year production was 473,400 units. This included 91,733 Tracers; 79,581 Topaz models, 110,256 Sables; 113,801 Cougars; and 109,054 Grand Marquis. There was a huge increase in the number of Lincoln-Mercury dealers to 3,640 franchises (874 exclusives). That kept model-year sales by domestic Lincoln-Mercury dealers on an upward trend, and the total was a healthy 683,214 cars. Of the vehicles they sold, 485,613 were Mercurys. This was up substantially from 470,644 sales in 1987, and from the 474,612 realized in 1986. Also imported from West Germany were 5,607 Merkur XR4Tis, and 8,661 Merkur Scorpios.

Mercury made its "50th Anniversary" model introductions of Tracers, Topaz models, Sables, and Grand Marquis on October 6, 1988. The most changed car of the year was the Cougar, which bowed about a month-and-a-half later on December 26, 1988. This was also the last year that Lincoln-Mercury dealers sold the Merkur, and Scorpio cars, which were sourced from West Germany. They again came as a Merkur XR4Ti three-door Hatchback model (with a turbo four), which was higher-priced at $19,759, and a Scorpio five-door Hatchback (with a six) priced at $25,052. The first offered 145 to 175 hp, and the Scorpio had 144 hp. Combined model-year sales, which ran just over 14,000 units in 1986-1988, were not reported for 1989, but some 9,000 were built in the model-year.

The 1989 Mercury Tracer looked virtually identical to the 1988 Tracer. It continued to be powered by the 1.6-liter (97.5-cubic-inch) inline four-cylinder engine with 82 hp. The two-door Hatchback ($8,556); the four-door Hatchback ($9,242); and the four-door Station Wagon ($9,726) all returned. The Hatchbacks could be ordered with the $268 Sport package.

Little changed in Mercury's compact Topaz Sedans, which got a moderate restyling for 1988. The grille had a new look with vertical louvers filling the entire opening, and a round Mercury symbol in the center. The plastic front bumper/fascia looked slightly revised, too. The Topaz came in two- and four-door GS versions, plus LS, and LTS four-doors, and the XR5 two-door. A driver's side airbag was now available in all, except the sporty XR5 two-door. The four-wheel-drive option was available throughout the line. The GS, and LS used the base engine, while the XR5, LTS, and all-wheel-drive models had a high-output version. Prices were $9,577 to $11,980.

Modest revision of Sable's front end included new headlamps, and park and signal lamps, as well as full-width illumination of the panel between the headlamps. Sedans changed their taillamp design. A new, optional 3.8-liter V-6 turned to sequential fuel-injection this year. It was teamed with the four-speed automatic transaxle that was standard with the base 3.0-liter engine. All Sables also got standard air conditioning, and all-tinted glass. Both the four-door Sedan, and Wagon came in GS, and LS trim. Prices were $14,101 to $15,872.

An all-new Cougar Coupe arrived for 1989. It was, again, closely related to the Ford Thunderbird. Though roomier inside, the new edition was smaller outside, but tipped the scales at some 400 pounds more. It also had its own, distinct low cowl/long hood look. Wheelbase grew by almost nine inches. Again rear-drive, the Cougar now had four-wheel independent suspension. A compact front suspension allowed the hood to slope down low. As before, a formal-style roof line was the main difference between the Cougar, and its Thunderbird cousin. Model availability was the same as the previous edition: a base LS, and sporty XR-7. The LS came with a 3.8-liter 140 hp fuel-injected V-6 (lacking the former balance shaft) and four-speed overdrive automatic transmission. The XR-7 featured a supercharged and inter-cooled version that developed 210 hp. A five-speed manual gear box was standard in the XR-7, with automatic transmission optional. No V-8 engine was available. LS Cougars now rode 15-inch tires, while the XR-7 used 16-inch performance tires.

217

Standard equipment included air conditioning, tinted glass, electronic instruments, power windows and mirrors, and AM/FM stereo radio.

Styling features of the XR-7 included monochromatic body treatment, and alloy wheels. Anti-lock braking was standard on XR-7, which used four-wheel disc brakes, rather than the disc/drum arrangement found on the LS. Adjustable shock-absorber dampening allowed the selection of a soft or firm ride. Extras on the XR-7 included a handling suspension, "Traction-Lok" axle, sport seats with power bolsters, and analog gauges. The Cougar LS Coupe had a list price of $15,448, while the hot XR-7 was $19,650.

"The Mercury Sedan buyer has two choices," said *Motor Trend* in 1989. "Get radical, and pop for the sleek Sable or be driven by the fear of change, and choose the old faithful, big-bumpered Grand Marquis." Little changed in the full-size Grand Marquis Mercury series, except that clearcoat metallic paint joined the option list this year. However, for dyed-in-the-wool "Big M" traditionalists, there was a 50th anniversary edition. It was released as a mid-year offering. The Grand Marquis four-door

The 1989 Scorpio XR4T1 was imported from Germany for Lincoln-Mercury dealers to sell. (Mercury)

Sedan came in GS ($16,701), and LS ($17,213) editions. The Grand Marquis Colony Park Station Wagon was $17,338 with GS trimmings, and $17,922 as an LS.

The Merkur, Scorpio, Tracer, Sable, and Grand Marquis power teams were direct carry-overs for 1989. The Topaz retained the base 2.3-liter four with 98 or 100 hp, but the XR5/LTS/4WD high-output four was discontinued. The Cougar's new 210 hp performance engine is described above. Also carried over for most models were the 1988 chassis specifications. However, the face-lifted Sable models each gained two inches of length and the Cougar had the following revisions: (Wheelbase) 113 inches; (overall length) 198.7 inches; (overall width) 72.7 inches; (overall height) 52.7 inches; (front track) 61.4 inches; (rear track) 60.2 inches; (base model curb weight) 3,553 pounds; and (tires) P205/70R15 on base model and P225/60R16 on Cougar XR-7.

A five-speed manual gear box was standard with the Cougar XR-7, and four-speed automatic was optional. Four-speed overdrive automatic was standard on the Cougar LS. Both Cougars had a "log spindle" short and long arm (SLA) front suspension with coil springs, gas shocks, upper A-arms, lower arms, tension struts, and stabilizer bars. The rear suspension was independent with coil springs, gas shocks, lower 'h' arms, upper arms and stabilizer bars. Other models had the same running gear used previously.

Again, Ross H. Roberts pulled the strings at Lincoln-Mercury Division. Mark Hutchins took over as general sales manager from Edsel B. Ford II. Dan Coulson was the division's latest comptroller, and Ian McAllister was the new general marketing manager. Model year production was 294,899 in the United States, and 495,017 total. This included 64,567 Tracers; 93,517 Topaz models; 119,050 Sables; 92,702 Cougars; and 127,152 Grand Marquis. Model-year sales were: 5,915 Merkur Scorpios; 2,878 Merkur XR4Tis; 62,693 Tracers; 93,348 Topaz models; 114,884 Sables; 97,246 Cougars; and 117,186 Grand Marquis.

Looking into a crystal ball, fortune tellers might expect the last-year Merkurs to be collectible someday. Naturally, the "50th Anniversary" Grand Marquis is assured some degree of special-interest status. Try to find one of these, in good shape, 10 to 15 years from now. Finally, do not overlook the Cougar as a good bet for a future collector car. Only 5.1 percent of all 1989 Cougars were super-charged XR-7 models, which calculates out to roughly 4,728 cars.

Cougar LS

Sable GS

Topaz GS

Tracer

Grand Marquis LS

The 1989 Mercury line-up included (top-to-bottom) the Cougar LS, the Sable GS, the Topaz GS, the Tracer, and the Grand Marquis LS. (Mercury)

Mercury in the '90s

1990 was essentially a carryover year for Mercury, except that the "Merkur experience" ended. All the other Mercury products remained closely related to models in the Ford lineup. Along with four domestically built models (Topaz, Sable, Cougar, and Grand Marquis) Mercury dealers sold the Mexican-built Tracer. However, Tracer production halted and, technically, there was no 1990 model. Mercury was awaiting a revised version. This new car, which bowed in April 1990, was promoted as a 1991 model.

Shoulder belts added to rear seats were the only notable change for the Mercury Topaz compact. Trunk and foot well lights became standard, as did floor mats. Wire wheel covers left the option list. As before, both the standard and high-output 2.3 liter four-cylinder engines were available, the latter standard in the XR5 and LTS Sedans and the AWD (all-wheel-drive) models. The two-door Sedan came in GS and XR5 editions, while the four-door also came as an LS. List prices ranged from $10,027 to $12,514.

Except for the addition of a standard driver's side airbag and optional anti-lock braking (on Sedans only), the mid-size Sable Sedans and Wagons were carry-over cars for 1990. Inside was a new instrument cluster, with a slide-out coin and cup holder trays. Tilt steering became standard and a compact-disc player was a new option. A 3.0-liter V-6 was standard again. Variable-assist power steering now came with the optional 3.8-liter V-6 engine. Both the four-door Sedan and four-door Station Wagon came in GS and LS trim. The price spectrum started at $15,009 and went as high as $16,789.

Not much changed for 1990 on Mercury's mid-size Cougar Coupes, which enjoyed a full restyling for 1989. The LS housed a 3.8-liter V-6 and four-speed overdrive automatic transmission. The XR-7 was fitted with a 210-hp super-charged, and inter-cooled version of that engine, mated to a five-speed manual transmission with overdrive. A four-speed overdrive automatic was optional. Anti-lock brakes became standard on the XR7. Prices began at $15,911 for the LS, and $20,217 for the XR-7.

Nearly all changes for the Mercury full-size Sedans and Wagons went inside. They included a driver's airbag, a new instrument panel, rear shoulder belts, and tilt steering as standard equipment. As before, the Colony Park Station Wagons could get optional third rear seats for eight-passenger seating. Sedans no longer had standard bumper guards, but they remained on the option list. Rear track width grew by 1.3 inches, because of a different rear axle. A single key now operated doors and ignition. Standard power train for all models was a 5.0-liter V-8 teamed with a four-speed

The Mercury "collector car" of 1990 would have to be the Cougar XR-7. This is the LS (Mercury)

A standard driver's side airbag and optional anti-lock braking for Sedans were new 1990 Sable features. (Mercury)

automatic transmission with overdrive. GS and LS trims were offered on both four-door Sedans and Wagons, with base prices starting at $17,633 and climbing to $18,920.

Ross Roberts continued to serve as a Ford Motor Company vice president and general manager of Lincoln-Mercury Division. There were 2,755 Mercury dealers in the United States as of January 1, 1990, plus 1,647 Lincoln dealers. The top dealership in the country was Libertyville Lincoln-Mercury, of Libertyville, Illinois, which sold 31,396 new-cars in 1990. Production of U.S.-built Mercurys for model-year 1990 totaled 242,537 units. This included 57,368 Topaz models, 81,240 Cougars and 103,479 Sables. Overall model-year output also included 70,510 Grand Marquis made in Canada, for a grand total of 313,047 units.

The Mercury "collector car" of the year 1990 would have to be the Cougar XR-7. Mercury fans just love the "Cat" and probably always will. One industry trade journal does not show a total for XR-7s, but indicates that only 4,129 of the 1990 Cougars were "turbo-charged." Since that figure is fairly consistent with the total of 1989 super-charged cars, we are guessing that they meant "super-charged" instead of "turbo-charged," which makes the 1990 XR-7 even rarer.

Mercury's 1991 model-year began with the April 1990 introduction of an all-new Tracer subcompact. This car evolved from a joint Ford-Mazda re-engineering effort. It was built in Hermosilla, Mexico. Tracers were now offered as four-door Hatchbacks ($8,969), and four-door Station Wagons ($9,990). The front-wheel-drive Tracer had a longer, 98.4-inch wheelbase. A fancy LTS (Luxury Town Sedan) Hatchback was $2,300 extra. The Hatchbacks were 171 inches long, and the Station Wagons stretched 172 inches. A Ford-built 1.9-liter single overhead camshaft, inline four-cylinder engine with fuel-injection was standard in most Tracers. However, the LTS featured a smaller (1.8-liter), but more powerful Mazda-made double overhead camshaft four, with 127 hp. The Tracer used what was known as Ford's CT20 platform.

A removable hardtop was available for the Australian-built 1991 Mercury Capri. (Mercury)

The second 1991 model to bow, in July 1990, was a new Capri. This $12,588 Convertible 2+2 was built by Ford's branch located in Broadmeadows, Australia. It had a 94.7-inch wheelbase, and a 167-inch length. It also came in XR2 Turbo format, for around $3,000 extra! The base engine was a 1.6-liter inline four with 100 hp. The turbo-charged engine was of the same displacement, but generated 132 hp. The Capri platform was designated SA30.

Four other cars, introduced in the fall of 1990, were the carryover Topaz, Cougar, Sable, and Grand Marquis. All had price cuts of 0.5 to 2.9 percent, due to the sluggish pace of 1991 car sales.

The "new" Topaz looked just like the old one, with the same 99.9-inch wheelbase, 177-inch overall length, 69-inch width, and P185/70R-14 tires. Power again came from a 2.3-liter four with 96 hp. A 3.0-liter V-6 with 135 hp was extra. The base GS series offered two- and four-door Sedans at $10,448, and $10,605. The four-door model was available in LS ($11,984), and LT ($13,008) trims. The two-door came as an XR5 for $11,447.

A new fascia identified the 1991 Cougars, which were built in Ford's factory at Lorain, Ohio. They had three-segment front lamps, a straighter hood lip and an inverted-trapezoid grille. The parking lamps were restyled, and moved further out on the bumper. The wheelbase remained at 113 inches, and length jumped one inch to 200 inches. A 3.8-liter V-6 with 140 hp was standard. The XR-

The 1991 Mercury Grand Marquis LS four-door Sedan got a blacked-out grille treatment and clearcoat paint. (Mercury)

7 came with a 5.0-liter H.O. V-8 that generated 200 hp. This motor was optional in base models. Cougars came as V-6s ($16,094), LS models with V-8s ($17,278), and XR-7 models ($21,139). Cougar's used Ford's MN12 platform, along with the Thunderbird.

The Sable was Mercury's version of Ford's popular, front-wheel-drive "jelly bean" car, the Taurus. The Sable version had a 106-inch wheelbase, and 193-inch overall length (194 inches for Station Wagons). It was built at plants in Atlanta, Georgia, and Chicago, Illinois. Power options included a 135-hp, 3.0-liter V-6 or a 140-hp, 3.8-liter V-6. Sequential fuel-injection was one of the year's improvements. Both body styles came in GS trim for around $16,000 to $16,100. They also came as LS models for about $1,000 more. Styling was virtually identical to 1990. The Sable platform was coded DN5.

Also looking a lot like its 1990 counterpart was the 1991 Grand Marquis, built on Ford's "Panther" platform. This rear-wheel-drive, full-size car came as GS ($18,199) and LS ($18,699) Sedans. It was also available as a Colony Park Station Wagon in GS or LS trims (with two or three seats) for $19,133 to $19,490. Assemblies of the big Mercurys were done in St. Thomas, Ontario, Canada. The Grand Marquis had a 114.3-inch wheelbase, and a 214-inch (218 inches for Station Wagons) overall length. The base engine was a 4.6-liter V-8 with 190 hp. A 210 hp version was optional.

The year 1991 began with Ross H. Roberts serving as general manager of Lincoln-Mercury Division, but during the year, Lee R. Miskowski stepped into the job. Model-year production of models built in the United States, and Canada, included 43,745 Topaz models; 96,698 Sables; 63,822 Cougars; and 91,075 Grand Marquis. Model-year sales of Capri Convertibles were 19,047.

Future collector cars from this model-year are likely to be the Cougar XR-7, the Capri Convertible (especially the Turbo version), and the "full-dresser" Grand Marquis, with all of the extra-cost goodies. This year's Cougar did not offer the supercharged V-6. However, only 15.9 percent of all 1991 Cougars, or 10,146 cars, had V-8 power.

The first 1992 Mercury to bow was the restyled Grand Marquis. It entered production in March 1991, and went on sale in April. It had a new "aero" body with a toothy grille, but the basic "Panther" platform was still the same as it was in 1979. Base price was $20,216. An LS option was $430 extra. The wheelbase was 114.4 inches, and overall length was 213 inches. A new single overhead camshaft 4.6-liter V-8 was used. It was rated at 190 hp, or 210 hp with dual exhausts. Late-1992

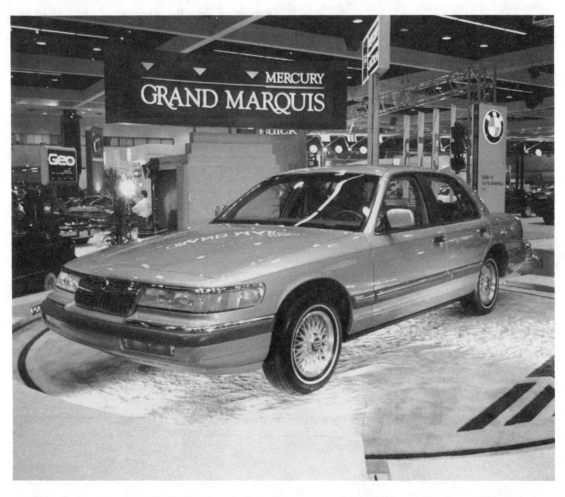

Completely restyled for 1992 was this Mercury Grand Marquis four-door Sedan at the Chicago Auto Show. (Ron Kowalke)

The base Capri 1992 came with a five-speed manual or automatic transmission. Turbos had only a five-speed. (Mercury)

New for 1992 was the first major redesign of the Mercury Sable. It was restyled inside, too. (Mercury)

models got an ETC (electronically controlled) four-speed automatic transmission. ABS (anti-lock brake system) braking was optional.

Mercury's Tracer again shared its CT20 front-wheel-drive platform with Mazda's Protege, although its styling was done at Detroit. There were virtually no changes from 1991. The two engines (one from Ford, and one from Mazda) were back again. The smaller (1.8-liter), but more powerful (127 hp) engine was standard in a new LTS model. Transmissions were a five-speed manual or a four-speed electronically controlled automatic. The same models were offered at prices from $9,773 to $12,023. The Tracer was a very space-efficient car. The Station Wagon had 67 cubic-feet of cargo room, with the rear seat folded. The LTS trim level was added in mid-1992. It offered more luxury-level features.

The Australian-built SA30 platform convertible again came in Capri ($14,452), and XR2 Turbo ($17,250) versions. All specifications were unchanged. The base model came with a five-speed manual or four-speed automatic transmission, but the Turbo came only with the five-speed. The XR2 also included alloy wheels; low-profile tires; a deck lid spoiler; an 8,000-rpm tachometer, and a pressure-boost gauge. A driver's side air bag was included, too.

Mercury's Topaz had no styling changes of significance. The base engine again had 96 hp. There was an optional new V-6 for the XR5 two-door, and the LTS four-door. Featuring a 3.0-liter piston displacement, it generated 135 hp. While prices on entry-level models dropped, or rose modestly (less than $50), the LTS and XR5 models with the V-06 were $1,200 to $2,000 higher.

The Mercury Cougar marked its 25th anniversary in 1992. To commemorate this, there was a special LS model with a monochromatic color scheme, a 5.0-liter V-8, BBS alloy wheels, and special trim. Styling, dimensions, and engines were unchanged. The LS Coupe with a V-6 was $16,460. The LS Coupe with a V-8 was $17,540, and the XR-7 was $22,054.

Mercury gave the 1992 Sable a makeover. New sheet metal was used, except on the roof, and the doors. Composite headlamps were added. They had a longer, narrower look. New 15-inch diameter wheels were used. There was also new upholstery, and amber-colored switch illumination was added to the instrument panel. Remote radio controls were new, too. GS and LS models were offered in four-door Sedan, and Station Wagon body styles. The 135-hp, 3.0-liter V-6 had new roller tappets. A 140-hp, 3.8-liter V-6 was optional. The Sedans featured MacPherson struts all around. The Station Wagons had coil springs, and control arms. Prices started at $16,418, and climbed to $18,395.

A modestly restyled Tracer was the first 1993 Mercury to appear. It was released in May 1992, as a 1993 model. There was a narrower new grille with a body-color panel across its top. The panel had the Mercury logo in its center. Models, dimensions, and engine specifications were the same as before. Prices ranged from $10,155 to $12,023.

The Topaz came out in September 1992, along with the rest of the 1993 Mercury models. It also had a new grille with a very thin, slot-like opening at the bottom of the body-color panel. There was a Mercury emblem in the center. Model offerings were cut back to GS two- and four-door Sedans at $10,809, and $10,976, respectively. Dimensions, specifications, and engine selections were the same, except that new 130 hp and 135 hp ratings were seen.

The Capri was back for 1993, also with no major changes. Prices went from $14,452 for the base model, to $17,250 for the XR2 Turbo. Later, Mercury slashed the Capri price range. It was listed as $13,640 to $15,390. Engines were the same 1.6-liter, 100-hp four, and 1.6-liter, 132-hp Turbo four.

Base Cougars were eliminated. The line was, again, simply called Cougar XR-7. There was one two-door Coupe with a V-6, and a list price of $14,855. The V-8 version listed for $16,045. This was $1,500 less than the year-earlier base Cougar! Specifications, and engines were the same as 1992, except the XR-7 now used the P205/70R15 tires that the base Cougar had the previous season. The P225/60ZR16 tires that came standard on 1992 Cougars were an extra-cost option.

The Sable had new exterior, and exterior trim. It did not look much different in basic format, however. Both the four-door Sedan, and the four-door Station Wagon came in GS, and LS trims. Prices started at $17,480, and topped out at $19,457. The base 3.0-liter V-6 had a higher 140 hp rating. The optional 3.8-liter V-6 was also rated 140 hp.

223

The 1993 Capri had no major changes. Prices were $14,452 for a base model and $17,250 for an XR2 Turbo. Later, Mercury slashed prices. (Steve Ellingboe)

A standard passenger-side air bag was a feature of the 1993 Mercury Grand Marquis four-door Sedan. It came in GS ($22,082), and LS ($22,609) editions. Leather seats were a $555 option. The 1992, and 1993 specifications looked identical.

The Tracer, Mercury's version of the Ford Escort, is the company's front-drive, small-size "family" car. Perched on a 98-inch wheelbase, it measures 171 inches from bumper-to-bumper. It is 67 inches wide. The 1994 Tracer comes in base four-door Sedan ($10,350), and base Station Wagon ($10,620) models, plus an LTS-level four-door Sedan ($12,660). The standard base-model engine is

Engines offered for the 1993 Capri were the 1.6-liter 100-hp four and 1.6-liter 132-hp Turbo four. Steve Ellingboe, editor of *Today's Collector* magazine, bought his Capri ragtop as a fun investment. (Mercury)

a 1.9-liter MPFI four that puts out 88 hp for adequate, but leisurely acceleration. The LTS has a Mazda-made 1.8-liter DOHC 16-valve four with 127 hp. It delivers strong performance. The LTS also includes anti-lock brakes as an option. Transmissions offered are a five-speed manual, or a four-speed automatic. The LTS features a taut suspension, too. For extra luggauge room, or cargo space, the rear seats fold forward. Tracers are built in the United States, and Mexico.

Counterpart to Ford's Tempo, the Mercury Topaz is a family compact with a 100-inch wheelbase, and 177-inch overall length. With us since 1987, the Topaz is due for replacement by a new car called the Mystique. *Road & Track* describes the Topaz models as "quintessential rental-fleet cars." The line includes the two- and four-door Sedans, which are both base-priced at $11,420. The standard engine is a 2.3-liter, 96-hp SEFI/HSC four. Optional is a 3.0-liter, 130 to 135-hp V-6. Available transmissions are the five-speed manual, or a three-speed automatic.

Mercury's Australian-built Capri was around for the start of model-year 1994, although scheduled for a phase-out. The front-wheel-drive Convertible came in base, and XR2 models. The former listed for $13,190, and the latter had a $14,900 window sticker. In reality, most (or all) Capris sold in 1994 were 1993-built models, and the prices were being discounted to move them out of the showrooms. The base models featured a 1.6-liter MPFI DOHC four with 100 hp, and the XR2 had a Turbo version of the same motor with 132 hp. Five-speed manual was standard, but mandatory with the Turbo Four. A four-speed automatic transmission was offered, for the base model only, at $790 extra. The Capri needed 10.8 seconds to go from 0-to-60 mph, and 18.2 seconds to cover the quarter-mile.

The "Cat" is back as Mercury's sporty, mid-size model. The Cougar is a Thunderbird clone, aimed at a higher-income market niche. The car dated way back to 1989. However, the 1994 model got a new grille, a revised interior, and a new "modular" 4.6-liter V-8. This engine was lighter, and more efficient than the 5.0-liter V-8, but nearly as powerful. Also new in the $16,360 XR-7 are dual airbags. The base XR-7 engine is the 3.8-liter SEFI V-6, rated at 140 hp. Optional, at $615 extra, is the 4.6-liter, 205 hp single overhead camshaft EFI V-8. The only transmission available is a four-speed automatic.

A highly rated, mid-size family car, the front-wheel-drive Sable is marketed in GS and LS car-lines in 1994. Both include a four-door Sedan, and a four-door Station Wagon. Prices start at $17,840 for the GS Sedan, and peak at $21,210 for the LS Station Wagon. Base engine is the 3.0-liter EFI V-6, rated for 140 hp. Optional for $630 extra is a 3.8-liter, 140 hp, EFI V-6 that is good for 9.9-second 0-to-60 mph performance. A four-speed automatic transmission is used with both engines.

Winding up Mercury's 1994 offerings is the Grand Marquis, a large, full-framed, V-8-powered, rear-wheel-drive car. It is available in two four-door Sedan models. The GS version retails upwards from $20,330, while the LS edition lists for $21,570. The standard power train combines the 4.6-liter SEFI "modular" V-8 with an electronically controlled, automatic overdrive transmission. The Grand Marquis does 0-to-60 mph in 10.5 seconds, and needs 18 seconds to cover the quarter-mile at 79 mph.

Capri
Tracer
Topaz
Cougar XR7
Sable
Grand Marquis
Villager

MERCURY
ALL THIS AND THE QUALITY OF A MERCURY

Mercury marketed seven 1994 car-lines: Capri, Tracer, Topaz, Cougar XR-7, Sable, Grand Marquis and Villager. (Mercury)

Canadian "Mercurys" 1946-1970

By R. Perry Zavitz

The Monarch

At the end of World War II, the Ford Motor Company of Canada revamped its dealer network, by separating Mercury from Ford. The established dealers sold Ford, while a similar number of new dealers were organized to handle Mercury and Lincoln. The Ford dealers were given a new car to sell in the Mercury class. It was called the Monarch.

Fundamentally a Mercury, the Monarch was a Canadian variation, with different chrome in the Mercury grille cavity. It had Ford-style oval taillights, and unique chrome trim on the fenders, and trunk. Styling changes went virtually unnoticed in the 1946 to 1948 period. A Ford-type instrument panel was used, and the motor was like that of the Canadian-built Mercury. Body types duplicated those offered by Mercury in the United States.

The all-new styling of the 1949 Mercury was copied for the Monarch. A unique grille of thick horizontal, and vertical, chrome bars dominated the front end. Mercury-style taillamps were used, but a unique trunk handle was fitted. A lion, reminiscent of the Lincoln greyhound, adorned the Monarch's hood. A Mercury dash, and other appointments, enhanced the interior for those privileged to "ride like a king" in a Monarch.

Minor front trim changes marked the 1950 models. A wide chrome trim outlined the same grille-work, and headlight rims were painted body color.

More extensive changes were made for 1951. A completely redesigned grille, made up of one heavy horizontal bar with five vertical bars on top of it, characterized the front. Chrome headlamp rims returned, and the rear fenders were restyled to look similar to a Mercury's. However, the tail-lamp lenses were more like a Lincoln's.

An unusual grille was a styling trademark of the 1959 Monarch.

The 1947 Monarch four-door Sedan was marketed in Canada. (*Old Cars*)

The 1949 Monarch two-door Sedan was called "a car you'll be proud to own." (*Old Cars*)

Like Mercury, the Monarch was new for 1952. The heavy bumper-grille was similar to Mercury's, except the vertical bars at the bottom were omitted. One single central bar appeared between the bumper and the top of the grille opening. By this time, gold-colored crowns were used to decorate the Monarch.

A new model, the Monterey, was added to the lineup. It was the first Monarch Hardtop. There were no pseudo-Hardtop Montereys, in Canada, in 1950 or 1951, as there had been in the United States. Monarchs used a 125-hp Mercury motor. Minor grille, and trim, changes were made for 1953. The Monarch grille featured seven thin, vertical pieces between the top of the grille and the top of the bumper.

Revisions for 1954 included a new bumper-grille, with the bumper guards spaced further apart than on Mercurys. The vertical connectors were located between the upper, and lower, bumper bars, and a long chrome strip was added to the rear fender chrome.

Monarch power came from the new overhead valve 161-hp Mercury V-8. The Lucerne line, a deluxe series, corresponded to Mercury's Monterey line. One of the Lucerne models was the Sun Valley, with a tinted, see-through roof.

Brand new styling came, again, for 1955, on both Mercurys and Monarchs. The bumper-grille used on both marques was similar, although the Monarch had five vertical bars in the lower part, instead of the Mercury's three. The upper portion on the Monarch opening featured a fine-textured chrome mesh.

For 1955, the Monarch came in three series. The lowest-priced line was given a name for the first time. It was called the Custom series. The middle series was the previous year's Lucerne line. The top offering was the new Richelieu series.

The same three series of Monarchs continued for 1956. The front end received some changes, which made a considerable difference from earlier Monarchs, and from Mercurys. "Dagmar" type bumper guards were placed fairly close together, near the center. Behind the bumper, was a chrome grille made up of a squared mesh, not unlike that used for the Thunderbird grille.

In mid-season, four-door Hardtops were added to the Monarch's choice of models. They were called Phaetons, like Mercury's four-door Hardtops.

Monarch had grown to be a very popular car. During the calendar years of 1953 through 1956, production of Monarchs exceeded Mercury's output in Canada. In 1954, Monarch production outstripped Mercury's by about 38 per cent.

The 1957 Monarch perhaps resembled Mercury more closely than in any other year. The Monarch grille consisted of straight horizontal ribs, rather than Mercury's "bug catcher" grille, with concave-vertical ribs. The Custom series was eliminated for 1957, but the Turnpike Cruiser line was added as the top offering.

Acceptance of the Monarch proved that a Ford product alternate, in the medium-price market, was a viable proposition, at least in Canada. This may have been one influence in the decision to introduce the Edsel.

At any rate, when the Edsel was put on the market, the Monarch was withdrawn. In Canada, Ford-Monarch dealers became Ford-Edsel dealers. Therefore, there were no 1958 Monarch models.

The unexpected sales failure of the Edsel prompted Ford of Canada to bring back the Monarch. So for 1959, Ford-Edsel dealers became Ford-Edsel-Monarch dealers. The revived Monarch was called the Mark II. It came in the three series: Lucerne, Richelieu, and Sceptre. The latter corresponded to the Mercury Park Lane line.

Styling was basically like that of Mercurys, except for the grille. It consisted of a single, rather small, horizontal bar. Seven rectangular chrome plates were mounted on it. The appearance was both simple and distinctive. The decorated panel, above the rear bumper, differed slightly from the Mercury's rear beauty panel. Monarch production, for calendar-year 1959, was more than three times that of Edsel in Canada.

Mercurys and Monarchs had considerable restyling done in 1960. Front and rear details were again different on the two marques. The Monarch grille consisted of a series of closely fitted, long rectangles. Within each of them were two horizontal strips, situated end-to-end. At the rear, the tail-lights were different, and within the chrome loops of the bumper ends, there were three small round lenses. The lowest were for the back-up lights. The others were red.

Few changes were seen in the 1950 Monarch Sedan-Coupe. (*Old Cars*)

Revisions to the grille were made on 1951 Monarchs. (*Old Cars*)

Eight new body colors were offered for 1952 Monarchs. (*Old Cars*)

The 1955 Monarch two-door Hardtop had a Lincoln look. (*Old Cars*)

Canadian models, like the 1954 Monarch Convertible, draw big crowds. (*Old Cars*)

The Monarch Lucerne four-door Sport Sedan was new for 1956. (*Old Cars*)

The same three series continued for 1960. For 1961, only the Richelieu was available. Its grille was quite distinctive, with a gold-colored crown in the center. On either side, was a series of chrome ribs angling upward, and outward. This same pattern was more or less duplicated on the trunk panel. Taillamp assemblies were of similar size, and shape, as Mercury's. Although, the lights themselves illuminated three lenses, the middle ones were clear. They were used for the back-up light function.

That was the last Monarch, or at least the last unique Canadian Monarch. After the Edsel flop, Ford approached the medium-price market from another angle. The company expanded the senior Fords into that niche. This move made the distinctive Canadian Monarch superfluous, so it was discontinued a second time.

Ford later used the Monarch name for a Mercury model made in North America.

The Meteor

When Ford Motor Company of Canada reorganized its dealer network, immediately following World War II, two branches were formed. One branch sold Fords, and Monarchs (described below). The other sold Mercurys, and a limited number of Lincolns. The Lincolns were *imported* into Canada, from the United States. The other cars were made in Canadian factories. The Canadian Mercury dealers were able to cover the upper end of the market with the imported Lincolns. However, they would have been weak, at the bottom end of the market, if a low-price Mercury had not been offered.

Called the Mercury "114," the low-price car was really a Ford with some Mercury styling features. The grille appeared to be like that of Mercury, but had some obvious modifications to fit the Ford front end. Mercury style taillamps were used. Double chrome strips, rather like the 1942 Mercury's trim, adorned the fenders of the Mercury 114. However, this chrome did not reach to the headlamps at the front, nor cross the trunk at the back. The parking lamps were different from both the 1946 Ford and Mercury styles. They were not located above the grille. Instead, they were round-shaped, and situated below the headlamps. This forecasted the 1947 to 1948 Ford parking lamp treatment. The instrument panel was essentially identical to that of Mercurys, although, in some models at least, it was a different color. The upholstery appeared similar to the material used in Mercurys, but was applied more in the Ford style.

The Mercury 114's motor was a 221-cubic-inch, 93-hp flathead V-8. This was the same engine used in Canadian-made Fords of the immediate postwar years. There were no six-cylinder motors available, for several years, in Canadian-made Ford products. When introduced, the Mercury 114 was available in the usual body types: two-door Sedan, four-door Sedan, Business Coupe, Club Coupe, Convertible, and Station Wagon. It would take Sherlock Holmes to note the differences between the 1946, 1947, and 1948 models, since very few changes were made in those model-years.

The designation "114" referred to the Ford wheelbase used for the smaller Mercury. The standard Mercury was, therefore, often called the "Mercury 118" in Canada. Possible confusion about the names was, wisely, eliminated. When the all-new 1949 models appeared, the Mercury 114 was replaced by a car named the Meteor. The Meteor conformed pretty much to guidelines set by the Mercury 114. Simply, it was a Ford with a Mercury-style grille. Meteor nameplates, and four-pointed-star emblems were used for identification. Because of the vast difference between 1949 Mercurys, and Fords, Meteors used fewer Mercury features than their

Mercury's relationship to the 1957 Monarch Lucerne Phaeton was obvious. (*Old Cars*)

The 1959 Monarch Sceptre came as a four-door Phaeton. (*Old Cars*)

The attractively styled 1960 Monarch Lucerne two-door Hardtop. (*Old Cars*)

The 1950 Meteor had a Mercury style grille. (*Old Cars*)

predecessors. The instrument panel was of Ford design. The upholstery was not identical to that of the Ford, but was quite similar, especially in its application.

Like Fords, the Meteors were offered in two series: DeLuxe and Custom. The Ford 239-cubic-inch, 100-hp V-8 powered all Meteors. The same body types offered by Ford were available, except there was no Meteor Station Wagon, or Convertible, for 1949. The 1950 Meteor car-line did, however, have both Station Wagon and Convertible body types. The chrome upper lip of the grille was deleted, and the parking lights were changed, for a 1950 face-lift. Meteors reflected a more independent styling trend with the 1951 models. Mounted in the grille cavity, was a long rectangular chrome loop with five vertical bars. Side trim consisted of a horizontal chrome strip, across the lower part of the front door, that ran onto the front fender. Near the front end of this strip was a circular Meteor emblem with a four-pointed star. A new body type for 1951 was the Victoria, a Hardtop similar to the Ford Victoria. There were no Crestliner models made or sold in Canada, by either Ford or Meteor, in 1950 or 1951.

Meteors for 1952 displayed more independence. The restyled bodies had Ford-like side trim, but Meteors retained a unique grille. It consisted simply of a single, broad chrome bar, running across the front, between the parking lamps. In the center, the bar was encircled by three ribs. Taillamp lenses, upon close examina-

A Crown Victoria model was offered in the 1956 Meteor Rideau series. (*Old Cars*)

The 1961 Canadian Meteor was based on a Ford. (*Old Cars*)

tion, appeared different from the Ford's lenses. The 1952 Meteors copied new Ford nomenclature, with Mainline, and Customline series. The Convertible, and the Victoria, were in the Customline series, since there were no Crestline models in Canadian Ford or Meteor car-lines then. The Ranch Wagon Meteor (a two-door) was a Mainline model. There were no other Station Wagons in either the 1952 or 1953 Ford, and Meteor, offerings.

Mainline Meteors used a Ford-type instrument panel, and a 110-hp 239-cubic-inch V-8 motor in 1952. By contrast, the 1952 Customline models were fitted with a Mercury style instrument panel, and Mercury's 120-hp 255-cubic-inch V-8 engine. The 1953 models had two changes. The Mercury engine was rated higher at 125-hp, and the Meteor engine was rated for 120 hp. The Crestline name was used on Canadian-built Fords, but not on Meteors.

The 1953 Meteor grille was another single-bar affair. It dropped at the center, something like its Lincoln cousins. Above this depression was a wide four-pointed star. Trim on the rear fenders of the Customline Meteors was a combination of the 1952 Ford style chrome, and the three horizontal accents seen on 1953 Mercurys.

Finally, in 1954, Meteors were offered in three series. The lowest-priced line had no name. The mid-range Customline was renamed Niagara. The Rideau was the new top-of-the-line nameplate. Two new body types were added. They included a Niagara two-door Ranch Wagon, and a Rideau Skyliner Hardtop. Grill-styling for 1954 was not changed extensively. The horizontal bar was angled downward, at its center, to form a "V" enclosing a four-pointed star. This may have influenced the design of the 1955 Ford truck grille. Engines for 1954 were the same as before, but with the Niagara, and Rideau, motors rated at 125-hp in the United States. The 1954 Ford, and Mercury, featured new overhead valve V-8 engines, but in Canada, only Mercury got such an engine. Ford had to wait another year. In midyear, a sub-series of Meteors was added. The Ford instrument panel was used in this line of cars called Niagara Specials.

The 1955 Meteors were just about as all-new as possible. Besides completely new styling, the new 272-cubic-inch, overhead valve, Ford V-8 was used. It was rated for 162 hp in the lowest series, and 175 hp in the Niagara, and Rideau models. The 1955 Meteor grille-work consisted of a series of small vertical pieces that formed a concave surface. It was again dissected, in the center, by a large "V." A four-pointed star was placed in the V.

Side trim was emphasized by most Meteors at this time, although the low-priced line had practically none at all. The Niagara series had a chrome strip running back from the headlamp rim. It curved gently downward to a point about midway between the front door, and the rear wheel opening. There, it joined a very wide chrome sash, which was angled forward at about 45 degrees. At the top of this, a chrome strip ran horizontally, back to the taillamps. Perhaps the 1956 Mercury's side trim was inspired by the 1955 Niagara.

A Ford-style instrument panel was used in Meteors, in 1955, and for some time thereafter. The same basic trim arrangement was applied to the Rideau, with the addition of a narrow strip of chrome, branching from the main piece, and running, almost horizontally, from the back of the front fender to the chrome sash. This formed a triangular area, which was usually painted a contrasting color. The available two- and three-tone paint combinations were, possibly greater on these Meteors,

In its second Merc-based year, the Meteor was Canada's fourth best selling car. (*Old Cars*)

than on any other car. Another model, the Crown Victoria, was added to the 1955 array of Meteors to satisfy desires for a sporty model. It was a welcome addition, as there were never any Meteor Thunderbirds. All Thunderbirds (early or otherwise) sold in Canada, have been imported from the United States.

Several different engines were used in 1956 Meteors. The 292-cubic-inch V-8, rated at 200 hp (or 202 hp with Merc-O-Matic transmission), powered Rideaus, and all Station Wagons. A 272-cubic-inch V-8 with 173 hp (176 hp with Merc-O-Matic), was used in all other Meteors. However, a six-cylinder motor was put on the Canadian market, at midyear. It was a reduced-cost option, used in place of the 272-cubic-inch V-8.

Side trim for 1956 Meteors was altered slightly. The lowest-priced series had no trim at first, but later, Mainline Ford type chrome was tacked on. The Niagara trim was about the same as on the 1955 Rideau, and the 1956 Rideau trim was a variation of this style. The forward-slanting chrome sash was shortened, at the top, by a round medallion. A broad piece of ribbed chrome, similar to that used on the 1956 Ford Fairlane, stretched from the round medallion to the taillamp. The narrow chrome, which formed the top side of the triangle on the Niagara, turned sharply upward, just aft of the front door. It then curved, almost concentrically, around the medallion, and ran parallel with the other chrome, back to the taillamp. The area between these two pieces of chrome was often painted a contrasting color.

The grille of the 1956 Meteor featured a sweeping chrome bar. It began at the back of each of the Ford-type parking lights. It then curved forward and upward, running to near the headlamps, then gently downward to the bottom-center of the grille. There, it formed a "V." Behind this was grillework of many thin, horizontal strips.

The 1957 Meteors reflected the same model, and size, shake-up that Fords underwent that year. On a 116-inch wheelbase were the Niagara, Niagara 300, and Station Wagon models. The Rideau, and Rideau 500, used a 118-inch wheelbase.

Niagara models used chrome, similar to Ford Custom trim, on their rear fenders. The Niagara 300 had side trim much like the Ford Custom 300, although it was placed lower, and towards the rear. Anodized gold accents were available. Rideau-style trim was simple. A chrome strip, about half-way up the door, started at the front wheel opening. It ran straight back to about the center of the rear door. There, it turned up and curved back, running horizontally to the taillamp. On the Rideau 500, a piece of chrome began near the headlamp. It gradually widened, as it gently curved downward to the rear wheel opening. At that point, it narrowed, and ran straight back to the rear bumper. Just above this long strip was a narrower piece of chrome, which ran almost straight from the front fender to just behind the front door. At that point, it curved upward, and followed the crease on the top of the rear fin. A contrasting color was usually applied between the two chrome strips.

The grille of the 1957 Meteor featured the familiar "V" and star in its center. Running horizontally from the outside edges of the "V," were several narrow chrome strips. They curved around the front corners, and ended at the wheel cutouts. There were 13 Meteor models for 1957, including four-door Victoria hardtops in the Rideau, and Rideau 500 lines. There was no Meteor version of the Skyliner retractable hardtop; the few retractables sold in Canada were built in the United States.

Ford side trim appeared on 1958 Meteors. Model choices remained the same as in 1957. Incidentally, the Meteor Niagara, and Ford Custom models, survived the full year, even though the Custom died during the season in the United States. The 1958 Meteor grille "floated" in the front cavity. It consisted of a slightly concave series of fine vertical bars. Across this was a very broad four-pointed star.

All Meteors went to a 118-inch wheelbase for 1959. The Niagara line was discontinued, but in midseason, a new upper line — the Montcalm series — was introduced. It featured a Thunderbird roof line, like the Ford Galaxie. A "Rideau 500" chrome script appeared on the trunk lid of the Galaxie, probably because it was integrated with the trunk lock, and too complex to remove. Side trim was somewhat like that of Fords. However, Meteors enclosed the bulge, along the top of the rear fender, in chrome. This was frequently painted a different color. The grille of the 1959 Meteors was of a type similar to the 1959 Mercury, although it looked different.

All-new styling, for 1960, caused the usual changes for Meteors. The grille was a succession of thin, vertical pieces, in a convex format. A gap across the middle, between the inboard headlamps, contained three small four-pointed stars. On Rideau, and Rideau 500 models (the Niagara 500 line was gone), a strip of chrome, reminiscent of the 1951 trim, was used. A diagonal cross-piece, located towards the front, formed a stylized four-pointed star. On Montcalms, this horizontal chrome went all the way to the rear. In addition, behind the rear wheel was a plate of bright ribbed metal. Lots of chrome seemed like a necessity on top-of-the-line models in that era. The 1960 Meteor taillights were simple. They consisted of a pair of small, round, protruding red lenses on each side of the cars. Montcalm models added a clear lens, with each pair, for use as back-up lights.

The last of this type of Meteor was the 1961 model. It was one of the cleanest designs, since these Canadian cars were really redecorated versions of the basic United States design. The 1961 grille was made up of many thin horizontal strips. At either end, the dual headlamps were placed wide apart, within an oval rim. Over the grille strips, between each pair of lights, was the typical Meteor four-pointed star. A chrome strip, running across the top of the grille, extended around the front corners, and along the fenders. At the front doors, it turned up. It then bent back the horizontal strip, at door handle level. It then went across the door handles, and onto the fins, extending all the way to the end. There, it bent downward, to the taillamps. The taillamps, and all the rear end elements, were revised from the basic Ford shape. The changes were rather simple, but the results were dramatically different.

A new mid-size Mercury Meteor made its debut in 1962. It replaced the Meteor 600, and Meteor 800 models, in the United States. It also replaced the Canadian Meteor. This car is included in the chapter entitled "All that glitters." It was created in the 1959 to 1960 period, when a recession in the United States created a

Of the 14 Meteor models in 1968, the LeMoyne was the fanciest. (*Old Cars*)

temporary demand for smaller, economy cars. However, by the time it hit the market, the American economy had bounced back. As a result, the Meteor failed to achieve its sales target, and disappeared after only two years.

When the mid-size Mercury Meteor was discontinued in 1964, Ford of Canada retained the Meteor name to use on a different car. Instead of having a Mercury series with the name "Monterey," two series of Meteors were developed. These were essentially the same cars as the Mercury Monterey models, but they were labeled, and sold, as Meteor and Meteor Custom models. Their exterior appearance was identical to the Mercury's, with "Meteor" nameplates being about the only trim difference. The interiors of the Meteors were trimmed very much like the Ford Custom, and Custom 500, cars. The 1964 engines were also from the Ford parts bin. Standard was a 223-cubic-inch, 138-hp six. Two optional engines were a 220-hp version of the 352-cubic-inch V-8, and the 300-hp, 393-cubic-inch V-8.

The grille of the 1965 Meteor was altered somewhat from that of the Mercury. The middle third had a frame. The bars were all the narrow type, and the name "Meteor" appeared across it. Whether this was a great enough difference to remove the Meteor from the richness of the Lincoln Continental tradition, I won't speculate. At any rate, a slogan suggesting this was not used for the Meteor, as it was for Mercury, although they were very similar. In 1965, the six-cylinder engine, for Fords, and Meteors, alike, was enlarged to 250 cubic inches. That boosted output to 150 hp. The two V-8s were optional, again. For 1965, as in 1961, there were three series of Meteors: Rideau, Rideau 500, and Montcalm. They included a total of 11 models.

In 1966, the Meteor car-lines offered 14 models. Added were a nine-passenger Station Wagon in the Rideau 500 line, and a second two-door Hardtop, and Convertible, in the Montcalm series. The latter two were given an S-33 designation, as well. This was revived from 1963 Mercury Meteor nomenclature. The full-width, flat grille, consisted of upper, and lower, pieces of finely squared chrome mesh. In a narrow gap, across the middle of the grille, were individual letters spelling "Meteor." Engine options were changed. Instead of the 352-cubic-inch V-8, the 289-cubic-inch job, rated at 200 hp, was offered. The 390-cubic-inch V-8 was altered to develop 275 hp. A third option was the 428-cubic-inch, 345-hp V-8, sometimes known as the 7-liter engine.

Yet another two-door Hardtop, and Convertible, were added to the 1967 model lineup. They both carried the name "Montego." The Rideau, and Rideau 500 two-door Sedans were dropped, but a two-door Hardtop was added to the Rideau 500 series. The 1967 Meteor grille was split horizontally, as in 1966. Grille-work above, and below, was made of small, horizontal rectangles. The center section protruded slightly. The same engines were available in 1967 Meteors, plus a 410-cubic-inch, 330-hp V-8. As in the Ford line, the "390" engine was offered in a choice of 270- or 315-hp versions.

The grille of the 1968 Meteors became more deeply contoured in its outer sections. Grille-work consisted of two rows of rectangles. Within each rectangle, two narrower rectangles "floated" one above the other. Ford (or Ford-style) interiors continued to be seen. Ford frequently seems to run short of model names. When the Comet was replaced in the United States after 1967, the name used on the 1968 mid-size car was Montego. It was swiped from the Canadian Meteor. As a result, Meteor's top-of-the-line two-door Hardtop, and Convertible, were re-badged as "LeMoyne" models. There was also a LeMoyne four-door Hardtop. Standard engine for LeMoynes was the 302-cubic-inch, 210-hp V-8. (This engine replaced the "289" V-8.) The six was standard in other 1968 Meteors, and other V-8 options were unchanged.

A new phase in the marque's history began with the 1969 Meteors. In the United States, after 1968, Monterey styling was changed from that of other Mercurys. Meteor used the Mercury Monterey body with no significant difference, except for nameplates and medallions. The same Meteor series were retained. There were four Station Wagons, despite the absence of that body type in the American 1969 Monterey. Interiors were finished like those of Fords, and they even included the Ford-type "flight cockpit" instrument panel. Engines were the same as those offered in full-size Fords, although the standard motor for the S-33 was a 302-cubic-inch V-8, instead of a six.

The Meteor situation remained very much the same from the 1969 model to 1976. Described in the simplest terms, late-model Meteors used full-size Ford engines, and interiors, in Mercury Monterey bodies, with Meteor model identification. At the end of that year, production of full-size Mercurys in Canada was concluded. For 1977, the marque name became Marquis Meteor, and the cars became stripped-down versions of Mercurys made in the United States. Unique versions of the sub-compact Bobcat also continued to be marketed in Canada, along with two "economy" editions of the Monarch

Another Canadian product was the Frontenac, based on the Ford Falcon. (*Old Cars*)

Other Canadian Mercurys

Described above are the Meteors, and Monarchs that Ford Motor Company of Canada built to bolster sales for its Mercury dealers. They were successful cars. The Meteor's life — spanning a quarter century —is evidence of its success. The Canadian Monarch lasted 15 years, and the name returned in more recent time. However, there have been other models added to Canadian Mercury dealers' catalogs.

Let's go back to the end of World War II. Mercury trucks, built for sale by Mercury dealers, were variations of Ford trucks. They were available in practically all Ford truck sizes, and types.

The 1946-47 Mercury trucks had horizontal grille bars. The amount of chrome used was surprising considering material shortages at the time and the lack of chrome on Ford trucks. Mercury trucks for 1948 to 1950 looked more like Fords. However, instead of five flat grille bars, the Mercurys had four bars. They were somewhat louver-shaped, with red pin striping.

After 1950, Mercury trucks were almost identical to Ford trucks, except for Mercury identification up the front and (where practical) on the back.

The Mercury name was not used on trucks, after 1967 models. Since then, Mercury, and Ford, dealers in Canada have sold Ford trucks.

When the compact Falcon was introduced for 1960, a companion car was offered at the same time by Mercury dealers in Canada. A variation of the Ford Falcon, it was called Frontenac. It was not a Mercury, nor a Meteor ... it was an entirely separate marque.

The Frontenac grille was completely different from the Falcon's grille. It consisted of two parts. On each side was a series of vertical strips, which formed a slightly concave front. Each of these sections came to a point near its center. In dead center, was a round medallion, through which was a horizontal bar connecting the whole affair to a single unit. The taillamps were another deviation from the Falcon. They were round and, although their size was probably the same as on the Falcon, the rims were much wider to accommodate small lenses. These lenses protruded and were reflected by the wide rims, giving the effect of lights the size as those of the Falcon. The lenses seemed to be simply red versions of those on dome lights used on several Ford models at the time.

Though successful, the Frontenac lasted for only one year and was replaced for 1961 by the Mercury Comet. No 1960 Comets were built or sold in Canada. The Frontenac was already in production. Over the years, the Comet followed the common trend of growing in size and price. As it did so, it created a vacuum at the low end of the Mercury-Lincoln-Meteor dealers' range. Drawn in to fill this vacuum (by 1968) was the Falcon, which kept its original size. So, until Falcon production ended in 1970, both Ford and Mercury dealers sold Ford Falcons.

When the Pinto went on the market in the United States, it was not sold by Mercury agents in Canada right away. However, a Mercury version of it was introduced later. It was called the Mercury Bobcat. Built at the St. Thomas Assembly Plant, in Canada, along with Pintos and Mavericks, the Bobcat had a squared-mesh grille, and chrome-trimmed headlamps. Its taillamps looked as if they were double the length of the Pinto's. Actually the inward extension was a red reflector. It was not illuminated. The Bobcat's interior was a little more luxurious than the Pinto's. Made available in the same three body types as Pintos, the Bobcat was powered by a 2000-cc four-cylinder motor. A 2300-cc four was optional. Unique versions of the Bobcat were marketed in Canada, including a model 62B two-door Sedan, and a non-Villager three-door Station Wagon.

(For much of this account, we gratefully acknowledge Ford Motor Company of Canada, Limited's former historical consultant, the late-Herman L. Smith.)

From a distance, the 1949 Mercury Pickup looks like a Ford F-1. (*Old Cars*)

A 1950 Mercury Stake Truck. (*Old Cars*)

Merc-O-Mobilia

Most Mercury buffs start with a car. It creates the spark that gets the collectibles fire going. Next comes the purchase of a sales catalog, an owner's booklet, or a shop manual. Then, before you know it, the little blaze turns into a conflagration. The "enthusiast" becomes a "one-marque collector" who will beg, borrow, or buy anything remotely associated with Mercurys. The possibilities include advertisements; belt buckles; cap pins; dealer promotionals; filmstrips; literature; magazines; models; press kits; toys; and videos.

Anyone who has kicked around the old car hobby long enough, realizes that there is no shortage of automotive memorabilia. This type of merchandise may show up in a car dealer's storage room, at an automotive swap meet, or in a neighborhood garage sale. Such merchandise is generally referred to as "automobilia." Playing off the name used for Mercury's automatic transmission, we are going to refer to Mercury automobilia as "Merc-O-Mobilia."

As indicated, there are many different types of auto-related collectibles to collect. Focusing on a single brand of cars does help to keep things focused a bit. It allows the collector to concentrate his or her efforts, and expenditures, in a single direction. This is likely to have a positive affect on the value of the total collection, as well. Once a large assortment of Mercury-only items has been brought together, the individual items will gain value. Each new acquisition moves the collection one step closer towards becoming the "ultimate" Merc-O-Mobilia collection. And the ultimate is usually worth the most.

In this chapter, we are going to review some of the Merc-O-Mobilia items that we ran across in researching, and creating this book. The review starts with a general description of Mercury advertisements through the years. The second part documents miniature Mercurys -- banks, models, toys, and childrens' cars -- that have been documented to exist. The third part gives a description of other Merc-O-Mobilia (particularly sales brochures) that we have acquired knowledge of. It's obvious that the information presented, although useful to Mercury collectors, is incomplete. We hope that this can be the beginning of a more comprehensive list of collectible items that are related to Mercurys. Please do not hesitate to send the editors additional information that could be used in subsequent editions of this book, or in other books published by Krause Publications.

Mercury Advertisements

Automobilia collections rarely start out as financial investments. Most collections spring out of love of a particular car, and a desire to learn more about it. In many cases, Merc-O-Mobilia collections begin with the purchase of vintage Mercury advertisements. These usually have at least two attractions. One is artistic, and the second is educational.

Old auto advertisements often have color artwork or photos. Illustrations were used in most pre-World War II Mercury advertisements. Some of the nicest of these are small-sized advertisements for the 1939 to 1941 models, which ran in magazine's like *National Geographic*. They have stylized drawings of the cars with attractive, muted colors. Advertisements printed in the early postwar period, through 1951, also had illustrations by commercial artists. These had a larger *Saturday Evening Post* or *Life* magazine-size format. They often depicted several Mercury body styles, in a single advertisement. They were usually painted various colors, and arranged to show different views, and features of the cars. Mercury continued to use illustrations in many 1952, and 1953 advertisements, but photography was employed, too. Illustrations and paintings continued to pop up in the mid-1950s. Poster-like, two-page advertisements, showing all FoMoCo models, were produced in 1956, and 1957. Another multi-page 1957 advertisement showed many details of the Turnpike Cruiser model.

The 1958, and 1959 Mercury advertisements had a mixture of artists' illustrations, and photography. In this period, the size of the Mercury and the heavy amount of chrome used to trim it was emphasized in the ads. Some showed details like headlamps, and tailfins, from dramatic angles. Luxury was emphasized by depicting tuxedo-wearing drivers chauffeuring women in high-fashion dresses, and fur coats.

A return to painted advertising art was made in the early-1960s, when the Comet arrived. One Comet ad depicted early models on a watercolor-wash background. Another showed a painting of one turquoise colored 1965 Caliente Hardtop that had completed a long-distance endurance run.

Gathered around the car was a group of drivers, wearing team jackets that complemented the color and graphics seen on the car. Another series of advertisements, from the mid-1960s, pictured the larger, upscale Mercury models, in sports settings, at posh locales. A Park Lane is depicted with a group of tennis players at the Delmonte Lodge, in Pebble Beach, California. Another Park Lane is shown in a skiing scene at Squaw Valley, Idaho.

From an educational perspective, most advertisements tell you something about the car they are promoting. Excessive hyperbole may be used at times, but the copywriters generally did a good job of describing standard, and optional equipment, or pointing out if a Mercury did well in the Mobilgas Economy Run, etc. The art and photography are also educational. They reveal what colors the cars came in, how the upholstery looked, and (sometimes) how wide the whitewalls were on the tires. Be careful, though, when it comes to engine colors seen in ads. The artists sometimes made their drawings of engines more colorful than the motors really were. Most Mercury advertisements seem to show the correct engine colors, but the creative people at advertising agencies were known to take liberties with how things looked under the hood.

Advertisements from the muscle car era often show accurate photos of engines, and do a good job of detailing standard, and optional, equipment. The sales pitch was very technical

Mercury advertisements are collectible. (Old Cars)

in those days, and the announcements reflect that fact. They often list all the "big-block," high-performance engines, and may list the availability of equipment such as bucket seats, four-speed manual transmission, and mag-style wheels. At least a couple of ads listed the Comet's drag strip victories, giving dates and tracks where records were set, the speeds, and the drivers' names. Such advertisements, reflecting Mercury history, have extra appeal to Merc-O-Mobilia lovers. In 1957, and 1958, there were at least two ads that showed entertainer Ed Sullivan, whose television variety show was sponsored by Mercury. Car advertisements showing historic highlights or famous people are very desirable.

Besides single advertisements placed by Lincoln-Mercury Division, there are two other types of advertisements you can seek. The first are Ford Motor Company "multi-line" ads, that show Fords, Mercurys, and Lincolns (as well as Thunderbirds, and Edsels, in some years.) A few of these multi-line promotions even focus on a particular body style, such as the Station Wagon, depicting a wide variety of "Ford family" wagons. There are also advertisements, placed by supplier companies, that feature Mercurys in them. Goodyear Tire & Rubber Company used an early 1950s Mercury in a tire test, driving the car over railroad tracks for about 100,000 miles. This test was depicted in a Goodyear advertisement. An oil company used a neat sketch of an early 1950s Mobilgas Economy Run Mercury to emphasize the good mileage customers could expect from its fuel blends.

Mercury advertisements can usually be collected at reasonable cost. Ads for late-model Mercurys can sometimes be obtained for free, by clipping them from current magazines. Ask you doctor, dentist, or barber to save their old magazines for you. Most big-time professional vendors sell auto ads for set prices, regardless of age or the kind of car they show. Typical prices are $2 for black-and-white examples, and $3 for color ads. Attractive, prewar advertisements rarely go over $5 each, unless they have oversize dimensions. Since many old car advertisements are framed and hanged as artworks, larger ones generally warrant slightly higher prices. These may also set you back as much as $5. You can sometimes find framed advertisements, in antique stores, where they sell for around $15 to $20. That's higher than you should pay. Shopping for ads at old car swap meets will get you rarer examples at lower prices. You'll wind up with enough left over to purchase a frame, and still come out ahead. If you are lucky enough to find stacks of old Life or National Geographic magazines at a garage sale, you may get a real bargain. Of course, you should check them, before you buy. Make sure the car ads are still intact. Someone may have clipped them.

55 Years Of Mercury uses representative Mercury advertisements to illustrate the appearance, and features of some cars. These are only a fraction of the many Mercury advertisements stored in the Old Cars library. There are many examples we do not have. One of the pleasures of doing this book was culling through the vintage Mercury advertisements. We enjoyed seeing the artwork, and learned many new things about older Mercurys.

Miniature Mercurys

Miniature Mercurys include toy banks, model cars, and toy cars. The toy banks we are referring to were a promotional item, usually given away by car dealers. Model cars are scale replicas of full-size cars. The earliest scale-models of cars arrived after World War II. They were cast in slush metal. Acetate-plastic dealer promotional models arrived next, followed by plastic "dealer promos." AMT, the largest manufacturer of plastic dealer promos, began making kit versions in the late-1950s. Plastic models, and kits, are most commonly done in 1/25th-scale. A couple of companies designed models in 1/18th or 1/32nd proportions. Die-cast models, and precision metal models are usually rendered in 1/43rd-scale. Toy cars are replicas of real cars that do not have exact-scale proportions. Some may look quite authentic, while others are crude representations. Another type of miniature Mercury is the child's car, designed for kids to ride.

The miniatures covered here will be of all these types. Both vintage miniatures, and current issues are listed, since Mercury enthusiasts often collect both varieties. In several cases, the current issues include what are called "resin-cast" models. Essentially, these are very limited-production, hand-made plastic models. Some of the 1/43rd-scale metal models are also done as limited-edition, custom-made items. Since the dies used to make them do not have a long life span, only so many models can be produced before the dies wear out.

You will not find as many Mercury models and toys available as there are miniatures depicting Chevrolets, or Fords (especially Corvettes and Mustangs). In fact, some of the miniature Mercurys are very rare. They are also very expensive, since relatively few were produced, and the number of serious Mercury collectors seems to be growing rapidly. On the other hand, most of these items will never be as "inexpensive" as they are right now, since prices promise to keep climbing. The miniatures will be covered in the order of the year of the car they represent, beginning with four versions of the 1939 Mercury, one from 1939, and the others from the early 1960s or later.

The earliest miniature Mercury produced, was probably the 1939 coin bank made by Banthrico, a company which (still) specializes in producing this type of dealer promotional item. Done in a scale slightly larger than 1/43rd, this is a fairly good representation of the original Mercury four-door Sedan. It was cast in slush metal, with a large coin slot on top of its cowl. The one we saw was painted light green. It was a 1939-1940 New York World's Fair promotional. There is no information on whether it was given away at the fair, or sold.

Issued in the early 1960s was a 1/25th-scale plastic kit of the 1939 Mercury made by ITC, which stands for Ideal Toy Company. It was their model number 78-8, and it came with a remote-controller. This kit was reissued, also in the early 1960s, with number 3878-6. Surviving examples are still few, and far between. In more recent years, a company named Motorsports Miniatures manufactured its number 39 handmade resin-cast kit of a not-very-accurate-looking 1939 Mercury.

Miniatures of the 1940 to 1948 Mercurys have probably been made, at one time or another, but information about any specific banks, models, or toys is lacking. However, there are at least 11 variations of small 1949 Mercurys, although eight of these are related spin-offs. A version that was contemporary to the car was a slush-cast metal four-door Sedan made by National Products Company. This was done, as a dealer promotional model, in a scale somewhat smaller than 1/25th.

In 1963, the AMT model company issued a 1/25th-scale 1949 Mercury two-door Club Coupe. It had front wheels that could be rotated by hand, an opening trunk, and an opening hood. It came with a stock Mercury engine, plus a Chrysler "Ram-Tuned" V-8 for hot rodding buffs. This kit was numbered 02-349. Later, the same kit was reissued with a new number, 2349. It was reissued, again, in 1967, as kit number 2449. Next, it was re-numbered T279. In 1973, the 1949 Mercury was reissued as T446. This time, it came with thrill show ramps. This version was reissued, in 1975, as T291. It next appeared, in 1980, as part of the George Barris "Cruisin' USA" series, with stock parts, and number 2258. In 1987, AMT/Ertl marketed it, again, as kit number 6594.

Besides the plastic kits, at least two 1/43rd-scale metal models of 1949 Mercurys have been designed. One is Brooklin's number 15, which replicates the two-door Club Coupe. The second is a 1949 four-door Sedan made by Tekno. A research footnote tells us there are several versions of the latter, although it does not give details on how they differ.

At least three 1950 "James Dean" Mercurys have been modeled, and one can be found in at least two variations. Zaugg's number 5 model was a 1/43rd-scale 1950 Club Coupe in stock trim. Ertl made a 1/43rd-scale 1950 Club Coupe with opening doors. Tootsie Toy made a crude-looking, die-cast version of the stock 1950 Mercury, then reissued it as a fire chief's car.

Banthrico did one of its 1/25th-scale slush-metal dealer promotional banks based on the 1951 Mercury. It was issued when the car was new. Another rare, and desirable 1951 Mercury model is a 1/25th-scale plastic kit, number 583, made by Aurora Plastics Company. It is a "Mod Squad" woodie Station Wagon, patterned after the car used in the television show of the same name. Television tie-ins make miniatures more valuable. This one, though not particularly accurate, is nice to have in a collection. There is also a modern, resin-cast reproduction of the Aurora "Mod Squad" kit made by Robert Antonucci's Scale Auto Replicas company.

At least a dozen scale-model, and toy versions of 1953 and 1954 Mercurys have been manufactured. Banthrico did a 1/25th-scale slush-cast four-door Sedan in 1953. Tootsie Toys also produced a four-inch-long die-cast metal model of the 1953 Sedan. Finally, TKM Models produced a modern, 1/25th-scale, resin-cast 1953 Monterey Hardtop.

A gray-and-black, tin toy copy of the 1954 Mercury, was made by Rock Valley Toy Company, of Japan in 1954. It is 9-1/2-inches long, and has a battery-powered motor. The car it is patterned after is the Monterey Hardtop. It has excellent detailing, two-tone finish, and whitewall tires, but the pro-

An authentic-looking precision model of the 1957 Mercury Cruiser Convertible Pace Car was available from Sinclair's Auto Miniatures in Erie, Pennsylvania. (Wayne Moyer)

Brooklin's 1/43rd-scale diecast model of the 1949 Mercury Coupe. (Dennis Doty)

portions are crude, like those of many Japanese tin toys. In another contemporary effort, the F & F Toy Company copied three 1954 Mercury Monterey models -- Sedan, Hardtop, and Convertible -- as three-inch long plastic toys. In more recent years, Solido's number 92, metal model of the 1954 Mercury Monterey Hardtop in 1/40th-scale, was issued, and Collectors' Classics, of Argentina, produced metal models of the 1954 Mercury Sun Valley glass-top (number C1-3U0), and 1954 Mercury Convertible (number C1-3DO). The latter came in two variations, with the top raised or lowered.

Lovers of the 1955 Mercury will also find a number of miniature versions available between the collectors' market, and current offerings. There is a Banthrico slush-metal model of the 1955 Mercury Hardtop done in 1/25th-scale with a coin slot in the plastic base plate, and electro-plated bumpers, and wheels. This was available only through Lincoln-Mercury dealerships, and it is a rare miniature. Apparently, in mid-1955, Mercury switched from Banthrico slush-metal dealer promos to Revell/AMT 1/32nd-scale plastic promos. Car dealers used the promotional models to show customers what the new cars looked like, and what styles or colors they could be painted. Some dealers also gave the models away to the children of regular customers or hot prospects. The new plastic models were a lot more detailed and brighter than the previous metal models. They did a much better job of representing the actual cars. The 1955 Revell/AMT item, a Montclair four-door Sedan (number H-1204), is also rare. This joint-venture between the two companies survived for only one year, into 1956. After that, AMT more or less took over the dealer promotional business, while Revell marketed to the public. In the late 1950s, AMT also started marketing different versions of its models to the public in its famous 3-in-1 customizing kits.

More recent versions of 1955 Mercury models include two hand-crafted, resin-cast models. TKM Models did the 1955 Monterey "woodie" Station Wagon in 1/25th-scale. John Heyer did the 1955 two-door Hardtop, also in 1/25th-scale. Finally, there is a toy-like, 1/18th-scale 1955 Montclair two-door Hardtop (number 428) that was produced by OSUL Toy Company.

Miniature versions of 1956 Mercurys start with a Revell/AMT plastic dealer promotional in 1/32nd-scale. The car modeled was the Montclair Phaeton. This four-door hardtop seems to have been made by modifying the 1955 four-door Sedan tooling. It was cast in two-tone orange-and-white (and possibly other color combinations) and numbered 4-1204-6. Later, a number H-1233 Montclair Phaeton Customizing Kit was released to the public under Revell's trademark. This kit could not be built to stock 1956 Mercury specifications. The date of its actual release is unknown, but it was probably sold in 1956 or 1957. A dandy tin toy version of the 1956 Mercury Montclair two-door Hardtop was also issued by Alps Toy Company. This 9-1/2-inch long toy is painted in a light-yellow-and-red two-tone color combination, and it has a friction-drive motor. Its features include bright metal trim, a realistic hood ornament, and whitewall tires.

In the reproduction segment of the market, at least three 1956 Mercury models have been resin-cast in more recent years. TKM Models has done a Convertible, and a Station Wagon in 1/25th-scale, and John Heyer worked up a two-door Hardtop in the same scale.

At least two models of 1957 Mercurys have been produced by the same modern source: S.C. Miller. The first is a Turnpike Cruiser two-door Hardtop, and the second is a Cruiser Convertible that has number 203C. It's also very likely that Japanese tin toy versions of 1957 Mercurys were produced, probably as police cars or ambulances. For some reason, the Japanese toy manufacturers liked to copy Fords, Edsels, Mercurys, and Lincolns. If they had used only Fords, we would guess the reason to be the marque's worldwide recognition. However, that they repeatedly copied all four Ford "family" marques suggests that Ford was not policing its design patents very carefully. The author is a collector of ambulance toys and models, and has a number of such Japanese tin toys. There are Fords, Edsels and Lincolns in his collection, but no Mercurys. He has, however, seen Mercurys at swap meets.

A very desirable item for any one-marque collector, but especially those interested in 1957 Turnpike Cruisers, is an electric-powered child's car called the "Mercury Jr." This is a very recognizable, miniaturized version of the 1957 Convertible Cruiser, big enough for most grade school children to ride. It was manufactured by the Power Car Company of Mystic, Connecticut. The same firm pro-

The "Mercury Jr." child's car was manufactured by The Power Car Company of Mystic, Connecticut, which also produced a similar T-bird. (Al Maticic)

Front view of Al Maticic's Mercury Jr. The bumper is non-original. (Al Maticic)

duced a similar replica of the Ford Thunderbird. Such toys must have made the children who owned them the envy of their sibblings, and playmates. The Mercury Jr. must be the absolute ultimate when it comes to Mercury toys.

There do not seem to be any scale-model kits of 1958 Mercurys, or later reproductions. However, there is at least one desirable tin toy made by Yonezawa, of Japan. It is a four-door hardtop with two-tone brown-and-white finish. This toy measures 11-1/2-inches long. It also has bright metal trim, a hood ornament, full wheel discs, whitewall tires, and a friction-powered motor. It was issued in 1958, and examples are hard to find. Asking prices for these tin toys can vary from $10 to $150, or more, though the general trend is towards ever-increasing prices. One nice thing about them is that damaged examples can be restored, so it pays to scout flea market spaces for banged-up examples with bargain prices. As long as all the parts are there, restoration is usually possible. A restored tin toy will probably be worth less to a *toy* collector, but a *mercury* collector who is more interested in design, than in condition, will often be happy with the lower-cost of a restored tin toy.

We seem to remember having a 1960 Mercury model on our toy shelf years ago, but have not been able to document specific details about any 1960 or 1961 miniatures. In 1962, a 1/25th-scale replica of the 1962 Meteor S-33 two-door Sedan is the first early-1960s model that we know was definitely produced. It was manufactured by AMT. The following year there were at least three different Mercury models. All of them were made by AMT. The first was a Meteor S-33 two-door Hardtop friction-motor promotional. The second was the same car in a 3-in-1 customizing kit, number 05-363. The third was a full-size Mercury two-door Hardtop with the fastback roof line. As this is getting to be one of the hottest Mercury collector cars, it sure would be great to see this kit reissued. One early-1960s kit that was re-issued several times was the 1964 Comet Caliente. It began as a 1/25th-scale AMT dealer promotional without a friction motor, and this version is rare to find today. It then appeared as kit number 4324 in AMT's "Craftsman" series. This version was later renumbered 4803. Still later, it was marketed as kit number C104. Finally, in 1969, it was reintroduced as the "Caliente Bandito." There was also a lime-green 1/25th-scale AMT model of the 1964 Mercury Breezeway two-door Hardtop.

The last annual, 1/25th-scale Mercury dealer promotional model manufactured by AMT was done in 1966. It was a Park Lane Convertible. It remained available until 1979 or 1980. By that time, the company was called AMT/Lesney. There are several other known Mercury toys, and models, dating from the late-1960s. Two are red, 1967 tin toy versions of the Cougar Hardtop, made by different Japanese companies. The smaller one, by Taiyo, is 10 inches long and battery-powered. The larger one, by Asakusa Toys, is 15 inches long and has a friction-powered motor. Besides these, Zaugg has done an expensive, hand-cast-resin, 1/43rd-scale version of the 1968 Comet GT. Cragston Toy Company made a 1/43rd-scale 1968 Cyclone plastic toy, which is out of production. Also no longer made is F & F Toy Company's three-inch-long 1969 Cyclone plastic toy.

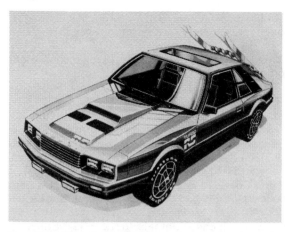

Revell offered a 1/25th-scale model kit of the 1979 Turbo Capri RS. (Revell)

MPC, another maker of plastic dealer promotional models, and scale-model kits, turned out two rare versions of the Montego Cyclone. The first was a 1970 kit numbered 2470. The second was the 1971 version, number 2471. There are also a number of models of the West German-built Capri, but the 1/43rd-scale Corgi number 303 and Solido number 26, plus the 1/24th-scale Nacoral number 3510 and Burrago number 0183, all show the early European Capri, rather than the Mercury version. The Mercury version was replicated in two Revell kits. Number 7201 was issued as the 1979 model, and number 7206 was the 1980 release. Another 1970s model is AMT's kit number T245, which can be built as a Ford Pinto or Mercury Bobcat funny car. It lasted until 1980.

A final "Mercury" model that turned up in our research, is a Merkur. Made by Intex or Zee Toys Company, in the "Grippers Pocket Racers" series, it is a three-inch-long, die-cast version of the 1985 to 1989 Merkur XR4Ti. We would be happy to hear about any information that would make this listing of miniatures more accurate or more comprehensive.

Mercury Literature

Like most automakers, Mercury has issued vast amounts of sales literature; showroom albums; product manuals; color and trim books; technical literature; press kits; dealer promotional items; and other collectibles over the past 55 years. Some of the items that we have used and documented in preparing this book are listed below. Each listing starts with a general description of the piece, its official title in quotation marks (these are written and punctuated as closely as possible to the factory's style), dimensions (width x height), number of pages, description of contents, code numbers (where used); and dates. A small amount of Canadian sales literature is also cataloged. (Editor's note: We would welcome any additions to this list with descriptions or photocopies of other pieces.)

Mercury Sales Literature (United States)

1939 Mercury full-line sales catalog. "New Mercury 8 For 1939." 11-7/8 x 7 inches. 20-pages including heavy stock cover. Green four-door Sedan, with chauffeur loading luggage, on cover. 1939 World's Fair Ford Rotunda on inside front cover. Drawings and illustrations of all models, Sedan interior, chassis, front, rear, trunk, instrument board and technical features. Production and testing procedures described. Dimensional drawing. Standard equipment list. Form number 7045, 10-38.

1939 Mercury full-line 12-panel sales folder. "New Mercury 8 For 1939." Folded size 10 x 5-5/8 inches. Four tri-folded pages with color illustrations and text on both sides. Green four-door Sedan, with chauffeur loading luggage, on cover. Drawings and illustrations of all models, Sedan interior, chassis, front, rear, trunk and instrument board. Standard equipment list. Form number 7047, 10-38.

1940 Mercury full-line sales catalog. "Mercury 8 For 1940." 10 x 8 inches. 20-pages including heavy stock cover. Profile of Roman God Mercury with winged helmet on gray/blue/white/yellow cover (brown lettering). Includes new Convertible Sedan. Drawings and illustrations of all models, Sedan interior, chassis, front, rear, trunk, instrument board and technical features. Safety features and testing procedures described. Standard equipment list on back cover. Form number 7208, 9-39.

1940 Mercury full-line eight-panel sales folder. "New Mercury 8." Folded size 11 x 8-1/2 inches. Two bi-folded pages with color illustrations and text on both sides. Profile of Roman God Mercury with winged helmet on gray/white/brown/pink cover. Drawings and illustrations of all models, Sedan interior, chassis, front, rear, trunk and instrument board. Standard equipment list. Form number 7209, 9-39.

1940 Mercury accessories folder. "Mercury Accessories To Give You Even Greater Pride In Your Mercury 8." Folded size 3-1/2 x 6 inches. Eight-pages. Photos and descriptions of factory accessories and car care products. Form number 7238, 10-39.

1940 Mercury full-line sales catalog. "Mercury 8 For 1940." 10 x 8 inches. 20-pages including heavy stock cover. Profile of Roman God Mercury with winged helmet on cover. Includes new Convertible Sedan. Drawings and illustrations of all models, Sedan interior, chassis, front, rear, trunk, instrument board and technical features. Safety features and testing procedures described. Standard equipment list on back cover. No apparent changes from September 1939 issue, but richer colors in illustrations. Form number 7208, 11-39.

1941 Mercury full-line sales catalog. "The Car That Dares To Ask Why?" 10 x 8 inches. Eight-pages. Front of Maroon car in blue/white circle on orange cover (black lettering). Drawings and illustrations of all models, interiors, underhood, and instrument panel. Form number 7357, 9-40.

1941 Ford, Mercury, Lincoln Accessory Merchandising Catalogue. 8-1/2 x 11 inches. 24-pages. Blue cover with yellow printing. Shows all accessories for cars. Very rare. Form number 7370, dated 12-40.

1941 Mercury sales catalog. "You'll Drive This One For the Fun of It." Color. 10 x 8 inches. Eight pages. Shows five 1941 Mercury models. Form number 7374, 1-41.

1941 Mercury sales catalog. "What the Birds Told Us." 10 x 8 inches. Eight pages, Full-color. Shows five Mercury models. Form number 7378, 1-41.

1941 accessory catalog. "Now! A foot control for your Ford or Mercury Roto-Selector Radio." 3-1/2 x 6 inches. Four pages. Two colors. Shows the radio foot control option. Form number 7381, 12-40.

1941 Ford Auto-Selector Radio Owner's Manual. 4-1/4 x 6-1/2 inches. Folds to 8-1/2 x 13 inches. Published by Philco Radio Company. Designed to be carried in glove box.

Maintenance folder. "You Can Cut Down Operating Cost and Engine Wear With a Ford Oil Bath Air Cleaner and Oil and Motor Filter." 3-1/2 x 6 inches. Unfolds to 14 x 6 inches. Color. Shows oil-bath air cleaners and oil filter. Form number 7382, 12-40.

Mailer. "Here's the New Idea Behind Mercury." 9 x 7 inches. Unfolds to 18 x 13-3/8 inches. Shows six late-1941 Mercury models. Color. Form number 7430, 4-41.

1949 Mercury accessories folder. "Mercury Styled Accessories." Folded size 10-1/4 x 7-1/2 inches. Designed as a tabloid-format, 14-3/4 x 10-1/4-inch, 16-page, stitched-and-trimmed glossy-stock booklet. Brown-toned illustrations. Photos and descriptions of factory accessories and car care products. No form number or date.

1950 Mercury full-line 12-panel sales folder. "Better than ever" 1950 Mercury." Folded size 11 x 8-1/2 inches. Four tri-folded pages with color illustrations and text on both sides. Front view of red Mercury with passenger entering on green/white cover. Drawings and illustrations of all models, interiors, engine, trunk and instrument board. Standard equipment list. No form number, dated 11-49.

1950 Mercury Monterey sales catalog. "... presenting the magnificent Mercury Monterey." 11 x 8-1/2 inches. Four pages. Burgundy car with black top in profile on gold/white cover with black/red/gold lettering. Shows features, colors, and special details of midyear Monterey model. Profile drawings of other Mercurys along top of back page on gold banner. No form number. Dated 6-50.

1951 Mercury full-line 16-panel sales folder. "Presenting The New Mercury For 1951" Folded size 11-7/8 x 8-1/2 inches. Folds out to 23-3/4 x 34-inch poster-size with four-color art and text on both eight-panel sides. Profile of Dark Green Mercury on cover. Drawings and descriptions of all models, interiors, engine, trunk, instrument board, and Merc-O-Matic Drive. Standard equipment list. No form number, dated 10-50.

1951 Mercury full-line sales folder. "for 'the drive of your life'...The New 1951 Mercury with Merc-O-Matic Drive." Folded size 11-1/8 x 10-1/8 inches. Folds out to 33-3/8 x 15-1/8-inch poster-size with two-color art and text on both sides. One side has 11-1/8 x 5-inch panels across top, with photos and text of car features. On bottom of same side are six 11-1/8 x 10-1/8 panels, five showing black-and-white photos of Mercury models, and the sixth with lettering. The obverse has upside-down 11-1/8 x 5-inch panels across top, with photos and text of car features (these fold-over on reverse side). On bottom are three 11-1/8 x 10-inch panels with cover, specifications, and features of Merc-O-Matic Drive. Includes photos and descriptions of all models, interiors, engine, trunk, instrument board, and Merc-O-Matic Drive. Standard equipment list. No form number, dated 10-50.

1952 Mercury accessories booklet. "Accessories styled in particular for your 1952 Mercury." Size 7-7/8 x 8 inches. 36-page stitched and trimmed booklet, including glossy-stock covers. Color-cover illustrations. Black-and-white photos, drawings and descriptions of factory accessories and car care products. Form number M-52-18. 3-52.

1956 Mercury full-line sales folder. "The Big M Mercury for 1956." Folded size 12 x 8-3/8 inches. Orange-and-white Montclair Coupe (two-door Hardtop) on cover. Illustrates all models with photos. Details styling, and technical features. Complete specifications on outside rear. Form number M56-101.

1957 Mercury full-line sales folder. "Straight Out of Tomorrow 1957 Mercury with Dream-car Design." Folded size 9 x 6-1/4 inches. Orange-and-white Turnpike Cruiser four-door Phaeton on cover. Illustrates all models with drawings. Details styling, and technical features. Complete specifications on outside rear. Form number M57-109.

1958 Mercury full-line sales catalog. "1958 Mercury Four Great Series With Sports-Car Spirit And Limousine Ride." 9 x 6 inches. 32-pages. Full-color. Illustrated with drawings, and photographs of all models, engines, interiors, and styling details. Options are illustrated and described. Major specifications on outside back cover. Form number M58-104.

1959 Mercury full-line sales folder; "Mercury '59 America's Liveliest Luxury Car." Folded size 9 x 6-1/4 inches. Metallic turquoise Park Lane four-door Phaeton on cover. Illustrates all models with drawings. Details styling, and technical features. Complete specifications on outside rear. Form number M59-104.

1960 Mercury full-line sales catalog. "Mercury 1960." 9 x 6 inches. 24-pages. Full-color. Illustrated with drawings, and one photograph of all models, engines, interiors, and styling details. Options are illustrated and described. Standard equipment, and specifications on outside back cover. Form number M60-103.

1960 Mercury three-panel sales fold-out for Mercury Station Wagons. "Mercury 1960 Country Cruisers." 11 x 8-1/2 inches. Six-pages. Full-color photographs of two Colony Park, and one Commuter Station Wagons. Detail photos of features, options, and engines. Illustration of red-and-white Colony Park interior. Dimensional drawing of Country Cruiser Station Wagon. Form M60-106

1960 Comet full-line sales catalog. "Fine Car Styling For The Economy-Wise." 10-1/2 x 5-1/2-pages. Heavy, pebble-textured cover, and center fold; glossy inside pages with one two-panel fold-out. Drawings of all models, interior details. Product descriptions. Color chart. Equipment, and specifications. Form C-60-101.

1960 Mercury. One-page, tri-fold flyer. "1960 Mercury the *better* low-price car ... now $174 less than in 1959!" 8 x 10 inches. Turquoise-and-black on white stock. Drawing of Monterey two-door Sedan. Ford, Chevrolet, Plymouth price comparison. Monterey features. No form number.

1961 Comet 12-horizontal-panels "accordion" sales flyer. Each panel is 9-1/8 x 3-1/2 inches. Six to a side on single folded sheet. Color illustration of each model and interior. Product descriptions. Colors, engines, extras, and specifications detailed in individual panels. Form number C61-105.

1961 Mercury sales catalog. "1961 Mercury, Meteor 600, Meteor 800, Monterey, Station Wagons ... the *better* low-price cars." 8 x 8 inches. 24-pages. Full-color illustrations of all models, and interiors. Product descriptions, color samples, fabrics, engines, transmissions, features. Form number M61-103.

1962 Meteor S-33 sales folder; "Mercury's nifty new number;" folded size 6 x 7 inches. Shows photos of light blue Hardtop, blue bucket seat interior, details, and selling points. Form number LM62-129.

1962 Meteor sales brochure; "Mercury Meteor '62;" 8 x 9 inches. Eight-pages. Color illustrations of all models; details; engines; equipment lists. Form No. LM62-119.

1962 Mercury 14-vertical-panels "accordion" sales flyer. "You have already won one of these wonderful prizes!" Each panel is 3 x 8-3/8 inches. Seven to a side on single folded sheet. Color photo of Comet, Meteor and Mercury offered as prizes in sales promotion. Photos of other prizes (i.e. television, flashlight, transistor radio). No form number.

1964 Comet. Flip-page sales catalog. "1964 Comet A Mercury Product." 11-1/8 x 5-3/4 inches. 24-pages. Color illustration of each model and interior. Product descriptions. Engines, extras, and specifications detailed individually. Illustrations of all options. Solid, and two-tone colors listed. Black-and-white mini-profiles of all models. Form number C64-111.

1966 Mercury. Full-line insert. "In the fine car tradition: Lincoln-Mercury presents the move-ahead cars for 1966." 10-3/4 x 6-3/8 inches. 12-pages (numbered 15 to 26). Inserted in *This Week* magazine, October 17, 1965 issue. Four-color on newsprint. Photos of models and product descriptions. Not coded or numbered.

1968 Mercury. Full-line. "Flip-style" sales booklet. 10-1/2 x 8-1/4 inches. 20-pages. Marauder, Montego, and Cougar on cover. Full-color. Photos and illustrations. Details on features of all models. Chart with profiles of full line. Form number M-68-102.

1968 Mercury. "Is it true that only station wagons have wood-tone paneling?"
Four-page brochure on wood-trim models. Heavy stock. 9 x 5 inches. Not coded or numbered. Dates from early 1968 calendar-year.

1970 Mercury. Full-line. "Flip-style" sales booklet. 10-1/2 x 8-1/4 inches. 20-pages. Orange and white cover with year '70, and Lincoln-Mercury badge. Full-color. Photos and illustrations. Details on features of all models. Chart with profiles of full line. Form number M70-104.

1970 Mercury. High-performance cars. "Mercury. Password For Action In The '70s: Cyclone Spoiler; Cyclone GT; Cyclone; Cougar Eliminator. Sales booklet. 9-1/8 x 10-3/4 inches. 16-pages including two-panel fold-outs of Cyclone Spoiler, and Cyclone GT. Product descriptions, specifications, power teams, options, and accessories. Full-color. Photos and detail photos. Form number M70-109.

1974 Christopher And Chauncey Coloring Book. 8-1/4 x 10-3/4 inches. 48-pages. Line drawings of 1974 models (Comet, Cougar XR-7, Montego, Mark IV, Marquis, Continental, Monarch) for kids to color. Introduced the Mercury Monarch. Form number LC-74-21.

1979 Mercury Capri sales catalog. "1979 Mercury Capri." 11 x 11 inches. 16-pages. Color illustration of each model and interior. Product descriptions. Engines, extras, and specifications detailed individually. Color chart. Illustrations of all options. Form number 79-201.

1981 Mercury LN7 sales catalog. "Mercury LN7." 10-1/8 x 10 inches. 16-pages (including two double-panel fold-outs. Color illustration of each model and interior. Product descriptions. Engines, extras, and specifications detailed individually. Color chart. Illustrations of options. Number 320M 3/81 form number P-115.

1983 Mercury Cougar sales catalog. "Mercury Cougar '83." 9 x 11 inches. 16-pages (including two double-panel fold-outs). Color photographs of models and interiors. Product descriptions. Engines, extras, and specifications detailed individually. List of all options. Litho in USA (702M) 11-82. Form number P-8075.

1983 Mercury Marquis sales catalog. "Mercury Marquis '83." 9 x 11 inches. 14-pages (including one double-panel fold-out). Color photographs of models and interiors. Product descriptions. Engines, extras, and specifications detailed individually. List of all options. Litho in USA (571M) 8-82. Form number P-8074.

1983 Mercury Marquis sales catalog. "Mercury Grand Marquis '83." 9 x 11 inches. 16-pages. Color photographs of models and interiors. Product descriptions. Engines, extras, and specifications detailed individually. List of all options. Litho in USA (466M) 8-82. Form number P-8076.

1984 Mercury Lynx sales catalog. "1984 Mercury Lynx." 9-18 x 10-7/8 inches. 24-pages with one two-panel fold-out. Color photographs of models and interiors. Product descriptions. Engines, extras, and specifications detailed individually. List of all options. Litho in USA (637.5M) 8-83. Form number P-251.

1984 Mercury Capri sales catalog. "1984 Mercury Capri." 9-18 x 10-7/8 inches. 14-pages with one two-panel fold-out. Color photographs of models and interiors. Product descriptions. Engines, extras, and specifications detailed individually. List of all options. Litho in USA (300M) 8-83. Form number P-241.

1984 Mercury Topaz sales catalog. "1984 Mercury Topaz." 9-18 x 10-7/8 inches. 20-pages. Color photographs of models and interiors. Product descriptions. Engines, extras, and specifications detailed individually. List of all options. Litho in USA (300M) 8-83. Form number P-8121.

1984 Mercury Cougar sales catalog. "1984 Mercury Cougar." 9-18 x 10-7/8 inches. 18-pages. Color photographs of models and interiors. Product descriptions. Engines, extras, and specifications detailed individually. List of all options. Litho in USA (800M) 8-83. Form number P244.

1984 Mercury Marquis sales catalog. "1984 Mercury Marquis." 9-18 x 10-7/8 inches. 14-pages with one two-panel fold-out. Color photographs of models and interiors. Product descriptions. Engines, extras, and specifications detailed individually. List of all options. Litho in USA (400M) 8-83. Form number P242.

1984 Mercury Grand Marquis sales catalog. "1984 Mercury Grand Marquis." 9-18 x 10-7/8 inches. 14-pages with one two-panel fold-out. Color photographs of models and interiors. Product descriptions. Engines, extras, and specifications detailed individually. List of all options. Litho in USA (600M) 8-83. Form number P243.

1986 Mercury full-line sales catalog. "Mercury '86/Sable/Cougar/Topaz/Lynx/Capri/Marquis/Grand Marquis." 11 x 4-1/2 inches. 28-pages. Photos of cars, and interiors. Listing of models. Service, leasing, and EPA information. Litho in USA (1100M) 9-85 P-9598.

1987 Mercury sales booklet. "Mercury '87. Sable/Cougar/Topaz/Lynx/Grand Marquis. 11 x 4-1/2 inches. 24-pages. Full color photographs of exteriors, interiors, and details. Shows and describes all models. (1,152M) 9-86 P-9434.

1988 Sable sales catalog. "1988 Sable The Shape You Want To Be In." 9-1/4 x 11 inches. 22-pages with one two-panel fold-out. Photos of cars, interiors, instrument panel, interior details, engine, and options. Product descriptions. Standard equipment list. Options list. Litho in USA. (772M) 8-87 P-4359.

1988 Topaz sales catalog. "1988 Sable The Shape You Want To Be In." 9-1/4 x 11 inches. 26-pages with one two-panel fold-out. Photos of cars, interiors, instrument panel, interior details, engine, and options. Product descriptions. Standard equipment list. Options list. Litho in USA. (650M) 8-87 P-4350.

1989 Mercury full-line sales catalog. "Mercury '89." Cougar; Sable; Topaz; Tracer; Grand Marquis. 8-1/2 x 11 inches. 20-pages. Full-color photographs of exteriors, interiors and details. Shows and describes all models. Charts of standard equipment for each car-line. (1,110M) 9-88 P-7179.

1989 Mercury Tracer sales catalog. "Mercury '89 Tracer." 8-1/2 x 11 inches. 16-pages with two fold-out pages. Full-color photographs of exteriors, interiors, and details. Shows and describes all tracer models. Chart of standard and optional equipment. (680M) 7-88 P-5214.

1989 Mercury full-line sales catalog. "Mercury; Cougar; Sable; Topaz; Tracer; Grand Marquis." 8-1/2 x 11 inches. 16-pages. Full-color photographs of exteriors, interiors, and details. Shows and describes all models. Chart of standard and optional equipment. (1,11M) 9-89 P-1023.

1989 Scorpio sales catalog. "Scorpio '89 XR4Ti. Imported From Germany For Lincoln-Mercury Division." 7-1/4 x 10-7/8 inches. Eight-pages. Photos and product descriptions. Specifications. Warranty information. Leasing information. Litho in USA (782M) 9-88 Form number P7165.

1994 Mercury. Full-line sales catalog. "1994 Mercurys "All this and the quality of a Mercury." 8-1/2 x 11-1/4 inches. 20-pages. Full-color photos of exteriors, interiors, and details. Shows and describes all models. Chart of standard and optional equipment, (1,000,000) 8-93 P-8126.

1994 Mercury Villager deluxe sales catalog. "1994 Mercury Villager. "If it were just another minivan, it wouldn't be a Mercury." 10-3/4 x 14 inches. Heavy coated stock. 16-pages. Color and black-and-white photographs of minivans, interior details, exterior details, etc. Phantom drawing of engine. Standard, and optional equipment list. Color chart. Litho in USA (700,000) 7-93 P-8099.

Mercury Sales Literature (Canada)

1949 Meteor 16-panel sales folder. "Advance Information 1949 Meteor A Product of Ford of Canada." Folded size 5-1/2 x 8-5/8 inches. Red/white/black cover. Black-and-white illustrations of cars, interiors, and technical features. Standard equipment list. Code AD 858.

1949 Monarch facts book. "Facts and Features of the New 1949 Monarch." 4 x 5-1/2 inches. 16 pages. Black and white illustrations of models. Product descriptions. Interiors, engines, technical features, and specifications. No code numbers or dates.

1949 Monarch announcement booklet. "Monarch News: New Monarch Makes Car News." 9-1/4 x 12-1/4-inch two-color, stitched-and-trimmed, newsprint "tabloid." Sales promotional booklet formatted in small tabloid newspaper style. Illustrations of models, product descriptions, technical features, styling details. Date-lined Windsor, Ontario, May, 1948. Code number AD 810.

1951 Mercury sales catalog. "the Mighty, ... Beautiful .... New 1951 Mercury .... ." 10 x 8 inches. Eight-pages. Blue/white/black cover. Black-and-white illustrations of cars, interiors, and technical features. Standard equipment list. Code AD 171.

1951 Monarch sales catalog. "Masterpiece by every measure 1951 Monarch." 10 x 7-1/2 inches. 12-pages. Red/white. Black-and-white illustrations of cars, interiors, and technical features. Standard equipment list. Code AD 102.

1951 Meteor sales catalog. "la nouvelle Meteor de 1951." 11 x 8-1/4 inches. 20-pages. Blue cover with part of green car. Color illustrations of cars, interiors, and technical features. Standard equipment list. Code Recl 150f.

1952 Monarch sales catalog. "Monarch 1952." 12-3/8 x 8-7/8 inches. 12-pages. Black cover, front view of blue car. Gold lettering. Color illustration cars, interiors, and technical features. Standard equipment list. Code AD 211.

The Mercury sales literature listed above, plus many other literature items of the same type, can generally be obtained from vendors who specialize in selling automotive literature. This is a rather large field, composed of both full-time dealers, and vendors who dabble in literature as a side-line business. *Old Cars* devotes an entire section of its classified advertising section to ads from literature vendors. We'll be happy to send you a free sample copy of the weekly news-magazine. Write to: *Old Cars*, 700 East State Street, Iola, WI 54990.

Magazines With Mercurys

One-marque enthusiasts love to get copies of old automotive magazines that published road tests on their favorite cars, when the cars were new. One of the best sources of such information for Mercurys was *Motor Trend* magazine. *Car and Driver*, and *Road & Track* also published a handful of Mercury road tests. The old magazines are generally inventoried, and sold, by the same vendors who deal in automotive literature. Prices for single copies of old magazines, in good condition, can range from less than $1 each to as high as about $15.

Here is a list of issues containing Mercury road tests, that you might want to collect:

Issue - Model-year and Model
(*Motor Trend*)
04/50 - 1950 Mercury four-door Sedan
04/51 - 1951 Mercury with Merc-O-Matic
10/52 - 1952 Mercury
03/53 - 1953 Mercury Monterey
01/54 - 1954 Mercury Sun Valley
05/54 - 1954 Mercury
04/55 - 1955 Mercury Custom
11/55 - 1955 Mercury Montclair
03/56 - 1956 Mercury Montclair
03/57 - 1957 Mercury Montclair and Turnpike Cruiser
12/57 - 1958 Mercury Park Lane
06/58 - 1958 Mercury Monterey
09/58 - 1958 Mercury Super Marauder V-8
03/59 - 1959 Mercury Montclair
03/60 - 1960 Mercury Comet
04/60 - 1960 Mercury Montclair
09/60 - 1960 Mercury Comet Station Wagon
03/61 - 1961 Mercury Monterey
05/61 - 1961 Mercury Comet
07/61 - 1961 Mercury Comet
05/62 - 1962 Mercury Monterey Custom/Meteor/Comet
10/62 - 1962 Monterey S-55 Convertible
03/63 - 1963 Mercury Monterey Custom
08/63 - 1963-1/2 Comet S-22 Hardtop
10/63 - 1964 Mercury Montclair
01/64 - 1964 Comet Endurance Run
03/64 - 1964 Comet Cyclone
05/65 - 1965 Comet Caliente and Cyclone
08/66 - 1966 Mercury Monterey S-55
09/66 - 1966 Comet Villager
10/66 - 1967 Mercury Cougar
01/67 - 1967 Mercury Cougar "289" and "390"
05/67 - 1967 Mercury Cougar
11/67 - 1968 Mercury Cougar, Marquis and Montego

Issue - Model-year and Model
12/67 - 1968 Mercury Cougar GTE
01/68 - 1968 Cougar
08/68 - 1968 Cyclone Cobra Jet
10/68 - 1969 Mercury Cougar XR-7
02/69 - 1969 Mercury Marauder X-100
03/69 - 1969 Mercury Cougar XR-7
07/69 - 1969 Mercury Marquis Brougham
01/70 - 1970 Mercury Cyclone
02/70 - 1970 Mercury Monterey
01/71 - 1971 Mercury Comet GT
03/71 - 1971 Mercury Monterey and Cougar XR-7
04/71 - 1971 Capri 2000/2300 GT
05/71 - 1971 Mercury Comet "202"
08/71 - 1971 Mercury Marquis
11/71 - 1972 Mercury Montego
12/71 - 1972 Capri 2600
11/72 - 1972 Mercury Marquis
(*Car and Driver*)
06/62 - 1962 Mercury Comet
12/63 - 1964 Mercury Comet Cyclone GT
10/66 - 1967 Mercury Cougar
12/67 - 1968 Mercury Monterey, Montego and Cougar GTE
03/68 - 1968 Mercury Cougar XR-7
12/68 - 1969 Mercury Cyclone GT
01/69 - 1969 Mercury Cyclone CJ
05/69 - 1969 Capri GT
05/70 - 1970 Capri 1600
04/71 - 1971 Capri GT
07/71 - 1971 Mercury Comet GT
12/71 - 1971 Capri 2000
01/72 - 1972 Capri 2600
07/72 - 1972 Mercury Comet
(*Road & Track*)
08/80 - 1960 Mercury Comet
06/70 - 1970 Capri 1600
09/70 - 1970 Capri Plus-50
10/71 - 1971 Capri 2000
03/72 - 1972 Capri 2600

Other Merc-O-Mobilia

We have little doubt that there are thousands of other Merc-O-Mobilia items available for Mercury enthusiasts to collect. The only other piece we were able to document by our deadline is the following item:

1964 Commemorative medal. Honoring the "Silver Anniversary" of Mercury 1939-1964. Heavily chromed medallion with a depiction of the 1939 Mercury represented on the medal.

Credits

As with any book of this scope, a number of automotive journalists, plus hundreds of Mercury owners, and experts have contributed photos, and information, that helped us to complete *55 Years of Mercury*.

Among writers whose research was referred to for this book are Dennis Doty, Bob Hall, Tim Howley, Tom LaMarre, Bill McBride, Phil Skinner and R. Perry Zavitz. For research on the 1943 to 1945 chapter, we are deeply indebted to Brooks Stevens and Alice Preston of the Brooks Stevens Automotive Museum. Lisa Alvarez, of *Motor Trend*, went out of her way to get permission for use of the photo of the Mexican Road Race Mercury. Mitch Frumpkin, of *Collectible Automobiles*, was equally helpful in providing a photograph of a rare Mercury Station Wagon with a Marmon-Herrington four-wheel-drive conversion. Finally, Timothy I. Chappell, of Lincoln-Mercury Division, provided photos and information on 1986 to 1994 Mercurys.

In addition to these contributors, special thanks go to Jerry Robbin, and all members of the International Mercury Owners Association. Mr. Robbins received a preliminary book manuscript to review. He made over 30 copies of individual sections of the book, and sent them to the IMOA technical advisors for proofreading. Due to tight production scheduling, listing all the advisors in this first edition was impossible. However, those that responded by our editorial deadline were: John Adamek, Greg Robinson, James R. Baron, Bill Moulton, Joseph Michaels, Bill Orr, Michael Timothy and Jim Tweedy. We are greatly indebted to all of the IMOA technical advisors for service above and beyond the call of duty.

Dozens of other Mercury owners, and *Old Cars* subscribers sent photographs of Mercurys in response to an advertisement in *Old Cars*. We appreciate each, and every one of these efforts. Final photographic selections are based on a variety of factors, including available space, contrast, format, and composition. Photographs used include credit lines with the name of the photographer and/or car owner. We thank all of the Mercury enthusiasts who loaned us photographs for this project. Limits on time and space are the only reasons that all of these photos were not used.

Additional major photo contributions came from R.L. Brown, Leroy Byers, Dick Dance, Lowell E. Eisenhour, James Gwaltney, Bernie Roehrig and Bob Thatcher.

Finally, we wish to thank all of the members of the following clubs for their interest in Mercurys, and their devotion to collecting the great cars that Mercury built.

Big M Mercury Club
5 Robinson Road
West Woburn, MA 01801

Cougar Club of America
0-4211 North 120th Avenue
Holland, MI 49424
(616) 396-0390

Early Ford V-8 Club of America
PO Box 2122
Sand Leandro, CA 94577
(619) 283-8117

Ford and Mercury Restorers Club
PO Box 2133
Dearborn, MI 48123
(313) 248-3400

'49-'50-'51 Ford/Mercury Owners
PO Box 30647
Midwest City, OK 73140-3647
(405) 737-6021

International Mercury Owners Association
6445 West Grand Avenue
Chicago, IL 60635
(312) 622-6445

Mid-Century Mercury Club
1816 East Elmwood Drive
Lindenhurst, IL 60046
(708) 356-2255

LINCOLN-MERCURY DIVISION
GENERAL MANAGERS

Lee R. Miskowski 1991-
Ross H. Robert 1988-1991
Thomas J. Wagner 1985-1988
Robert L. Rewey.. 1984-1985
Gordon B. Mackenzie 1980-1984
Walter J. Oben 1977-1980
Walter S. Walla 1975-1977
William P. Benton... 1973-1975
Bennett E. Bidwell 1970-1973
Matthew S. McLaughlin 1968-1970
E.F. Laux 1966-1968
Paul L Lorenz.. 1964-1966
Ben D, Mills.. 1958-1964
James J. Nance 1957-1958
Ben D. Mills (Lincoln) 1955-1957
F.C. Reith (Mercury) 1955-1957
Benson Ford.. 1948-1955
Thomas Skinner... 1945-1948

MERCURY RACE RECORD 1950-1959
NASCAR GRAND NATIONAL/AAA/USAC

Year	Firsts	Seconds	Thirds	Fourths	Fifths	Rank	Notes
1950	2	2	3	2	6	5	
1951	2	3	3	0	1	6	
1952	0	0	0	0	0	0	None in top 5
1953	0	0	0	0	0	0	None in top 5; 11 Mercs raced
1954	0	2	0	2	3	5	20 times in top 10
1955	0	0	0	0	0	0	Chrysler dominated with 27 wins
1956	5	14	7	7	2	5	67 Mercs raced; 67 times in top 10
1957	1	0	4	8	4	4	115 Mercs raced; 46 times in top 10
1958	0	2	2	2	3	5	61 Mercs raced; 17 times in top 10
1959	0	0	1	1	1	7	21 Mercs raced; 7 in top 10

Photo Contributors

Norman F. Abston; John Adamek; Thomas C. Amandale Sr.; Barbar J. Bahr; Maxie L. Ballenger; James Barlion Jr.; Ron Batease; John D. Baxter; William E. Belk; Jerome Bergdorf; Kenny Berogan; R.L. Brown; Leroy Byers; Donald F. Cady; Tim Caffery; Steve Calavetta; Jim Carlson; Frank Cassello; Timothy I. Chappell; Beatrice M. Chisholm; Tom Christofferson; Bowen Cochran; Edward Dalitian; Dick Dance; Richard Defendorf; Kirk Dillery; Charles J. Dodson; Ron Donott; P. Scanlon D. Dugal; Chris Dunn; Robert T. DuPont; David G. Eager; Larry Edus; Harry E. Edwards; Lowell E. Eisenhour; Jerry L. Emery; Steve Engeman; W. Eschback, Jr.; Wayne Feindt; Paul Ferguson; Jay Findlay; Merle A. Fourez; Dick Garstang; Richard Gibson; Dale Gillespie; Louis Gorenz; James L. Gwaltney; Ron Handy; L. Hockenburg; G. Palmer Humphrey, Jr.; Charles Hunckler; Imperial Palace; Robert B. Lade; Elmer Larson; Dale Lawson; Gerald W. Lyon; Al Maticic; May Motors; DeWitt McCrary; John W. McFadden; W. McKiernan; R. Dale Miller; Paul Morse; John J. Muller; Bill Nappi; James P. Nelson; John Nevestich; L.E. O'Dell; William L. Opfer, Jr.; Michael Patzuh; Louis D. Possehl; Bernard Pranica; Bernie Roehrig; Gene Salzman; James B. Saxe; D. Scott; W. Sevie; CR Shipman; Hagin Stewart; George Stringos; Larry Sullivan; Bob Thatcher; Coy Thomas; Robert Twohey; Bob Vest; Walter Villa; Cliff Walraven; Richard A. Weber; Paul Yount; Robert R. Ziemer.

Due to last minute contributions, some photographers or car owners not listed here will appear in photo caption credits only.

A Gallery of Collectible Mercurys

A 1939 Mercury Sedan at a show in Zephyrhills, Florida. (Robert A. Selle)

Jerry Emery's 1939 ragtop has factory draft deflectors. (Jerry Emery)

Richard Defendorf bought a 1939 Convertible in 1978. He got it running good enough to drive to Ford V-8 national meets until 1983, when he did a five-year restoration. (Milton Gene Kieft)

This 1939 Mercury Convertible was restored in 1984. (C.R. Shipman)

Ballard Crooker, Jr. with his 1939 Mercury Convertible in an old photo.

Bernard Pranica sent photos of a 1939 Mercury Convertible.

This 47,000-mile 1940 Mercury is a fine original. (James Barlion, Jr.)

Donald F. Cady photographed his "jazzed-up" 1941 Mercury in 1955.

This 1941 Mercury ragtop sold for $32,500 at Auburn '92. (James L. Gwaltney)

A 1946 Mercury Coupe at a Dearborn, Michigan show. (Lowell E. Eisenhour)

Dynamic Maroon paint brightens this 1946 Mercury Coupe. (Paul A. Emptage)

This 1946 Mercury Convertible is owned by Ron Batease.

A Pheasant Red 1948 Convertible restored by owner Ron Donott.

The collector plate on this 1947 Mercury Coupe is from Minnesota.

Robert R. Ziemer is proud of his 1948 Mercury Convertible.

Bill and Nina Belk's Tampico Red over Bermuda Cream 1949 Sport Sedan.

A 1949 Mercury Woodie at a Brooklyn, Michigan show. (Lowell E. Eisenhour)

This 1949 Mercury Sport Sedan belongs to Robert T. DuPont.

In 1954, Rose Gillespie visited Joplin, Missouri with a 1950 Merc. (Dale Gillespie)

Old photo shows Lou Goren's white 1950 Mercury Coupe.

At a 1993 Titusville, Florida show is a 1950 Mercury Monterey. (Robert A. Selle)

A 1950 Mercury brought $15,900 at the 1993 Daytona Beach sale. (Robert A. Selle)

Hopped up V-8 in a 1950 Monterey at Titusville, Florida. (Robert A. Selle)

Walter L. Villa owns this 1950 Mercury Sport Sedan with skirts.

Merle A. Fourez of Classic Mercury Parts has a 1950 Convertible.

Mid-'50s photo shows rear view of 1951 Sedan with Merc-O-Matic. (Dale Gillespie)

Beatrice M. Chisholm's 1951 Mercury "hunting car" had 200,000 miles on it.

Photo of Bob Thatcher's 1951 Mercury four-door Sedan was snapped at the 1993 Grand National Early Ford V-8 show in Dearborn, Michigan. It took a first in class.

Custom touches set off this 1951 Merc with original flathead V-8. (DeWitt McCary)

Wearing Texas license plates is a dressed-up 1951 Monterey. (James L. Gwaltney)

Wisconsin collector tags mark this 1951 Merc as a Badger State car. (James L. Gwaltney)

A Sedan has 1951 Ohio plates and a number of accessories. (James L. Gwaltney)

A 1952 Sport Coupe was at a 1992 Monroe, Michigan show. (James L. Gwaltney)

Rare 1952 Mercury Convertible with wire wheel hubcaps. (James L. Gwaltney)

An Iola Car Show "Blue Ribbon" winner is this 1953 Monterey. (Jerry Bergdorf)

This 1953 Monterey has a Tahiti Tan top over a Bittersweet body. (Kenny Berogan)

A 1953 Mercury Sedan owned by Bill Lawrence of Florida. (Robert A. Selle)

A 1953 Monterey Hardtop at a show in Casselberry, Florida. (Robert A. Selle)

In the 1950s, Ballard Crooker, Jr. bought his 1953 Mercury two-door Sedan in Alabama. He traded-in his 1939 Mercury Convertible to buy it and drove it almost 100,000 miles.

David Weiner had a 1953 Mercury at Melbourne, Florida. (Robert A. Selle)

A Palm Bay, Florida meet included this 1953 Monterey. (Robert A. Selle)

A 1954 Mercury Convertible from Ohio. (John Baxter)

There are 67,000 miles on this 1954 Mercury Monterey. (Dale T. Lawson)

Lou Gorenz's fourth Mercury was a special-order black and white Montclair with a 198 hp V-8 purchased in December 1954. He used in to move from Texas to California.

Even Chevrolet restoration specialist Jim Carlson, of Holmen, Wisconsin, has a place in his heart for cars like a 1955 Mercury Montclair two-door Phaeton. (Jim Carlson Auto Center)

This 1955 Montclair Hardtop has 86,000 original miles. (Lloyd E. O'Dell)

Perfect for top-down driving is a 1955 Montclair Convertible. (Barbara J. Bahr)

One of eight Mercurys in a collection is this stock 1956 Montclair. (Chuck Dodson)

Chuck Dodson also owns a customized Montclair with tiara roof band.

A third Merc in the Dodson collection is a 1955 Montclair ragtop.

Rear vents indicate this 1956 four-door Phaeton has factory air. (Wayne Fiendt)

This show featured a 1956 Mercury Custom two-door Phaeton. (James L. Gwaltney)

This 1956 Montclair is painted Lauderdale Blue and Classic White. (Louis Possehl)

1950s pop art decorates the continental tire on a 1956 Mercury. (Pauline Scanlon)

A 1956 Montclair ragtop is one of three Mercs in George Stringo's collection.

John Bernhardt's 1956 Montclair four-door Phaeton has 35,400 miles.

Florence Bernhardt's 1956 two-door Phaeton is nearly a twin to John's four-door

This 1957 Colony Park wagon is a one-owner Los Angeles car. (Paul Morse)

This 1958 Mercury was at a Dearborn, Michigan show in 1990. (Lowell E. Eisenhour)

A 1959 Mercury Monterey four-door Sedan. (James L. Gwaltney)

David G. Eager poses with his 1960 Monterey Convertible.

This 170,000-mile 1961 Monterey has had one owner since 1962. (Carl F. Price)

A 1961 Mercury Convertible at a North Baltimore, Ohio show. (Lowell E. Eisenhour)

A 1963 Mercury Comet Convertible was at a Milan, Ohio car show. (Lowell E. Eisenhour)

John W. McFadden's 1963 Monterey Custom has New York plates "63 Brzway."

Edward Dalitian of Fresno, California owns this 1963 Mercury four-door Hardtop.

A 1963 Merc ragtop was seen in Bowling Green, Ohio in August 1992. (Lowell E. Eisenhour)

This 1963-1/2 Mercury Marauder has traveled 345,000 miles. (Elmer Larson)

This 1963 Meteor S-33 Sport Coupe is mostly original. (William L. Opper, Jr.)

This 1964 Montclair Breezeway Sedan is a well-preserved, one-owner, original car. It was bought new, in Casper Wyoming, in 1964. There are 123,510 actual miles on its "390" V-8. (Harry E. Edwards)

Harry Edward's 1964 Mercury is finished in Pink Frost with a White top.

The engine in this '64 is untouched, except for tune ups and maintenance. (Harry E. Edwards)

The interior is original, as well as the spare tire. (Harry E. Edwards)

This 1964 Merc has "XXV" on steering wheel to mark 25th year. (Harry E. Edwards)

V-8 powered 1964 Comet ran like a top on a recent trip. (Tom and Mona Christofferson)

This 1964 Colony Park was purchased new by current owner's parents. (Chris Dunn)

Frank Cassello is the owner of this original 1966 Colony Park Station Wagon.

A 1967 Mercury S-55 Convertible with a "428" V-8. (Robert L. Brown)

This 1968 Marquis has 157,000 original miles. (John Adamek)

John Adamek collects 1968 Mercurys, especially "woodies."

This 1968 Colony Park Station Wagon looks new. (John Adamek)

Less than 200 of the 1968 Parklane Convertibles had wood trim. (John Adamek)

This is believed to be the only 1968 Mercury Monterey Fastback ever built with simulated wood-grain trim. It was probably a special-order car. (John Adamek)

Steve Engeman's '68 Park Lane "Colony Park" has factory-correct trim.

Tim Caffery of Racine, Wisconsin owns this 1968 Cougar Hardtop.

This 1968 Mercury Park Lane Convertible is also owned by Robert L. Brown.

This 1970 Cougar XR-7 has the "351 Windsor" V-8. (Robert L. Brown)

This 1972 Cougar is one of about 300 XR-7s sold with the "351" Cleveland "Cobra Jet" V-8. It also has a four-speed "top loader" gear box and Hurst shifter. (G. Palmer Humphrey, Jr.)

Charles and Diane Hunckler's 1978 Cougar XR-7 has been dressed up with Keystone wheels and Goodyear Eagle GT tires. Under its hood is a modified "351" two-barrel V-8.

Gene Salzman of Pardeeville, Wisconsin, owns a 1979 Cougar XR-7 Coupe.

Wood trim continued to identify the 1988 Colony Park wagon. (Robert A. Selle)

This is a 1989 Mercury Grand Marquis "50th Anniversary" model. (William Eschbach, Jr.)

Bob Vest posed his 1992 Grand Marquis next to his 1941 Town Sedan.

Mercury
Experimental Cars

Front view of the 1954 Mercury XM-800 concept car. This early 1950s "dream car" made its debut in February 1954 at the Detroit Automobile Show. The XM-800's hooded headlights and front wheel opening contours later appeared on the 1956 Lincoln. (Mercury)

Rear view of the XM-800. The "dream car's" body was constructed of fiberglass and was approximately five inches wider than a 1954 Mercury Monterey. Four individual seats with vinyl upholstery were found inside the car. The seats were separated by stationary armrests. (Mercury)

Side view of the 1954 Mercury XM-800. Seen inside the cockpit of the concept vehicle were full gauges including a tachometer, plus warning lamps. The engine used in the "dream car" had dual exhausts, but was otherwise a stock Mercury V--8. (Mercury)

Mercury's 1956 XM-Turnpike Cruiser was designed with fast, long-distance driving in mind. President Eisenhower was pushing completion of an Interstate Highway System, which inspired this concept vehicle. A special truck and trailer were used to haul it from city to city. (Mercury)

The trailer used to haul the XM-Turnpike Cruiser was a mobile showcase. Picture windows were built into each side of the trailer to make a dramatic traveling display for the latest Mercury experimental car. With the glass lowered at stops, the Turnpike Cruiser could be shifted crosswise on a turntable. (Mercury)

Customizer George Barris created the 1964 Super Marauder for Mercury. It was powered by a high-performance 427-cubic-inch V-8 and toured the country as part of Ford's show car fleet. It had twin torpedo-shaped headrests that carried the rear turn signal indicators. A "two-handle" steering system replaced the conventional steering wheel. The exhaust system was integrated into the rocker panels. (Mercury

A high-performance image was the heart of the 1969 Mercury Super Spoiler show car. This was tied into the fact that Mercury's NASCAR team was taking many checkered flags in superspeedway competition. The spoiler on the car was more decorative than functional. Based on the Cyclone/Cyclone GT production models, the Super Spoiler was finished in brilliant Canary Yellow. (Mercury)

The 1970 Mercury El Gato was an experimental modification of the 1970 Cougar. It was shown for the first time at the Detroit Auto Show on November 15 to 23, 1970. Mercury described it as "one hot cat!" Both the windshield and sloping back window were designed with extremely rakish angles to enhance the low, sleek look of the car. It was the first fastback Cougar. Unique green body finish was lighter in hue above the sculptured character line, with a tapered paint stripe calling attention to the color break. The front end design featured a split grille with a strong center motif of impact-resistant material that harmonized with the flush-mounted bumper. (Mercury)

The 1991 Mercury Cyclone was a sleek, smooth, high-tech concept car that turned in an appearance at the 1990 Chicago Auto Show where it was photographed by Ron Kowalke, managing editor of Krause Publication's Automotive Books Department. (Ron Kowalke)

High-performance and luxury features were wrapped up in the dramatic design of the 1991 Mercury Cyclone concept specialty car, seen here in profile view. Among the many futuristic features of this car was an electrochromic roof. (Mercury)

From behind, the 1991 Mercury Cyclone concept car looks extremely aerodynamic for a four-door model. A closed-circuit television system was used to provide the driver with rear vision, instead of exterior side-view mirrors. (Mercury)

Index

Books for Old Car Fans!

Standard Catalog of Military Vehicles
• Profiles all U.S. military vehicles built from 1940-1965
ONLY **$29.95**

Imported Cars, 1946-1990
• 165 foreign car manufacturers profiled
ONLY **$24.95**

The Fabulous 50s
• A photo-journey back to an unforgettable automotive era
ONLY **$14.95**

Weird Cars
• 500 photos from the Batmobile to the Wienermobile
ONLY **$16.95**

Collector Car Digest
• Presents the "Best of Old Cars Weekly" from 1987-1988
ONLY **$24.95**

Antique Car Wrecks
• Wreck photos from the 1900s to the 1960s
ONLY **$14.95**

Old Cars Questions & Answers
• Collecting tips, restoration hints & investment advice
ONLY ....**$ 6.95**

Guide To American Muscle Cars
• 300 photos and information on muscle cars from 1949-1992
ONLY **$19.95**

American Volunteer Fire Trucks
• 600 photos of rural brush rigs across America
ONLY **$16.95**

American Motors, The Last Independent
• The complete corporate history of American Motors
ONLY **$19.95**

Standard Catalog of American Motors
• Facts, figures and photos for AMC models from 1902-1987
ONLY **$19.95**

Standard Guide to Cars & Prices
• Today's prices for vehicles built from 1901 through 1986
ONLY **$15.95**

Krause Publications

Book Dept. YDH1, 700 E. State St., Iola, WI 54990-0001

*Add $2.50 shipping 1st book, $1.50 each additional.
Wis. residents add 5.5% sales tax.*

MasterCard/VISA Cardholders
Order Toll-Free By Calling...

800-258-0929

Dept. YDH1, Mon.-Fri., 6:30 am - 8 pm,
Sat. 8 am - 2 pm, CST